MUSIC TRADITIONS
CULTURES &
CONTEXTS

MUSIC TRADITIONS
CULTURES &
CONTEXTS

Edited by Robin Elliott and Gordon E. Smith

Wilfrid Laurier University Press

WLU

Wilfrid Laurier University Press acknowledges the financial support of the Government of Canada through the Book Publishing Industry Development Program for our publishing activities.

Library and Archives Canada Cataloguing in Publication

Music traditions, cultures, and contexts / Robin Elliott and Gordon E. Smith, editors

Festschrift in honour of Beverley Diamond.
Includes bibliographical references and index.
Issued also in electronic format.
ISBN 978-1-55458-177-1

1. Diamond, Beverley, [date]. 2. Music—History and criticism. 3. Ethnomusicology.
I. Elliott, Robin, [date] II. Smith, Gordon Ernest, [date]

ML55.D53 2010   781.620092   C2009-904919-8

Music traditions, cultures, and contexts [electronic resource] / Robin Elliott and Gordon E. Smith, editors

ISBN 978-1-55458-199-3

ML55.D53 2010a   781.620092   C2009-904920-1

Cover design by Graham A. Blair. Text design by Catharine Bonas-Taylor.

© 2010 Wilfrid Laurier University Press
Waterloo, Ontario, Canada
www.wlupress.wlu.ca

This book is printed on FSC recycled paper and is certified Ecologo. It is made from 100% post-consumer fibre, processed chlorine free, and manufactured using biogas energy.

Printed in Canada

To Beverley Diamond, in admiration and friendship

Contents

List of Illustrations

The photographs section appears between pages 16 and 17.

List of Music Illustrations

Chapter 10, "Father of Romance, Vagabond of Glory: Two Canadian Composers as Stage Heroes," by John Beckwith

Acknowledgements

We would like to thank all who have contributed to making *Music traditions, cultures, and contexts* a reality, including, first and foremost, the book's contributors: John Beckwith, Rob Bowman, Virginia Caputo, Beverley Diamond, Charlotte Frisbie, Jocelyne Guilbault, Ellen Koskoff, Pirkko Moisala, Bruno Nettl, Kip Pegley, Regula Burckhardt Qureshi, Neil V. Rosenberg, and Kay Kaufman Shelemay, as well as the group of Bev's students who so generously and enthusiastically supported this project and contributed their reminiscences about Bev for the book's website. We are grateful to all of these people for their excellent contributions to the book, and for their patience during the genesis of this volume.

We are indebted to those who have read these texts at various stages and have provided valuable feedback, including colleagues, friends, external assessors, and copy editors. We take this opportunity to thank two former students, Erin Bustin and Vincent Spilchuk: Erin transcribed some twelve hours of interviews between the editors and Beverley Diamond that were recorded in St. John's, and Vincent provided valuable editorial assistance in the final preparation of the book typescript. A special word of thanks to Graham Blair, Memorial University, who created the splendid cover design for the book. Thanks also to Brian Henderson, Leslie Macredie, Lisa Quinn, and Rob Kohlmeier at Wilfrid Laurier University Press: Brian for his help and encouragement from the very beginning of the project early in 2006, and Leslie, Lisa, and Rob for shepherding it through the final stages of production.

Our sincere thanks go to Beverley Diamond and Clifford Crawley for their hospitality and generosity during our research visit to St. John's in May 2007. We also take this opportunity to thank Bev for her assistance in providing us with ideas and information through all stages of the preparation of this book, and for her knowledge, inspiration, and much valued friendship. Working on this book, which is a tribute to her exemplary scholarship and collegiality, has been an honour and a real pleasure for both of us.

For financial assistance in the production of this book, we would like to thank the Faculty of Arts and Science at Queen's University and the Institute for Canadian Music at the University of Toronto.

Finally, we would like to thank our families and partners, who have encouraged and sustained us throughout this project. To them, as always, we owe everything.

R.E. and G.E.S.

Preface

Music traditions, cultures, and contexts is a tribute to Beverley Diamond to celebrate her sixtieth birthday, which fell on 4 June 2008. Together with the volume's contributors, we offer it to Bev[1] in recognition of her outstanding scholarly accomplishments, and with sincere thanks for the collegiality and friendship that she has shared with us all and with countless others over many years. The volume contains fourteen contributions by leading ethnomusicologists and music scholars, including a collaborative contribution from a group of Bev's former and current graduate students; a chapter by Bev herself on the life and music of her partner, Clifford Crawley; and two short chapters by popular-music specialist Rob Bowman. An appendix lists Bev's publications and lectures, demonstrating the scope of her research and her prolific scholarly activity for over thirty-five years. An added feature of this book is a related website that contains dialogue and commentaries by Bev's students, past and present: http://www.press.wlu .ca/press/Catalog/elliott/shtml. It is our belief that these multiple texts are distinguishing features of the book, and will broaden notions of the traditional Festschrift as a tribute volume to encompass how the work of an individual such as Bev can inspire us to find ways to do research and to produce knowledge that is accessible, interactive, and reflective of goals of equity and the human dignity of those with whom we work.

Overview of Chapters

Collectively, the chapters in *Music traditions, cultures, and contexts* present narratives about music drawn from a broad range of contexts and perspectives. Each one can be read as articulating themes in Bev's work in various and engaging ways, often invoking contested ideas, positions, and voices. We open with a chapter in which we, the editors, engage in dialogue with Bev about her life experiences, teaching activities, and research trajectories. This opening chapter is complemented in Chapter 2 by "Conversations with Clifford Crawley," in which Bev writes an engaging account of the composer's childhood, early years, and education in England, as well as his life in Canada since the early 1970s. Based on interviews with Crawley and his two children, Alison and John, this oral history is linked to a discussion of Crawley's musical philosophies, as well as an examination of his musical styles through selected musical compositions.

Next, we have grouped the chapters in an ordered thematic sequence, starting with the three contributions from Bruno Nettl, Ellen Koskoff, and Kay Kaufman Shelemay, in which the authors argue respectively about disciplinary notions related to ethnomusicology. In his chapter, "Ethnomusicology critiques itself: Comments on the history of a tradition," Nettl discusses how the practice of critiquing the discipline of ethnomusicology is part of the identity of the field, and one that can be traced back to ethnomusicology's origins in comparative musicology of the 1880s. Invoking a series of case studies, Nettl considers several important historical precedents (Ellis, Stumpf, Adler), the "definitional" work of "arch critic" Alan Merriam in the 1960s, as well as contemporary "Y2K" discourse on critiquing ethnomusicology. As Nettl notes, "A number of Beverley Diamond's powerful contributions to ethnomusicology" have contributed to the "newly developing critical perspective [in ethnomusicology] dominating the period since 1990" (p. 85).

In "Is fieldwork still necessary?" Koskoff considers fieldwork both as "defined" by the discipline and as an everyday process of "coming to terms with difference." Following a discussion of theoretical models, Koskoff illustrates her argument with three reflexive scenarios drawn from her own fieldwork: an encounter with a Lubavitcher informant; a concert of Tuvan throat singers; and a contextual learning encounter with the gamelan *angklung* (the latter two scenarios were at Koskoff's university home, the Eastman School of Music). Koskoff argues that as ethnomusicologists we need to broaden our knowledge of the forces that shape our approaches to fieldwork, beginning with trying to understand difference—how we recognize it, react to it, and integrate it into "new understandings of ourselves and others" (p. 111).

In "Toward a history of ethnomusicology's North Americanist agenda," Shelemay continues the theme of reflecting on historical precedents and ideas in ethnomusicology, as well as contemporary thought in the field. She poses the question as to whether there is "a divide or ... rather a common Canadian–US Americanist music agenda," and uses Bev's work as a departure point for exploring similarities and differences between these two national contexts. Shelemay's article emphasizes "common ground," especially what she refers to as "the transnational moves that have characterized the twentieth century" (p. 114).

The authors of the next three chapters explore aspects of musical performance in three different cultural and social contexts, and from three different critical perspectives. In her chapter, "Encountering oral performance as total musical fact," Regula Burckhardt Qureshi emphasizes the importance of understanding music as a series of contextual processes. Qureshi contends that "oral performances are more than enactments of already extant musical texts; they are total musical facts that encompass everything that makes the music happen" (p. 129). To illustrate, Qureshi presents three examples: the first is based on her long and extensive research on the Sufi music of India and Pakistan known as Qawwali. This discussion is followed by references to Jane Sugarman's work on Albanian weddings and to Michael Asch's work on the Dene drum dance. In all three contexts, Qureshi emphasizes the theme of thinking of music "outside of itself" in ways that can open up "room for exploring all music as aesthetically coded social action revealed in performance regardless of cultural status, sonic complexity, or degree of acknowledged orality" (p. 141).

Invoking a personal perspective on performance, Charlotte Frisbie begins her chapter, "You also work as a church organist? Whatever for?" by linking her topic to "Bev, who, besides being a scholar and educator, is herself extraordinarily talented as a musician and pianist" (p. 145). Frisbie provides a lively account of her long-standing work as church organist and how, as an anthropologist, she has come to view the musical world of a church organist through multiple critical lenses. Drawing on historical and current theoretical models from anthropology and ethnomusicology, Frisbie argues that performance and scholarship are often intertwined and that each can inform and inspire the other.

In "The politics of organology and the Nova Scotia banjo: An essay in honour of Beverley Diamond," Neil V. Rosenberg draws on his background as a folklorist and a banjo player to present a fascinating account of the banjo in the Canadian maritime province of Nova Scotia. A US émigré to Newfoundland in 1968 and a colleague of Bev's at Memorial University of Newfoundland, Rosenberg begins by making reference to the telling question Bev posed in her keynote address to the fiftieth anniversary of the Society for Ethnomusicology in 2005: "I suppose I speak from the margins of North America, but is that position distinct or different from that of my US colleagues?" (p. 181). Rosenberg's chapter reconsiders a conference presentation on the Nova Scotia banjo that he read at the American Folklore Society conference in New Orleans in 1975 and offers a series of reflections on important musical, social, and other kinds of identity issues, then and now.

Reflecting on identity issues is also an important theme in the following chapter, "Strategies of survival: Traditional music, politics, and music
education among two minorities of Finland," by Pirkko Moisala. In her
study, Moisala examines factors and strategies in the process of incorporating orally transmitted music into educational programs in Finland.
Drawing on music traditions from among the oldest minorities in Finland,
the Sámi *joiku*, and Finnish-Swedish fiddling or *spelmansmusik*, Moisala
combines theories of social movements (Sidney Tarrows) with the concept of "assemblage" (Gilles Deleuze and Félix Guattari) as a means of
articulating the social, discursive, and material frameworks behind the
learning of traditional music in the context of Finnish music education.

Reflecting on identity issues through history is also an overarching
theme in John Beckwith's "Father of romance, vagabond of glory: Two
Canadian composers as stage heroes." In this chapter, John Beckwith
examines two Quebec musical stage works from the 1940s and discusses
the musical world of their composer, the Montreal critic, church musician, and teacher Eugène Lapierre (1899–1970), as well the protagonists
in each piece: the French-born composer and writer Joseph Quesnel (1746–
1809) and "the outstanding musical personality of nineteenth-century
Canada, best known as the composer of 'O Canada,'" Calixa Lavallée
(1842–1891) (p. 228). Beckwith describes the genesis of both works, discusses literary and musical details, and emphasizes Lapierre's typically
romantic approach to writing Canadian "history" through music.

The next three contributions in the book deal with topics related to popular music. These chapters are a tribute to Bev's long-standing interest in
Aboriginal popular music, and to her enthusiastic support of the Canadian
branch of the International Association for the Study of Popular Music. The
two short chapters by Rob Bowman originated as conference presentations. Bowman presented "Funk and James Brown: Re-Africanization, the
interlocked groove, and the articulation of community" at the International Association for the Study of Popular Music's Americas conference
in Cuba in 1994. This chapter focuses on the "re-Africanization" of Black
culture in the 1960s in the US, and how James Brown's music, and his
development of funk, can be regarded as exemplifying changes behind the
re-Africanization movement. In developing his argument, Bowman also
problematizes it, pointing out the importance of different readings of
stereotypical musical gestures, and social and cultural interpretations.[2]
The second chapter by Bowman, "On the one: Parliament/Funkadelic, the
mothership, and transformation," was read at the Toronto 2000 Musical
Intersections mega-conference. In this chapter, Bowman investigates the

theoretical ideas of Richard Schechner, drawing on Schechner's "Towards a poetics of performance," in which the author locates the essential drama of performance "in transformation—in how people use theatre as a way to experiment with, act out, and ratify change" (p. 269). To illustrate, Bowman discusses Schechner's theoretical ideas as they apply to performances by the funk ensemble led by George Clinton, alternatively known as Parliament, Funkadelic, and P-Funk, in the years 1976–78.

In "Politics through pleasure: Party music in Trinidad," Jocelyne Guilbault offers an ethnographic perspective on the popular Trinidadian musical and dance genre known as soca. Pointing out that while the commercial value of soca is widely acknowledged, its "socio-cultural and musical accomplishments … remain contentious and contested" (p. 279). Specifically, soca is criticized by many for not engaging the "political" and for failing to address the country's social problems. In her chapter, Guilbault focuses on live soca performances and what she highlights as their "transformative capabilities," including both pleasure *and* political persuasion. She also refers to relevant historical and critical literature to build her argument that, as a national musical genre, soca is a potent agent of emergent social and political identities in contemporary Trinidad.

The final contribution in the book is "A Festschrift for the twenty-first century: Student voices." Having discussed aspects and perspectives of teaching in Bev's work in Chapter 1, and considering the overall, ongoing importance of pedagogy in her professional career, we leave this discussion open-ended here. In addition to this chapter by Kip Pegley and Virginia Caputo, readers are encouraged to visit the "Student" link under this book title (cf. Wilfrid Laurier University Press website).

Finally, in addition to paying tribute to a wonderful scholar, colleague, and friend, it is our belief that the contributions in *Music traditions, cultures, and contexts* bring together many of the important, vital, and critical themes in Beverley Diamond's work. Read alongside her own scholarly writings, these chapters reinforce the idea that music traditions, cultures, and contexts are always nuanced and never static. It is our hope that this book underscores for all of us the power of music as lived human experience.

Notes

1 In keeping with the spirit of friendship that surrounds this project, we refer to Bev by her first name in this preface, as do a number of the contributors in the book.

2 Bowman told us (email message, 29 August 2008) that this International Association for the Study of Popular Music conference occurred at the same time as a graduate seminar in popular music he was teaching at York, and that several students, including Kip Pegley (see "A Festschrift for the twenty-first century: Student voices"), went with him to Cuba for the conference, a point that links in interesting ways to Bev's comments earlier in Chapter 1 about teaching, and the impact of graduate students on teaching.

ONE

Beverley Diamond
Life Stories, Academic Directions and Teaching, Research and Scholarly Activity

ROBIN ELLIOTT
GORDON E. SMITH

N REFLECTING ON HOW WE MIGHT write about Bev's life and work in this opening text, we have chosen to let Bev's own voice "speak" her story, rather than have us write that story. In opting for this approach, we are cognizant of the kinds of dialogic, experiential models that have increasingly inspired Bev's own work, as well as the real value of asking deep questions, articulating alternative critical stances, and searching at the boundaries of ideas, rather than struggling to find definitive answers or the "right" story. Of great importance here, too, is Bev's work on life stories in various research domains. In the introduction to the "Telling lives" section of *Music and gender* (2000), for instance, Bev notes that musicology has traditionally prioritized "telling lives" of influential figures in the Western art tradition, and goes on to observe: "More recently, we have become attuned both to the perspectives and factors that ascribe historical significance to lives and to the critical problems of 'telling'—representing, and interpreting—the enormous complexities of human musical experience" (Moisala and Diamond 2000, 95). Along these lines, Jeff Titon emphasizes that life stories are "personal narratives" even if the story gets transferred to the written page. Titon (1980, 276) also underlines the reflexive nature of the processes surrounding this kind of research: "The storyteller trusts the listener(s) and the listener respects the storyteller, not interrupting the train of thought until the story is finished. That is not to say the listener is passive as a doorknob; he nods assent, interposes a comment, frames a relevant question; indeed, his presence and reactions

1

are essential to the story. He may coincidentally be a folklorist, but his role is mainly that of a sympathetic friend."

Aware of these contextual considerations, over a three-day period in May 2007, we had a series of conversations with Bev at her home in St. John's, Newfoundland. Initially, we conceived of our visit with Bev and the ensuing conversations as a kind of fieldwork and, in the planning stages, we imagined them as interviews, complete with some prepared questions, a tape recorder, and even a camera. To this end, we planned six morning and afternoon sessions over Friday, Saturday, and Sunday on the following selected topic areas: (1) research and fieldwork perspectives in the 1980s, the SPINC project, *Visions of sound* (1994); (2) Bev's article (for this volume) about the life and music of her partner, Clifford Crawley; (3) Bev's life story (family, schools, musical training, university education); (4) Canadian music topics (e.g., thinking in decades: 1930s, 1940s, 1950s, 1960s, etc., "Narratives in Canadian music history" [1995], *Canadian music: Issue of hegemony and identity* [1994], "What's the difference? Reflections on discourses of morality, modernism, and mosaics in Canadian music" [2001], "Overview: Musical culture in Canada" in *The United States and Canada*, volume 8 of the *Garland encyclopedia of world music* [2001], etc.); (5) perspectives on fieldwork, Inuit work in the 1970s, First Nations work in the 1980s and 1990s, Sámi and other recent fieldwork, changes in ethnomusicology as a field of study over thirty years, feminist studies and music and gender, music technology; (6) teaching, university and institutional environments; collaboration with consultants, colleagues, and students; teaching and research. Significantly, the sessions turned into a collaborative ethnographic experience; they did not end up being interviews in any formal sense but rather three-way conversations with Bev's voice as the focal point. And, needless to say, the sessions flowed into each other, and into lunches, dinners, and a visit to the recently opened provincial cultural centre, The Rooms, and another to spectacularly scenic Cape Spear, the easternmost part of North America.

Reflecting back, in adopting this interactive, experiential framework we were attempting to avoid what might be called, among other things, an ethnographic "crisis of representation" (Marcus and Fischer 1986, 7–16). As it turns out, we ourselves became part of the framework, an aspect of the research we had not anticipated, and one that all three of us found inspiring and memorable. Without deliberate intent on our part, we became part of a "metaphor of dialogue," which has influenced many ethnographers over the past two decades, stimulated in part by the writings of such scholars as Clifford, Marcus, Fischer, and Rosaldo. Referring to this shift as from "Reading over the shoulders of Natives" to "Reading alongside Natives," Lassiter has articulated about the movement to writing collaborative and reciprocal ethnographies: "They [recent scholars] have thus sought to develop ethnography along dialogic lines and have in their individual accounts shifted the dominant style of writing from authoritative monologue to involved dialogue between ethnographer and interlocutor" (2005, 3).

We begin with Bev's "life stories" as she told them to us. These stories—and we deliberately use the plural here to reflect the multiplicity of ways we can speak about our lives—are presented as a continuous narrative. We have provided endnotes to assist in understanding the various contexts referred to by Bev in this narrative, especially with regard to the identities of individuals and places. "Life stories" is followed by a discussion of the academic directions in Bev's career: her teaching, her research, and scholarly activity.

We have interspersed our discussion with commentary by Bev, again deriving from the St. John's interviews, as well as a few related excerpts from her writings. To facilitate this discussion, and for coherence and representational completeness, we invoke chronological as well as thematic paradigms. Sensitive to details of accuracy, ethics issues, and representational integrity, we followed an authorized university ethics review procedure for the St. John's interviews, continued to consult with Bev during the writing stages, showed her a final draft of this introduction, and include interview excerpts here with her permission. To facilitate following this discussion, we have used italic typeface for the interview excerpts.[1]

Life Stories

I grew up on a farm about 125 kilometres west of Toronto, near the town of New Hamburg.[2] It is located midway between Stratford and Kitchener, just south of what is now a main highway.[3] We had [forty hectares] and we grew grain and corn, [and] raised several hundred chickens and a dairy herd.

My mother is a second-generation immigrant. Her father emigrated with the potato famine Irish; three of the grandparents on that side of the family are Irish. My mother was really intelligent and would have done well in university, but her mother was ill at the point when she had to enter high school. She had to stay home for four years and look after her mother. She went off to secretarial school, but got sick just before the final exams; she just had the darnedest time! She met a medical doctor, who realized

*that she was somebody who could learn quickly, so she became a doc-
tor's assistant. Her ambition for me was that I would become a lab assistant, she told me at one point, but that had to do with her loving her
work with that doctor at that time.[4]*

*My father was English; I suspect there were some French roots in the
family, but all I know are two English grandparents. I was born in Kitchener, Ontario, but my parents lived in the little town of Baden[5] where
the doctor my mother worked for was based. We moved to my paternal
grandfather's farm—they had been there for maybe three generations—
when I was two. I am not from a family of intellectuals. They were farm
people and community-minded people. My mother was a smart woman,
involved in numerous organizations, but particularly the Women's Institutes, and my dad, who had not had the opportunity to acquire much
education, nonetheless gained some prominence in local government,
eventually becoming county warden.*

*I have one brother, Douglas Diamond, who is a couple of years older
than me. He became a veterinarian. Due to health problems, he has been
unable to be active professionally since his forties. His daughter is my
dear niece, Terry Diamond. She's like a daughter to me, and she treats
me like a second mom. She got a Ph.D. in psychology from York, and her
specialization is working with autistic children.*

*When I was growing up we attended a little rural church, but for us
it was more social than religious. It was a United Church, now used by
the Mennonite community, at the corner of Diamond Road (which ran
along the edge of our farm) and Bean Road (which ran by the farm of Ell-
worth Bean, who would become my stepfather). My father was killed in
a car accident at the age of sixty-two; my mother was alone for a decade.
Then her best friend died, and after some years, she married her best
friend's husband, my dad's best friend. Needless to say, the two families
had always been close and it was quite special to renew the bonds when
the two remaining parents were in their late seventies.*

*I lived on the family farm until I went to university. My elementary
school was one of the last one-room schools, eight grades in one room. For
me that one-room school experience was phenomenal, although I think
that for people who needed extra attention, it was probably not great. I
was reading fluently before I began school. Although I must have learned
to read at some point, it seemed to be something I always knew how to
do. You could listen in on other classes, so I could pay attention to whatever grade's work I wanted to. Because the lone teacher in such schools
could not teach more than one grade at a time, there was lots of time to*

*use the library (it was just a corner in the single classroom) and read.
Even more extraordinary opportunities for independent learning came
when I was in grade eight along with one other child. The teacher had so
many other kids on her hands that she said, "I'll give you two access to
the teacher's room. I want you to go write a book." So we did. We wrote
stories, we drew pictures, we wrote poetry; that's what we did for the
year. I guess that was the beginning of my collaborative urge! I helped
with the music teaching in that school as a student. The teacher would say,
"Could you get them to play the rhythm band?" or "Could you accompany while we do this little song?" Whoever was in the room helped out
however they could.*

*I did not have much opportunity growing up to listen to music. My
parents had only two LP recordings, both country-and-western music,
which they paradoxically claimed to dislike. We had a radio in the barn
to increase milk production, according to my father. I played the organ at
our little church from about the age of thirteen. The Kitchener–Waterloo
Symphony was a pretty amateurish thing at that point, and I did get to a
couple of their concerts, but only after I was old enough to drive. I knew
only a little of the world of classical music until I got to university. I still
often wish my classical repertoire was bigger, but I don't do as much about
it anymore because I also wish my popular and world music repertoires
were bigger!*

*I went to a regional high school, Waterloo-Oxford District High School,[6]
with an exceptional music teacher, a man named Ed Ferguson. We had quite
a good choir that performed widely and did well in at least one Toronto
music festival, as I recall. He was a good choral conductor and, together
with the English teacher there, had us do a fully staged Gilbert and Sullivan operetta every year.*

*We had a piano at home and I started taking piano lessons at age three.
My brother had started taking lessons, and I was imitating what he was
playing by ear. My parents thought that was a bad thing that interfered
with the ability to learn to read music. I took lessons in New Hamburg
from Grace Klassen, who charged twenty-five cents a lesson in the early
days. One year I won a prize at the Kitchener Music Festival that gave me
twenty-five dollars. My parents said they weren't going to cycle that back
into music lessons since they could afford the music lessons, so I could use
it for anything I wanted. So I took one year of figure skating lessons on
my twenty-five dollars.*

*I did the Western Conservatory[7] and then the Royal Conservatory
music and theory exams. When I was about fifteen, the wonderful pianist*

and composer, *Ruth Watson Henderson, moved to Kitchener.*[8] *I really needed a teacher who knew repertoire more extensively and had professional technique. I studied with her for several years before I went to university. She was an interesting teacher, a Guerrero student.*[9] *I remember when I played my ARCT*[10] *the examiner said, "Who did you study with? You have Guerrero technique." I knew who Guerrero was and I knew Ruth had studied with him, but I had no idea what I had picked up by way of that technique. I remember her saying, "People will say 'play soft,' but probably nobody's told you how to do that." She would explain physically what to do. I probably had terrible habits like many young players do, but she managed to teach me to have a sufficiently relaxed technique that I never had problems with tendonitis.*

When I entered the University of Toronto in 1966, all I really knew was performance. I studied with Clifford Poole[11] during my undergraduate degree. I see in retrospect that he taught me a lot about phrasing. More importantly, he allowed me to explore—new music, big concertos that were much too hard for me. I was hungry to get to know the big pieces of the repertoire. I would take a Liszt concerto in and say, "Could I work on this?" And he'd say, "Yeah, spend a few weeks … but you won't do that on your jury." I did quite a lot of performing as a university student. Twentieth-century music was a hugely exciting discovery. A lot of my peers didn't like to learn it, but I did. I developed a modest reputation for being willing to accompany people doing twentieth-century repertoire. There were composers in our class—Clifford Ford and John Fodi[12]—and so sometimes we would work on pieces by our classmates.

By the end of the first year—having discovered, as university students often do, that there is more to music than performance—I realized I liked the academic side as well as performance. I remember going with fear and trepidation to Harvey Olnick's[13] office to say I wanted to be a history and literature major. If he had laughed at me, I might have run away and never returned, but he didn't. I was so timid; as an undergraduate, I didn't want to open my mouth about anything.

From second year on I was in the history and literature stream. There were four of us in my year: Cindy Shuter, who ended up playing in the Montreal Symphony, Dorith Cooper, Nicholas Schmidt, and me.[14] Elaine Keillor[15] came in when we were in second or third year. She was about a decade older than us, and had all this international experience as a performer. I remember her coming into ear-training class; we were doing three-part Kodály exercises, where you had to play two lines and sing the other in tonic sol-fa. We were sitting there singing very slowly and barely *picking out the tunes. Then Elaine came in one day and sang up to speed. And it was a* musical *performance! Well, that raised the stakes, and never again did any of us do anything less than up to speed.*

Mieczyslaw Kolinski *was doing ethnomusicology and acoustics courses at that time. He was sixty-five when he was hired at the U. of T. and had never taught before, so he was not very confident teaching undergraduate classes. It was hard for him. He had been working as a music therapist in New York City hospitals; before the war, he had been a psychology student of Erich M. von Hornbostel. Of course there were other important teachers, but John Beckwith stands out for his encouragement to value the musics in our midst as much as the classics from elsewhere. That was radical pedagogy in the 1960s.*

Initially I lived in residence in a house on St. George Street, where Innis College is now. Two old houses there were informally called the music residences. I married Bob Cavanagh after my third undergraduate year. He was a graduate engineering student at the University of Waterloo, but it was through music that we met. He is a talented singer. Over time, our values and interests diverged and so we went our separate ways, but he was a good fellow.

I started out in the master's program in 1970, wanting to do twentieth-century music. I was going to be a historical musicologist with a twentieth-century specialization, probably Canadian-oriented. I felt ethnomusicology was too big; I had so little background. How could I take on the whole world when I didn't know as much repertoire as people who had grown up in cities? But halfway through the first year I thought, "What I really want to do is ethnomusicology," so I switched. Kolinski had Balikci's Inuit collection in his office.[16] He said, "Somebody should work on this. Why don't you listen to it?" I liked the music. I thought the songs were intriguing, so that's what got me into Inuit studies. I was easily led in those days. I remember sitting in my faculty office at McGill thinking, "How the heck did I get here?" I hadn't made a very conscious decision about career directions, and had just kind of fallen into things. Luckily, they seemed to be the right things and I've had the rare privilege of making a living doing the things I love.

There were academic jobs open at U. of T. and McGill, both in 1973. My doctorate was far from finished: I had just done my first field trip! But, in those days, there were not many jobs, and so I thought, "Maybe I should apply for these and see what happens because maybe this is the only time there will be a job in the next fifteen years." Jay Rahn[17] got the U. of T. job that year, at a salary 12 percent higher than mine at McGill; that seemed to be the gender gap at that time. Bob said, "If you get that McGill job, I can find work in Montreal." It was easy for engineers with comput-ing skills in those days, and he had exceptional hardware skills. I'm sure he still does![18]

I linked up again with Cindy Shuter in Montreal, my undergraduate friend. Among the new friendships that developed, Sandra Mangsen[19] *and I started what has become a close and lasting one.*

A former colleague of Bob's had come to run the computing centre at Queen's University and offered him a job there. I left my tenure-track job to take a one-year appointment at Queen's. Of course these days it would be insane to do that, but in those days you had a vague hope something might come of it, and it did. Istvan Anhalt[20] *was very helpful to me, and very supportive in all kinds of ways, so he was instrumental in my stay-ing. I got along well with Istvan and enjoyed that association. I felt like a musician as much as an academic at Queen's. We started the Windsong trio with Carol-Lynn Reifel and Donelda Hunter and I, and then Ireneus Zuk replaced me.*[21] *We did a lot of work with the CBC. I did not get really serious about performance in some ways until the Queen's years.*

Ultimately of more importance, though, was the opportunity to develop ethnomusicology courses with no interference, and to develop more ambi-tious and socially conscious research plans. I formed the SPINC group at Queen's because I really felt I needed people to talk to about professional issues and my struggle to work ethically in First Nations contexts. I invited Franziska von Rosen and Sam Cronk to join a research team, and while our project was not without moments of "adventure"—largely because I had no experience running such a project—we remain good friends and professional colleagues.[22]

My favourite colleague at Queen's was composer Clifford Crawley. After a decade of teaching together, we decided we were rather more than colleagues, although we married only after Cliff took early retirement and joined me in Toronto in 1992. And so the Crawley family became an important part of my life. I even acquired two wonderful grandchildren, Evan and Jill.

The move to York University was part of a larger pattern in my life; it's weird, but every fifteen years an opportunity emerges that I didn't plan but can't resist. The master's program was already established at York; in the late 1980s, it was the only place in Canada with a group of faculty ethnomusicologists. York was a great place to be! It was not easy, but it was really the right thing for me. After I had been at York for a year

*I remember having coffee with Les Monkman,[23] who had done his grad-
uate degrees at York, and I said, "You know, I feel like my thinking has
moved ahead light years since I've been at York." And he said, "Mine did
too. Isn't it amazing for that?" There was creativity in the air. Everybody
was socially engaged and ready to experiment. It was easy to work across
the disciplines, and I loved that. At that point I really wanted to do everything. I was on the Robarts Centre[24] board, the Ontario Council for Graduate Studies, umpteen committees, and eventually I did a fair bit of
administrative stuff, both as associate dean in the Faculty of Fine Arts, and
as the grad program director in music for six years.*

*David Mott[25] was the head of music when I went to York. Bob Wit-
mer[26] had been there pretty much his whole career. Alan Lessem[27] was a
big influence; I really wanted to learn how Alan thought. [He was] a
lovely man, and [it was] a tragic loss when he died. Jim Tenney[28] was
also a tragic loss more recently. There was an event I wish we had recorded,
especially now that both Alan and Jim are gone. We had a kind of thought-
piece seminar one of the first years I was there, at which the three of us
addressed two articles: Susan McClary's "Terminal Prestige,"[29] which neither of them liked, and a conservative article by Edward Rothstein. I
remember that being a great public discussion! I wanted to have those
kinds of public debates.*

*At York I began to see how difficult but also how possible and fruit-
ful interdisciplinarity is. York does interdisciplinarity in a way that is
sometimes flaky, but at other times quite brilliant. They are willing to
take the all-important risk. In addition to friends in ethnomusicology,
especially Bob Witmer and Rob Bowman, at York some of my closest colleagues were from outside the music department—for instance, my dance
colleagues, Nina De Shane and Mary Jane Warner. I still feel I have got
lots of friendships all across that campus.*

*I've been lucky to enjoy good friendships and professionally support-
ive relationships with amazing women in my field. My Canadian "sisters"—Jocelyne Guilbault and Regula Qureshi—continue as important
and inspiring friends. Jocelyne once compared our friendship to those of
earlier generations, suggesting that our mothers might have exchanged
recipes, but we exchange bibliographies. Ethnomusicologist Pirkko Moisala
(with whom I co-edited a book more or less by happenstance) also remains
a close friend. During a magical six months when I taught at Harvard in
1999, Kay Shelemay took me under her wing. I fondly recall many dinners in the area of Harvard Square with Kay, Ingrid Monson, Carol
Babiracki, and Ginny Danielson that were as intellectually transformative*

as they were fun. There's a wonderful core of truly caring women who do Native American studies and feminist studies. Being an academic enables a huge network of friendships, of course, but these are some of the ones that really sustain me.

The chance to move to Newfoundland in 2002 was like a gift from heaven. The rugged beauty, the ocean, the incredible music (and unparalleled love of music), feisty friends, so many fine writers/thinkers/artists.... It's clichéd to say it feeds my soul like no other place I've lived, but that's what it does. I have world-class colleagues in both Folklore and Music and an enviable job description, thanks to excellent support from the CRC program and MUN. The Research Centre for Music, Media, and Place (MMaP) that I established in St. John's gives me a base for a more reciprocal style of research both with indigenous musicians globally and communities locally. I've had the good fortune to be able to contribute to the establishment and development of a second graduate program in ethnomusicology, and I've had the good luck to teach stellar students in both. Some of my earliest graduate students at York—Virginia Caputo, Kip Pegley, Andra McCartney among them—set the bar high. So have the first graduates of the MUN Ethnomusicology program—Kelly Best, Judith Klassen, and Janice Tulk—here in St. John's.

Since coming to Memorial University the interdisciplinarity has continued, but now it is between the School of Music and the Department of Folklore. The hope was that the new graduate program in ethnomusicology would be a bridge between the two, and it has happened. One thing that I have to juggle is that I'm trying to be part of the traditional music community, and also part of the classical music community, and they don't mix much. My musical skills as a keyboard player are useless in the traditional music scene here. I'm struggling to learn the button accordion, which is by far the most counterintuitive instrument I've ever attempted, but my academic life has never been more demanding and so there is little time.

Academic Directions and Teaching

As Bev comments in the preceding narrative, her career as a teacher, researcher, and a scholar is linked in fundamental ways to the contexts of her academic appointments: Lecturer at McGill University in Montreal (1973–75); assistant, then associate, professor at Queen's University in Kingston, Ontario (1975–88); associate professor at York University in Toronto (1988–2002); and Canada Research Chair (Tier I) and professor of ethnomusicology at Memorial University of Newfoundland (2002–present). In addition, Bev was visiting assistant professor at the University of Toronto in 1980–81, and visiting associate professor at Harvard University in the winter term of 1999. One of the overarching themes in Bev's academic career is her continuous, vibrant emphasis on teaching, and how teaching stimulates her perspectives on research. We therefore consider it to be a fitting departure point for this discussion. The following are excerpts around teaching and academic directions from the St. John's interviews.

I had no teaching experience when I went to McGill. I'd had a couple of TAships, but that was it. I taught everything at McGill—four courses a term, including tonal harmony, music history, twentieth-century music courses, and world music courses. Even then I remember how elated I was [about teaching]. I'd come out of classes high on the energy of the music and the discussion. I recall that when I went to McGill I went through huge crises about whether I was more interested as a teacher in conveying information or stimulating thinking. I still think that's a difficult issue. What is it we're teaching?

Some people are happy staying in one place all their lives, but for me, I've learned so much from different institutional cultures. It seems like every fifteen years I've moved [referring to her moves from Queen's to York to Memorial]. At Queen's I felt so junior and so insecure, but under the radar for a long time and hence free to experiment.

I think you have to accept the fact that you've got a different role at different stages of your career. I didn't realize that I'd developed any idiosyncratic teaching approaches until I went to York, and I realized that I was not doing what was expected there. Reflexive teaching was not popular. For another thing, they were really into big issues. I remember during my first year at York I taught a grad course on [Marius] Barbeau. York students (and colleagues) were more interested in my having proposed something on some huge theoretical issue. At York I did learn how to teach the big issues. The classes there were the most challenging ever, for many reasons. The cultural diversity was one of them. Students' perspectives were diverse and often at odds. And when that worked, it was fantastic. I remember a class where the African-American students got talking about their experiences of race, and it remains to this day one of the most insightful discussions I read or heard anywhere. What impressed me so much was that their interventions were heartfelt and the narratives were lived. They totally understood the artificiality of the construct of race and yet its persistent power. They discussed how variations in skin tone might impact the respect they got, the music they preferred, the career choices they were encouraged to make. They understood how histories of immigration helped shape the power dynamics among the cultures of different national groups. They felt it when a reductionist phrase like "Caribbean music" was used to homogenize radically different histories and experiences. We talked about relative differences in the authority of African as compared to Caribbean, or Jamaican as compared to, say, Haitian identities. It was dynamite.

But then there were other times when teaching at York was far from easy. I remember one class where the jazz guys (they were mostly guys) all sat in the back corner of the room, and it was a North American music course, so I had to teach about jazz. They knew very well that I didn't know much about jazz. I would say at the beginning, "You know what I am going to teach is for those people who don't have a jazz background. We're going to do some introductory stuff here, and those people in the jazz program may want to chip in about one thing or another." And at the best of times they did. I would get them involved, or have them come and do a demonstration. I think it worked.

Having graduate students at York and at Memorial was/is for me a wonderful thing. It has taught me so much. Working on so many different topics with bright students you can see the potential for making a difference in the worlds that we live in by not just spending your own time and energy, but being able to mobilize a whole lot of other time and energy. As every teacher knows, learning happens in two directions and that continues to be what I think is transformative.

I have always struggled with teaching. It's very rare that I come home and say that I had a wonderful class today. There's always something that I wanted to do better, that I'm not happy with. There are days when I come home and say, "I had a wonderful class today!" But not a lot of them.

In conjunction with these excerpts, readers may consult the student contribution to this volume for reciprocal perspectives on Bev as teacher, mentor, and friend. Referencing her work with graduate students at York and Memorial and facilitated by Kip Pegley and Virginia Caputo, Bev's former and current students took part, and *are* taking part in a student web Festschrift as a means of reflecting honestly and interactively on Bev's work with them. As explained in "A Festschrift for the twenty-first century" (295), this process led to the articulation of lifelong lessons learned, the exploration of difficult issues and, at times, contested perspectives. As Pegley and Caputo note, "Our attempt to craft this work in Bev's honour by exploring an electronic medium through which to engage a diversity of voices as a way to work with/in/through the intensities of relationships in the intellectual community surrounding Bev is part and parcel of her influence on us as growing scholars and teachers. She instilled in us the desire to push back at conceptual boundaries both theoretically and practically; she taught us to seek out and envisage ways to see obstacles as productive events in and of themselves" (Pegley and Caputo, 303–4).

Research and Scholarly Activity

Bev's research trajectory extends from the 1970s to the present, and includes a wide range of topics and critical/theoretical approaches, which derive in fundamental ways from contextual perspectives linked to her life story as well as to her development as a scholar. As noted earlier, Bev's output is incredibly prodigious; highlights include seven books, seventeen book chapters, twenty-one refereed articles, thirty-three reviews, and nearly one hundred conference presentations and invited lectures—a list that is substantial and expands significantly every year. We would like to emphasize that our discussion of Bev's research in what follows is a partial one, and is not intended to be a complete overview, nor a particular critique of her work. Rather, we wish to provide some of the perspectives that Bev herself focused on in her interviews with us, perspectives that we also recognize as good entry points to knowing about her work. In keeping with the dialogic structure of this discussion, we highlight Bev's words, and ask that readers consult the Appendix for related publications to various works referred to in the following.

Bev's early work in the 1970s focused on gaining knowledge about ethnomusicology as a field of study, as well as her fieldwork and research on Inuit musical traditions that led to her doctoral dissertation. The following are some related comments on her academic background and early fieldwork.

Well before the reflexive turn in ethnographic work, we had to try to figure out what fieldwork was by reading very early sources. [Franz] Boas as fieldwork advice? Hmm. I remember the day that I discovered the report of the Fifth Thule Expedition in the library at the University of Toronto, and I was struck by the fact that to do our work, we ethnomusicologists venture into parts of the library that many of our music colleagues rarely venture into. It sounds naive to say that now, but the gap between the realms of knowledge that shape our work is, of course, a fascinating topic.

I had no training in fieldwork methods at U. of T. Kolinski had been on his way to do some fieldwork when the war broke out and he had never done it. He remained an "armchair ethnomusicologist." I took Inuktitut as a private student of Mick Mallon, who developed some of the earliest Inuktitut courses in Canada. He had moved to Toronto from the North on a sabbatical and kindly offered to teach me. But, when I first arrived in the Arctic, I didn't know what I was doing in terms of fieldwork. I had a translator, a wonderful Inuit woman from Gjoa Haven named Rebecca Qitsualik, who helped with the translations and explained to me that she had trained many previous scholars to work with Inuit. I was grateful for her guidance. Her husband was one of the first ordained Anglican clergymen from the Inuit community.

On my first [field] trip in 1972, I was introduced to some amazing elders who were willing to record drum dance songs in particular, and that first collection—which is still by far the most significant collection that I have made anywhere in my whole career—came together in about a month. This is the collection that I partially transcribed in volume two of my thesis. There was a guy in Pelly Bay, named John Ningark. I think he subsequently became a member of Parliament.³⁰ He said, "Well, let's go around and get you a schedule!" I kept saying, "You're not supposed to do this in ethnomusicology, you're supposed to hang out for months." But within two days he had introduced me to many important singers and culture bearers, explaining to them that "She'll come Wednesday morning. She'll come Thursday afternoon...." My experience reminds me of a comment that Carol Babiracki has made about acquiring "the hard-won wisdom that choices would be made" for her.

In the 1980s Bev carried out research on Innu musical traditions, using her first grant (of many) from the Social Sciences and Humanities Research Council (SSHRC) to help finance a series of field trips to Innu communities in northern Quebec and Labrador. As she explained:

Innu tradition was utterly different from the Inuit one where I encountered such openness. The Innu tradition is a "received" (not "composed") song tradition, and my interest in the dream songs, which are very private things, was met with understandably guarded reaction. Some people were reluctant to talk about that repertoire; others did share a lot, often advising me about the inappropriate use of what they recorded or taught me. There was a vibrant hymn singing tradition there as well. That was easy and more appropriate to research, [and] important too as a window on colonialism. And storytelling: Innu related the classic atnuhana *and music was part of the narration of those great myths. Labrador Innu were struggling against a lot of problems in the late twentieth century: NATO's low-flying aircraft training program that disrupted hunting and endangered lives; easy access to alcohol and drugs; dislocation from their traditional lands. I was of little use in these struggles and my narrow interests seemed trivial in the face of such issues. After considerable soul-searching, I opted to curtail research in Labrador, although I continued Innu work in northern Quebec throughout the 1980s. Together with Franziska von Rosen, I got more involved with First Nations communities near where I lived, and institutions (notably the dismal national Prison for Women in Kingston) in which Aboriginal peoples needed support. I decided to abandon research in remote Aboriginal communities in which I could not commit to live usefully, and, for much of the 1990s, opted to leave Aboriginal research to Aboriginal peoples, a decision that I slowly rethought during that decade. Little did I suspect in 1980 that it would be the contemporary creative artists and musicians who would be the ones to articulate memory and vision with such power. When I returned to indigenous projects in the late 1990s, I focused on indigenous modernity and the powerful popular music that was emerging.*

This fieldwork helped to open new horizons, and coincided with exciting shifts in ethnomusicological research, which were increasingly interdisciplinary, and embracing of innovative perspectives that sought to consider music as a socially constructed and a lived process, as well as the more traditional approach that considered music as a sound product. A critical theme that emerged in Bev's work in the 1980s is collaboration—working with others, which is essential to doing fieldwork, for sure—and something that Bev considers foundational in her work over the past twenty-five years. In addition to her collaborations with informants and consultants in ethnographic work, in the 1980s Bev initiated a collaborative project with two undergraduate students. Importantly, this project received two substantial SSHRC grants, one of the first research projects of its kind (i.e., on First Nations music culture) to receive this level of government support.

Without anybody else as an ethnomusicologist in the department, and without graduate students around [at Queen's], I didn't feel I had colleagues that I could talk to about the kind of issues that I really wanted to think about: fieldwork ethics, different ways of knowing, so, in a way, the SPINC project was motivated as much by my wanting to invent a team as it was by the research itself. I just felt that I needed more discussion—ongoing discussion—with colleagues doing First Nations work.

I think what might be considered different about SPINC [and the resulting Visions of sound *book], and certainly about the textbook project I just did [*Native American music in eastern North America*] is the belief that [Native] issues relate to research elsewhere in the world. I think that there are important intersections between issues of indigenous peoples everywhere and the issues of ethnomusicology in general. And I wanted to be part of that conversation. In SPINC we had those "conversations" at the beginning of each of the chapters [in* Visions of sound*] and they have been justifiably criticized because we didn't involve Aboriginal participants, but we wanted to be part of this conversation about how we were learning what we were learning, and we thought that was the way to do it. Other people might find these sorts of things self-indulgent and dislike these sorts of reflexive exercises, but I don't make apologies for those conversations. I think they served a purpose.*

Indeed, the collaborative aspect was essential in *Visions of sound*, as it was in *Canadian music: Issues of hegemony and identity,* a collection of essays published in the same year (1994). *Canadian music: Issues of hegemony and identity* contains twenty-two previously published essays, nine essays written especially for the book, and an introduction and "bridging" essays for each of the sections. Bev co-edited the book with her colleague at York University, Bob Witmer, with whom she shared fourteen years of collegiality and friendship during her period at York. *Canadian music: Issues of hegemony and identity* can be considered as a wide-ranging gathering together of "voices" on topics from various scholarly disciplines, which address aspects of critical importance to Canadian music, many of which were influenced by current theoretical issues in the humanities and social sciences. The book as a whole pushed back at embedded notions of history, invoking questions about power relationships, such as "the greater prominence to interpretations grounded in the 19th-century, Euro-centred belief in the autonomy of musical language," in favour of exploring other contextual paradigms (i.e., social construction of music), and questioning academic conventions and "the very abstraction of music itself" (1994, 1). *Canadian music: Issues of hegemony and identity* broke important new ground in Canadian music studies, not only because of its innovative approaches to historiography, theoretical issues, and varied musical emphases, but also because of its collaborative, interdisciplinary scope.

Bev and her brother Doug Diamond, ca. 1951 (photo by their mother, Florence Diamond)

Windsong ensemble (Queen's University) in 1983: Carol-Lynn Reifel, soprano; Donelda Hunter (Gartshore), flute; Bev, piano (photo by Bob Cavanagh)

Bev and Cliff Crawley, backyard of John Crawley and Amy Smith's former home near Cobourg, Ontario, 2000 (photographer unknown)

Bev, Rosemary Diamond, Terry Diamond, and Cliff Crawley, Cape St. Mary's, Newfoundland, 2003 (photo by a tourist)

Bev and Charity Marsh at the University Club in the University of Regina, March 2006; Bev's visit was funded by an Indigenous Peoples Project Education Grant at the University of Regina (photo by a student)

Sadie Buck, Six Nations Reserve, and Bev at Memorial University, March 2006. Sadie's visit to St. John's was in conjunction with Bev's work on her (then) forthcoming book, *Native American music in eastern North America* (photo by Cliff Crawley)

Bev with the MMaP team at Memorial University: Spencer Crewe, Mauréen Houston, Janice Tulk, and Tom Gordon, director, School of Music, Memorial University, 2007 (photo by Chris Hammond and used with the permission of Memorial University)

Cliff in his cottage office, Holyrood, Newfoundland, 2008 (photo by Beverley Diamond)

Gordon, Bev, and Robin at The Rooms, St. John's, Newfoundland, May 2007 (photo by a visitor)

Bev's highly influential article, "Narratives in Canadian music history" (Diamond 1995), provided further challenges to the field of Canadian music historiography. In this article she examines three Canadian music texts from multiple "narrative" perspectives (e.g., intent, proportion, organization, metaphor), and compares Canadian and American ways of narrating music history. In an important sequel to the "Narratives" article (Diamond 2000), Bev explores ways of reinterpreting Canadian music and cultural history by examining how social difference has been articulated through discourses on morality, modernism, or mosaics in different historical and contemporary contexts.

Another major collection of essays that embodies the collaborative and innovative spirit of Bev's work in the 1990s, as well as an emerging focus in her research, was *Music and gender* (2000), co-edited with her colleague, the Finnish musicologist (and contributor to this volume), Pirkko Moisala. Ellen Koskoff (2000, ix; also a contributor to this volume) notes in the foreword that the book includes research on music and gender from "an unusually diverse set of scholars from the United States, Canada, and Europe," and she points out the eclectic mixture of disciplinary approaches (ethnomusicology, historical musicology, feminist studies, music composition, education, popular music studies, music technology, and sociology) in the book's essays. Innovative for its topical and critical diversity, *Music and gender* also points to another manifestation of the collaborative theme in Bev's work, namely, her interaction with colleagues, not only in Canada and the US but across the world, an aspect of her work she continues to consider extremely important. Bev comments on the importance of global perspectives:

To this day, I continue to feel that my favourite society is ICTM [International Council for Traditional Music]. I'm drawn to its philosophy, the whole idea of really making sure there's a grassroots discussion across the whole world. As I've often said to people, at SEM [Society for Ethnomusicology], we talk about difference, but at ICTM we encounter it or we participate in it. You begin to see that the esoteric topics that we do as academics may not be relevant for colleagues in Africa, or for the new East European block or some other part of the world. It just always transforms me, the ICTM meetings.[31]

As a part of a process of repositioning our thinking about identity modelling in musical contexts, we can consider dialogue on multiple levels, including individual, local, regional, national, and transnational ones, as a critical aspect of Bev's work. As she reminds us (see below), dialogic processes have expanded and been transformed by technology across the world, a point that needs to be considered in research on music. Indeed, dialogue is a theme that pervaded all of our interview sessions, including, needless to say, the interviewing process itself. As she has written, "By the 21st century, it is obvious that Indigenous music, once thought to be the most local of traditions, is widely implicated in globalization. Indigenous musicians are using transnational networks and media sources for local purposes; they are defining the potential of new technologies, and articulating the social issues that constitute modernity" (Diamond 2007, 1). As an alternative to "identity studies," in this article Bev proposes "alliance studies" as a more encompassing means of understanding music and modern indigeneity, inspired in large part by her work on Sámi *joik*, including renowned Sámi musicians such as Frode Fjellheim and Wimmi Sari. Drawing on her Sámi research, as well as her Inuit and Innu research, in this article Bev explores "alliance studies" along an axis of "mainstreamness" and "distinctiveness," including genre and technology, language and dialect, citation and collaboration, and access and ownership.

Until recently, Bev's books were collaborative in the sense that they were multi-authored in different ways (i.e., collections of writings, etc.). *Native American music in eastern North America* (2008) represents a departure from this model, a departure that Bev addressed at the beginning of the book's preface. Because of its significance with respect to the *Native American music in eastern North America*, and its significance with respect to Bev's work overall, we quote it here:

Until I decided to accept the invitation to write this book, I had always vowed that I would never write a textbook. I am more interested in exploring the uses and limitations of authority than setting down what students inevitably would regard as an authoritative version, a truth about the musical practices of a group of people. As it turns out, by working with a group of Aboriginal advisors whose knowledge was so deep and whose capacity to discuss issues of representation was so capable, I found the preparation of this book one of the most rewarding projects I have ever undertaken. I hope that the differences among our perspectives remain clear and that this textbook, then, can never be read simply as a univocal authoritative text. (Diamond 2008, xiii)

Bev's Aboriginal advisers in this project were Sadie Buck, Stephen Augustine, and Karin Kettler. Along with providing valuable indigenous

perspectives on Haudenosaunee, Mi'kmaq, and Inuit traditions and culture, these advisers helped to stimulate dialogue among individuals and
across cultures, as noted earlier, an aspect Bev believes to be an essential
part of the process of learning and knowing. Bev underlines the challenge
of incorporating indigenous perspectives and the relatively small (though
growing) number of ethnomusicologists of First Nations, Métis, or Inuit
descent. In explaining this as a challenge behind the book project, she
comments on her struggle with speaking as an outsider about cultures that
have such articulate spokespeople, and again emphasizes the need for far-
reaching levels of dialogue: "In addition to indigenous perspectives, however, I believe that we need dialogue: dialogue that does not gloss over the
shared responsibilities that we have toward social justice, the environment, and peaceful coexistence" (Diamond 2008, xiii–xiv).

In this chapter we have drawn on multiple narratives with the aim of
presenting Bev's life stories, as well as aspects of her academic career,
research, and teaching. Inspired by her own collaborative approach to
scholarship and teaching, we have also engaged reflexively with the "telling"
of these stories, drawing on our conversations with Bev in May 2007, and
our subsequent reflections on those conversations with each other, and
also with Bev. Collaboration and interactive engagement are also overarching themes in Bev's chapter on the life story and music of her partner,
Clifford Crawley, in Chapter 2 and also in a number of other chapters in
Music traditions, cultures, and contexts.

Notes

1 Over the course of three days we recorded twelve hours of interviews with Bev. We are
   grateful to Erin Bustin, former graduate student at the University of Toronto, for tran-
   scribing these interviews. With Bev's permission, we have taken the liberty of editing and
   integrating the excerpts given in the following.

2 Although Native peoples had long lived in the area, the first European immigrants
   arrived in the area of what is now New Hamburg in the early nineteenth century. Early
   European settlers were German and Swiss (Lutheran, Catholic, and Amish/Mennonite),
   along with farmers from Britain and France. The current population of New Hamburg
   is 7,000. See Paul Knowles, *A history of New Hamburg* (New Hamburg: English Garden, 2002), and Ernst F. Ritz, *New Hamburg as it really was* (New Hamburg: Ritz,
   2003).

3 The farm is on Diamond Road, which is about four kilometres south of Ontario Provincial Highway 8; this highway runs from Stratford to Kitchener–Waterloo.

4 There is a biography of Beverley Diamond's mother, Mrs. Clarence Diamond (née
   Florence Fallis), on the website of the Federated Women's Institutes of Ontario
   (FWIO): www.fwio.on.ca/Contribute/about/Mrs.C.Diamond.asp (accessed 19 Sep-
   tember 2008). She was born in Wellington County, attended Weller Secretarial and

Business College, and served as a receptionist and office manager for a medical doctor before marrying Clarence Diamond and moving to his family's farm. After her husband's death she moved to New Hamburg. She served as president of the FWIO from 1977 to 1980.

5 Baden, which has a population of under 1,000, is 6.5 kilometres northeast of New Hamburg.

6 Waterloo–Oxford District Secondary School's (http://wodss.wrdsb.on.ca/) motto: "Take charge of your success." The school is located just outside of Baden, about thirteen kilometres from the Diamond family farm.

7 The Western Conservatory of Music was a teaching and examining body that operated from 1934 to 1997 and was affiliated with the University of Western Ontario in London, Ontario. In 1997 it merged with the Western Board of Music (which operated in Alberta, Saskatchewan, and Manitoba) to create Conservatory Canada.

8 Ruth Watson Henderson (b. Toronto 1932) is a pianist, organist, teacher, and composer, best known for her many published choral works. She lived in Kitchener from 1962 to 1968, and then returned to Toronto.

9 The Chilean-born pianist Alberto Guerrero (1886–1959) lived and taught in Toronto from 1918 until his death. His pupils included many eminent Canadian musicians, including Glenn Gould, R. Murray Schafer, John Beckwith, and William Aide. See John Beckwith, *In search of Alberto Guerrero* (Waterloo: Wilfrid Laurier University Press, 2006).

10 The performance curriculum of Toronto's Royal Conservatory of Music consists of eleven graded examinations, culminating in the ARCT (Associate, Royal Conservatory of Music of Toronto) diploma.

11 Clifford Poole (1916–2003) was a pianist and composer who toured widely as a part of a piano duo team with his wife, Margaret Parsons. He began teaching at the University of Toronto in 1963.

12 Clifford Ford (b. 1947) is a composer and writer, and was a co-founder of the Canadian Musical Heritage Society. John Fodi (1944–2009) was a composer and music librarian; he was on staff at the University of Toronto music library from 1974 until his retirement in December 2007. Both men graduated with B.Mus. degrees in composition in 1970, the same year Bev completed her B.Mus. in history and literature.

13 Harvey Olnick (1917–2003) taught musicology at the University of Toronto's Faculty of Music from 1954 to 1983, and was head of the Graduate Department of Music there from 1954 to 1971.

14 Dorith R. Cooper (b. 1948) went on to complete a Ph.D. in musicology at the University of Toronto in 1983 on the subject of opera performances and opera repertoire in Montreal and Toronto. In the *Alumni directory* for the University of Toronto's Faculty of Music (Toronto: Institute for Canadian Music, 1990), a fifth history and literature student is listed as graduating in 1970: Christopher Wilson.

15 Elaine Keillor (b. 1939) began her professional career as a pianist at the age of eleven. She completed a B.A. in music in 1970, and in 1976 she became the first woman to complete a Ph.D. in musicology at the University of Toronto. In 1977 she began teaching at Carleton University, where she is currently a distinguished research professor in the School for Studies in Art and Culture.

16 Asen Balikci (b. Turkey, 1929) was an anthropologist at the University of Montreal who made extensive recordings and films documenting Inuit life for the National Museum of Man (now the Canadian Museum of Civilization).

17 The music scholar Jay Rahn completed his B.Mus. degree in history and literature at the University of Toronto in 1969, one year before Beverley Diamond. He went on to complete a Ph.D. in the field of Renaissance music at Columbia University in 1978, and began teaching at York University that same year.

18 Bob Cavanagh is currently on staff at Queen's University as the director of technology for the School of Business.

19 The harpsichordist and musicologist Sandra Mangsen is currently a faculty member at the Don Wright Faculty of Music in the University of Western Ontario.

20 Istvan Anhalt (b. 1919) is a Hungarian-born Canadian composer; he was a faculty member at McGill University from 1949 until 1971, and at Queen's University from 1971 until his retirement in 1984. He was the head of the Department of Music at Queen's from 1971 to 1981.

21 Windsong, founded in 1983, was a trio with the soprano Carol-Lynn Reifel and the flutist Donelda Gartshore Hunter, both faculty members at Queen's University. Carol-Lynn Reifel, Donelda Gartshore, and Ireneus Zuk continue as applied music faculty members today. Ireneus Zuk was director of the School of Music at Queen's from 1997 to 2003.

22 SPINC (Sound-Producing Instruments in Native Communities) was a research group at Queen's University from 1985 to 1988; Sam Cronk and Franziska von Rosen were full-time research associates in SPINC for four years. One outcome of the SPINC project was *Visions of sound* (1994).

23 Leslie G. Monkman (Ph.D., York University, 1975) is an emeritus professor of English at Queen's University and a specialist in English-Canadian literature.

24 The Robarts Centre for Canadian Studies was founded at York University in 1984. It is named after John P. Robarts, a former premier of Ontario and chancellor of York University.

25 David Mott (b. 1945) is a US-born composer and saxophonist; he was appointed to York University in 1978 and became head of the Music Department in 1988, the same year that Bev began her fourteen-year-long appointment there.

26 The ethnomusicologist Robert Witmer (b. Kitchener, 1940) joined the faculty at York University in 1971 and was the founding director of York's program in jazz studies. He co-edited *Canadian music: Issues of hegemony and identity* (Toronto: Canadian Scholars' Press, 1994) with Bev.

27 The Rhodesian-born musicologist Alan Lessem (1940–91) was a founding member of the Department of Music at York University in 1970 and taught there until his death in 1991.

28 The composer James Tenney (1934–2006) taught at York University from 1976 until 2000.

29 Susan McClary, "Terminal Prestige: The Case of Avant-garde Music Composition," *Cultural Critique* 12 (Spring 1989): 57–81.

30 John Ningark is a hunter from Pelly Bay (renamed Kugaark in 1999). He was first elected to the Legislative Assembly of the Northwest Territories in a by-election in 1989, and was re-elected in 1991 and 1995. With the creation of Nunavut in 1999, he retired from elected political office.

31 Noteworthy here is Bev's recent research on music and issues of ownership and indigenous property (see Publications and Conference List). In addition, a recent example of Bev's ongoing concern for including global perspectives in discussions about issues of

indigenous property is Indigenous Music and Dance as Cultural Property: Global Perspectives, an ICTM colloquium that was co-sponsored by Memorial University and the University of Toronto, and was held at the University of Toronto in May 2008. Bev played a key role in including participants from around the world in this event. In 2011, the ICTM biannual meeting will be held in St. John's, Newfoundland, largely a result of Bev's work in the society and her international renown, generally. The St. John's conference will be the second time in the ICTM's more than sixty-year history that the society has met in Canada. (The first time was in Quebec City in 1960.)

References

Diamond, Beverley. 1994. *Canadian music: Issues of hegemony and identity.* Toronto: Canadian Scholars' Press.

———. 1995. "Narratives in Canadian Music History." In *Taking a stand: Essays in honour of John Beckwith.* Edited by Timothy J. McGee. Toronto: University of Toronto Press. 273–305.

———. 2000. "What's the Difference? Reflections on Discourses of Morality, Modernism, and Mosaics in the Study of Music in Canada." *Canadian University Music Review* 21, no. 1: 54–75.

———. 2006. "Canadian Reflections on Palindromes, Inversions, and Other Challenges to Ethomusicology's Coherence." *Ethnomusciology* 50, no. 2: 324–36.

———. 2007. "Music of Modern Indigeneity: From Identity to Alliance Studies." *Journal of the European Seminar for Ethnomusicology.* The John Blacking Distinguished Lecture for 2006. Online at http://www.marta-dahlig.com/esem/pdf/ml/JBML2006-Diamond.pdf (accessed 2 July 2009).

———. 2008. *Native American music in eastern North America.* Global Music Series, edited by Bonnie C. Wade and Patricia C. Campbell. New York: Oxford University Press.

Lassiter, Luke Eric. 2005. *The Chicago guide to collaborative ethnography.* Chicago: University of Chicago Press.

Marcus, George E., and Michael M.J. Fischer, eds. 1986. *Anthropology as cultural critique.* Chicago: University of Chicago Press.

Moisala, Pirkko, and Beverley Diamond, eds. 2000. *Music and gender.* Urbana: University of Illinois Press.

Titon, Jeff Todd. 1980. "The Life Story." *Journal of American Folklore* 93, no. 369: 276–92.

Conversations with Clifford Crawley

BEVERLEY DIAMOND

WHEN GORDON SMITH ASKED who might write a chapter about Cliff for this book of essays, I responded "Could I do it?" without a moment's thought. For years Cliff and I had talked about recording his stories, his memories, and his ideas as a family project. This opportunity gave us the push to do it, while also moving the boundaries to include professional circles. It was more difficult than I had expected to shift from soulmates to oral history collaborators. All the good conversation topics that have energized our relationship initially evaporated in the face of the microphone, but we eventually relaxed and recorded about ten hours of conversation.[1] Of course, my perspective as both a colleague and, for more than two decades, his life partner is a particular one. I know his views rather well and had easy access to the boxes of memorabilia, tapes or CDs, and the cabinets full of scores.[2] But I hardly claim objectivity. I can only write this with enormous love and professional admiration, and in a style that is personal rather than academic.

Article-length professional biographies often start with authority figures in the relevant art or discipline, with a pedigree of teachers and influences. They often ignore the formative influences, families, and childhood experiences. Unless they are autobiographies, they may ignore the way in which individuals narrate their lives. I want this "portrait" to have some of those often-ignored features. I've attempted here to convey not just the historical information, but something of the way in which Clifford Crawley stories his life and his work.

From England to Canada

> There are magical moments in life and they often come at unexpected
> times. I think we don't really want to analyze them too much. Otherwise,
> the magic might disappear.

Clifford Owen Crawley[3] was born on 29/1/29—that is, 29 January 1929,
a date he likes written as a palindrome with the 29s mirrored[4]—in Dagenham, on the outskirts of London, England. He describes it as "a bit dreary,"
a place where "all the houses were the same." Most houses in the area
were rented in this working-class district. His parents were able to buy a
home in nearby Rush Green, not far from Romford, when Clifford was
about four years old. Of German origin, his mother, Lottie Becker, came
from a large family of bakers. His father, Thomas Owen, was a lorry driver,
after serving with distinction in the army in World War I. His father's
father had been a minister in the German-based Catholic Apostolic Church.
Cliff's most illustrious ancestor is arguably a distant relative on his father's
side, Thomas Hill, who invented the postage stamp.

While his family history includes tradespeople, clergy, and inventors,
Cliff characterizes his beginnings as "working class." As he chats about
his life, I note that he is keenly aware of class culture, but emphasizes a
capacity to move across social boundaries; he has an eye for the quotid-
ian, even the seemingly banal; and he pays close attention to turning points,
tragic or lucky. His life, as he tells it, has dramatic "magical moments"—
and so, as it happens, does his music.

Neither he nor his older sister Anne recalls much music in their parents' home, though both of them would pursue professional careers in
the arts. Cliff recalls his mother picking out tunes on their upright piano,
and his lifelong love of radio was inaugurated by the Home Service and
Forces Program on the BBC. There he heard the big bands of the day—
Stanley Black, Henry Hall, Glenn Miller, and Robert Farnon, the Canadian who was much better known in England than in Canada—as well as
singer Vera Lynn. He took piano lessons from a local teacher who routinely
fell asleep during lessons and he served as a choirboy in an Anglican church
in Romford from the age of seven. He also loved to buy printed music in
Romford, or later at Foyles bookshop—still one of his favourite places in
London. "My first score was Schubert's *Unfinished Symphony* ... because
that was the cheapest one—only two movements, fewer pages," he explains.
By the age of seven or eight, he had composed his first piece, Andante in
G for piano.[5] Much later, he became deeply conscious of social class and
was attracted to comedians such as Peter Cook and Dudley Moore—the

latter also from Dagenham[6]—who parodied the differences between elites and working-class folks.

Both Cliff and his sister Anne were sufficiently talented to win the economic support they needed to pursue their arts and, retrospectively, they acknowledge a sort of pride in one another and a bonding because of this. Anne commented: "I think he was thrilled that I was in shows, and I was thrilled that he was doing what he wanted to do, but we didn't really discuss it much. I have heard him talk since about people that I was in shows with and he would say 'I remember her,' or whatever, but we didn't talk about it much at the time.... We were the only two as far as I know. Nobody else in the family[7] had danced or were musical." Similarly, Cliff says: "We get on well together. We have sort of similar interests, but they are still isolated because the rest of our family is not particularly interested in music or dancing." Anne started ballet lessons as a therapeutical measure after she sustained an injury. While her parents could not afford dance lessons over the long term, she was so talented that she was very quickly asked to tutor the beginners at a Romford dance school run by the well-regarded teacher Marjorie Davies. Older than Cliff by five years, Anne entertained the troops as a part of the Entertainment National Service Association during the later years of World War II, and that experience changed her career ambitions from ballet to the popular dance shows in London theatres. She aimed high and succeeded, dancing as the lead in Ivor Novello's *The Dancing Years* and *Perchance to Dream* for which she served as the ballet mistress as well as lead dancer. She thought highly of Novello, describing him as "a very kind person" who appreciated hard work and "always kept you in work." Neither child was particularly encouraged in their artistic interests, however. Anne describes how she "used to go home to my mother and cry because I was so upset. I'd gotten told off. And Mother would say, 'Well, give it up. You don't have to do it.' But I wouldn't."

On a scholarship from the Guildhall School of Music, Cliff was given an opportunity to take piano lessons (with Frank Griggs), history (with Orlando Morgan),[8] and theory classes several days a week. He describes his early attraction to composition with typical self-deprecation: "I think I liked the writing because I found it easier than learning someone else's music." Guildhall required that composition students ask permission to publish. "I didn't. I just changed my name," says Cliff. Hence his first publications, mostly songs and instrumental arrangements, appeared under the name Clifford Curwin. While the pseudonym was for very practical reasons, it is but one of the things-are-not-quite-what-they-seem qualities in Cliff's work. He retained this name for all publications prior to his immigration to Canada.

During his student days at the Guildhall, he discovered what would be a lifelong love of French music. Once again, there was a significant event, a magical moment that sparked this interest: a recital by Francis Poulenc.

> France had just been freed from the Germans. It was still wartime and Poulenc came over on tour with Pierre Bernac. Actually he was hailed as a resistance fighter, although he did little to resist the Germans. He just kept quiet, stayed away from Paris, and kept writing. I remember many of his songs and in his accompanying of Gounod's "Sérénade," I thought the piano playing was so spectacular that I wanted from that moment to be an accompanist. I loved his playing; it had an elegance about it, although, by today's standards, he used far too much pedal, but that was his style. Pierre Bernac, I thought, had an unremarkable voice, but created an absolutely beautiful line; he knew exactly how to phrase. A wonderful duo.

The war was the first major dramatic event of his personal narrative. From a child's perspective, the war had many elements of excitement, at least initially. He was in the church choir when war was declared:

> I remember the declaration—it was a Sunday morning and we were in church, and the vicar went to the pulpit and announced that Mr. Chamberlain had declared war. It was eleven o'clock on a Sunday morning and the sirens went off almost immediately, so everyone dashed out of the church into the air raid shelters. It was a false alarm.

Like many London children, he was evacuated for a short while to a home near St. Ives in Cambridgeshire. After a British plane crashed in the village, presumably calling the "safety" of the countryside into question, many evacuees were sent home—"in time for the Blitz," as Cliff describes it.

> A tragic moment of huge import was the bombing of the Crawley home. It was just a Sunday night and I think my dad had gone to bed and suddenly, without warning, everything collapsed around the house. A V2 rocket was the cause. When they fell fairly close, you didn't actually hear anything, although people a little way away would hear the really loud explosion.... My piano—it wasn't a very expensive one, but it was new—it had all the strings hanging out.

That image of the ruined piano is etched in his memory. He told me that story a number of times before I learned that both his parents were injured and taken to hospital in the bombing. A further change marked this event for him: his first cigarette.

I think that rescue people were quickly there and ambulances, but it was the curate of the church where I was a choirboy whom I remember most. He came 'round and gave me a cigarette to calm my nerves.

At the age of seventeen, when the war was already over but strife in the Middle East was heating up, he was called up to do National Service. His two-plus years in the army are not fond memories. "A terrible waste of time, uninteresting, boring," he mutters. Work in the quartermaster's store in Portsmouth, where he was eventually posted was, on the other hand, less onerous than that of the men who were sent to Palestine. He played piano in a dance band many evenings. When we discuss the narrow period of years that circumscribes most people's concept of "their" popular music, Cliff claims, "We played the popular music of the day, which I still love."

The day in 1949 when he left the forces was the next turning point in his personal narrative.

Two or three of us were "demobbed" at the same time. We caught a train and travelled up to London. On the train I sold some of my equipment to a fellow who was in the same compartment as me. I sold him my army boots and then we had a good day in London. It just felt so wonderful.

His release from the army meant a return to composition and to professional training. His first published song, written when he was sixteen, before he was called up, was "The Early Morning," with words by Hilaire Belloc. This and other early works were published by J.B. Cramer, Curwen, J. Williams Paxton, Chappells, or in the journal *Child Education*. In need of money, he sold most of his early songs to J.B. Cramer outright, hence losing the royalties.

For three years after he left the army, he attended an Emergency College to train as a teacher. Many of his instrumental works in the late 1940s and early 1950s were written for the ensemble, Dalbec,[9] a group that did school concerts in conjunction with and following their teacher training program, as well as public performances. Clifford comments:

They were short of everything, including teachers in those days. This college was the Southern Music Training Centre in Surrey, near Epsom. [It was] a small college, but there were some interesting students there, most of them older because they were people who had come out of the services.

One of the "interesting people" he met there in Epsom was a young Welsh woman named Ennis Roberts, a part-time student at the Southern Music Training Centre, who would soon become an important part of his life. Already a teacher, she was doing a short course there and subsequently taught at a school in nearby Cheam. Clifford's first job was teaching at St. Mary's Secondary School in Richmond, a short commute from the town of Kingston where he lived—the first of two Kingstons in his life. Ennis continued to teach at Cheam.

During the Kingston (UK) years, he also took measures to improve his technique as a composer. He had taken a few composition lessons from Dr. Edith Bathurst, a composer who was deputy principal of the Emergency College.[10] He felt, however, that he would like to have lessons with one or more of the other composers whose music he truly admired.

> So I had the nerve to write to a few people I admired. I wrote to Michael Tippett, who wrote back a really nice letter, saying—I can't remember his excuse, but it was a real excuse. I wrote to Arthur Benjamin, who said he was just off to Australia, but he would write to me immediately when he got back home. He died. I wrote to E.J. Moeran, who recommended his teacher, John Ireland. I wrote to Gordon Jacob, who said he was just so busy [teaching at the Royal Academy] that he couldn't take any private students. I wrote to Lennox Berkeley, who said, "Yes, come and see me." He lived in the Warwick Avenue area of London and I went to his house for a few lessons.
>
> I liked him because he was one of the few, perhaps the only, English student(s) of Nadia Boulanger and his music had a French wit, which I rather liked. I was particularly fond of his Divertimento and his piano music. Anyhow, I had some lessons with Berkeley, who I thought was absolutely terrific. He was a gentlemanly person, but a man who got enthusiastic about things. We just talked for an hour or two and I would come away wanting to write more music. He was a good teacher because he didn't just "instruct." He talked and showed me some of the music he was working on and played some of mine on the piano. He introduced me to J. & W. Chester, who published my *Six French Nursery Songs* for piano duet, which I still rather like. They were clean and crisp and simple arrangements. Chester's published Berkeley's music and a lot of French music, including much of Poulenc's.

Clifford and Ennis would marry in 1954. They decided to move to Devon, where Cliff got a job as music teacher at two schools in Plympton, half-time at the secondary modern school and half-time at the grammar school.[11] The next "magic moment" was the birth of his daughter Alison in 1955, a day that also coincided with his finding Stentaway House, in Plymstock, a beautiful Georgian house with stone-walled garden, to live in.

Stentaway was a big house; we had a third of it. It was a gorgeous old house. That day Alison was born was a big day. We were getting desperate to find somewhere [to live]. There wasn't much money available then either.

Ennis gave up full-time teaching after the birth of Alison, her first child. In 1958, their son John was born. Cliff describes Ennis as a good wife and mother, and the portraits of their children attest to the fact that she was the steady, loving one. Later, she would take courses toward a mathematics degree and return to some part-time work.

Cliff's two children, Alison and John, have written about their father. With wit that matches his, they describe important aspects of their family life and their relationship with him and his music.

Alison Jennings Reflects

The following are random recollections of my father and how he made an impact on my world when he lived in England. My memory is such that I can't vouch for the accuracy of any facts, but it makes these very brief summaries no less familiar. The longer I sit and write, the more comes flooding back, as I'd expected, especially as I see him as a complex person. In fact I'm sure I could probably write my own book, but I've edited it down to what I see as a summary of the most significant points.

As a child, I saw my father as a very strong person. My memory is of a man of few words who could either be very exciting, or occasionally, when I had transgressed, rather frightening. When we were together we were generally doing things rather than just sitting talking or watching TV. I associated my mother with the constancy of everyday life and my father with the less routine events.

My paternal grandmother came from a family of larger-than-life characters, but the thing that struck me most about the ones I met was their sense of humour and of fun. The banter was fantastic! That's not to say it was consistent as there were times when they were as difficult as they were funny at others. My father and his sister have definitely inherited that humour, though, and it's most evident when they are together. I still think they are recognizably siblings both in their appearance and their mannerisms, and they have retained an incredibly strong bond despite their geographical dislocation.

My overriding recollection of houses we lived in was the presence of a baby grand piano. My father would sit at it playing, writing, replaying, and rewriting for many hours, although (sadly) I don't think I ever wondered exactly what he was doing, assuming it was part of his job as a teacher to create music. By the time I was of an age to think about such things, it was just too routine to even notice. This occupation was, however, a very useful source of ideas for presents for a man who used to throw aftershave down the toilet and disliked fancy soaps. On the limited budget we had (and, with hindsight, limited imagination too), he was spoiled with such gifts as staff paper and things with pianos or notes printed on them for every birthday and Christmas for many years.

Most of our holidays were spent with relatives. I always thought that my father did not relish trips up to his in-laws in Cheshire as he usually seemed to be at a bit of a loose end there. To add a little excitement to those visits, he would sometimes get John and me up before the other adults arose. We would walk about half a mile to a bridge over the main railway line from Euston. From there we could see the trains as they steamed past. I loved those little excursions. I don't know what it was about trains and buses as his interests didn't seem to extend to any other form of transport, but I think they were boyhood passions.

I remember a variety of family days out, mostly at the seaside when we lived in Devon and in London once we had moved to Essex. My father took obvious delight in the trips to London and the excitement levels used to rise as we approached the outskirts. Apart from knowing his way around what seemed, to a child, to be the most enormous network of roads, he knew about the buses (even now he appears able to recite what number bus is needed to get to any London destination) and how to find everything of interest.

He must have been about forty when he realized a lifelong ambition to drive a bus for a few weeks during the summer holidays. I always thought it rather a shame he didn't get to drive red double-deckers in his beloved London,[12] but he chose instead to ferry the residents and tourists of Clacton-on-Sea from A to B, on one occasion reversing part of the way from B to A, a manoeuvre that I believe was illegal while passengers were on board. I never had the impression that my father was bothered by convention.

I have inherited a love of geography largely because of poring over various maps and atlases with him. When travelling somewhere in the car, he would give us spelling tests or quizzes on capital cities. He used to send us into fits of giggles by waving to passing strangers, who would then turn and stare at us and the car, trying to figure out who we were.

My father never seems to have lost the ability to see things through a child's eyes, which I'm sure must explain in part why he has been so successful in writing music for children. This trait was never clearer to me than when seeing him with his grandchildren. I remember wondering who would tire first of whatever they were playing at together. He has always been playful with his cat too, and would get down on the floor for a bit of "rough and tumble" even when his own joints were complaining. He certainly used to frighten the living daylights out of my timid little "moggie" (cat) with his enthusiastic approach, just as every child had scared her.

John Crawley Reflects

As I actually remember comparatively little of my own childhood (mostly due to a very bad, or perhaps a very unfocused, unstructured memory), I have only vague remembrances of my father in daily life. I do remember that I was a little afraid of him and that he seemed to be a person with a shortish temper and also a lot of passion.

Our house was filled with music in my early life. If it was not something being played on the piano or gramophone, it was the radio. I always thought that Sundays were a time to listen to classical music on the radio, something that I still think I believe today.

Growing up we seemed to have one dominant piece in the house, a grand piano. Apart from being a great place to compose music for my father, I always thought it made a great place under which to play, such as putting up the train set or race-car set at Christmas. I remember my father playing the piano to us, especially around the holidays. He would play music and make up funny little endings or change keys halfway through, and I thought that was just wonderful. I think that of all the things I remember from my youth, this was one of my fondest.

I remember asking him when I was twelve or thirteen why he did not write music for films or TV, as I thought that would have made us rich. (I was always staunchly more conservative than him, even at a young age.) I do not think that was something that he gave too much thought to, however, much preferring, I think, to do his own thing and do what he loved.

I did try my hand at music lessons in the form of piano playing. I cannot remember if it was [he or] my mother ... [who] suggested this. I must admit that I had no talent in this area, but I do not remember Dad expressing disappointment in me when I did not continue lessons. I did not give up on music forever, though, as I did decide to try trumpet and join a brass band.

I belonged to a brass band in Clacton-on-Sea and Dad was asked to write a piece for the band. I do not remember the name of the piece, but I do remember it was quite tricky to play. I do remember other members, the less talented ones like me, having troubles with the rhythms. I did manage to play my part in the arrangement, and the piece was well received within the band. More importantly, perhaps, it was well received by the audience. I can still play the main theme of the piece.

My father does have a love of steam locomotives. On trips to my grandparents outside of Chester, he would sometimes take us to the bridge to see the trains rushing by underneath us. He would tell us that in his day, there were more steam engines and could tell us the numbers of the trains and where they would go. I think my knowledge that he liked trains was the only reason I did not get him socks or underwear for every single birthday or Christmas. If I saw a book on locomotives, I would think it a suitable present for him.

When we lived in Clacton on the east coast of England, we lived for a time at the Hadleigh, a men's residence for the college where my father taught. There was a billiards table there upon which my father taught me to play snooker, to which I attribute my exceptional talent of sinking white balls.

Moving to Canada seemed like a big step, but one that Dad was very enthusiastic about. We spent the first little while in a one-room apartment close to the university. We did not talk much about his acclimatization into his new job, but I got the impression that he was happy with the move and the challenge.

I have memories of my days in the Kingston Youth Orchestra where Dad was the conductor. I thought he did a great job with all the kids, and it was a truly enjoyable experience having him lead. He had a good way of working with us and made it enjoyable to be part of the orchestra.

I have always thought that my dad's music was generally not the easiest to listen to. As I have grown older, I have re-listened to it and found that while I would not exactly call it easy to listen to, and definitely not the easiest to hum along to, it is something that becomes more interesting each time you listen, and you realize that there is more to it than you first thought.

As I grow older, I think I see where I got my sense of humour from. I had not seen it in my father as I was growing up as I think our communications were very limited. As I became an adult, however, I found myself "in tune" with him and genuinely enjoying his company. Sometimes we have laughed so much over something we both found extremely funny that we would end up in tears. Typically I think it would be something that others at the conversation would not even find that amusing.

I saw my father much more when he lived in Toronto at his house by the Humber River. Being in Toronto on business and also travelling for my job and flying from Toronto airport quite often made Dad and Bev's place quite a nice stopping-off point. During this time I think I became much closer to him and realized the many things we have in common. It was easy to talk to him, and having the same type of humour meant we laughed at many of the same things and could appreciate our time together. I also share his love of all things Tim Hortons and Canadian Tire. I get the feeling that all the things in the world could be fixed by a visit to one or the other or both of these places.

Growing up when I was younger, we did not have pets, so I did not see him as an animal person. However, seeing him with his cat makes me wonder why. It can easily be seen that he has a great affection for his animals. In fact, his tolerance for the animals seems to be greater than for many other things.

To supplement his income, Cliff did musical theatre, conducting a number of productions for the Carmenians, a good amateur theatre group in Plymouth. He conducted *Oklahoma,* and Vivian Ellis's musical *And So to Bed,* based on Samuel Pepys, among others. A highlight of the Plympton years for Cliff was his school's production of Benjamin Britten's *Noye's Fludde,* the world's second performance just after the Aldeburgh premiere. In 1958[13] the coordinator of music for Devon encouraged him to apply for the plum teaching job in the county, in Crediton, north of Exeter. He described the attraction the Crediton school had for him:

> The grammar schools there had a really big musical reputation. The oldest one was a boys' school and next door to it was a girls' school. They were boarding schools. The headmaster of the boys' school was a very enthusiastic amateur musician and insisted on lots of music in the school. The two schools combined together for choral and orchestral rehearsals, and they had a tradition of doing the *St. Matthew Passion* one year and the *St. John Passion* the next year, a tradition that I continued.

Among other works that Cliff had performed at Crediton were several of his own works, including a piano concerto performed by John Wood, a visiting teacher who became a good friend. They remounted *Noye's Fludde*. The schools' choirs and orchestras also did church services in Crediton and Evensong at Exeter Cathedral a couple of times. He began to develop his approach to teaching music creativity, described below.

Cliff often observes that his life seems to have been divided into ten-year segments with relatively major life changes after about a decade.[14] Indeed, after nearly a decade in Devon (1954–63), he decided to take a job teaching at a College of Education in Clacton in Essex, affiliated with the Cambridge University Institute of Education. Here he established the St. Osyth's College Orchestra. Since the majority of teacher trainees at this college were potential elementary schoolteachers, his orientation changed from high school-age curricula to those of junior and infant schools. This was a decade when the Orff and Kodály techniques and the innovations of John Cage and Cornelius Cardew were beginning to attract the attention of music educators in different countries, and Cliff was among those who made the teaching of improvisation and composition a central curriculum component.

He also decided to get academic credentials and applied to Durham University, one of the few universities that offered "external" degrees in music[15]—with flexible admission requirements. The program required three or four major papers in theory and music history, questions that were to be answered by means of imitative composition, as well as an original composition. He wrote a string quartet for his B.Mus. He became an admirer of Arthur Hutchings, who was still the professor of music. He subsequently took the newly devised M.Mus. degree,[16] a program devoted exclusively to contemporary music, devised by Australian composer David Lumsdaine. For this degree he wrote an orchestral work, *Fast Sinks the Sun*. Durham recommended that Cliff seek out a tutor for this work, and he consulted with Humphrey Searle on a couple of occasions. Another work for string quartet (his *Overture, Air and Dances*, 1971) was accepted in fulfillment of the requirements to become a fellow of the Trinity College London.

The family bought a house in Clacton, but after a couple of years, an opportunity emerged to live in and supervise the men's residence, the Hadleigh. The college was housed in a number of seafront hotels, deserted during World War II as "the coastline was out of bounds." The men's residence opened a bar, "the most popular one in Clacton," he explains. As the licensee, Cliff had to deal with problems of rowdy clients, but he enjoyed the billiard room, and remembers how the residence was an adventure for the Crawley children, as well as their friends and cousin (Anne's daughter Suzanne).[17] "[During holiday times] they used to have the whole hotel to themselves. There were probably a hundred rooms and the children would wander around the corridors, get lost, play hide and seek."

Cliff explains that the Essex years brought some measure of marital problems. A young teacher had captured his affections. Eventually the job became less exciting. Hence, in the early 1970s he again began to look elsewhere, this time further afield in Canada, among other places.

Istvan Anhalt, the head of the Music Department (later the School of Music) at Queen's University in Kingston, Ontario, made a recruiting tour in the UK in the early 1970s. In particular, he hoped to bring innovative dimensions of the British style of music education to Queen's. As a composer himself, the emphasis on creative listening and composition were more attractive to Anhalt, no doubt, than the performance-oriented, band-centred programs still dominant in Canada. R. Murray Schafer's innovative books on music education were especially influential and popular at this time, but Anhalt was aware that Schafer's work was complemented by that of British educators such as John Paynter, Bernard Rands, and George Self. The two innovative faculty he was about to hire—namely, Denise Narcisse-Mair and Clifford Crawley—were engaged in developing innovative curricula and had extensive classroom experience, which was essential testing ground for any innovative educational approach.

In 1973, Cliff moved with his son John to Kingston to embark on what would be the longest phase (twenty years) of his teaching career.[18] Ennis and Alison stayed behind temporarily, so that Alison could finish her General Certificate of Education (or A levels). When Ennis arrived in Kingston, they moved to a home on Nelson Street. Although she visited Canada for one term, Alison remained in England, where she still lives. Cliff remained committed to Ennis throughout her life, although they formally separated and lived apart for many of the Queen's years. She died in 1991 after heart surgery.

Over the course of the Kingston period, Cliff's professional focus became less music-education-oriented and more directed to composition, teaching duties he shared with electroacoustic composer David Keane and Istvan Anhalt, who taught one course and a few private composition students. Cliff served twice as acting director of the School of Music at Queen's, resisting his colleagues' repeated urging to accept a longer administrative term.

He reflects on the strength of composition at Queen's and on the relationships he had with his fellow composers:

Istvan [Anhalt] had a different aesthetic about composition from me, but I respected what he did and I loved the way he was immersed in music.... He didn't want to write music for amateurs. His music was difficult because that was the way he thought. His thoughts were complex and the only way he could express them was in complex terms. Mine were less complex, perhaps, but that doesn't mean to say they were less important. It is not a question of value; it is just a different approach.

Not surprisingly, given his own interest in writing for amateurs as well as professional musicians, he admired the practicality of Fred Clarke's music: "his anthems and his good practical church music and some of his orchestral music; he was a competent craftsperson." He notes that David Keane had "lots of terrific musical ideas" and understood the electronic music studio well, as did Kristi Allik, whom he also admired. He felt that he had "more in common compositionally with John Burge," whose bridging appointment to Cliff's retirement actually positioned him as Cliff's replacement. Similarly, he found Marjan Mozetich's music "fascinating."

In addition to the university work, he was involved with the Suzuki institutes held annually in Kingston, for which he wrote two concerti for pianist Valerie Lloyd-Watts, co-director of those institutes. He conducted the Kingston Youth Orchestra and Queen's University Orchestra in the mid-1970s, and the Eastern Ontario Concert Orchestra in the early 1980s. He was extensively engaged with local school music programs, creating many of his youth musicals for production in area schools. He had a close personal association with an innovative teacher and choral conductor, Brenda Hunter, who facilitated the production of a number of musicals and other projects.

His relationship with his colleagues was cordial, but he only occasionally socialized with them, partly since he was so busy with commissions, but partly, according to his own self-analysis, because he was not a "buddy sort of person," and never felt completely at home in the university context. For recreation, he was more inclined to head to the racetrack than the faculty club. He took me to the one and only wrestling match I have ever attended in my life. He had more time to pursue an interest in (spectator) sports, including wrestling and cricket in his earlier life in England, and again after he retired, he enjoyed Toronto Blue Jays games when we lived in Toronto.

He has never been particularly interested in organized religion, noting that "I went to church because I was a choirboy and I quite liked singing in the choir ... but after that, the only reason I went to churches was to hear beautiful music."

A further reason for his minimal association with social circles in Kingston was the fact that his professional work extended far beyond Kingston and Queen's University. He became actively involved with the Ontario Arts Council's Creative Artist in the Classroom as well as the Canadian Music Centre's Composer in the Classroom program, doing creative projects in northern Ontario, Sudbury, Deep River, Oshawa, and other places. After one of the projects he did, a reporter for the local newspaper noted that "Pupils gave him a child's equivalent of a standing ovation: they asked to skip recess."[19] The *Walkerville Suite* was one product of these projects.

In almost every domain of his professional life, he encouraged creative work by students. One such project was the *Young Composers Anthology*, a co-publication in 1989 by the Frontenac County Board of Education (directed at that time by his good friend, James Coles) and the Queen's University School of Music. He also collaborated with Ottawa-based Opera Lyra in still other creative projects and one full-length, two-act opera, *Angel Square,* which has been given a full stage production twice. Other commissions during the Kingston years came from the Kingston Symphony Orchestra, as well as the many local instrumentalists and singers. Cliff is pleased that audiences found his music accessible, albeit sometimes demanding, and that they looked forward to new works.[20]

He was associated with the Canadian Executive Service Overseas and undertook two projects for them. The first was a contract to create a music curriculum in Honduras. His hosts wanted a classical music program, somewhat to the frustration of Cliff, who wanted to incorporate some local and vernacular styles. He had an opportunity to do this when, in 1985, the Malaysian government hired him to record local music in Borneo and make arrangements for use in their schools.

In the 1980s, he became an examiner for the Royal Conservatory of Music, with an eye to travelling to different parts of Canada and beyond, including Bermuda. He had always enjoyed work as a music festival adjudicator. Indeed, one of his first assignments in this regard was in Newfoundland, and he still speaks about how moved he was by a family performance of "Bridge over Troubled Water" in Grand Falls on this assignment. His frequent travel to the easternmost province convinced him that it would be a wonderful place to live, and so it has been since 2002.

Cliff and I have been partners since 1985 and were married in 1992; after his retirement, we were happy to give up weekly commutes between Kingston and Toronto. In his post-retirement years in Toronto (1993–2002), he continued to do a lot of adjudicating and examining, including one assignment in Trinidad and Tobago, where he came to admire the skilful arrangers of steel band music. Commissions for new compositions scarcely slowed down, but he views these years as less productive. His compositional aesthetic was at odds with the Toronto mainstream. He acknowledges that he "was happy living there because I did work, but it was never really connected with Toronto in any way." For both of us, a six-month interlude in Boston in the winter of 1999 was, on the other hand, a very exciting time.

In 2002, we moved to St. John's—back to the sea as he had been in Plymouth and Clacton[21]—where, if anything, Cliff became more involved again in university and community. He even returned briefly to teaching at the age of 74, doing two sessional composition courses for Memorial University. Atlantic Canadian performers—such as the Newfoundland Symphony Orchestra, Jane Leibel, Maureen Volk, Duo Concertante (Nancy Dahn and Tim Steeves), the Rhapsody Quintet (from Halifax), traditional music performer Pamela Morgan, and others—all commissioned new works or arrangements. He reflects on the move to St. John's:

> It hasn't changed the way I work, but I find the place more congenial. We've been to a lot more concerts. Some were quite brilliant. Even the ones that were less so were often interesting and there is a lot of new music around of various sorts.... I've enjoyed the folk music here. I admire the way it keeps going and growing.

While Cliff denies that place has much impact on his work, arguing that he can work anywhere, he seems to be deeply affected by place on a personal level. The joy he gets by living near water, particularly the sea, is palpable. The rugged coast of Newfoundland suits his temperament particularly well. Even in his seventies, the energy he has when he visits his other favourite port city, London, is astonishing. This great city was, from his early teens, the connecting point, the hub of his life in student and army days and later. Russia similarly has magic for him. A few days in St. Petersburg in the late 1990s were powerful intensifications of his love of Tchaikovsky and Shostakovich. Just as significant events in his life held a kind of miraculous significance in his oral narratives, so certain places also had similar qualities.

In music and in life, he reflects: "I'm happy that they [the magical moments] came."

The Integration of Teaching and Composition

> I think it is just a question of attitude. You don't have to have ten years of theory before you start writing music any more than you do to write words or paint pictures.

I first intended to write separate sections about Cliff's teaching philosophy and his compositional activity, but quickly realized that it would do a disservice to his fundamental belief in the integration of these two. This points to one of the several differences between the philosophies and systems of music teaching in England and in Canada about which Cliff has spoken extensively over the years.

He often notes that most twentieth-century English composers of high repute have written important works for amateurs, works that might, in some cases, be designed for them to perform, and in other cases, for them to listen to. The most famous example of the latter is undoubtedly Britten's *Young Person's Guide to the Orchestra*; he also wrote works such as *Noye's Fludde* and *Let's Make an Opera* with parts for young performers. Britten, Maxwell Davies, Holst, and Vaughan Williams all wrote significant works for amateurs to play. As mentioned earlier, in the late 1960s there were initiatives in England, Canada, and the US to engage children creatively and stimulate their capacity not just to perform but to create music. With the exception of Schafer, there were arguably fewer composers of stature engaged with music education in Canada vis-à-vis England at this time. Most Canadian composers who wrote for young people in the 1970s and 1980s often wrote "teaching pieces" rather than work in major genres that was easy enough to play or sing without advanced skill, and many of these composers were either women (Coulthard, Pentland, Telfer) or composers affiliated with the Royal Conservatory of Music and not often represented as part of the compositional mainstream. Even fewer composers were interested in enabling children to develop their own creative instincts. There was, then, in those decades at least, an implicit hierarchy in Canada when Cliff arrived here, that undervalued music for amateurs as less serious and less important than music for professional musicians. I have often thought this was a colonial legacy, a deeply ingrained attitude among Canadians that leads us to believe we have to be extra complex or serious to be noticed on the world stage. Cliff shares this view, noting "a little bit of insecurity" among both American and Canadian composers who are, in his opinion, "more worried about the image." He explains other factors, however, noting fundamental distinctions between the English and Canadian music education systems:

I think the Canadian one had much more emphasis on playing and singing—performing music—whereas the British one tended to play and perform, but not in class time. If there was an orchestra in the school, it would rehearse after school. If you joined a choir, that was extracurricular. Music was an academic subject, like Art or English where you learned about other creators as well as the act of creation.

He notes that a great deal more music history and analysis was done in Britain than Canada, and consequently, many British students knew more classical repertoire than their Canadian peers of the 1970s and 1980s. Most significantly, composition was a central part of music education. Performance, in Cliff's view, comes along with invention. Steps were taken in Canada to get composers to write for students,[22] but it was only in the late 1960s with various "composer in the classroom" initiatives[23] that composers enabled students themselves to write music and still only with short-term (usually week-long) residencies.[24] Composition, then, was at best a special, once-a-year treat at the pre-university level rather than a basic part of music training. As noted earlier, Cliff was a very active participant in these programs. He describes his approach:

> We did various things. Sometimes I started music projects with words because kids didn't feel too uptight about writing poems. Sometimes we would take a local legend and work on that. I tried to find something that was meaningful to that particular school. At other times, my approach was a more spontaneous one: "Let's make some music" then "Let's find a way to notate it."

Improvisation played a role, as the last phrase of the quoted statement implies, but Cliff always valued the opportunity to teach music literacy and noted that students felt they achieved a great deal when they had created a score. In part, this reflects his own pleasure in creating handwritten scores, often saying that he loves to make little dots on pages for a living. He acknowledges that "this is old-fashioned now because you can record it straight away," but explains that "I was keen to get young people to notate because I think you learn to read music by writing it just as you learn to read English by writing and you learn to write by reading. It is a two-way process."

He admires Murray Schafer's approach and used some of the intersensory techniques of creating music based on pictures or found objects, but his own approach was arguably more analytic and very often theatrical. I've watched him show children how to work with the rhythms of words, how to make a tune with the letters of a name, how to find pattern in random pitches, how to create an accompaniment for a tune they know. He often explores background music, showing students how to increase or decrease tension, or make a moment scary or relaxed. At one point, he said, "You engage more of their being somehow." This describes a lot about Cliff's work with children.

One of the secrets of Cliff's success in these projects was quite simply his own fluency as an arranger/orchestrator, and his capacity for hard work. He would, for instance, take a group of tunes that students had composed one day, arrange and orchestrate them overnight, creating a complete score and copying out all the parts by hand, so that the class orchestra or band could do a performance the next day. He often ties creativity to the capacity for observation:

> You notice things in works of art if you have handled that sort of material yourself. You get children to draw pictures almost immediately. You buy them a paint book for Christmas and they may make a horrible mess, but the experience of doing it is part of education and you notice the personality of children emerging. Some do very, very neat lines and individual, contrasted colours; others put one colour on top of another. There is self-expression there. I think, then, we look at pictures in a different way because we have been involved in making them ourselves. Language and drawing are very similar to music. Just performing music is not enough. You have to try and invent it as well.

His own capacity for observing children fed back into his composition. He was keenly aware of how children and young adults thought and what they were interested in. In particular, he could relate to their sense of humour. As described further, in the next section, the work he writes for children engages them at many levels. His lyrics avoid the stereotypes that are often put forward as "appropriate for children," and instead have the freshness of their issues, their subjects.

Developing the capacity for observation was equally central to teaching more advanced students. He drew on elements of pop culture, challenging students to notice their sonic surroundings. Robin Elliott recalls a particularly memorable explanation of "balanced phrase structure, illustrated amusingly at the piano with a rendition of the McDonald's theme song ("You deserve a break today ... ")" (email, 26 March 2007).

For many years at Queen's University, Cliff taught a required twentieth-century composition course that was, in my opinion, one of the most innovative aspects of the curriculum. Few professors would have been able or willing to teach composition classes with upwards of sixty students and to mark their compositions every week. Cliff found a way by exploring models from different twentieth-century compositional schools, explaining that he based some of his "imitative composition" ideas on Arthur Hutchings's concepts in *The invention and composition of music.*[25] With Hutchings, he recognized that the majority of the students would not become composers, but that their capacity to hear the nuances of music would be greatly enhanced. His course design, however, was uniquely Crawley:

> We usually covered about six different areas.... Debussy was a starter to get students straight away out of harmony exercises—lovely parallel chords which you dare not do in harmony exercises, whole-tone scales, single notes, becoming much more conscious about, not the notes themselves, but the colours they produce. We certainly looked at Bartók, who I found was really important. We explored serialism, Schoenbergian type to start with, but then we looked at Stravinsky's and Webern's. I also felt Messiaen opened new doors, his modes of limited transposition, *ragas* and *talas* [his exercise in total serialism], *Modes de valeurs et d'intensités*, etc. Every course had some sort of improvisation, new notation, aleatoric devices with more than a glance at John Cage. Toward the end [of my teaching career], Philip Glass and Steve Reich and Terry Reilly and a return to near traditional harmony, but elasticized. I also spent some time on word setting because that was often a mystery to some people.

Former Crawley student Robin Elliott recalled another aspect of this course.

> My recollection [of Cliff's twentieth-century composition class] is that another innovative aspect of it was that for one assignment he asked us to write a pop song. Moreover, he informed us that it was just as hard to write a good pop song as it was to do any of the other pastiche assignments for that course. From a pedagogical standpoint, one thing that I admire about that assignment (in retrospect) is that for many of the students in the class, it provided a validation of their own pop music interests in a way that few (okay, none) of their other classes/profs did. My own first attempt at a pop song was utterly dismal (in the style of Wagner, if I recall correctly),[26] and deservedly got a low grade (my impression is that Cliff was always a fair grader). But Cliff let me do it over again, and my second attempt was a bit better. That struck me as another great pedagogical strategy—we could do any of our assignments over again as many times as we wanted. The message was that getting it done on time was not as important as getting it done to the best of our ability. Or, to put it another way, assignments were about the learning process, not the grading process.

I asked Cliff how he taught risk taking. His response reflects his conscious encouragement of rule breaking, but also indicates that he does not see any disjuncture between this and the imitative composition techniques he values:

I used Peter Maxwell Davies' *Eight Songs for a Mad King* sometimes. In those days and probably even these days, Davies "pushes" things to the utmost with screeching clarinets, extended vocal techniques. I used *Nouvelles Aventures* by Ligeti. That pushed things too.

We have frequently discussed gender issues in relation to composition, generally, and risk taking specifically. It was Clifford Crawley, not I, who first raised concern about the gender imbalance in composition classes at Queen's University in the 1970s and early 1980s. Young women excelled in music theory, but few chose to do composition.[27] He urged that the next hire in the composition area be a woman so that a role model was available for both men and women. Indeed, that happened with Queen's University's appointment of Kristi Allik in 1988, and the gender imbalance changed noticeably.

In the process of nominating Clifford Crawley for a teaching award in 1991, a group of his students reflected on what they had learned from his courses in a letter written in support of the nomination:

As a teacher, he manages to bring out the best in his students.... They must be willing to take risks, to reach inside of themselves, and share what they find with both Professor Crawley and the rest of the class. He creates an environment in which this daunting task of "being creative" is not only possible, but often desirable. Experimentation is required, mistakes are permitted and learned from, in an environment of total acceptance. Professor Crawley's sense of humour and gift for telling relevant anecdotes make class very enjoyable, even in the awful time slot of 8:30 Friday mornings. We've learned much more from him than how to compose or how to be creative. We've learned not to be afraid of expressing our own personal feelings, and how not to be afraid of making mistakes.... Through the impact he has made on us, as future educators, many young students will also be affected by his excellent teaching skills and ideals. [Letter from three students, dated 25 January 1991]

Robin Elliott describes a similar experience of feeling Cliff's respect for his students:

I fear that I may have been something of a pest for him when I was an undergraduate, for I did not always agree with his ideas about music, and as a brash youth, I may have said so on occasion, but … he always treated me as an adult and was never condescending, never exerted power over me, and always gave my views his careful consideration. The older I get, the more I appreciate what Cliff had to offer all those years ago.

The Compositions

I need to look around every so often. Perhaps the music is like that too.

There's not much value in consistency.

I suspect that dance is something I envy.

Cliff has often claimed that he became a composer because he could not be anything but a composer. The single-mindedness of this assertion is curiously at odds with the breadth of his interests, experiences, and tastes. It simply reflects the intensity of his passion for creating music of many kinds. When I first knew him, he used to joke that so long as he could compose music twelve hours a day, he didn't mind what else he was asked to do at work or at home. The long hours are not far from a true picture. The range of his work is enormous, encompassing children's songs and piano pieces, operas and musicals, vocal works, chamber music, orchestral works, piano and other solo pieces, as well as arrangements. He has written well over 150 unison children's songs, another twenty-three two-part songs, and nine musicals for children, as well as a full-length youth opera. For professionals, or combinations of professional and amateur performers, he has created six operas. Other vocal works include seventeen song cycles and numerous individual songs, as well as twenty-six choral works (many with varying instrumentation). Among his twenty-four orchestral works are several overtures, suites, a sinfonietta and divertimento, as well as more evocatively named pieces; he has also done seven concert band works and composed ten concerti (five for piano and one each for two violins, cello, tuba/trombone, and violin). His keyboard works include sets of teaching pieces and arrangements, but also virtuosic inventions, toccatas, and improvisations, among others. His oeuvre thus far includes seventy-eight chamber works. He works quickly, revises little,[28] and keeps no sketches (in spite of protests from the musicologist in the family). Clearly he thinks more about performances than posterity.

The three quotations at the start of this section point to important philosophical tenets that underpin his work. The first suggests the groundedness of his work, its connections with the local, with a community of musicians, music learners, and others. "Looking around" also implies his cherishing of the details of ordinary things, a quality that both of his children noted about him. The second quote points to the often noted eclecticism of his style as well as the unique combination of the serious and humorous in many works.[29] The third hints at the important influence of dance, an influence that I think partially derives from his admiration of his sister's career.

His work has sometimes been situated in the British tradition: "carrying on the tradition of Benjamin Britten and Malcolm Arnold," as F.R.C. Clarke described it in the *Encyclopedia of music in Canada* (2nd ed., 328). I tend to see him as equally connected to French music, its wit, rhythmic originality, and strong links to dance. Cliff dislikes assessments that focus too much on influences, however, arguing that while they may demonstrates the writer's experience with music, they simultaneously undervalue the personality of the composer.

> When you reduce everything to what somebody does to influence somebody else, it is like saying that you can't speak English anymore because somebody else has already said those words. It gets to a ridiculous state. We've known people who can't listen to anything without saying who it reminds them of and that is absurd.

While he acknowledges that if you admire the music of someone, you may accidentally draw on some of his or her characteristics, he urges musicologists to focus on the craftsmanship and personality of individual composers.

Cliff draws on a wide range of modernist techniques in his work, and he flirted briefly with electronic composition in his Clacton days. Though he has only occasionally written serial music, he sees value in such techniques "because one thinks in wider terms." Nonetheless, he has generally preferred to write music that has tonal elements and occasional references to familiar musical idioms. In his words, he believes that "originality is not necessarily something new but often [the result of] looking at the familiar in a different way" (quoted on the Canadian Music Centre website, www.musiccentre.ca/home). In addition, however, he has strong opinions about the exclusivity of "new music," believing that the fundamental importance of memory and familiar references were too often denied in the late twentieth century. New Music concerts that present only modernist work often bound their audiences too narrowly in his view.

> [They] should have a feeling of: "Look what's happening now. Isn't it exciting?" Sometimes [instead] it's: "You need to be clever to understand this music; you need to know this is not fun; this is something different."

As soon as he says this, he reflects that perhaps he has been unfair to the range of new music initiatives in various Canadian scenes, but there is a modicum of truth in his words.

His style has changed relatively little over the course of his career. Already in his early published work, the *Six French Nursery Songs* (1952) for piano duet, he colours a repeat of a diatonic melody with surprises, flat-six or Neapolitan harmony, for instance, uses hints of bi-tonality, impressionistic parallel fourths and fifths, or tone clusters. While these are rather mild departures from tonal harmonic language, they signal the sorts of stylistic elements that Cliff would exploit.

On the other hand, there are noticeable distinctions among genres. Consider, for example, some contrasting uses of dissonance and serialism. At times, like Berg in his Violin Concerto, to name one famous example, Cliff uses tone rows in ways that are fundamentally rooted in tonality. He has turned several times to a famous atonal theme by Ebenezer Prout, effectively a twelve-tone row before the label existed, a theme about which Prout claimed "a succession of sounds which by no conceivable stretch of imagination can be called a melody" (1893).[30] The most recent Crawley reworking of this theme is in his *Fantasia for Violin and Orchestra,* a work premiered by Scott St. John in 1995. Robin Elliott remembers performing an earlier work based on the Prout theme, the *Divertimento on a Theme of Ebenezer Prout*:

> His explanation that he had decided to write an entire composition based on this "non-melody" by Prout I found to be both amusing and inspirational. It reminded me of George Orwell's pithy statement about why he took up a career as a writer—"To prove that my parents were wrong." Cliff certainly proved that Prout was wrong! I can still recall the twinkle in his eye as he conducted it.

By arranging the theme so that it gravitates to D, he meets Prout's challenge, while taking us on a chromatic adventure.

His piano works are often atonal and some, such as *Naditas, Inventions*, and *Aubade*, have serial elements.[31] In works such as *Three Shades of Dark*—arguably his emotionally darkest work—and the *Toccatas*, the structures are quite innovative as well. Motives and gestures reoccur in different toccatas, with a tightly integrated economy of material, while the contrasts between movements are still distinct. The following examples (Figure 2.1) show touches of quartal harmony, bi-tonality, and whole-tone scales, idioms that he moves between fluidly in his *Toccatas*. The brilliance of the piano writing is enlivened by articulation contrasts, strong dynamic

FIGURE 2.1 Short excerpts from *Toccatas*

(a) quartal harmony, expanding intervals in the 4/8 measures

(b) bitonality

(c) sudden register changes

(d) four-note segments of alternating whole-tone scales

FIGURE 2.2 Excerpt from *Grey Island*

FIGURE 2.2 *(cont'd)*

FIGURE 2.3 Opening of "Thunder and Lightning"

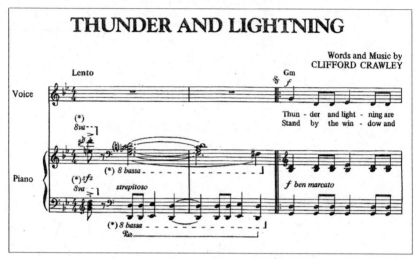

changes, unpredictable shifts in melodic contour, and sudden changes of register.

In orchestral works, on the other hand, he uses dissonance more often as colour, complementing his skilful orchestrations. His songs for children are firmly based in tonality, but dissonance is frequently introduced as an element of surprise or simply contrast. His vocal music and chamber works, on the other hand, rely more extensively on whole tone and other modes of limited transposition, and on other characteristics one might associate with French modernism, even though he uses these in quite an individual manner. I associate arpeggiated whole-tone scales (or the two whole-tone scales juxtaposed) as a sort of signature gesture that occurs particularly in songs for voice and piano, but even more characteristic is the fluid way he moves between diatonicism, chromaticism, and whole-tone passages, consciously reflecting the meaning or emotion of the text as he does so. Figure 2.2 demonstrates: in the first two phrases, the harmonies are chromatic, first moving to d minor (via e minor and D-flat major and then to a minor (via b-flat minor and G major), with key words—"sight," "alphabet" "tower," and "air"—emphasized by harmonic changes. But then the voice enters a new realm on the line "nothing higher eagle god." The whole-tone scale, lacking the closure of a leading tone, has the unending quality that mirrors the hints of infinity in the text. There are, of course, many exceptions to the patterns I have observed, but he agrees with my observation of these tendencies.

The differences between short and long music, and between texted and untexted music, are distinctions that interest him more deeply than questions of his harmonic language. He insists that writing short and long pieces are two different ways of thinking, and that neither was better or more difficult than the other. He notes that some composers such as Beethoven thought in larger terms, while others such as Debussy are arguably more at ease in shorter ones, "just as some people are good at writing short stories and some are good at writing novels or feel more comfortable with one or the other. Some can do both really well." Cliff has done both successfully. He emphasizes that it is no easier to write a short unison song for schoolchildren than a twenty-minute concerto, but the process is qualitatively different. Long works not only have to present more ideas, but, as he explains with reference to verbal genres, the structural plan must be different:

> When writing a novel, you don't reveal everything immediately—characters don't all appear on the first page. You set the scenes and the interplay between them, introducing characters, scenarios, plot, etc., over pre-calculated time, playing with tensions and maintaining interest as part of the fun/skill.
>
> When writing short pieces, calculations are very different. Your intentions have to be made known quickly, even though there may be a surprise or two. As with journalism, the headline often says it all.

His short pieces only partially bear out his words. Some of his school songs, such as "Thunder and Lightning" (Figure 2.3), "Gremlins," or "There's Magic in the Air," start with dramatic or catchy gestures; others introduce an attractive melody or simply set the mood with a sort of rhythmic vamp or bass line.

Surprise elements in these songs occur, however, most often at the end: the sneeze that follows "I can catch a cold" in the song "Catching," a lyric that well represents Cliff's delight in wordplay; the whispered "BLACK" that ends "Lights"; the rapid accelerando that ends "Trolls" (Figure 2.4); the long descending chromatic line in "Thunder and Lightning" that conveys the distress of "the dogs and the cats and the mice and the rats and the wasps and the bees and the birds in the trees and the rabbits and the hares and the wolves and the bears" over the thunder and lightning children find "very exciting."

These examples point to his skilful lyrics for children. "Catching," for instance, plays with the polysemy of the title word: "I can catch a bus and I can catch a train, / And I can catch a raindrop sliding down a window pane. / And I can catch a falling star, At least that's what I'm told, / But one

FIGURE 2.4 Ending of "Trolls"

thing that's for certain is that I can catch a cold. / ACHOO!" A number of children's songs explicitly "teach" about "ordinary" phenomena, but there is never any didacticism in the language. Consider "Clouds," one of *Three Songs of Science for Juniors* (Leslie 1979), where he distinguishes cloud types quite accurately but poetically: "Delicate gentle Cirrus looks like feathers floating by. / Some folks call them mares tails; They sail like ships on high. / Like balls of cotton, Cumulus comes with weather that is dry, / It sometimes has a silver edge; it's known as mackerel sky." He was sometimes asked by his publisher, Joan Leslie, to write about unusual topics (magic, trolls, pelicans, for instance), but he manages to connect such things to the world of children, to their actual fears and their "pretend fears" as well. He explains that he had to research "trolls" before he wrote the song about them. But it is his sense of play (allowing children to scream in the middle of a song, for instance, or using vernacular language) that is ultimately the "hook" in the latter part of the song: "Make a noise like thunder or give a screeching piercing shout. {!} Trolls can't stand many decibels. It almost freaks them out. These hairy red-capped creatures, they can't stand a lot of noise, / And they don't like mistletoe or bonfires, And they don't like girls and they don't like boys / Who seek them in their hideouts, for they'd rather not be seen. / But I'm told that you can tempt them with ripe bananas and ice cream. But I'm not prepared to try this. It might be a troll-like trick, / So my best advice if you see one, is move, move, move, move, move move, move, move, move, move, move, move, quick!" Cliff feels that his best children's lyrics were done in the late 1970s and early 1980s when he was working with children and collaborating closely with a number of Kingston-area music teachers.

Surprise elements are not restricted to his children's songs. He uses the unexpected to end a number of works for professional musicians as well. The non-cadencing, rhythmically asynchronous spiral off the keyboard and ever upward in flute and soprano motives that ends the "In paradisum" section of his *Stabat Mater*; the spoken afterthoughts ("why me?" "oh yeah") that follow cadences in movements of *Personal Column*, are examples. Within pieces, the surprises are often references to familiar styles: the "Foxtrot" in *Tenapennypieces*, the "British Grenadiers" march in the "Progression" movement of his *Seven Stevie Smith Songs* (Figure 2.5a), the seasick variant of "What shall we do with a drunken sailor" in the "All at Sea" movement of *Pieces of Eight,* the varied rendition of "Good King Wenceslas" in the orchestral overture *Koleda* (Figure 2.5b), to name only four of many examples. In other cases, the wit is in the structural surprises, particularly the unexpectedly short movements.

FIGURE 2.5 Transformed themes: (a) The twist on "British Grenadiers" in "Progression," one of the *Stevie Smith Songs*; (b) "Good King Wenceslas" in the overture *Koleda*

(a)

(b)

The sets of short pieces for professional players, within which these surprises occur, however, invariably have well-calculated overall structures, albeit ones that he seems to arrive at intuitively without a lot of preplanning. The placement of long and short movements, or familiar tune references, within these sets is part of the overall architecture, one that often relies on symmetry (in one dimension or another) or on Fibonacci proportions. Consider the *Seven Stevie Smith Songs*, for instance. Here the symmetries include the placement of the familiar march centrally, as well as the framing by means of outer movements that are metrically and harmonically diverse and through composed. Adjacent to each (as movements 2 and 5) is a very short, single-idea movement. In terms of length, however, the march is closer to five-eighths of the way through the work, a Fibonacci placement. There are connections in the tonal relationships of adjacent movements (3 and 4, 5 and 6) and a tendency for minor third harmonic adjacencies within movements; these factors lend coherence to the stylistically diverse set.

The overarching structures, however, are not always readily evident. In *Tenapennypieces*, the dance movements are movements 4 (tango), 6 (polka in 5/8), 8 (waltz), and 9 (foxtrot)—neither symmetrical nor Fibonacci related. The tempi crosscut the styles with a fast movement as 1, 3, 5, and 8 (one could read this as a grouping of movement 1, 2+3, 4+5, 6+7+8, 9+10 or 1+2+2+3+2)—Fibonacci overtones, but not quite. The movements with regular phrase lengths are 2 and 9. Two is also the shortest movement and 10 the longest. All of these patterns create a counterpoint of structural contrasts in a complex way that "the notes dictate," according to the composer.

In *Koleda,* a work that is more organic in its integration of motive and development of basic materials, an unconventional but well-conceived architectural plan is again apparent. The principle thematic materials— namely, the opening fanfare theme and the "Good King Wenceslas" theme—are mirrored in reverse order in the final section. The relationship between the extension of the fanfare theme (a descending motive with a 3+3+2 rhythm) and a new lyrical theme introduced in the *Poco meno mosso* section, or the ways in which the GKW rhythms infiltrate the transition sections, however, are subtler structural elements. The orchestration of the fanfare theme, in particular, is slightly contrasted with almost every repetition, building to a brilliant finish.

In discussing such structures, Cliff refers to his love of pattern, sometimes referencing such things as a quilt, noting that "patterns cross each other sometimes, like counterpoint." More often, however, he uses metaphors of architecture:

> To cover a whole railway terminus with one big arch or two small arches and one big arch, you've got to think a hell of a lot more about structure than if you were just making a shed: where the tension is coming from, how to make the structure solid enough to hold up, and whether it serves its purposes. I think in a way music does the same.

The contrasts between different genres and magnitudes of writing have fascinated both of us and are a frequent topic of conversation in our household. I often distinguish journalism and academic work in terms that are a bit like Cliff's distinction between short and long, although I tend to introduce a time factor: journalism is essential because it is relevant to the moment, while scholarship's value is in its longer periods of reflection and its consideration of a wider body of evidence. When I reminded Cliff of this idea, he immediately connected other music genres:

> So does a lot of pop music [express what is relevant to the moment]; it's what life is about. You tend to think journalism is not as valuable as a novel, but that is not true. It's just different and we have to get over that with pop music [too]. It is not less good than the symphony, but a different art form. I don't like all pop music, but I don't like all classical music [either]. We get muddled with what we like, but I think if we dismiss one form completely, we don't understand what it is about, what music is about.

Of course, I replied, "I love to hear you say that. It is so what I believe."

Another distinction that Cliff speaks about frequently is the difference between texted and instrumental music.[32] He is convinced that we not only create, but also hear the two types differently. Except where the voice is used as an instrument (examples that came to mind as we chatted about this were some twentieth-century works such as the Berio *Sequenza 3* or Sámi *yoiks*),[33] texted music is "like a portrait. There is a model even though it is subject to many kinds of interpretation." In instrumental music, on the other hand, the "sounds must speak for themselves."

Like many composers he is concerned about the balance between what can be said textually and musically, particularly in his dramatic works. He describes his work with Canadian poet David Helwig as the most satisfying of any of his collaborations with writers, particularly commending David for the libretto of his opera *Barnardo Boy*.[34] Even there, he mentions that "he [Helwig] wanted to explain everything in words and sometimes I wanted to explain it in music," but they worked out their differences well.

In his vocal music for professionals, as well as children's songs, he frequently writes his own words (*Personal Column*),[35] but draws on other poetry in Latin (*Stabat Mater, Laudate Pueri, Laudate Dominum*) and French as well as English. He sometimes interleaves texts. The large-scale work that he wrote as a "Millennium" project, *Aetas Nova* (1999), juxtaposes texts by Alphonse de Lamartine, Longfellow, and a Kingston, Ontario, writer, Peter G. Davies. *Childermas*, a Mass for the Innocents, is the most complex example of a composite text, partially his own, but also quoting Longfellow, Francis Bacon, Thomas Gray, James Montgomery, John Milton, Philipp Nicolai, Charles Wesley, Matthew Arnold, the books of St. Luke, St. Matthew, the Philippians, and Isaiah, Shakespeare, Binyon, Rossetti, Tolstoy, Wordsworth, and the Book of Common Prayer. Like the musical style shifts in many of his works, the juxtaposed images of prophecy, children's play songs, urban despair, adult pronouncements on children, references to Herod's slaughter of the innocents, modern consumer goods, Third World poverty, a nativity scene, and words of inspiration ("Children arise!") together create a moving portrayal of the human condition. The disparate styles and text scenarios are somewhat analogous to his use of different musical styles in the song cycles, although *Childermas* is a large, continuous work.

His delight in linguistic play is also evident in the expressive markings and sometimes also the titles in his scores, many of which have sent performers to their Italian dictionaries to decipher: "Affrettando," "Guerriero" "Allegro strepitoso" "Rilassamento," among others, are interspersed with more familiar expressive markings. One work in which he took particular delight in challenging the performer's knowledge of Italian expressions is his *An Album of Piano Pieces* (2000), where one finds *frizzante e regulare, caldamente, ondeggiamente ma poco indistinto*, and *sfacciato*—"sparkling and regular," "warmly," "swaying but not vague," and "impudent."

Closely related to this sort of play is his love of symbolic musical references, both local and historical. Each movement of the *Twelve Preludes* for piano centres on successive pitches in the tone row of Berg's Violin Concerto.[36] The cover of the *Young Composers Anthology* (1980) features a treble clef on a staff with the pitches F-C-B-E, a reference to the Frontenac County Board of Education, which co-commissioned the project. His "Symphony S.B." (also expressed by a musical fragment with the notes E-flat–B) refers to Simon Bolivar. For a family wedding, he once did a piano tribute that incorporated pitches based on the names of the bride and groom. One of his titles references a well-known composer with the letters of his name reversed. These are the sorts of playful (and affectionate?) gestures that Cliff loves to offer in his music to those who can decipher them.

A distinctive element of Cliff's work is his orchestration. Paradoxically, he is colour-blind and one wonders if his aural sensitivity to colour compensates for his visual impediment in the same way that his love of dance idioms masks the fact that he maintains that he cannot dance. He approaches the orchestral palette with an eye toward the intensity of the energy he needs, but he also realizes that less is often more.

FIGURE 2.6 Excerpt from *Serenade for Cello and Orchestra*, first movement

FIGURE 2.6 (*continued*) Excerpt from *Serenade for Cello and Orchestra*, first movement

His Christmas Overture, *Koleda*, commissioned by the Kitchener–Waterloo Symphony Orchestra (conductor Raffi Armenian), has a sparkle that
he regards as appropriate for a celebratory piece. Perhaps he refers to the
lush harp and woodwind glissandi upbeats, or perhaps the rich horn transition leading into the "Good King Wenceslas" theme, or maybe just the
rich resonance of the open fourths and fifths in the strings whenever the
initial theme returns.

As an orchestrator, he likes some instruments (horns) better than others (clarinets as orchestral soloists), but generally avoids analyzing his own
process, preferring instead to cite other orchestration that impresses him.
He loves the brilliance of early Mendelssohn, "his good use of woodwind
solos" and the way "he can make the strings bubble." While he will rarely
admit to his own achievements, he acknowledges that he managed "a nice
bit of bubbling" in the opening movement of his Cello Serenade. While
Figure 2.6 might not exactly be the "bubbling" effect he had in mind, it
illustrates how he energizes a phrase with cross-rhythms in the celli and
bass, percussive touches on upbeats, cadential harp flourishes, and motivic
cascades through the strings.

He often, however, discusses orchestration in terms of restraint: a single note that can give the right accentuation, for instance. He emphasizes
restraint the most in conjunction with percussion.

> I can't remember who [said it], but [they said that] one clash of the cym-
> bals is the most exciting thing you can do in music. Two is okay. Three is
> ho-hum. Four is "Oh gosh, I don't want to hear that anymore." Tchaikovsky
> was good at doing percussion. He overdid ever such a lot of things, ... but
> I think he knows when to strike the cymbals and when to make the tim-
> pani do a low roll rather beautifully. Brahms never understood percussion
> at all.[37]

His skill at making arrangements also reflects his orchestral ear, although
it has often been a reverse process—reducing the timbres and the instrumental forces for a smaller number of players, as in the case of his reworking of Rimsky-Korsakov's *Scheherezade* for string quintet and wind quintet,
or his arrangements of jazz standards and opera arias for the violin-piano
Duo Concertante. His arrangements manage to capture the energy of the
original and the nuances of style. The jazz arrangements in particular have
enabled classical players who have little familiarity with jazz to learn the
swing, all carefully notated by Cliff.[38] Compare the beginning of three
choruses in his arrangement of the Dizzy Gillespie classic "Night in Tunisia"
(Figure 2.7).

FIGURE 2.7 From Crawley's arrangement of "Night in Tunisia" for violin and piano; (a), (b), and (c) are the openings of three choruses

He also emphasizes the fit between orchestration and musical content, arguing that some composers tend to separate the two: "Colour is part of the sense of the music. They are not separate things and I think the best orchestrators know that."

Cliff has occasionally written for instruments that are outside of the conventional classical roster, as in the *Ban Righ Overture* for bagpipe,[39] snare drum, and orchestra, composed for the sesquicentenary celebrations of Queen's University in 1991. Here, he exploits the very misfit in dynamics to good theatrical advantage. After an orchestral beginning, the bagpipe and snare drum enter from the back of the hall, playing a tune that resembles a folk tune (but is, in fact, a Crawley invention) as they walk on stage, pause momentarily, and then walk out of the hall again. The loud bagpipe not only overpowers the entire orchestra but causes the ears of the audience to readjust so that when the bagpipe leaves the hall, listeners see an entire orchestra playing, but initially they can't hear it. Only slowly do ears readjust so that the orchestra sound is again audible. The power of this instrument, then, is manifest both in its presence and its absence. Of course, as an ethnomusicologist, I hear this piece as a sort of showdown between traditional and classical styles and love the outcome.

While Cliff values coherence, or at least integration of orchestration and musical content, and while his formal structures are strong and clear (albeit not calculated), his style changes are radical, unexpected, and generally a lot of fun. He elaborates on his controversial statement, quoted as an epigram at the beginning of this section: "There's not much value in consistency."

> I can't think of any of my favourite composers who are particularly consistent.... I think in great art you get surprises all the time. That's what's exciting.... Mahler does the most surprising things sometimes. You hear a very solemn movement and then there is a little marching tune played by a piccolo or other unexpected instrument. Life isn't consistent. The form and construction of Mozart is beautiful. The joins don't show, but look at the variety of ideas in that little piano concerto we were playing this morning. The A-major one.... Too much variety doesn't make sense if is a jumble, but the Prairies are consistent, and isn't it a relief to get to the mountains at the other end?

When I asked him whether he was a "postmodernist," he deflected my suggestion by saying he "was never quite sure exactly what it means." We have already seen his incorporation of diverse styles in the very logical overall structure of the *Seven Stevie Smith Songs*. Similarly, most of his sets of pieces incorporate short and long, atonal and tonal, dance and non-dance, familiar idioms and totally original ones. While he has written both, he tends to prefer sets of short pieces to continuous, developed long works. The opportunities for style contrasts afford greater theatricality, and ultimately, Cliff is a theatrical composer most of the time.

Furthermore, multi-movement sets also enable him to exploit his gift for writing fine melodies, often ones that arguably serve less well as modules for "development" in the classical sense, although in his work they are frequently reinterpreted, parodied, or recontextualized sometimes for witty and sometimes profound effect, perhaps in the same way that he twisted the familiar Christmas carols that his son John recalls.

> I think people remember fun things much longer [than serious ones]. I think you can use humour sometimes to say something important. Humour isn't merely fun. It can be significant sometimes.

His sense of theatre is, of course, most fully realized in his operas and musicals. He has written six operas, several of them incorporating parts for both amateur and professional performers. The two that have been fully staged are *Barnardo Boy* and *Angel Square*. The most ambitious work is *Barnardo Boy*,[40] written for the Kingston Symphony Association in association with the Frontenac Board of Education and the Kingston Youth Orchestra, and mounted at the Grand Theatre for a four-day run in May 1982. The institutions founded by Thomas John Barnardo in England (which still exist) worked to place 30,000 orphans in homes in Canada. They were familiar to Cliff:

> I'd been to school with Barnardo boys. There was a home not far away just east of Romford. Also, every year in church they used to have little boxes to collect money for Dr. Barnardo's homes, so it meant quite a lot to me and obviously it did to David Helwig. It seemed a good dramatic story because a lot of it took place in Canada, so there was a combination of England and Canada, which worked well.

The narrative contrasts intergenerational perspectives. It begins when a young girl emerges from a dance hall, where a rock band was performing, to find an old man beaten up by some of her young peers. She helped him home and he began to tell his story as a Barnardo boy. The opera shifts to show Barnardo children at an English dockyard, preparing to sail across the Atlantic. The boy came to a farm on the Prairies and was treated very roughly by his new family. Act 2 shifts to a World War I battleground, where the boy, now a young man, fights alongside his best friend and watches him die. He reflects on all these experiences as the scenes shifts back and forth between the conversation with the girl (who does much of the narration) and the dramatization of episodes from his life. The program for the Kingston production explains some of the source material:

> The story includes a good deal of documentary material. The comments made by the philanthropists in the London scene are taken from Charles Booth's pioneering work of sociology, *Life and Labour of the People of London*. The story of Jim Jarvis, which Barnardo tells at Liverpool, is one that he used many times in pamphlets describing his work. Both words and music of the hymn in the Liverpool scene are those used on such occasions, and a brass band of Barnardo Boys was always present. Barnardo died of a heart attack not long after seeing off a group of children. The words of the chorus in the World War I scene are taken from an actual set of field orders of the time and from a list of casualties in the official Canadian War History. (*Barnardo Boy*, program 1982)

The work had a strong impact in eastern Ontario. In letters to the local Kingston paper (*The Whig Standard*), and even conversations where complete strangers stopped Cliff on the street, various people came forward to tell their own stories as Barnardo boys. For many, the stigma of being a poor orphan had silenced them, and only the production of this opera gave them courage to reveal their own histories.

The lead role of the old man, Albert, had been written for a tenor, but Jan Rubes was approached and eventually hired for the part. This is by far the most demanding role in the work and the only one for which a seasoned professional was essential. Cliff had to rewrite much of the score to accommodate Rubes's baritone range.[41] Janice Coles sang the role of the girl and librettist David Helwig played Dr. Barnardo. James Coles served as music director and Gordon Love as dramaturge.

The two-act opera draws upon a range of twentieth-century styles. While much of the dialogue between Albert and the girl is atonal and rhythmically quite fluid, the orchestra provides tonal underpinning for such things as Albert's reminiscences about his mother. Dr. Barnardo speaks in rather short, chromatic phrases, much less lyrical than those of Albert and the girl. Vernacular music of various types is used as appropriate to the scene: a street seller's calls to set the initial London scene, Anglican chant-like delivery for a group of "philanthropists." A march for the Barnardo children when they describe their hard life transforms into the bustle of the Liverpool dockside, the hymn "God Be with You Till We Meet Again" as the children depart for the New World. Act 2 opens with a scene in which the children are looked over by prospective families. As they sing an ostinato of fourths and fifths, the orchestra betrays their fears and nervousness. Young Albert becomes a soldier and scenes from the front in World War I incorporate rhythmic speech (of the soldiers) and popular music of the day. The score is filmic in its musical dimensions, implying perhaps that John Crawley's suggestion to his father that he write film music was not such a bad idea.

The same freshness of approach is evident in the musicals that he has written for children. The fantastic figures in those based on fairytales and his keen eye for everyday things plays well in his most ambitious children's opera, *Angel Square*, composed for Opera Lyra (Ottawa), under the direction of Jeanette Astor and Janet Irwin. Based on a novel by Brian Doyle, the libretto for *Angel Square* was by Irwin. The edgy social issues of religious and racial conflict in the schoolyards of 1940s Canada (specifically the now upscale area of Rockwood in Ottawa) are crosscut by a mystery and a boy who fantasizes that he is the equivalent of the hero of the radio drama, *The Shadow*.

Although dance idioms do not play a large role in Cliff's operas, they are ubiquitous in his other work. As John Burge said in an introduction to the concert that the School of Music at Queen's University produced in celebration of Cliff's seventieth birthday, the "nature of dance" is rarely far away in Cliff's music. I recall Cliff's dismay that so few could get the waltz rhythm right in the second movement of his *Suite for Flute and Piano*. He has used many waltzes, but additionally a foxtrot, tango, gavotte, and others. The dance movements in his work often evoke laughter from audiences, and we have frequently discussed why this should be. Is the body embarrassing in classical music? Does a vernacular dance simply seem incompatible with the rhythmic fluidity of the music that surrounds it? Or are people's memories touched so deeply that a physical response is invariably evoked?

Even where dance is not specifically referenced, the "nature of dance," as Burge described it, is often implicit in the rhythmic energy of his writing, moments of "bubbling" orchestration described earlier, or the sweep of a phrase. Part of this quality may relate to his own wartime participation in a dance band and his subsequent arrangements in which he found ways to notate the grooves that popular musicians generally improvise. But, as signalled earlier, I think the dance career of his sister, whom he admired so deeply, had a very big impact on him.

But what of the serious—the spiritual even—in the music of Clifford Crawley? He resists the conversation, joking that "spiritual" is often simply a word used when the music is slow.

I don't know why "spiritual" should be slow. Or why heaven is always calm. It just gets a bit boring after a while. It is all light and no dark, no surprises.

While he acknowledges that "some people obviously do have spiritual ideas and think in those terms," he notes that most composers were practical and down-to-earth. He prefers to think of the spiritual in terms of listeners' engagement with sound. "One always hopes ordinary ideas have some relevance for some people," he says, "some beauty or significance." Again he turns to architecture to elaborate:

Why do we like the look of certain buildings? We are impressed with them. They don't all have to be Taj Mahals. It might be a house that you would like to live in. It is very difficult to explain, but it immediately attracts our attention and then when we look at it in more detail, it becomes even more attractive. I think you can do that with a piece of music.

His remarks resonate as I contemplate what I regard as works that have profound spiritual dimensions in his output. I might think of his recent song cycle, *Grey Island*, a setting of poems by John Steffler, which reviewer Nancy Anne Brydges described as the "highlight of the album" *Songs and Sonnets*, an "extraordinary work [that] portrays the spiritual journey of reconciliation between place and self" (*CAML Review* 34, no. 2 [August 2006]: 47–48). His *Serenade* for cello and orchestra, however, would top my list of "profound" works by Clifford Crawley. Is it the energy of the first and fourth movement, the improvisatory cello writing in the second, or the simplicity of the dialogue between cello and orchestra in the third? To some extent it is the fact that these movements precede the ultimate simplicity of the final one (Figure 2.8), somewhat like Messiaen's final movement in the *Quartet for the End of Time*. Its beauty lies in the slow unfolding of the lyrical cello theme over two alternating chords (D major, A/G), the fact that when the cello line becomes most intense, it becomes almost inarticulate, able simply to reiterate one note in the middle section before the lyrical theme returns. And, indeed, the tempo is slow, an unexpected conclusion in the concerto genre that often highlights virtuosity.

To signal that music such as *Grey Island* or the cello *Serenade* are somehow more serious or more spiritually profound than some of his other works, however, is to miss part of the point of Cliff's work. Earlier, there have been indications that Cliff takes some delight in things that are not always what they seem, both in his life and his music. I refer not just to the pseudonym, or the cryptic incorporation of initials into his thematic

FIGURE 2.8 Opening theme from final movement of the *Serenade for Cello and Orchestra* (piano reduction by the composer)

material, not just to the surprise elements in his music, but also to a more profound tension that underpins his intellect and his artistry. Cliff claims to be neither an intellectual nor a writer, but reads prodigiously, having once complained that he wished the Queen's library would order more biographies because he had read them all. And he writes words with the same incisiveness as his music. He is thought to be prolific because he writes quickly while, in fact, he is prolific because he works constantly and intensely. He is often acknowledged as a composer of children's songs, but is less recognized as a composer of operas, concerti, etc. Wit and spontaneity are the masquerade for carefully planned patterning and structuring. He claims to observe the everyday, but in those observations, he finds a profundity that is often missed. This is equally true of works that have apparently more serious themes and ones that are overtly humorous. Compare, for instance, his

Stabat Mater with his song cycle, *Personal Column*. In the former, he sees the complexity of Mary's emotional response to the crucifixion, sorrow and intense love at times (in the sweetness of the parallel thirds in soprano and flute lines at the beginning of the work), rage at other times (in the contrapuntal atonality of the middle section), and resignation in the end (in the pentatonic spiral, uncoordinated with the flute and voice, that ascends to the top of the keyboard at the end). At first glance, *Personal Column* seems like a very different sort of work, a lighthearted parody of the classified ads in a daily newspaper. But again, his own lyrics introduce characters that are multi-dimensional and tragicomedic: the clients at an escort service, the woman who must sell beloved belongings to make ends meet, and so on.

Ever anti-heroic, Cliff's modesty about his own role in this process is, however, unbreakable.

> What I am more interested in is something that is practical and workman-like and suitable for the occasion, not a great monument for the future. Sometimes by accident things work out well, something has clicked.

The passion he instilled in his students and the courage to create certainly clicked, as testimonies by his former students demonstrate. So, too, the love his children learned for old maps, trains, billiards, cats, or Tim Hortons, as Alison Jennings and John Crawley described in their reminiscences. They convey something of the combination of intensity, together with a capacity to see the ordinary in new ways, with humour and delight. Cliff's work occasionally has monumentality in spite of his assertions to the contrary. It inevitably has connection, however. The power to make children want to skip recess, to influence students to trust their abilities to create, to engage audiences so much that they eagerly await the next Crawley premiere—these are rare qualities among composers of the twentieth and twenty-first centuries. Wherein lies the magic? It's the poignant tension of the ludic and the serious, the tension of life, that is, for me at least, the compelling quality and the deeper significance of Clifford Crawley's work.

Notes

1   I am grateful to my assistant at the MMaP Research Centre, Maureen Houston, who transcribed all the interviews, well over one hundred pages. All quotations in this article are from those interviews unless otherwise specified. I took the liberty of editing the conversations, juxtaposing some statements about the same issue from different interviews, with the composer's approval. Cliff was then invited to do further editing of his own words.

2 Thanks to Jeremy Strachan for digitizing the musical examples. Many thanks to the co-editors for their excellent comments on an earlier draft of the article.

3 I chose to begin writing the biographical part of this article during a visit to see Cliff's daughter Alison and his sister Anne and family in the UK. The visit, as always, was a marathon of reminiscences. The close relationship between Anne and Cliff brings stories to life.

4 Certain patterns and numbers have special significance for Cliff. The number nine has been his favourite throughout his life. We joked that the title of this article should perhaps have been "Congenial, content, and sometimes controversial conversations with cute Canadian composer Clifford Crawley" so that we could include a ninefold alliteration.

5 Regretably, the music has been lost.

6 Dudley Moore attended the same school as Cliff, though in different years.

7 Cliff and Anne were the only two siblings in their immediate family. Her comment, however, may also reflect that neither their cousins nor their children were interested in a career in the arts.

8 He is known for his fingered and annotated edition for Edwin Ashdown of Bach's *Well-Tempered Clavier* (1923).

9 The name consists of the initial letters of each of the musicians' first names; the final "c" stands for Clifford. Other members of the ensemble included J. Lesley Pound (flute), Barbara Graham (oboe), Alan Hantwell (clarinet), and Dennis Dorey (clarinet). I have not yet identified the person associated with the initial "e."

10 An enterprising musician, she organized a concert series and set up a composition prize to encourage young composers. Cliff won in the second annual competition.

11 In comparison with education in Canada, the English school system was more hierarchical with two grades of high school. Students had to pass an examination called the eleven-plus to be admitted to a grammar school. Without this qualification, students could attend a secondary modern school.

12 He did drive double-decker buses in London at one point.

13 I have had trouble verifying the date; it may have been 1959.

14 This pattern broke somewhat in Kingston, Ontario, where he spent twenty years teaching at Queen's University.

15 Cliff was awarded the B.Mus. in 1968 and the M.Mus. in 1973.

16 While most of the work toward this degree was done while Cliff was in England, the revision of his M.Mus. composition and the actual awarding of the degree occurred shortly after he moved to Canada.

17 Anne's second daughter, Elizabeth, was an infant at this time.

18 Cliff explains he didn't know much about the place, although the family of one of his early students, Keith Hamel, had befriended the Crawleys during a sabbatical year in the UK and they had provided Cliff with some sense of life in Canada. He reflects: "The job just looked attractive because it was a combination of music education and composition."

19 *Hamilton Spectator*, 7 January 1993, T4.

20 In a review of *Three Shades of Dark*, David Barber noted that "hearing a Crawley work, new or old, is always a cause for celebration" (*Kingston Whig Standard*, 25 March 1988, 8). Barber goes on to note the dark intensity of the new work and the challenges it offered for listeners.

21 We tend also to include Kingston in this list of water-edged places since the lake was a huge presence there.

22 The John Adaskin project of the 1960s was the first of these. Guides to Canadian music for teachers by Patricia Shand, the establishment of Canada Music Week, the Contemporary Showcase competitions, and other projects of the Alliance for Canadian New Music were among other initiatives.

23 As mentioned earlier, Cliff did a number of Composer in the Classroom projects for the Canadian Music Center and Artist in the School projects for the Ontario Arts Council.

24 In rare instances, creative/composition projects extended over a complete term.

25 Published by Novello (London, 1958).

26 Robin Elliott jokes about being a "raving fanatic about Wagner" in his student days, noting that Cliff probably liked Wagner even less than Brahms. "I recall in particular a discussion with him about Wagner and Nazism—a subject on which he had insightful views that have only gotten a fuller airing from musicologists in more recent years. In this, as in many respects, he was way ahead of the academic curve" (email, 26 March 2007).

27 Among Cliff's composition students, there are several highly successful women composers, including Micheline Roi and Jacqueline Legatt. Several male composers have also distinguished themselves, among them Keith Hamel and Kirk Elliott.

28 He does, however, "revisit" works often and has incorporated many early ones into later pieces, fully reworked. He is also known to respond with generosity when asked to rearrange or re-orchestrate a work for a different ensemble or even a different soloist. I suspect that few composers would rewrite an opera to accommodate a soloist with a different vocal range, or orchestrate chamber works (often in an extremely limited time frame) on request.

29 Both this feature and the dance qualities of much of Cliff's music were noted by John Burge in his cogent introduction to a concert staged by the Queen's University School of Music on the occasion of Cliff's seventieth birthday.

30 Quoted on the title page of the *Fantasia for Violin and Orchestra* (1995).

31 *Mayday* for wind ensemble is another serial work.

32 He does, on the other hand, often give his instrumental works evocative titles. Many of his post-1973 orchestral works have had Canadian themes or references, as in *Group of Seven*, *Tyendinaga*, or the *Loyalist Suite*.

33 In both cases, there are words, but their rhythms and structures do not dictate the musical delivery.

34 He also sometimes tells the story of how the Crawley dog ate a piece of Helwig poetry written for an earlier collaboration.

35 The title leads one to believe that Cliff used actual newspaper advertisements, and he rather encourages this illusion, but in fact, he wrote all these "columns" himself.

36 A gesture that hints at the complex symbolism in Berg's own work.

37 My love of Brahms and Cliff's relative dislike of his music is an ongoing debate in our household.

38 His piano arrangements for Valerie Lloyd-Watts have attracted attention from a wide range of pianists, including Ontario politician Bob Rae, who wrote a thank-you note to Cliff at one point, stating that he enjoyed playing them.

39 Other classical compositions with bagpipe include Peter Maxwell Davies' *Orkney Wedding and Sunrise* (1985) and John Beckwith's *A New Pibroch* (2002).

40 The unfortunate, more recent associations of the name Barnardo with a mass murderer (Paul Bernardo) rather than the doctor who brought orphans to Canada probably

means that this work could not easily be remounted without a name change. Robin Elliott has written about this work in "Barnardo Boys," *Intersections* 28, no. 1 (2007): 120–33.

41 An instance of his willingness to accommodate collaborators even when it requires a great deal of extra work.

Recordings of Music by Clifford Crawley

Aeolian Winds. *Home Suite Home* (IBS Music IBS1037, 1998); Aeolian Winds with guest artists, the Penderecki String Quartet; *Scheherezade* (arr. Rimsky Korsakov) for wind quintet and string quartet

Aulos Trio. *Playing Tribute* (CanSona Arts Media CAM9502, 1998); Nancy Maloney (flute), Timothy Maloney (clarinet), Dina Namer (piano); *Pieces of Eight*

Bending the Bows (Take a Bow Music CD TABM001, 1993); Ed Minevich and Frank Leahy; "Foxtrot" from *Tenapennypieces*

Canadian Compositions for Young Pianists/Compositions canadiennes pour jeunes pianists (Studea Musica, BR1336, 2000); Elaine Keillor (piano); three movements ("You're Welcome," "Yes Sir!," "I'm Sorry") from *Exchanges*

Contrasts at Play (CBC Saskatchewan, 2005); Ed Minevich (violin), Pauline Minevich (clarinet), Leslie De'Ath (piano); "Will You, Won't You?," "The Butter's Spread Too Thick," "Fritter My Wig" from ... *of Cabbages and Kings*

Let There Be Music (Nahani Way Productions, 1993); "Nahani Song"

London Pro Musica. *Canadian Voices* (London Choral Foundation, LPM 2004, 2004); Aeolian Winds; *Airs and Graces* for wind quintet

Luba & Ireneus Zuk: Piano duo (Montreal, SNE-602-CD, 2007); *Three Shades of Dark*

Lynn Harting-Ware. *Americas*. (Acoma GXD 5736, 2000); Lynn Harting-Ware (guitar); *Phantasia*

Rhapsody Quintet. *Rhapsody in Red* (Rhapsody Quintet RHAO CD004, 2004); "Tuckamore," "Blind Date," "The Butter's Spread Too Thick"

Songs and Sonnets (Memorial University of Newfoundland 0206808, 2005); Francesca Swann, producer; Jane Leibel (soprano), Kristina Szutor (piano); *Grey Island*

Trio Chanteclair. *Canadian Premiere Performances* (Queen's University TCC-200109, 2001); Thomas Davidson (piano), Tracy Davidson (soprano); *Toccatas 1–5* for Solo Piano, *Piano Sonata no. 4*, "When Soft Voices Die"

Twentieth-Century Canadian Chamber Music (Queen's University Music 9101, 1991); Donelda Hunter Gartshore (flute), Carol-Lynn Reifel (soprano), Ireneus Zuk (piano); *Stabat Mater*

Valerie Lloyd-Watts. *Great Movie Themes* (Renaissance Music, CD106, 1998); twenty-one arrangements by Clifford Crawley

Works List

Many of Clifford Crawley's unpublished works are in the Canadian Music Centre. See www.musiccentre.ca.

Vocal/Choral

SOLO/UNISON FOR CHILDREN (pseudo. Clifford Curwin)

"The West Wind" (1944), text by John Masefield; "The Early Morning" (Cramer, 1945), text by Hilaire Belloc; "The Awakening" (1949, revised 1986), text by Sir William Watson; "The Centipede" (1950), text by Mrs. Edmund Craster; "The Clown's Song" (Paxton, 1951), text by William Shakespeare; "The Lord's Prayer" (Cramer, 1954), for St. Mary School, Richmond, Surrey; "This Is England" (1955), text by Lawrence Bin Yon; "The Pilgrim" (Cramer, early 1950s), text by John Bunyan; "A Christmas Lullaby" (University Carol Book, 1955), text by Diane Bennetto; "The City Child" (1956, revised 1986); "The Flower Seller" (Cramer, 1957), text by Eleanor Farjcon; "Now Welcome Summer" (1958, revised 1986), text by Chaucer; "Widge, Squidge & Bother" (J. Williams, 1958), text by Ivy Sedgwick; "The Elephant" (1950s); "Dawn" (1961, revised 1986, published by Leslie 1988), text by Thomas Ford; "Country Vegetables" (Cramer, 1962); "Everyday Things" (Curwen, 1964), text by Jean Ayer; "Skippets" (Curwen, 1964), text by Christine Bradley; "Thrice Welcome Christmas" (1964), text by George Wither; "My Dog Spot" (Curwen, 1965), text by Rodney Bennet; "The Tortoiseshell Cat" (Cramer, 1962); "The Devon Maid" (Cramer, 1963), text by John Keats; "Go Pretty Child" (Cramer, 1965), text by Robert Herrick; "The Nativity" (Cramer, ca. 1960s); "The Honeysuckle" (Cramer, 1965), text by Cicely M. Barker; "A Country Walk" (Cramer, 1966), text by Kathleen Boland; "The Voice" (Cramer, 1966), text by Kathleen Boland; "Praise" (Cramer, 1966), text by Mary Anderson

Unison Songs published in *Child Education, 1965–72*

"Caravans," "Pictures," "Day," "Marketing," "Tall Trees," "Zoo Manners," "Little Things," "My Hut," "Thoughts on a Cold Day," "The Song of the Poppy," "The Song of the Herb Robert," "Three Dogs," "A Little Brown Bird," "The Lost Snowflake," "Madcap March"

SOLO/UNISON FOR CHILDREN (for solo voice and piano unless otherwise indicated; titles of song sets are italicized, but individual song titles are not)

"Clocks" (1972); "My Shadows" (1972); "Christmas Is a Time of Love" (1974); "Hand in Hand" (1975); *Aroundabout Christmas* (Frederick Harris, 1976); *Three Songs of Science for Juniors* (Leslie, 1979): "Clouds," "Long Ago," "Cold Winter," "Hark the Glad Sound" (1960s, published by Warner/Chappell, 1980); *Five Songs for Halloween* (Leslie, 1981): "Trick or Treat," "The Witches Ride," "Grizelda"; *Merry Merry Christmas* (Leslie, 1981, except nos. 2 and 5): "Merry Merry Christmas," "Weather," "December," "A Card for Santa," "Other Folks," "We're Busy

Buying Presents," "Santa Claus Parade," "Our Christmas Tree"; "Halloween Song" (Roberton, 1983); "Late at Night" (Roberton, 1983); *We Love to Sing* (Leslie, 1984): "It's Not Easy," "Wishes," "Thunder and Lightning" (Leslie, 1984); "Let Us Remember" (Leslie, 1984), unison with descant, also arranged for SAB with optional descant and piano or organ; *Once upon a Christmastime* (Leslie, 1984): "Once upon a Christmastime," "Lullaby Loo," "Listen," "Santa's Pets"; *Everyday Things* (Leslie, 1985; except no. 3 and 4): "I Like Food," "Lights," "The Corner Store," "There's a Mouse in My House," "Cars," "Busy," "Catching"; *Creatures Great and Small* (1984; Set 1 published by Leslie, 1986; Set 2 published by Leslie, 1988): Set 1: "Dragons," "Gremlins," "The Unicorn"; Set 2: "Little Leprechaun," "Beautiful Mermaid," "The Phoenix"; *Songs of the Settlers* (nos. 1, 3, and 5 published by Leslie, 1984): "I've Crossed the Sea," "Our Homestead in the Flatlands," "We'll Blaze a Trail to the Rockies," "What Shall I Do?," "Northwards"; *Magic in the Air* (Leslie, 1987, except no. 4): "There's Magic in the Air," "Abdul the Magician," "Magic Carpet," "Abracadabra"; "I'm Feeling Very Happy" (1987); "O Little Town of Bethlehem" (arr. 1987); "Ambitions" (1987); "It's Christmas" (1987); "Christmas Is a Time of Love" (1987); "The Star of Bethlehem" (1987); "Mrs. Dinosaur" (Leslie, 1988); "Penguin Dance" (Leslie, 1988); "Humpy the Camel" (Leslie, 1988); "The Fox" (Leslie, 1988); "Pelicans" (Leslie, 1989); *Circus Songs* (Leslie, 1989, except no. 3): "Clowns," "Lions," "The Tight-rope Walker," "Horses," "Elephants," "The Circus Band"; "Doubles" (1989); "Tinkerteller" (1989); "Storybookland" (1990); "We Can Make a Difference" (Leslie, 1990); "Hand in Hand" (1992); "Paddy" (1993); "Montague" (1993); "The Magic Paintbox" (Leslie, 1993); "Nahani" (1993); *Six Songs for Aladdin* (1994); "Trolls" (Leslie 1994); "Only Half" (1998); "School Song for Forest Glen Public School" (2002); "Graceful Gavotte" (2005); "The Haunted House" (2005); "Red Canoe" (2005); "Sleuths" (2005)

TWO PART FOR CHILDREN

"A Song of Autumn" (Cramer, 1966), pseudo. Clifford Curwin, text by Kathleen Boland; "Listen to the Lambs" (Cramer, 1973), arr. traditional, pseudo. Clifford Curwin; "Sometimes" (1987); "The Grass Is Always Greener" (1987); "The Star" (1987); "Dawn" (Leslie, 1988); "Shadows" (Leslie, 1988); "Thanksgiving" (1987, published by Leslie, 1989); "Green and Blue" (Leslie, 1989); "Butterflies" (1991), text by Lynn Harting-Ware; "Late at Night" (Leslie, 1995); "Participate," for speaker(s), SA, keyboard and percussion (Leslie, 1996); "The Moon" (1997), text by Wordsworth; "The Man in the Moon" (1997)

SOLO SONGS AND SONG SETS (for solo voice and piano unless otherwise indicated; titles of song sets are italicized, but individual song titles are not)

1946 "Loveliest of Trees"; text by A.E. Houseman

1949 "Brigg Fair"; arr. traditional; tenor and two violins

1951 *Three Nocturnes* (2. "Owl" published by Alberta Keys, 2003); text by Osbert Sitwell

1951   *Two Songs: A Carol and Spanish Song*; texts by Ronald Duncan

1955   *Philip Sparrow's Funeral and Other Songs*; text by Robert Skelton

1955   *Two 16th-Century Lullabys*; anonymous; voice and string quartet

1957   "The Fiddler of Dooney" (revised 1983); text by John Keats

1958   "Now Welcome Summer" (revised 1986)

1961   "Dawn" (revised 1986); text by John Ford

1976   *Hymns Ancient and Victorian*; text by various poets

1977   *Grotesques*; text by Robert Graves

1978   "Wedding Song"; text by Diane Gordon; for voice, piano, and cello

1982   *Songs of Duke Redbird*; texts by Métis poet, Duke Redbird

1983   "Everyone Sang" (published by Alberta Keys, 2003); text by Siegfried Sassoon

1983   *Five Traditional Songs*: "The Bonny Lighter Boy," "Johnny Was a Shoemaker," "Golden Slumbers," "Robin Adair," "Lasses and Lads"; for soprano, piano, and flute obligato

1983   "Penillion." "In the Vale of Llangollen" (revision of an earlier work); for solo voice and SATB

1984   "My Wild Irish Rose" (arr.)

1984   *Stabat Mater*; for soprano, flute, and piano

1985   *When Soft Voices Die*: "Listen," "Wisps of Sound," "O What Joy," "The Rainbow," "A Child in All"; text by Lisa Marsh

1986   "Psalm CXIV"; for mezzo-soprano and piano

1987   *Ayres*; sixteenth-century texts; soprano and harpsichord/piano

1988   "Bird That Never Was" (1988); text by David Helwig; mezzo-soprano with clarinet

1988   *The Winter Galaxy and Other (Early Canadian) Songs*: "Song of the Thousand Islands" (text by Agnes M. Machen); "Our Life Is Like a Forest" (text by Charles Sangster); "Indian Summer" (published by Waterloo Music, 1999, text by Wilfred Campbell); "Lord of My Heart's Elation" (text by Bliss Carmen); "The Rickety House" (text by Alexander McLachlan); "Winter Evening" (text by Archibald Lampman)

1989   "Blow the Wind Southerly" (arr. traditional); contralto, alto, flute, and piano

1990   *Danses Macabres;* twelve songs for soprano, clarinet(s), and piano; texts from medieval lyrics, arranged by Judith Pond

1990   *Personal Column*; seven songs for soprano, clarinet, and piano; texts by Clifford Crawley; premiered by Stephanie Bogle in 1991

1995   *Trois Vocalises*

1997   *Seven Stevie Smith Songs*: "A Dream of Comparison," Some Are Born," "November," "Progression," "Coeur Simple," "From the Greek," "Not Waving But Drowning," "Encore—My Hat"

1998   Songs by Wolf, Poulenc, and Keel (arr.); for voice and woodwind quintet

1999   "Spirit of Delight" (1999); text by Percy B. Shelley

2003 *Grey Island*: (1) "The Things You Look at"; (2) "Clear Day"; (3) "On the Line"; (4) "Today a Sadness"; (5) Day by Day"; texts by John Steffler; five songs for soprano, clarinet, and piano

2004 *The Sounds of Many Waters*: (1) "Full Many a Gem"; (2) "The Seas Are Quiet"; (3) "Noah," (4) "The Rainbow"; (5) "A Jollyrodgered Shantisea"; (6) "A Ship Is Floating in the Harbour"; (7) "Willy Nilly."; (8) "Sea Fever"; (9) "On One Side Lay the Ocean"; (10) "Dark Blue Ocean"; (11) "Earth and Oceans"; (12) "The Rising World of Waters"; miscellaneous texts compiled by Clifford Crawley; (very) short songs for soprano, flute, percussion, and bass

2005 "Labrador Carol" (arr. Abass); for Festival 500 in Labrador

2005 *In a Summer Seson When Soft Was the Sonne*: (1) "Sumer Is a Cumin in" (anon.); (2) "It Is Spring" (text by Simon Steele); (3) "Screened" (text by Joanne Edwards); (4) "Young and Simple" (text by Thomas Campion); (5) "October" (text by Carolyn Smart); (6) "Summer Suns Are Glowing" (text by Walsham How); for soprano, flute, lute, cello, and keyboard

2005 *Overheard at Mrs. Beeton's Kitchen Party*: (1) "The Mistress"; (2) "Miss Nightingale's Notes"; (3) "To Smoke Hams at Home"; (4) "A Pretty Dish of Oranges"; (5) "The Height of Excellence Is a Pheasant"; (6) "Food and Its Preparation for Children"; texts by Clifford Crawley, adapted from *Mrs. Beeton's book of household management* (1861), reprinted in the Oxford World's Classics series (2000).

2005 "Nancy and Thomas" (arr. traditional.); for voice, piano, and string quartet

Choral

1950 *Two Canticles*: Psalms 98 and 100; SATB; broadcast by the West of England Singers

1950s *Gloria in Excelsis*; SAB and organ.

ca. 1950 *Our Risen Lord, an Easter Cantata*; SATB and organ

1960 *Sigh No More, Ladies* (arr.); SATB

1961 *Magnificat and Nunc Dimittis*; unison voices and organ

1962 "A Celtic Lullaby" (Cramer); arr. traditional; pseudo. Clifford Curwin; SSA; text by A.P. Graves

1973 *Missa Brevis*; SATB

1974 *The King of China's Daughter*; text by Edith Sitwell; voices and instruments

1975 *A Festal Te Deum*; SATB and organ

1976 *Psalm 104*; SATB and organ

1977 *Nemesis*; text by Diane Gordon and others; SATB, string quartet and percussion

1977 *McAvity*; text by T.S. Eliot; SATB; for David Barber and the Queen's Singers

1978 *Laudate Pueri*; text anonymous; seven motets for voice; SATB, brass quintet, and organ; premiered by the Pro Arte Singers, Kingston, Ontario (David Cameron, conductor)

1978 *Before the World Was Made*; text by W.B. Yeats; SSSAAA

1979 *A Night among the Pines*; text by Robert Louis Stevenson; SATB

1979 *Childermas—Mass for Holy Innocents*; composite text by various authors; soloists (SSATB), chorus, piano-duet, and strings

1979 *The Miracle Child*; text by David Helwig; SAB, band and optional strings

1981 *The Lord Is King* (Leslie); text Psalm 93; SATB with organ

1983 *Children of the Heavenly King; Sing Joyfully*; text by J. Cennick; SSA

1984 *Peter Piper* (Lawson Gould, 1988); text anon.; SATB

1984 Juanita (arr.) (revised 1984); SATB version

1984 *Close of Spring* (Lawson Gould, 1989); SATB

1984 "The Harvest of Life"; words paraphrased by Brian Yelland; SATB

1986 *Laudate Dominum*; text Psalm 150 and excerpts of Milton's "Il Penseroso"; for SATB, brass, percussion, strings, and organ

1987 "I Love Thee, O Lord"; SATB

1988 "Bird That Never Was"; text by David Helwig; SATB with narrator and percussion

1988 *Missa Brevis*

1990 *The Sorrows of Werther* (Lawson Gould); text by W.M. Thackeray; originally for male-voice quartet, arranged for SATB for publication

1992 "Hark the Glad Sound" (Lawson Gould, 1995); text by P. Doddridge; SATB with brass quintet and organ

1992 "Peace" (Leslie, 1993); S(SA) and piano

1999 *Aetas Nova*; text by Alphonse de Lamartine, Longfellow, and Peter G. Davy; chorus and orchestra; millennium project for the Kingston Symphony Orchestra; premiered by them in 2000

Orchestra

1971 *Fast Sinks the Sun/Sol/Praceps Rupitur*; composed in partial fulfillment of the M.Mus. requirements (University of Durham); for thirty-eight players

1972 *Divertimento on a theme of Ebenezer Prout;* for the Queen's University Symphony Orchestra

1973 *Prelude* (arr. Chopin); for the Kingston Youth Orchestra

1975 *Overture on a Canadian Theme (or Two)*; recorded by the Ottawa Youth Orchestra; also performed by the Kingston Youth Orchestra

1976 *Greek National Anthem and Olympic Hymn* (arr.); commissioned for the 1976 Olympic Games

1980 *Koleda: A Christmas Overture* (Berandol, 1980); eight mins; 2222/4331/timpani, percussion (three), harp, strings; for the Kitchener–Waterloo Symphony Orchestra, conducted by Raffi Armenian, who premiered the work in December 1981

1982 *Symphony S.B.* (1982); based on E-flat–B, a reference to Simon Bolivar

1983 *Tyendinaga;* for the Kingston Symphony Orchestra

1983 *Canadian Dances—Set 1* (1983); for the Kingston Symphony Orchestra

1984 … *of Cabbages and Kings: Five Quotations from Lewis Carroll* (1984); see Chamber works re. original version; commissioned by the Kingston Symphony Orchestra (conductor Brian Jackson) for Canada Music Week, 1986

1984 *The Loyalist Suite* (1984); commissioned with support from the Ontario Arts Council for the Eastern Ontario Concert Orchestra

1985 *Threnody*; commissioned with support from the Ontario Arts Council for the Eastern Ontario Concert Orchestra

1987 *Sinfonietta;* original version was for symphonic band

1991 *Ban Righ Overture* bagpipes and orchestra; commissioned by Queen's University for the university's sesquicentennial

1992 *Changes*; for the Eastern Ontario Concert Orchestra who premiered the work in 1993

1998 *Overture—King Coles*

2003 *After Dark*; premiered by Symphony Nova Scotia, 2004

2005 … *For Mozart's 250th Anniversary*; orchestra, two pianos and voices; for the Newfoundland Symphony Orchestra's Mozart celebrations of 2006

String Orchestra

1951 *Suite in G*; for the Epson Symphony Orchestra

1976 *Four String Things*; for the Frontenac County Junior Strings

1978 *Overture, Air, and Dances*; for the Victoriano Lopez Music School, San Pedro Sula, Honduras, CA

1979 *Blue Peter. Eight Sea Songs for Elementary Strings*

1982 *Suite Victoria*; on themes by the grades seven and eight students of Victoria School, Kingston, Ontario

1984 *Pavane and Galliard for String Nonet or String Orchestra*; for the Prince Edward Island Orchestra

1987 *A Group of Seven*; double string orchestra with optional keyboard; for the Kingston Symphony Orchestra; subsequently performed by several orchestras, including the Hamilton Philharmonic (Boris Brott, conductor); each movement based on line drawings by Group of Seven artists

1988 *Walkerville Suite*; for Elementary string orchestra or string quartet with optional keyboard/guitar continuo; written with the students of Walkerville Collegiate Institute, Windsor, Ontario; also arranged for concert band

1990 *Overture on "The Pink Panther"*

2002 *Pastime with Good Company;* string quartet and string orchestra

2005 *Canzona da Sonare;* for the Regina Symphony Orchestra; premiered by them

2006 *Let's Join in;* buckets, audience, and orchestra; commissioned by the Kingston Symphony Orchestra

Orchestra with Solo Instrument(s)

1968   *Piano Concerto*; premiered by John Wood and High Schools in Crediton, Devon, UK

1972   *Concertino in D* (arr. Clementi); for piano and orchestra; for the Clacton-on-Sea Concert Orchestra

1973   *Gymnopédie* (arr. Satie); for oboe and orchestra; for the Kingston Youth Orchestra

1982   *Concertino for Piano and Orchestra*; for the Eastern Ontario Concert Orchestra

1985   *Concerto for Piano and Orchestra*; for Valerie Lloyd-Watts

1988   *Concertino no. 2 for Piano and Orchestra*; for Valerie Lloyd-Watts

1989   *Gemini Dances*; for two violins and orchestra; commissioned by the Kingston Symphony Association and premiered by Ed Minevitch with the KSA, 1989

1989   *Serenade for Cello and Orchestra*; premiered by Jill Vitols with the Kingston Symphony Orchestra, 1990

1993   *Concerto for Tuba and Orchestra*; reworked as *Concerto bouffe* (see below)

1995   *Fantasia for Violin and Orchestra*; based on a theme by Ebenezer Prout; commissioned by the Kingston Symphony Orchestra and premiered by them with Scott St. John (violin)

2002   *Concerto bouffe*; trombone and string orchestra; reworked version of the *Concerto for Tuba and Orchestra*

Band

1977   *MayDay*; for the Queen's University Wind Ensemble

1978   *Tyendinaga. Legend for Concert Band*; for the Napanee High School; also scored for orchestra (first performed by the Kingston Symphony Orchestra, 1983)

1981   *Concerto for Piano and Band*; arranged for orchestra, 1982, and first performed by the Eastern Ontario Concert Orchestra

1983   *Proclamation for Concert Band*

1984   *Fanfare for Youth and the Arts*; for six trumpets, four horns, four trombones, two tubas, and three percussion; commissioned by Frontenac County with a grant from the Ontario Arts Council; premiered at the Donald Gordon Centre, Kingston, January 1985

1985   *Canadian Heritage*; based on traditional airs and themes by Dunbar Moodie (1797–1869) and students of Centennial High School, Belleville, Ontario; a Composer in the Classroom project

1987   *Sinfonietta* (1987); for the Queen's University Symphonic Band (conductor Gordon Craig)

1990   *Tlah Nanavtsi* (1990); suite for flute and clarinet choirs

Keyboard (for piano unless otherwise indicated)

(undated) *Song and Dance*; see *Suite for Flute and Piano*

(undated) *Partipieces*; incorporated into later pieces

(undated) *Three Short Pieces*

(undated) *Mr. Gunn's Lesson* (arr. Bartolmo Gunn); versions for organ and piano

1940s *Six Miniatures*; some incorporated into later pieces

1952 *Six French Nursery Songs* (Chester); pseudo. Clifford Curwin; for piano duet; multiple BBC broadcasts and other performances

1952 *Elegy for Organ*; incorporated as the slow movement of *Sonata Giocoso*

1952 *Canon à 7 for Two Pianos*

1957 *Sonata Giocoso* (revised 1984)

ca. 1959 *Blue Peter* (arr. traditional)

1959 *Two Pieces for Two Pianos*: "Aubade" and "Outward Bound"

1960s "Decadent Dance," "Blind Date," "Vacation," "Tuckamore," "Royal Parade," "Peaches and Cream"; rearranged in 2005 for the Fantasy Quintet, Halifax, Nova Scotia

1962 *Welsh Airs and Dances* (Galliard); pseudo. Clifford Curwin

1963 *Tunes from Ireland* (Galliard); pseudo. Clifford Curwin

1972 *Improvisations on a Theme of Ebenezer Prout*; see *Divertimento* for orchestra

1974 *Arabesques on Medieval Themes*; for organ; for F.R.C. Clarke

1975 *Aubade*

1975 *Four Inventions*

1978 *Naditas*

1978 *Toccatas*; see recordings

1983 *In Memoriam Randall Marsh*; for organ

1986 *Three Impromptus*

1987 *Sonata no. 4*; for Thomas Davidson; see recordings

1987 *Three Shades of Dark*; for two pianos; commissioned by Ireneus and Luba Zuk with support from the Ontario Arts Council

1988 *Twelve Preludes*

1988 *Sonata Semplice*

1988 *La ficelle d'or*; for Valerie Lloyd-Watts

1989 *Spirituals*; five movements for organ

1989 *Kalamalka*; for piano duet; for Rosdal Duo, British Columbia

1990 *Four Uneasy Pieces* (published by Frederick Harris, 1994); for piano duet

1993 *Exchanges* (1993, published by Frederick Harris, 1996); see recordings

1994 *24 Arrangements of Movie Themes for Valerie Lloyd-Watts* (1994) Commissioned by Valerie Lloyd-Watts, who recorded twenty-one of the arrangements on *Great Movie Themes* (1998)

1998 *Three Piano Duets*

1999 *Formations*; commissioned by the Euromusic School, Markham, Ontario

2000   *An Album of Piano Pieces*: (1) "Genesis"; (2) "Rush Green"; (3) "All Dressed
       up and No Place to Go"; (4) "The Woods Are Lovely, Dark, and Deep";
       (5) "Bdellium"; (6) "Happiness Is No Laughing Matter"; (7) "Galump";
       (8) "Cumulus"; (9) "L'un ou l'autre, plus ou moins"; (10) "Machinations";
       (11) "Soliloquy"; (12) "Envoi"
2001–2 34 *Pieces for Piano*; the following twenty were published by the Canadian
       National Conservatory of Music, in *Northern Lights* (2006) or *Making
       Tracks* (2006), or *Expeditions in Canadian Music* (2006): "Seashine," "A
       Rant," "Musette," "From C to C," "Stepping Lightly," "Out of Town,"
       "Quite Contrary," "Going, Going, Gone," "My Red Canoe," "Kicking
       Horse Pass," "Neverland Nocturne," "Morning Fog," "Wishing Well," "The
       Laird of Lochleven's Lament," "Fiddlesticks," "Boomerang," "Shuffle,"
       "Cushions," "Shenanigans," "Short Change"
2002   *Lark in the Clear Air* (arr. for piano)
2002   *Profiles/Portraits for Piano*; nine short pieces
2004   *In the Wake of the Aftermath* (2004); premiered by Clifford Crawley at the
       Newfound Music Festival, St. John's, 2006

Chamber Music

1950   *Sonatina for Unaccompanied Cello*; premiered by Sela Trau and the Soci-
       ety for the Promotion of New Music (London, UK) in 1951
1950   *Threnody for Recorder and Piano* (arr. Ireland)
1951   *Divertimento for Woodwind Quartet*; flute, oboe, two clarinets; for the
       Dalbec ensemble
1951   *A Suite for Flute and Piano*; for the Dalbec ensemble; revised for oboe
1951   *Suite for Oboe and Piano* (1951); for Barbara Graham and the Dalbec
       ensemble; see *Suite for Flute and Piano*
1951   *Sonatina for Clarinet and Piano*; for the Dalbec ensemble
1952   *Four Short Pieces*; two clarinets; for the Dalbec ensemble
1952   *Three Dances for Bassoon and Clarinet*; for the Dalbec ensemble
1952   *A Bach Suite* (arr.); for the Dalbec ensemble
1952   *Suite in F from the Water Music* (arr. Handel); for the Dalbec ensemble
1952   *Les Petits Riens* (arr. Mozart); for the Dalbec ensemble
1952   *Five Traditional Songs for Woodwind Quartet*; for the Dalbec ensemble
1952   *Waltz, Intermezzo, and March*; violin and piano; for Rosemary Utting
1956   *Scherzo for Clarinet and Piano*; arrangement of last movement of Sonatina
       no. 3
1959   *Four Pastorals*; oboe, clarinet, and piano; premiered by the BBC West of Eng-
       land Players in 1962
ca. 1960s *Equali*; based on Paganini's Op. 1
1960s *Two Pieces for Two Flutes* (arr. W. Bates)
1961   *Air with Diversions*; recorder trio; for Brian Crispin and ensemble
ca. 1962 *Two Pieces*: "Level," "Rant"; violin or clarinet and piano

1963 *Ricercare*; oboe and piano; BBC broadcast by Ian Black and Wilfred Parry

1963 *Prelude and Hornpipe* (arr. James Hook); trio

1963 *Three Toccatas for Woodwinds* (arr. Loesehorn)

1964 *Divertimento*; flute, oboe, and clarinet

1964 *Divertimento for Violin and Piano*

1964 *Georgian Dances*; clarinet and piano

1965 *Suite for Three* (arr. Hook) (Chappells); three clarinets; pseudo. Clifford Curwin

1965 *Sonatinas* (arr. Hook) (Chappells); three clarinets; pseudo. Clifford Curwin

1965 *Guida di Musica* (arr. Hook) (Chappells); two clarinets unaccompanied or with string orchestra; pseudo. Clifford Curwin

1965 *Flourishes for Brass* (arr. William Bates) (Chappells); two trumpets; pseudo. Clifford Curwin

1966 *Adagio & Allegro* (arr. Felton) (Chappells); oboe and piano; pseudo. Clifford Curwin

1968 *String Quartet*; original composition in partial fulfillment of the requirements for the B.Mus. degree at Durham University

1971 *Overture, Air & Dances for String Quartet*; original composition in partial fulfillment of the requirements to be recognized as a fellow of Trinity College, London (FTCL)

1971 *Four Songs without Words* (arr. Mendelssohn); for instrumental quartet

1972 *Variations for Violin and Piano*; Certificate of Secondary Education recording

1972 *Minuet*; for violin, clarinet, and cello

1973 *Sonatina for Brass Trio*; later renamed *Trio Sonata*

1973 *Boutade*; four saxophones

1974 *Foray*; woodwind quintet

1974 *Quintessence* (published in the *Canadian Music Educator*); for instruments and/or voices

1975 *Three or Four Bagatelles for Solo Clarinet*

1977 *New Year Dances*; clarinet and piano

1978–79 *Gallanteries*; original version for trombone choir; arranged for brass quintet

1980 *Four Pieces for Handbells*; named after Crawley's places of residence: Waresfoot, Hadleigh, Rush Green, Stentaway; "Hadleigh" won first prize in the Regina Bell Ringers Competition, 1980

1983 *Harlequinade for Clarinet Choir*; for the Queen's University Clarinet Choir

1983 *... of Cabbages and Kings: Five Quotations from Lewis Carroll*: (1) "Will You, Won't You?"; (2) "Curiouser and Curiouser!"; (3) "The Butter's Spread Too Thick"; (4) "Off with Her Head!"; (5) "Fritter My Wig"; flute/violin, clarinet/viola, and piano; three movements recorded on *Contrasts at Play* (2002); also scored for small orchestra (1984); premiere of the orchestral version by the Kingston Symphony Orchestra, 1986

1983   *Sonata for Viola and Piano*; slow movement is an arrangement of the slow movement from the *Oboe Sonata*

1984   *Tenapennypieces* (1984); clarinet and piano: (1) "Prelude" (from *Suite for Flute and Piano*); (2) "Cavatina"; (3) "Capriccio" (from *Three Short Pieces for Piano*); (4) "Tango" (from *Dances for Clarinet and Piano*); (5) "Pezzatrena" (from *Dances for Clarinet and Piano*); (6) Allapolka (from *Four Pastorals* for flute, clarinet, and piano); (7) "Intermezzo"; (8) "Waltz" (from *Suite for Flute and Piano*); (9) "Foxtrot" (from *Dances for Clarinet and Piano*; (10) "Theme and Variations"; "Foxtrot" arranged for violin and orchestra (see recordings)

1985   *Six Miniatures for Recorder Trio*

1986–87   *Song and Dance*; flute and guitar

1987   *Slow Movement* (1987); flute and piano/organ

1987   *Gems*; for recorders and/or Orff instruments with optional guitar; twelve pieces

1987   *Trio Sonata*; for three brass instruments or saxophones

1989   *Pieces of Eight*; flute/violin, clarinet/viola, and piano; see recordings; (1) "Outward Bound"; (2) "All at Sea"; (3) "Solo for Flute/Violin"; (4) "Panjandrum"; (5) "Jeremiad"; (6) "The Rocky Road to Dublin"; (7) "Solo for Clarinet/Viola"; (8) "Roulade"

1989   *Divertissements*: "Level," "Eclogue," "Rant"; brass instrument and piano

1990   *Phantasia for Guitar* (Acoma, 1990); for Lynn Harting-Ware; see recordings

1990   *Recitatives and Arias*; oboe and piano; three movements

1991   *Four Allegri*; alto saxophone/clarinet and piano; premiered by Patrick Vetter and Allison Gagnon

1991   *Beverley*; for the Regina Bell Ringers

1991   *Broderie Perse*; for violin and cello

1992   *Aquarelles*; violin and piano

1993   *Solstice*; clarinet and piano; for Brian Jackson and his daughter

1994   *Scheherezade* (arr. Rimsky-Korsakov); re-orchestration for woodwind quintet and string quartet; commissioned by the Aeolian Winds and Penderecki String Quartet; see recordings

1994   *Plainte*; cello and piano

1995   *Airs and Graces*; ten pieces for wind quintet; commissioned by the Aeolian Winds; see recordings

1997   *Urban Pastorals*; five movements for flute and bassoon; (1) "Playgrounds, Parks, and Picnics"; (2) "Sanctuary"; (3) "Sidewalk Sale"; (4) "Through a Glass Darkly"; (5) "Juxtapositions"

2000   *Sextet*; woodwinds and piano

2001   *Sonata*; horn and piano; four movements

2001   *Quadrilles*; string quartet; (1) "Wending"; (2) "With Measured Tread"; (3) "Pale Blue"; (4) "Issues"; (5) "Once upon a Time"; (6) "Insouciance"; CBC broadcast by the Atlantic String Quartet, 2007

2002 *Suite for Bassoon and Piano*

2002 *Song and Dance for Bass Clarinet and Cello*; for Paul Bendza's sixtieth birthday concert

2002 *Suite Badine*; trumpet and piano

2003 *Antiphons*: brass and saxophone quintets; for ensembles at Memorial University

2003 *Sonata for Unaccompanied Cello*; for Thomas Lowenheim; three movements; rewrite of 1950 *Sonatina for Unaccompanied Cello*

2003 Variations (on a Newfoundland Song); unaccompanied cello; for Thomas Lowenheim

2003–4 Arrangements of early piano pieces by Crawley for the Rhapsody Quintet: "The Butter's Spread Too Thick," "Tuckamore," "Blind Date," "Blue Peter," "Vacation," "Decadent Dance," "The Lark in Clear Air," "Peaches and Cream"; for nos. 1, 2, and 3, see recordings

2004 *Duet for Two Violins*; for James and Beverley Coles, on the occasion of their fiftieth wedding anniversary

2005 *Trio*; three movements; clarinet, French horn, and piano; for members of the Aeolian Quintet

2005–6 Arrangements for Duo Concertante: "Samson and Delilah" (Saint-Saens); "Barcarolle" (Tchaikovsky); "Tico-tico" (Zequinha de Abreu); "It's a Grand Night for Making Love to a Beautiful Girl on a Carousal in Vienna" (Rogers and Hammerstein); "Madame Butterfly" (Puccini); "Solveig's Song" (Grieg); "Night in Tunisia" (Dizzy Gillespie); "Black Orpheus"(Luis Bonfa); "Sabre Dance" (Khatchachurian); "Ronda alla Turca" (Mozart); "Oh, Lady Be Good" (George Gershwin); "The Sorcerer's Apprentice" (Dukas)

Opera

1974 *The Slaughter of the Innocents*. An opera for performance in church; libretto compiled from medieval sources by Robert Wright; for soprano, three mezzo-sopranos, five baritones, four non-vocal stagehands, chorus of men, women, and children, with participation from audience/congregation; small orchestra; premiered in Clacton, 1974; subsequent performances at St. Martin's Cathedral, Leicester, UK (1975), and St. Georges Cathedral, Kingston, Ontario (1977)

1977 *The Creation: An Opera*; for St. George's Cathedral, Kingston, Ontario; premiered May 1978

1981 *The Trouble with Heroes*; libretto by Guy Vanderhaeghe; for baritone, string quartet with bass, one percussion, and piano/conductor

1981 *Barnardo Boy*; opera in two acts; libretto by David Helwig; for rock band (pre-recorded), large cast of adults and children, and orchestra; performed 12–15 May 1982 with Jan Rubes in the lead role, James Coles, musical director, Gord Love, director, and Reginald Bronskill, designer

1989   *The Pied Piper*; libretto by David Helwig; soprano and tenor, large cast of
        adults and children, small orchestra; concert performance by Glynn Evans
        (tenor) and Carolyn Lynn Reifel (soprano).
1996   *Angel Square*; opera in two acts; libretto by Janet Irwin after novel by Brian
        Doyle; for adult or teenage performers, and children with accompaniment
        for piano/synthesizer, or piano/synthesizer, string quartet, and percussion

Children's Musicals

1956   *The Rivers*; for Plympton Grammar School; producer Alan Rowe
1983   *Fe-Fi-Fo-Fum*; libretto by Clifford Crawley; arranged for puppets by David
        Smith, 1993; for First Avenue Public School, Kingston, Ontario
1984   *Goldie and the Three Brown Bears*; libretto by Clifford Crawley; a musical
        for children with piano accompaniment; for J.E. Heston School, Kingston,
        Ontario
1984   *The Ring of a Thousand Wishes*; libretto by Clifford Crawley; a musical for
        children with piano accompaniment; for First Avenue Public School,
        Kingston, Ontario
1985   *The Adventures of Little Red Riding Hood*; libretto by Clifford Crawley; a
        musical for children with piano accompaniment
1987   *Porky, Snorky, and Corky* (The three little pigs) (Novello); libretto by Clif-
        ford Crawley; a musical for children with accompaniment for piano and/or
        Orff instruments and/or small orchestra; for First Avenue Public School,
        Kingston, Ontario; orchestral version for the Eastern Ontario Concert
        Orchestra
1987   *Santa and the Idle Elves*; libretto by Clifford Crawley; a musical for chil-
        dren with piano accompaniment
1988   *Santa and the Reindeer Rocket*; libretto by Clifford Crawley
1991   *Starship Twinkle*; for orchestra and Suzuki strings, or piano and Suzuki
        strings; libretto by Beverley Diamond; commissioned by the Kingston Suzuki
        Music Association
1993   *Tom*; libretto by Clifford Crawley after Mark Twain; for baritone and many
        children; for Lord Strathcona Public School, Kingston, Ontario; revised
        1993 for Opera Lyra

Other

1976   Improvised music for a film depicting the history of Queen's University
1980   Electronic call–signals for CFRC
1999   *Things to Do with Strings* (1999); theatre piece with string quartet accom-
        paniment; see *Quadrilles*; libretto by Gordon Love; commissioned by the
        Kingston Symphony Association

Ethnomusicology Critiques Itself
Comments on the History of a Tradition

BRUNO NETTL

ORE PERHAPS THAN THE PRACTITIONERS of other disciplines, ethnomusicologists have been critical of their own field. One might almost say that the practice of critiquing the discipline as a whole is part of the identity of this field, and goes back to its roots at the beginnings of the twentieth century. Periods in which this kind of self-critique was significant have arisen several times, alternating with periods of relative satisfaction. At the beginning of the twenty-first century, a good many scholars have again begun to look at what they and their colleagues have been doing as a population of scholars through a sharply evaluative lens.

A number of Beverley Diamond's powerful contributions to ethnomusicology have participated in this critical perspective. To be sure, her publications have not ordinarily set out to claim explicitly that her field has gone off in undesirable directions. It seems reasonable, nevertheless, to see much of her work as contributing to a newly developing critical perspective dominating the period since 1990. Thus, her edited works dealing with Canadian traditions insist on the specialness of the musical cultures of Canada (Diamond and Witmer 1994), maintaining that they may be fundamentally different from those of the United States and of Europe, which have all along been seen as the norm of both ethnic traditions and methodology. *Visions of sound* (Diamond, Cronk, and von Rosen 1994) stands as a critique of normal organology of the past and proposes an essentially "emic" approach. Unquestionably, the whole field of gender studies—or gender-oriented ethnomusicology—is a critique of much (most) of the ethnomusicology done before, and Beverley Diamond has been in the intellectual leadership of this movement (e.g., Moisala and Diamond 2000). Her bibliography also gives evidence of her superb talent for collaboration. It seems appropriate, therefore, to honour her contributions by examining, commenting on, and speculating about what may have become a tradition of critique.

After Y2K

Although this contribution follows a historical plan, let me work, for the first few paragraphs, in reverse chronological order and mention three critical trends that have been gathering steam in the first years of the twenty-first century, beginning a few years earlier, trends that suggest that major changes in the identity of ethnomusicology may be in the offing. All of them speak to the basic character of ethnomusicology, and/or its place in the academy.

During the spring and summer of 2006, the Society for Ethnomusicology Internet discussion list hosted a debate that began with well-founded accusations of a particular insularity of American ethnomusicologists, leading to the issue of scholarly hegemony paralleling political hegemony, and eventually moving to the question of ethnomusicology as an international or a nation- and culture-specific discipline. To the underlying question, of long standing in our field—"Are data, facts, conclusions, and interpretations the result of 'objective' observations and universally recognized theory?"—issues such as these were added: "What kinds of people should ethnomusicologists be? Should the answer depend on a scholar's national and cultural identity?" The notion that there are many ethnomusicologies—American, but also African American, Indian, Chinese, etc.—was aired, and to understand all of them became a desideratum. It was pointed out, for example, that in The new Grove dictionary of music and musicians (2nd ed.), no Indian or Chinese scholars identified as ethnomusicologists were listed, as compared to dozens of Europeans and North Americans. This accusation requires further analysis, for we know that many scholars from these two most populous nations don't like the term ethnomusicology and prefer to be known as musicologists, even if their interests intersect with North American "ethnomusicologists." Even so, the tone of the Internet discussion suggested that American ethnomusicologists weren't happy with their role in the world of scholarship, and some ethnomusicologists elsewhere agreed with them. There was discussion of the insularity of all nationally defined groups of scholars, but the political and economic power of the US gave the tendency of American scholars to isolate themselves from the rest of the world an especially undesirable air. Everyone engaging in this discussion wished to increase the opportunity for crossing cultural and national academic boundaries.

A second illustration: Recently, there appeared an article by Martin Greve, the accomplished scholar of the musical culture of the Turkish population of Germany, "Vom notwendigen Verschwinden der Musiketh- nologie" (Greve 2002), arguing that the kinds of research with which ethnomusicology was associated in the minds of most academics—the study of the musical and cultural "other" and the notion of fieldwork in a foreign environment—needed no longer (*could* no longer) be carried out, and that one should therefore subsume the work now being done by ethnomusicologists in the larger discipline of musicology. Greve proposed that because of the changes that the world of music has undergone in the last twenty years—in technology, communication, and politics—ethno- musicology had ceased to be justified as a separate field. In Germany, where academic positions in ethnomusicology have been declining in num- ber, Greve's article, published next to an article criticizing the configura- tion of musicological training in Germany at large (Adam, Heesch, and Rode-Breymann 2002), made a considerable splash, and a debate ensued about the continued usefulness of traditional ethnomusicology, with its configuration of methods centring on fieldwork and comparative study. It was all about getting rid of or holding on to disciplinary boundaries.

A third area of critique involves the erasure of boundaries in another way. Today we read far less about the special characteristics of art music, folk music, and popular music. Indeed, these terms are used far less in our literature than had been the case, for example, in the 1960s, when North American and European scholars were eager to demonstrate that other musical cultures *did* consist of various strata of music-making, and that they all *did* have something like folk, classical, popular, or sacred and secular traditions. Now we're not sure that these distinctions work so well in any society. Indeed, the concept of the world of music as consisting of distinct and separable "musics," one of the paradigms of the second half of the twentieth century, has covertly been under attack. To be sure, the world of music has changed more, perhaps, in the era since ca. 1990 than ever before (can one, however, measure these degrees of difference?), not so much in the creation of new sounds, styles, and genres, but in the ways in which music is communicated and in the experience of musical perception. "Musics," if we can still use the term, are changing to be more like each other (for discussion and bibliography, see Keil and Feld 1994; Nettl 2002, 2005). Western harmony and Western instruments encroach on once contrastive traditions, African and African-derived rhythmic structures and practices invade, and concepts such as concerts and virtuosity play an increased role. Musical diversity in the world has probably decreased in ways similar to the drastic decrease in natural languages (chronicled by Nettle and Romaine 2000), while the number of "dialects" in music (and the number of dialects of dominant languages such as English, Spanish, Chinese) has increased. But in the face of all this homogenization, the normal musical experience of the typical individual, who has access to radio, the Internet, and all the marvels of modern technology, has become more heterogeneous. In a possible interpretation of the world's music history (and admitting the difficulty of measuring degrees of diversity and defining personal music repertories), one might suggest that the world has become musically poorer, but the individual musically wealthier.

Recognizing this—more by implication than expressly—ethnomusicologists have begun to change their approaches, looking less at musical cultures at large (as did Merriam 1967, for example, or Berliner 1978), and more at specific cases: events, genres, individuals, institutions, pieces (e.g., Meintjes 2003, Danielson 1997). And they seem to wonder whether this approach should not have been followed earlier on, and whether it would have tied them more closely to the traditional musicologists.

I have mentioned three groups of events that suggest that ethnomusicologists find themselves now in an era of critique of their discipline. I would like to argue that this practice of self-critique has periodically characterized the history of our field, and my purpose in the following paragraphs is to make some forays into the history of this tradition. No doubt similar trends could be identified in other kinds of music scholarship, but I would suggest that possibly ethnomusicologists have made more of a project of it. Perhaps, following what Alan Merriam (1964, 3) said, ethnomusicology has always been "caught up in a fascination with itself."

The Early Ethnomusicologists as Naysayers

In important ways, the field of ethnomusicology has functioned as a critique of general musicology. A good deal of its literature is couched as a response to the typical academic's view of music, contradicting and correcting conventional wisdom and accepted generalizations. When I was a student, one of only two or three in my institution studying what would later come to be known as ethnomusicology in the presence of a much larger group of music historians, I found myself constantly responding to generalizations about world music with "Yes, but in Central Africa they don't do this," or "It's quite different among the Arapaho." And when confronted with assertions about the specialness of Western music and its theory, I would say, "No, they have something equally complex in India." At that time, if someone had told me that ethnomusicologists were interested in universals, I would have contradicted by pointing to the specialness of each culture (Nettl 2002, 5; 2005, 42).

I didn't know it at the time, but the publication that is often cited as the beginning of ethnomusicology, A.J. Ellis's "On the musical scales of various nations," ends on a similar tone: "The final conclusion is that the Musical Scale is not one, not 'natural' nor even founded necessarily on the laws of the constitution of musical sound, so beautifully worked out by Helmholtz, but very diverse, very artificial, and very capricious" (Ellis 1885, 526–27). The tenor is one of contradicting conventional wisdom.

Actually, the first article to speak to the special problems and methods of comparative musicology (Hornbostel 1904–5) also distances itself from traditional musicology. Three points struck me as especially interesting: (1) "Comparison is the principal means of scholarly comprehension" (Hornbostel 1904–5, 85); (2) Comparative musicologists must broaden their perspective of the kinds of phenomena in music that should be examined, going far beyond "tones" to a great variety of sounds, including those that are intermediate between music and speech, music and noise; (3) Music is changing rapidly, and one must "save what can be saved, before airplanes are added to automobile and electric trains and all of Africa is dominated by 'tarara-boomdeyay'" (Hornbostel 1905, 97).

In the light of these considerations, an early quotation by Carl Stumpf that is clearly trying to correct widely held assumptions (it appears in a review essay about the earliest publications on Native American and First Nations musics) sounds interestingly up to date: "Die indianischen Leitern, wie wir sie bisher kennen, gehören also keineswegs einem 'archäischen' oder gar 'primitiven' Musikzustand an … Die Beziehung zwischen den Tonauffassungen ganz andrer Art sein, ebenso die psychologische und die historische Enstehungsweise" (Stumpf 1892, 142). [The Indian scales, as we know them thus far, don't by any means belong to a "primitive" or "archaic" state of music…. It may concern totally different conceptions of music, and involve, historically and psychologically speaking, different kinds of origin.]

The tone of these classics differs from the enormously influential article by Guido Adler, laying out the discipline of musicology in a positivistic style and an optimistic mood, seeing a process of consistent progress toward a clear goal: "Jeder Schritt, zu dem Ziele [Lösung grosser wissenschaftlicher Aufgaben] führt, jede That, die uns ihm näher rückt bedeutet einen Fortschriftt menschlicher Erkenntnis" (Adler 1885, 20). [Every step that leads to the solution of major scholarly problems, every act that brings us closer to this solution, represents progress in human understanding.] In contrast to Ellis and Hornbostel, Adler wants to look forward; he does not look back and does not suggest that his earlier colleagues had been on the wrong track.

If this tiny sampling of citations suggests the contrastive moods of the musicologies a century ago, then comparative musicology entered the academy with the task of providing a corrective to widely held beliefs. It continues to fulfill this function, looking critically at the hegemony and hierarchy assumed by historians of European music, trying to broaden the perspective of educational institutions, hoping to institute a vision of music as a universal, and of a world of musics. In doing this, however, ethnomusicologists have found themselves in a plethora of intellectual, social, political, and ethical problems that have led, I believe, to the tradition of self-criticism that has characterized the discipline.

A landmark of the critical mood early in the history of SEM was a set of two panels that dominated the 1958 annual meeting, formally titled "The Scope and Aims of Ethnomusicology," later titled "Whither Ethnomusicology? A brief report" (McAllester 1959), which summarizes papers and the ensuing discussion, shows this to have been a very wide-ranging debate, in which each speaker proposed what should be done in his or her area, with a lot of criticism of past practices implied. These include excessive concentration on analysis (e.g., interval-counting), neglect of cultures close to oneself, and failure to respect one's informants. In the discussions, however, the speakers spoke past each other, and it is clear that there was little agreement on where ethnomusicology should go. The most conclusive statement telling us to change direction came from Charles Seeger: include Euro-American music, and persuade music historians to study the history of other cultures (McAllester 1959, 102).

Alan P. Merriam as Arch-critic

Outstanding among the many contributions of Alan P. Merriam was his continued insistence that ethnomusicologists, as a defined group of scholars, must decide who they are and what their task is, and that what he perceived to be an uncomfortable diversity should be replaced by a unity of purpose. Throughout much of his career, he was critical of the people who called themselves ethnomusicologists, and a number of his writings emphasize this issue; the statements of his unhappiness were, to be sure, always expressed with moderation and with respect for divergent views.

Merriam's first significant publication on the subject, titled simply "Ethnomusicology: Discussion and definition of the field" (1960), was published shortly after he had completed his term launching the SEM newsletter and journal as the first editor. Noting that the literature of ethnomusicology was dominated by description and analysis of music, particularly melodic and pitch phenomena, and by interest in taxonomy of musics and the origins of music, he hailed as a significant change the broadening conceptualization of this field, praising what he saw as pioneering steps to include all (and not just non-Western) music, and all aspects of musical life. Although his criticisms of earlier practices are gentle, it is clear that Merriam wanted this article to signify a major turning of a corner, that emphasis on studying music as sound alone should be abandoned. He ends: "While the study of music as a structural form and as a historic phenomenon is of high, and basic importance, in my own view it holds this position primarily as it leads to the broader questions of music in culture" (Merriam 1960, 113).

"Music in culture" was the definitive characterization—a kind of coat-of-arms—of ethnomusicology in Merriam's (1964) most influential book, but he continued later to be perplexed by the multiplicity of definitions in use and published, not long before his death, a major critique of the subject (Merriam 1977). Citing, comparing, and classifying about forty definitions culled largely from American publications, Merriam believes that the proper way of defining a field is not on the basis of observing what its practitioners do, but of what it ought to be. He appears in this article to have given up the desire to unify, closing by saying, "I have no doubt that new definitions of ethnomusicology will continue to be proposed and that they, too, will reflect the growing maturity of the field and its practitioners" (Merriam 1977, 198). Still, a tone of frustration appears in his discussion of definitions that stress "form"—that is, the materials or peoples to be studied—as against those focusing on "process," i.e., the ways things are done, which he clearly favours. I should think that the field has indeed moved in Merriam's direction. Nevertheless, one may be bemused to find that the Society for Ethnomusicology avoids any specific definition, tending rather to dissimulate: in its mission statement, SEM aims to "promote the research, study, and performance of music in all historical periods and cultural contexts." The constitution says that we exist "to promote research and study in the field of ethnomusicology." The journal *Ethnomusicology* says that it publishes articles in the field of ethnomusicology, "broadly defined." It is amazing that a society with such a vague notion of what it includes can have been so successful. The International Council for Traditional Music's history is similar. When I was about to become editor of its yearbook for a three-year term, I asked ICTM president Klaus Wachsmann whether I shouldn't make an editorial statement of what this publication stood for. "Oh no," the president said, "you could get into a lot of trouble telling people what they should or shouldn't include in 'ethnomusicology.'"

Relating to the World's Musicians

The 1970s seems to have been a period in which North American ethnomusicologists were particularly concerned with a critical look backward and the need to change directions. A number of facets of this movement may be distinguished, but mostly they concern issues that are fundamentally social and/or ethical, involving the differences in power relations between Western and non-Western scholars, between scholars and their informants or consultants or teachers, and within the North American ethnomusicological community.

Before ca. 1955, little thought may have been given to the complex problem of these relationships, but it was not completely ignored. Already in the first substantive analytical article on Native American music, Carl Stumpf (1886) commented on the differences between one's own culture and another in the perception and interpretation of music, in speaking of Nutsiluska, his principal informant in the band of Bella Coola people who were touring Germany, presenting songs and dances. In his case, the relationships were opposite to those subject to criticism later, for he claims that he could appreciate (he didn't claim "understand") Nutsiluska's songs, but Nutsiluska would not have apprehended Bach's B-Minor Mass. Never mind Stumpf's perhaps unjustified claim for himself; he tells us at least that there is no universal aesthetic standard.

Only gradually did ethnomusicologists come to embrace the (now laughably obvious) idea that one should find out how the members of a host society think about and analyze their music. How strange this concept may have seemed at an earlier time is illustrated by the obscure position of one of the first articles on the subject, "Music in the thinking of the American Indian" by George Herzog (1938), which touches on the fundamental concept of music of a number of Native American traditions in a few pages; later on each of these points would have been the subject of extended discourse. I have always been astonished that these concepts did not play a major role in Herzog's better known and larger works on the same musical cultures, and that this article, which appeared in the most obscure of journals, was not quickly reprinted in a major journal.

It took some decades for the idea that perhaps we couldn't understand someone else's music at all to come forward, and longer yet for this critique to be joined by a related one: What are the social and political implications of doing research "on" people frequently designated as "the other?" The first of these two connected developments may be dated as beginning in the 1960s, and associated with the development, in anthropology, of "the new ethnography," which emphasizes the importance of discerning a society's own perception and appraisal of its culture. This, in turn, produced the concept of the "emic-etic" contrast, and in the end cast doubt on the possibility of positivistic objectivity. It is a view that pervaded, through the 1990s, the fields that participated in postmodernism, and in ethnomusicology its earliest statement may be Merriam's (1964, 209–10) discussion of "folk" and "analytical" evaluations in ethnography.

The coalescing of these issues has to do with the recognition, by Western academic society at large, of the need to face issues of intercultural (and intracultural) power relations.

The development of the emic-etic interface in the 1970s may be the starting point, but beyond that, it seems fair to claim that during this decade more than any other, the papers read at meetings of SEM and the special panels looked at the past quite reproachfully. An uncommonly large number of paper titles begin with the words "Towards a ...," suggesting the need for supplanting earlier methods and approaches and proposing new ones.

Thus, SEM in 1970 established a Committee on New Directions whose charge was to study and make recommendations for the improvement of relationships between ethnomusicology (learned society and profession at large) and the societies whose music they study, and the public they serve. Although it did not accomplish much, it marked the beginning of a permanent component of the organization (represented by a succession and variety of committees, study sessions, and policy discussions) that now characterize the field, much in contrast to other societies for the study of music—e.g., the American Musicological Society, International Musicological Society, and Society for Music Theory—in which these matters are left to individual discretion.

Throughout the 1970s and 1980s, one of the most prominent critical voices was that of John Blacking, calling into question many concepts of conventional wisdom: tradition, change, musicality, nature and nurture of music, in a number of important publications, some of whose titles suggest that we should turn a corner: "Some problems of theory and method in the study of musical change" (Blacking 1979), "Towards a theory of musical competence" (Blacking 1971), "Challenging the myth of ethnic music" (Blacking 1989). The rhetoric of his most influential book is full of normative statements: "we must be able to describe exactly what happens to any piece of music ... we shall never be able to do so until ..." (Blacking 1973, 89). Reading Blacking over the years, I always had the feeling that, despite his polite respect for earlier publications, he wanted to assert that the field had taken wrong turns and must be redirected.

Among the many influential publications that date from this period and are central to the tradition of critique, one of the most vehement is K.A. Gourlay's "Towards a reassessment of the ethnomusicologist's role in research" (1978), which argues for an active political and social involvement of the researcher in order to liberate and save music (and not just by archiving it) and its people(s), and disputes the possibility of pure objectivity. Gourlay ends with a bleak picture of what may happen if we don't change our ways:

> When the oil runs out, coal reserves are exhausted, and solar energy discovered to be pie-in-the-sky, the seas polluted with atomic waste and the lands so overpopulated that there is no room for crops, the Karimojong [of Uganda] may yet have the last laugh, as they trudge around the periphery of their land in search of water, driving their cattle before them, and entertaining themselves with a new song to celebrate the mounds of useless motor-cars, the unplayable tapes of their own music rotting in the archives of the West, and a people who have recovered the use of their legs but have forgotten how to sing. (Gourlay 1978, 32)

What Are We Doing There?

Late in the twentieth century, the most significant self-criticism of ethnomusicology may be called "What are we doing there?" The entire course of intercultural study, the validity of participant-observer fieldwork, the intellectual and political implications of cross-cultural study, the translatability of cultures, were and continue to be called into question. One thrust of this field of consideration concerns what has broadly been called "ethics," and includes a suddenly growing kind of self-reflection and self-awareness of scholar within environment. According to Slobin (1992, 329), publications that speak to the issue were rare or absent before 1970, and a brief statement by Barbara Krader (1980, 280–81) was the first mention of it in a standard reference work.

A second strand signals the rise—or renewed attention to—"ethnomusicology at home," however "home" may be defined. This type of research was once considered the closest thing to "armchair ethnomusicology" and thus was relegated to a kind of second-class status supposedly requiring less effort, knowledge, commitment, and perhaps courage, but it has recently been revived. Among the most influential publications have been those of Kofi Agawu, one of whose critical tenets (see Agawu 1995, 2003) is that the unified concept of "African music," as held by mainstream ethnomusicologists, was an invention of Western scholars.

There were many who believed, by the late twentieth century, that the central ideas of the previous hundred years had been misguided, and that in certain respects ethnomusicology as a discipline on the American and Western European model had been a failed enterprise. The point was driven home to me at a 1988 conference attended by American and (then) Soviet scholars, in which the two groups exchanged views. The Soviet scholars did not appreciate the Americans' desire to do fieldwork all over the world, thought that this was a kind of scholarly colonialism that took unfair advantage of musicians and local scholars, and were convinced that it resulted in inadequate scholarship. Instead, they promulgated the practice of doing research in your own nation or region or community where, to be sure, they would—as scholars—be seen as "outsiders" in any event.

The considerable increase in the proportion of papers on music at "home," though, to be sure, taking account of the increased diversity of each "home" ground, such as the development of ethnic, national, generational, and economic minorities, shows the effectiveness of this line of criticism. Naturally, "What are you doing here?" is the question behind the increased disinclination of Native American communities in the US to tolerate fieldwork by outsiders. The concept of the "field" has been thoroughly reconfigured.

"What are we doing here?" is a question that also applies to the growing understanding that the position of the observer, and the person of the participant, are essential considerations in fieldwork and interpretation. Most significantly, the large literature of gender studies in ethnomusicology is perhaps the largest body of writing in which ethnomusicologists critique their past. The total thrust of works such as Moisala and Diamond (2000) seems to me that we should all start over, with a different perspective, different methods, and different forms of interpretation. This is not at all an unreasonable directive were it possible to undo the past, and certainly one that is appropriate for the future. This thrust is, of course, part of the strong movement of gender studies in academia worldwide, but one should, in ethnomusicology, also see it as part of the tradition of self-critique that has—uniquely, I would argue—developed in this field.

The most evident self criticism of ethnomusicologists in the late twentieth century has concerned this relationship of scholars to various kinds of environment, and this has led to a dispersal of thought: we worry about who we are in relation to the people whose musical culture we study vis-à-vis scholars outside the Euro-American sphere; in terms of gender differences and of who we are, individually, in the context of our societies; in relation to other disciplines; about the identity of the "field"; and about the taxonomy of musics. This focus tends to lead to a situation in which each researcher does his or her own "thing," each problem requires an individual methodology, each culture tells us, as it were, only about itself.

A second strand, following Merriam's critiques of excessive diversity and lack of focus, argues for greater unity, seeking a model of research and a concept of music and culture that can be the basis for any kind of study. For Merriam, it was the threefold model of music, although he did not propose that it should be the discipline's coat-of-arms. The recent version of this approach is best illustrated by articles by Timothy Rice, who, on the basis of a critique of Merriam's model and others associated with it, produced what he considered to be a statement of the field's fundamental question, a kind of umbrella for all research, under which individual projects would, of course, occupy small spots. Rice's basic question for the field of ethnomusiology was: "How do people historically construct, socially maintain, and individually create and experience music?" (Rice 1987, 473). Later Rice (2003, 172) reformulated his idea, but continued a three-dimensional model, abandoning the static model of cultures that he considered (Rice 2003, 151) characteristic of ethnomusicology in Merriam's time, and emphasized their dynamic nature, looking to ethnographies that "trace the movement of subjects in location, metaphorical understanding, and time, and the differing experiences that such movements entail" (Rice 2003, 174).

Conclusion

My contention that ethnomusicology has been more prone to self-criticism—criticism of the practices and procedures of the discipline going far beyond correction of details and culture-specific findings—than other fields of music research, leading to subsequent changes of direction, is certainly impressionistic and not based on any hard data. But comparison with the practices of historical musicology and music theory suggests that comparative musicologists and ethnomusicologists have changed their ways frequently and dramatically over the last century, perhaps, if we compare today's practices with those of 1905, beyond recognition. The changes parallel changes in technology both in musical culture and in research techniques; changes in the world's politics, economics, and social organization; changes in the world's societies' conception of music; and more. They also result from the fact that we interact not only with written and recorded and filmed data, but, much more importantly, with human beings.

And so, many of our publications—more than those of our colleagues in the humanities—are not principally about field data or analysis, but about how we, as a profession, go about our work, and much of this concern appears, as well, in the culture-, repertory-, and musician-specific studies. Around and shortly after 2000 CE, however, we are seeing an unusually large body of critique, while at the same time the world of music changes more rapidly than ever before. It is proposed that we have all along been concerned with the wrong things. Many ethnomusicologists have become uncomfortable with the "e" word and wonder whether it explains what they do, and what it may suggest to others. So one begins to wonder whether ethnomusicology will change its name (to socio-musicology? cultural musicology? reclaim the general term *musicology*?), or whether it will change in its purposes and methods so much that the name will no longer mean anything. In other words, will we have critiqued ourselves out of existence? Certainly scholars in many nations who do the kind of research that is done by ethnomusicologists in North America prefer, as I said above, different labels. Is it possible that the twentieth century will eventually become known, in the world history of music and musics, as the ethnomusicological century?

References

Adam, Nina, with Florian Heesch, and Susanne Rode-Breymann. 2002. "Über das Gefühl der Unzufriedenheit in der Disziplin." *Musikforschung* 55: 251–73.

Adler, Guido. 1885. "Umfang, Methode und Ziel der Musikwissenschaft." *Vierteljahrschrift für Musikwissenschaft* 1: 5–20.

Agawu, V. Kofi. 1995. "The Invention of African Rhythm." *Journal of the American Musicological Society* 48: 380–95.

———. 2003. *Representing African music*. New York: Routledge.

Berliner, Paul. 1978. *The soul of Mbira*. Berkeley: University of California Press.

Blacking, John. 1971. "Towards a Theory of Musical Competence." In *Man: Anthropological essays in honor of O.F. Raum*, edited by E.J. Jaeger, 19–34. Cape Town: Struik.

———. 1973. *How musical is man?* Seattle: University of Washington Press.

———. 1979. "Some Problems of Theory and Method in the Study of Musical Change." *Yearbook of the IMFC* 9: 1–26.

———. 1989. "Challenging the Myth of Ethnic Music." *Yearbook for Traditional Music* 21: 17–24.

Danielson, Virginia. 1997. *The voice of Egypt: Umm Kulthum, Arabic song, and Egyptian culture in the twentieth century*. Chicago: University of Chicago Press.

Diamond, Beverley, with M. Sam Cronk, and Franziska von Rosen, eds. 1994. *Visions of sound: Musical instruments of First Nations communities in northeastern America*. Chicago: University of Chicago Press.

Diamond, Beverley, and Robert Witmer, eds. 1994. *Canadian music: Issues of hegemony and identity*. Toronto: Canadian Scholars' Press.

Ellis, Alexander J. 1885. "On the Musical Scales of Various Nations." *Journal of the Society of Arts* 33: 485–527.

Gourlay, K.A. 1978. "Towards a Reassessment of the Ethnomusicologist's Role in Research." *Ethnomusicology* 22: 1–36.

Greve, Martin. 2002. "Writing against Europe: Vom notwendigen Verschwinden der 'Musikethnologie.'" *Musikforschung* 55: 239–51.

Herzog, George. 1938. "Music in the Thinking of the American Indian." *Peabody Bulletin*, May, 1–5.

Hornbostel, Erich M. von. 1904–5. "Die Probleme der vergleichenden Musikwissenschaft." *Zeitschrift der internationalen Musikgesellschaft* 7: 85–97.

Keil, Charles, and Steven Feld. 1994. *Music grooves*. Chicago: University of Chicago Press.

Krader, Barbara. 1980. "Ethnomusicology." In *The new Grove dictionary of music and musicians*, edited by Stanley Sadie, 275–82.

McAllester, David P., reporter. 1959. "Whither Ethnomusicology?" *Ethnomusicology* 3: 99–105.

Meintjes, Louise. 2003. *Sound of Africa! Making music Zulu in a South African studio*. Durham, NC: Duke University Press.

Merriam, Alan P. 1960. "Ethnomusicology: Discussion and Definition of the Field." *Ethnomusicology* 4: 107–14.

———. 1964. *The anthropology of music*. Evanston: Northwestern University Press.

———. 1967. *Ethnomusicology of the Flathead Indians*. Chicago: Aldine Press.

———. 1977. "Definitions of 'Comparative Musicology' and 'Ethnomusicology': An Historical-Theoretical Perspective." *Ethnomusicology* 21: 189–204.

Moisala, Pirkko, and Beverley Diamond, eds. 2000. *Music and gender*. Urbana: University of Illinois Press.

Nettl, Bruno. 2002. *Encounters in ethnomusicology: A memoir*. Warren, MI: Harmonie Park Press.

———. 2005. *The study of ethnomusicology: 31 issues and concepts*, new ed. Urbana: University of Illinois Press.

Nettle, Daniel, and Suzanne Romaine. 2000. *Vanishing voices: The extinction of the world's languages*. Oxford: Oxford University Press.

Rice, Timothy. 1987. "Toward the Remodeling of Ethnomusicology." *Ethnomusicology* 31: 469–88.

———. 2003. "Time, Place, and Metaphor in Musical Experience and Ethnography." *Ethnomusicology* 47: 151–79.

Slobin, Mark. 1992. "Ethical Issues." In *Ethnomusicology, an introduction*, edited by Helen Myers, 329–36. New York: Norton.

Stumpf, Carl. 1886. "Lieder der Bellakula Indianer." *Vierteljahrschrift für Musikwissenschaft* 2: 405–26.

———. 1892. "Phonographierte Indianische Melodien." *Vierteljahrschrift für Musikwissenschaft* 8: 127–44.

Is Fieldwork Still Necessary?

FOUR

ELLEN KOSKOFF

THIS CHAPTER EXAMINES THE NATURE of fieldwork, both field-work as defined by ethnomusicology, which uses it as a major method of data collection, and fieldwork as a more general everyday process of coming to terms with difference. I use here some of my own fieldwork and life experiences as illustrations, trying my best to communicate the essence of the process through these words, understanding that all words are mere shadows of experience.

My immediate reason for writing this chapter is my concern over two trends I have seen in recent postmodern scholarship in ethnomusicology, one questioning fieldwork as a primary method of data collection and the other responding to changing notions of the field itself. My concern focuses on what I see as a moving away from real people in on-the-ground social and musical contexts where real differences are confronted and negotiated in a face-to-face reality.

It is often difficult to confront difference and I'm not suggesting here that I have answers. In fact, as you will readily see in my examples, my own struggles to deal with social and musical differences did not always end satisfactorily. It has always been easy for me to profess a tolerance for difference, but actually being tolerant, especially of my own intolerance, is far more difficult, especially in the on-the-ground reality of the fieldwork process, where one is face to face with differences of all kinds.

Earlier in my life as an ethnomusicologist, I worked with Lubavitcher Hasidim, mainly in Crown Heights, Brooklyn, using participant observation as my main method of collecting data. I went to live for periods of time in Crown Heights, went to *schule* and to the kosher eateries with my "community," slept in their houses, watched them cook, pray, and do music. In ethnomusicology, fieldwork at that time was defined as "the observational and experiential portion of the ethnographic process," in which we sought musical meaning in different contexts (Barz and Cooley 1997, 4).

In retrospect, I see that a certain amount of exoticism permeated this practice. After all, I had chosen the "field site" assuming difference—I was not like Lubavitchers, or so I thought. My job was to document this difference, process it, put it into understandable categories, and bring it back, so to speak, to an academic audience in a recognizable form. In short, my job was to reify difference, spin it through ethnographic theory, and perform it for a (mostly) friendly family.

In the mid-1970s we did not have a good handle on how to understand the fieldwork process itself as implicated in larger power dynamics. This was uncovered later, in the 1980s and 1990s, during the so-called "crisis of representation," which is well documented elsewhere. (See, for example, in Timothy Cooley's introduction to his and Gregory Barz's book, *Shadows in the field: New perspectives for fieldwork in ethnomusicology*, 1997.)

One of the most powerful ideas to emerge from this self-conscious moment was the notion that fieldwork, like most human interactions, was a power-laden process in which subtle codes and cues that signalled various social structures and positions of status, deference, and opposition were continuously performed by socially situated actors. As early as the mid-twentieth century, sociologists, such as Herbert Blumer (1969), who coined the term *symbolic interactionism*, and Erving Goffman (1959; 1967), among others who refined this theory, were examining how "in time," largely symbolic human interactions could be analyzed to uncover social structures in ritual, drama, and even in everyday life.

Later scholars, such as Richard Bauman (1986), Edward L. Schieffelin (1998), and Judith Butler (1990), among others, developed some of these ideas into a theory of performativity, the "expressive processes of strategic impression management and structured improvisation through which human beings normally articulate their purposes, situations and relationships of everyday social life" (Schieffelin 1998, 195). Further, writes Schieffelin (1998, 205), "performativity is not only endemic to human being-in-the-world but fundamental to the process of constructing a human reality." A certain anxiety set in: What was the point of writing ethnographies if reality was socially constructed and performed into being by constantly changing selves and others? Who, exactly, was participating in the field experience? Was any of this "true"? Perhaps it was time, hinted major scholars, such as James Clifford and George Marcus (1986), and Clifford Geertz (1988), among many others, to give up fieldwork altogether or to use our ethnographic data to construct fictions.

Anthropology in the 1990s also began to take another turn toward theorizing globalism. Thus, for the first time in a generation, basic core values of anthropology and ethnomusicology were questioned. Scholars, such as Arjun Appadurai (1990), Bryan Turner (1994), and Marilyn Strathern (1995), pointed to the profound social, technological, and economic transformations of the late twentieth century that rendered older, more easily managed concepts of culture and fieldwork obsolete, for what was the "field" now? Shifting notions of the "field" in ethnomusicology seemed to result in a move away from researching individual people or small, discrete societies, and toward examining issues affecting music through commodification, mass media, local/national/global politics, and quickly changing economic systems that favoured Western capitalism.

Works, such as Veit Erlmann's *Music, modernity, and the global imagination* (1999), Mark Slobin's *Subcultural sounds* (1993), Thomas Turino's *Nationalists, cosmopolitans, and popular music in Zimbabwe* (2000), Timothy Taylor's *Global pop* (1997), and Lise Waxer's *Situating salsa* (2002), to name a few recent titles, began to examine various non-Western musical cultures—not always using the method of fieldwork—and theorized their work in terms of cultural studies-derived postmodern ideas centring on construction and deconstruction, ideas that they shared with historical musicologists. Had the fields merged somehow without my noticing? "Regular folks" and their musics were somehow lost in this effort to filter everything through ever-denser lenses of cultural and technological theory and other forms of mediation.

What the changes of the past thirty years or so have brought about, it seems to me, is a deep insecurity, even a fear of confronting and dealing head on with musical and social difference. We seem to have theorized ourselves into a sort of paralysis. Granted, it is difficult dealing with difference in the moment of its happening. It often creates uncomfortable feelings, moves us into default (and not always appropriate) patterns of behaviour, or causes us to lose our sense of self, but it is only in these moments that real change can occur and real understandings take place. So, if ethnomusicologists are truly committed to promoting tolerance for musical and social difference, we must first understand the nature of difference and how to manage its destabilizing power. I see the process of confronting and dealing with difference as divided into three experiential stages: noticing, processing, and integrating difference. To illustrate the difficulty of recognizing and separating these stages, I present three different scenarios describing my own coming to terms with various differences, all connected in some way to my life as an ethnomusicologist.

The first is a true fieldwork experience—that is, an experience consistent with the ethnographic methods of my discipline—one we would all recognize as fieldwork, where I, the ethnographer, am engaging with an informant; the second presents an experience, perhaps not formally "fieldwork," but sharing much of its structure; and the last is an experience of encountering difference in music during a "fieldwork" situation. Each highlights an extraordinary moment where I had to quickly notice and process difference and come to terms with its meaning. Each of these experiences led to a profound change in my understanding of myself, of music, and of its connection to contemporary human life.

Scenario 1: "Miriam and Ellen's Play"

Here is one small snippet of conversation that took place between Miriam Rosenblum, one of my main Lubavitcher informants, and me, which I jotted down in my diary in 1974. This dialogue eventually made its way into my book, *Music in Lubavitcher life* (Koskoff 2001), as data substantiating the prohibition against men listening to a singing female voice, about which I have written extensively. Here, though, I use this same dialogue to illustrate the shifting perspectives between Miriam and me and point to the changing voices that emerged in our conversation as it moved along, somewhat like the entrance of a cast of characters in a play.

I have been invited to a *Shabbos* dinner with the Rosenblums. We have just finished dinner and the singing has begun, with Rabbi Rosenblum and his six children (all under the age of ten) shouting out the Lubavitcher *nigunim* I have come to hear.

Soon a familiar tune pops up. Miriam is humming. I begin to sing along.

"Shh," Miriam leans over and whispers in my ear. "Stop singing."

"Why?" I whisper back.

"I'll tell you later. Just be quiet."

The singing continues into the night. Rabbi Rosenblum has a beautiful baritone voice and sings with tremendous feeling and gusto. He and the kids are really enjoying themselves.

"So, why can't I sing?" I prod Miriam later. "I know women and men can't sing together in the synagogue, but does that extend to the home as well?"

"The idea is that a woman's voice is beautiful. It has a lot of qualities that would be enticing to a man. This is a fact known anywhere, so it's better that you don't sing. It would distract my husband."

"Hmm," I think, "Am I really that attractive?" I try another tack.

"Wait a minute," I suggest. "I might think that the sound of your husband's voice is enticing, so why is he allowed to sing in front of me?" I can see by her face that I've missed the point. She glances at her husband.

"Ephraim, Ellen wants to know why she can't sing in front of you, but you can sing in front of her." They both smile patiently at me as though I'm a wilful but lovable child. "Because the Torah forbids it, that's why," says Rabbi Rosenblum, expecting me to simply accept this. "And the Torah is the will of God."

I am not happy with this explanation and begin, once again, to argue.

Miriam says, "Ellen, this is the way it is. It's been looked over a lot because liberated women are pushing away all of their ideas about being different. But for us in the Torah way, it is like this. Woman is woman and man is man. Women have certain aspects which are appealing to men, and they cannot be taken away. Now, one of the halachic [legal] considerations is that when a woman sings, it has a very appealing aspect to a man who is not her own husband." She finishes with a look that says this conversation is closed.

I am annoyed. These people look so reasonable! How can they believe this?

Two days later, I am talking with Miriam about this incident:

EK I knew I shouldn't have done it [sing], and I remember turning to you and saying, "I know I shouldn't be singing, but I don't know why," and then you explained it, and then I said....

MR You got on the defensive.

EK No, I didn't, I said that a man's voice is just as enticing.

MR "You're not gonna' make me religious," you said. [*laughing*]

EK No, no, that's not what I said.

MR It came around through what you said, I think. [*still laughing*]

EK I said to you, "But a man's voice is just as enticing," and you laughed.

MR I guess it's not.

EK It is to me.

When I came to write up this scene in my book, I had tremendous difficulty in framing it. On the surface this dialogue was evidence for the Lubavitcher position concerning *kol isha*. But, under the surface, it was also a mediation of difference, where Miriam and I seemed to "perform" our political positions, actually structuring the "reality" of the conversation as it went along. Maybe Goffman had been right. So, I began to ask questions of the data: Who was speaking in this dialogue and why were we having this conversation? Analyzing this bit of dialogue closely, within the context in which it occurred, seemed to reveal a multitude of voices, performed through subtle changes of tone, attitude, body position and so on, that reoriented the perspectives of the speakers, creating new dialogues between new actors. Just who were the characters that I played in this scene? First, I was at the beginning of fieldwork and was carrying into the field all of my assumptions about Hasidic Jews and about Hasidic women learned from my parents, my Reform Jewish community, the society at large, and from the many books I had read.

One thing I had already learned about Lubavitchers, one of the behaviours that separated them from other Hasidic groups, was that they proselytized—a real no-no in "mainstream" Jewish culture—and they had already started on me, so part of my beginning fieldwork personality included a person with tremendous resistance to becoming "Lubavitch." Next, I was a musician, and in fact, it was the sound of music that originally attracted me to Hasidic culture. And, as a musician, I could perhaps cut across other social boundaries, such as being a woman, that might better position me vis-à-vis Hasidic culture, which seemed to greatly value music. The musician was my least problematic personality in this situation. I was also a young feminist, in the very early stages of seeing the Big Picture of sexism in my own cultural context—remember, it was 1974! I was set to be angry, looking for confrontation, and ready to save my Jewish sisters. This was my most openly angry voice.

But perhaps the most fundamental Ellen was also here: the trickster, the comedian, the "little devil girl," who would do almost anything to get a laugh. She is the oldest of the identities present, formed from countless interactions with scary and out-of-control situations in her youth. She is perhaps the most entertaining, but also the most deeply problematic in this fieldwork situation—the most subtly angry and the most controlling.

What cast of characters did Miriam play? (I might point out here that the "construction" of Miriam I am presenting in this analysis is based on knowledge that I gained about her and about Lubavitcher women generally, not only at the time of the original conversation, but through many later conversations and through Miriam's own critique of my portrait of her.) Miriam was the quintessential Lubavitcher "handler" for young female newcomers to the community. She was the one who took young women under her wing, taught them the half-forgotten prayers, the laws of *tzniut* (modesty), and *kol isha* (women's voices)—anything one would need to know as a woman entering the community—obviously that was what I was doing from her perspective.

Miriam was also a protector of her husband and children. She was protecting them from me, a secularized Jew, who has entered her house to work on music with her husband. Although fairly certain that he would not be tempted to follow me to ruin, she was nonetheless cautious and worried about my motives. Miriam was also confrontational, and, in this context, slightly annoyed with me. She accused me of being defensive, and perhaps I was, given my distaste for proselytizing. But she was also annoyed at my resistance—she has seen this for a number of years with other young women, many of whom are dealing with new social and sexual freedoms and are either questioning their more traditional Jewish values or running toward a more conservative environment to escape such freedoms. As our conversation went on it became clear that Miriam could not understand why I didn't plainly see the "truth" of the Hasidic way of life. Why didn't Ellen understand that women have a profound and holy obligation to maintain sexual boundaries and to act correctly according to the laws of modesty? Even if Ellen *was* sexually stimulated by my husband's singing, she'd better control it!

I, for my part, simply became more resistant and rebellious as I plodded on in this interaction. After all, my new feminist consciousness said that I have the right to express my sexuality, although I may choose not to under these circumstances. I wasn't going to let a religious law tell me what to do! Why didn't Miriam understand that religious systems like hers are simply cultural rationalizations for White, male hegemony?

Scenario 2: Tuvan Throat Singers Come to Eastman

In 1993 the Tuvan throat singers, Huun-Huur-Tu, came to the Eastman School as part of our World Music Series. Yes, I understood going in that this performance in the snow-capped plains of Rochester, New York, was far removed from its original context, was "constructed" for Western audiences, and was politically representative of a newly emerging Tuva. But, I was not prepared for the front man, a former Russian rock star, or for most of the musicians in the group, to be already firmly entrenched in the hyped-up world of global music commodification. What had happened to the five guys in front of the yurt that Ted Levin had "discovered"? Okay, maybe I was being too protective—trying to keep this performance "pure," trying to preserve a constructed Tuvan past uncontaminated by Western greed, a past that probably had not existed. But, while I recognized my inherent paternalism, even racism here, I also felt a sense of loss, a loss of idealism, of the direct face-to-face experience and wonder of live musical performance in its original context. Was this performance a true cultural exchange, or a carnival of mediation?

Of course, I had confronted these differences before. As early as the late 1980s, I had begun to recognize that I was no longer in sync with the students I was teaching, or with my junior colleagues, that we had vastly different orientations to people, to music and to musical perform-ance. They didn't understand my jokes any more, and they tended to roll their eyes when I voiced my standard phrases: "All you really *do* need is love," and "Hug the person next to you and you are less likely to kill him." Most of them, by this time, thought I was hopelessly naive, even dorky, a remnant of a 1960s hippie past. "It's a generational thing, they would say."

Sitting in my seat in Kilbourn Hall, I leaned over to my student who had come with me to the concert and began to voice my concerns:

"Hey, aren't you tired of all this mediation and construction? Don't you wish you could just see five guys singing in front of a yurt?"

He was a young ethnomusicology-friendly student, whom I assumed would understand, maybe even share, my discomfort. His response: "Oh, you're too sensitive; everybody does this now; we all know this is con-structed! But, where else would I get to hear Tuvan music performed live? I'm not going to Tuva!" Indeed, why should he, when Tuva had come to him? Was his generation oblivious to these political issues, or were they all-knowing, consciously cynical?

I knew I had been caught between my idealistic notions of musical directness and purity and the reality of today's musical commodification, between my naive, preservationist stance, and the knowledge of how pater-nalistic that stance was. And, I also recognized that my student, like many in his generation, had been able to successfully separate music as a com-modity from the people who had made it. I accepted it, but it saddened me nonetheless.

Scenario 3: "Lembu Bajan" and the Merry-Go-Round

In the early 1990s the Eastman School purchased a gamelan *angklung* from Bowling Green State University. Knowing absolutely nothing about playing Balinese music, I contacted José Evangelista, a composer who had set up a gamelan program at l'Université de Montréal. For the first few years of our program, we shared teachers brought in each year from Bali. Our first year of sharing brought Pak Wayan Suweca, one of the most renowned Balinese musicians alive today, to the Eastman School. My job was to be his best student, to learn enough about Balinese music that I could teach it myself some time in the future. In short, I was to do "fieldwork" on Balinese music, while playing it in Rochester, New York.

Pak Suweca wanted to teach us a representative repertoire of Balinese music and chose pieces from the so-called classical, or *tua angklung* repertoire, as well as some of the new ones in the *gong kebyar* style. We had been working for a while on an old classical piece, "Lembu Bajan" ("Young Cow"), learning it, as we did everything, in the traditional Balinese oral method. This meant using no notation and coming to know the pieces from the ground up, so to speak, absorbing the musical material tiny chunk by tiny chunk until it assumed a whole shape. Concentration was high, and we were all incredibly focused because if we missed something—anything—we were lost. We kept repeating the sections over and over and over until everyone in the group had it. There were no recordings of this music, so none of us (except Suweca, of course) had any idea of the larger forms, what was repeated, where the end of a phrase was, what constituted a musical unit, where it was all going. In short, we were totally clueless and could only rely on the musical information we were receiving second to second, trying to build up our understanding of the whole as we went along.

What we had all picked up, though, in a more or less visceral way, over many hours of work, was the inexorable "two-ness" of it all. As there was no gong structure in this section to orient me, I found myself focusing on the tawa-tawa, that wonderful Balinese beat-keeping instrument that helps us stay honest (i.e., together). The tawa-tawa was subdividing everything into duple units, so if I could focus on that I could find my way. By now I had come to expect this unrelentingly duple world and assumed it would go on forever. So far, we had learned almost the entire first section. Then Suweca added the last little bit to the section that finally brought it around for the first time to complete the circle, with the gong signalling the end and beginning. Whoa! A sudden shift from two to three!

I started to laugh; I couldn't stop! I laughed so hard I fell over! I was totally delighted. When I first heard the rhythmic shift from two to three that signalled the end of the cycle, I could feel my body moving as though on a swing or a merry-go-round. I experienced that exhilarating, slightly scary sensation of dizziness, of almost falling, of being out of control.

Part of the joy of this feeling was the sense that I was not experiencing it alone, that I was sharing it with my students, with Pak Suweca, maybe with everyone in the world. For an instant, I lost consciousness of where I was, I was free, and all there was was my body moving in the music. For an instant, I was the music.

If we go back to the stages that I outlined earlier, those of recognizing, mediating, and integrating difference, and apply this model to the three scenarios, what can we learn about human and musical interactions? First, what does it mean to notice a difference? Simply noticing difference implies an assumption of agreement or sameness, and it is in the assumption of sameness that the heart of the problem lies. Postmodernists call this assumed understanding "intersubjectivity"—the assumption of "common sense, shared meanings constructed by people in their interactions with each other and used as an everyday resource to interpret the meaning of elements of social and cultural life" (Seale website). When intersubjectivity fails, it causes destabilization or disruption.

In the first scenario, I went in assuming that Miriam would share a certain orientation to women with me, despite the many differences I recognized in her world view and religious practice. I'm not sure why I thought this; maybe I just hoped it would be the case. After all, she was a Lubavitcher and I had chosen to work with her precisely because I assumed she *would* be different. That I was immediately destabilized, thrown off guard, responding confrontationally to this difference, surprised me— made me notice the difference as a difference. Mediation of difference— the second stage—didn't work here. On we went, constructing an argument for which there was no immediate solution or give and take. And, I'll admit it: I was angry (one of my many default positions)! Of course, I knew that I shouldn't have been arguing with my informant—that's not what you do in a fieldwork situation. But, is fieldwork so different from life, I rationalized, and she was being so unreasonable!

As I began to notice that I was resisting Miriam's difference, I realized that I was not really hearing what she was saying in my effort to fight off the implications of her words in my newly formed feminist world. I was closed off to her. Even my attempts to over-theorize this dialogue for an academic paper did not lead me to a solution as to how to integrate this satisfactorily into my work. Objectifying, reifying, and categorizing difference is perhaps a common strategy for academics, but it was not satisfying here.

In the second scenario, I assumed that my student and I would share a basic orientation to the event of the Huun Huur-Tu concert. In our brief exchange, I recognized the differences in our world view, but I was not angered by them. I felt more of a sense of loss, not the loss of getting older so much, but that of not being able to share my true ethnomusicology spirit with my student. We agreed to disagree and now when we meet, this experience has become something of a private joke between us.

In the third scenario, that of experiencing a piece of Balinese music, I was simply overwhelmed by difference. There were vast differences in teaching and learning styles; major differences in what constituted even a unit of music; and most importantly, a difference in the organization of musical time within the small unit that set me off into giddiness. It was a special moment of merging, with the music, with my students, with Pak Suweca, losing all boundaries, becoming free, even free from the self who was responding to the difference.

If, as ethnomusicologists, we wish to promote tolerance for musical and social difference, we must first learn to recognize difference, understand our own reactions and resistances to difference, and integrate difference into new understandings of ourselves and others. Accomplishing that will allow us to continue, I believe, with some sense of a bygone hope and even naive idealism that seems to have been lost in our recent theorizing and mediating.

Is fieldwork necessary? Yes, but not only in its narrow disciplinary sense, as a necessary process of data collection for ethnomusicology, but also in its more general life sense, as the conscious awareness, mediation, and integration of differences of all kinds. Fieldwork, in this more general sense, is not only necessary, it is vital to our social and musical health.

References

Appadurai, Arjun. 1990. "Disjuncture and Difference in the Global Cultural Economy." *Public Culture* 2, no. 2: 1–24.

Barz, Gregory F., and Timothy J. Cooley, eds. 1997. *Shadows in the field: New perspectives for fieldwork in ethnomusicology*. New York: Oxford University Press. 2nd edition, 2008.

Bauman, Richard. 1986. *Story, performance, and event: Contextual studies of oral narrative*. Cambridge: Cambridge University Press.

Blumer, Herbert. 1969. *Symbolic interaction: Perspective and method*. Englewood Cliffs, NJ: Prentice-Hall.

Butler, Judith P. 1990. *Gender trouble: Feminism and the subversion of identity*. New York: Routledge.

Clifford, James, and George E. Marcus. 1986. *Writing culture: The poetics and politics of ethnography*. Berkeley: University of California Press.

Erlmann, Veit. 1999. *Music, modernity, and the global imagination: South Africa and the West*. New York: Oxford University Press.

Geertz, Clifford. 1988. *Works and lives: The anthropologist as author*. Stanford: Stanford University Press.

Goffman, Erving. 1959. *The presentation of self in everyday life*. Edinburgh: University of Edinburgh Social Sciences Research Centre.

———. 1967. *Interaction ritual: Essays on face-to-face behavior*. Garden City, NY: Anchor Books.

Koskoff, Ellen. 2001. *Music in Lubavitcher life*. Urbana: University of Illinois Press.

Schieffelin, Edward L. 1998. "Problematizing Performance." In *Ritual, performance, media*, edited by Felicia Hughes-Freeland, 194–207. London: Routledge.

Seale, Clive, ed. *Researching culture and society*, http://people.brunel.ac.uk/~hsstcfs/glossary.htm.

Slobin, Mark. 1993. *Subcultural sounds: Micromusics of the West*. Hanover, NH: Wesleyan University Press/University Press of New England.

Strathern, Marilyn. 1995. *Shifting contexts: Transformations in anthropological knowledge*. London: Routledge.

Taylor, Timothy. 1997. *Global pop: World music, world markets*. New York: Routledge.

Turino, Thomas. 2000. *Nationalists, cosmopolitans, and popular music in Zimbabwe*. Chicago: University of Chicago Press.

Turner, Bryan S. 1994. *Orientalism, postmodernism, and globalism*. London: Routledge.

Waxer, Lise, ed. 2002. *Situating salsa: Global markets and local meanings in Latin American popular music*. New York: Routledge.

FIVE

Toward a History of Ethnomusicology's North Americanist Agenda

KAY KAUFMAN SHELEMAY

N THE BEGINNING, OR SO THE ORIGIN myth might recount, early ethnomusicologists worked in many regions of North America. Alice Fletcher, Franz Boas, Frances Densmore, Marius Barbeau, Diamond Jenness, Helen Roberts, Gertude Kurath, Ida Halpern, David McAllester, and others were among a stream of folklorists, anthropologists, comparative musicologists, and, finally, ethnomusicologists who made Native American musics their focus over the course of the twentieth century. They and others have inspired those who came after them: Charlotte Frisbie (1978) with the Navajo; Bruno Nettl (1989) with the Blackfoot; Beverley Diamond (Cavanagh 1982) with the Netsilik Inuit; Judith Vander (1988) with the Shoshone; Victoria Lindsay Levine (Howard and Levine 1990; Levine 2002) with the Choctaw; Tara Browner (2002) with the Lakota and Anishnaabeg, and so on. The study of Native North American music traditions frames the broader tale I will recount, both setting a standard for North American musical studies in the ethnomusicological past and linking that past to the present.

In *America's musical life*, Richard Crawford (2001, 3) notes that "the preservation and study of Indian music by Western scholars since the 1880s forms an important part of the story of American anthropology and ethnomusicology." I concur: The engagement with Native American music cultures is a broad and deep one in ethnomusicology; it also provides a provocative entry to a discussion of the intellectual history and politics of

ethnomusicology as a discipline, one that forces us to contend with the
US–Canadian divide.

I dedicate this chapter to Beverley Diamond, whose brilliant career
has contributed in so many formative ways to establishing North America as a site for ethnomusicological research as well as strengthening its many
institutional settings. In Diamond's recent article, "Canadian reflections on
palindromes, inversions, and other challenges to ethnomusicology's coherence," she discusses the relationship of Canadian musical scholarship to
history, asking if we can write histories that would help assess the impact
of our work (Diamond 2006, 331). The present chapter seeks to explore
the place of North Americanist musical research in the history of the ethnomusicological canon. It both acknowledges and interrogates Canadian
and US scholars' engagement with musics of the continent they share. It
begins with attention to the formative role of Native American/First Nation
musics, the study of which set the stage for work in other domains of
North American expressive culture. This discussion also seeks to cut across
the Canada–US border and to examine differences in national policies and
perspectives.

Is there, in fact, a divide or is there rather a common Canadian/US
musical agenda? Can we effectively approach scholarship in the United
States and Canada as a single unit of analysis? Like Diamond (2006), who
raises this question in the article cited above, I would observe that there
are both similarities and differences; while Diamond cites some differences, such as the higher number of Canadians involved over the course
of the last century in the "field at home," here I will focus more on common ground, especially the transnational moves that have characterized the
twentieth century. In addition to their early and continuing concern with
indigenous musics, scholars in ethnomusicology followed roughly parallel paths on both sides of the border. They shared methods of musical
ethnography, drawing on common theoretical sources from folklore and
anthropology. There were also shared institutional connections. For
instance, the University of Toronto's Mieczyslaw Kolinski was a founder
and early president of the Society for Ethnomusicology. But Kolinski,
although generally perceived as a Canadian ethnomusicologist, led a life
that graphically illustrates the difficulty in defining a Canadian–US divide
without attention to broader biographical and historical contexts. Born in
1901 in Warsaw, Kolinski was educated in Berlin and resided in both
Prague and Belgium before he immigrated to the United States in 1951.
After obtaining US citizenship in 1961, he moved to Toronto in 1966 to
found the ethnomusicology program, becoming a Canadian citizen only

in the last decade of his long career, which ended in 1976 (Beckwith 1982, xvii–xxiv). The professional paths of many others raise similar issues of blurred national identities and complicate categorizing ethnomusicologists by nationality given their status as "border crossers." For instance, Gage Averill, who received his Ph.D. at the University of Washington and taught in the United States at Wesleyan and then New York University until he assumed the deanship of the University of Toronto's Faculty of Music in 2004, recently became a landed immigrant in Canada.[1] The identification of a scholar as US or Canadian may thereafter refer variously to place of residence, immigration status, and/or passport at a given time. It is often further complicated by prior immigration or long-term residency in multiple sites abroad. Most ethnomusicologists spend substantial periods of time in the field; these long-term residencies give them additional geographical and national connections that may be as powerful in their own concepts of their identity as their formal places of residence.

There are surely substantial national political and policy differences that colour the careers ethnomusicologists pursue on different sides of the Canada–US border. For instance, it must be noted from the outset that Canada and the United States have had quite divergent policies toward diversity. Canada was much earlier and forthrightly supportive of multiculturalism; the 1969 Report of the Royal Commission on Bilingualism and Biculturalism resulted in recommendations for new Canadian federal policies endorsing minority cultures through multicultural grants, culture development programs, ethnic histories, Canadian ethnic studies, and teaching of official languages (Qureshi 1972, 381; Potvin 1972, 514).[2] In contrast, US policy was until the last decades of the twentieth century still struggling to emerge from the residual influence of the "melting pot philosophy," which gave rise to recurrent "allegories of assimilation" in which immigrants enter the American arena only to emerge as a "new race," letting go of their culture and history (Hollinger 1995, 45). Today, despite official acknowledgement in the US of cultural diversity, one still finds frequent (and successful) ballot initiatives against bilingual education and, particularly post-9/11, a widespread suspicion of cultural differences. A second difference between the Canadian and US arenas is in their populations; while both are home to a wide range of Asian and Caribbean communities, the US has far larger African-American and Latino populations, both proportionately and numerically. With these issues on the table, we can resume a discussion of ethnomusicology's North Americanist agenda.

To return to the early study of Native North American musical traditions, it left an enduring shared legacy for US and Canadian scholars, one
that extends beyond scholarship to cut a clear and distinctive path through
ethnomusicological pedagogy. Indeed, major ethnomusicology textbooks
still bracket music of Native American peoples within a separate Native
American time and space. Of particular interest here is the way in which
Native American musics have often served as the primary marker for an
otherwise unmarked ethnomusicological North America, a synecdoche
for American musics at large.

For instance, in Bruno Nettl's textbook *Excursions in world music*
(1997; see Figure 5.1) one finds a chapter titled "Native American Indian
music" amid ten other chapters treating countries, regions, subcontinents,
or entire continents. Similarly, Jeff Todd Titon's *Worlds of music* (2002;
see Figure 5.2) has a North American chapter focusing on the Navajo, the
first of a series of chapters looking (variously) at other Native or ethnic communities, musical genres, regions, countries, and subcontinents. While it
is clear that ethnomusicological pedagogy in these and other texts moves
uneasily and unevenly across territory defined by rubrics ranging from
the geographical to the national to the subcultural, it is striking that North
America in particular is consistently represented by Native American music.
Otherwise, inclusion of North American music in Nettl's *Excursions in
world music* extends only to "Old World Cultures in North America,"
perhaps reflecting the editor's Europeanist roots, while in Titon's *Worlds
of music*, one finds a North America extending to Black American blues,
a specialization of its editor. Beyond Native America, North America is in
fact largely absent from these two admirable pedagogical excursions. North
America remains a largely empty signifier alongside other, more richly
documented areas that constitute, for most ethnomusicologists, the world
of music.

This quick glace at the study and pedagogy of Native North American
music sets the stage for a critical discussion of ethnomusicology's North
Americanist agenda. I will argue that, for much of the twentieth century,
certainly until well into the 1980s, in fact, ethnomusicology did *not* have
a North Americanist agenda. With a few exceptions following the wave of
early North American studies before 1950, most North American ethnomusicologists promptly moved abroad, along with composers and eth-
norecordists as well as anthropologists. They rarely looked back, and
through most of the second half of the twentieth century, Native North
American studies continued on a largely separate track, with Native North
Americans approached primarily as bounded communities of descent

FIGURE 5.1 Table of Contents, *Excursions in world music*

Chapter 1	Introduction
Chapter 2	The Music of India
Chapter 3	Music of the Middle East
Chapter 4	China
Chapter 5	Japan
Chapter 6	The Music of Indonesia
Chapter 7	The Music of Sub-Saharan Africa
Chapter 8	Europe
Chapter 9	Music in Latin America
Chapter 10	North American Indian Music
Chapter 11	Old World Cultures in North America

Bruno Nettl et al., *Excursions in world music*, 2nd ed. (Upper Saddle River, NJ: Prentice-Hall), [1992] 1997.

FIGURE 5.2 Table of Contents, *Worlds of music*

Chapter 1	The Music-Culture as a World of Music
Chapter 2	North America/Native America/Navajo
Chapter 3	Africa/Ewe
Chapter 4	North America/ Black America/Blues
Chapter 5	Europe/Bosnia
Chapter 6	India/South India
Chapter 7	Asia/Indonesia
Chapter 8	East Asia/Japan
Chapter 9	Latin America/Ecuador
Chapter 10	Discovering and Documenting a World of Music

Jeff Todd Titon et al., eds., *Worlds of music*, 4th ed., Shorter Version (Belmont, CA: Schirmer/Thomson Learning), 2002.

whose musical practices were assumed to be congruent with the regions in which they live.

While ethnomusicologists worked around the globe to connect (mainly ethnic/traditional) musics within local cultural matrices and to interpret these practices in relation to a wide range of factors, regional and national, Native North American musical studies remained a curiously cloistered field of inquiry. It continued as a scholarly discourse that did not, for the most part, engage with changing theoretical concerns or with broader issues in North American society. Here the interest of composers in Native North American music provides an exception, as do some individual studies such as those by Diamond (Cavanagh), that directly interrogate the rate of change in Inuit music, "especially as a result of contact with European and North American music" (Cavanagh 1982, vi).

If Native North American musical research did not engage until recent decades with broader cultural issues, and may be said at moments to have "naturalized" the post-colonial and subaltern status of First Nations, by the early twenty-first century one finds studies of Native North American history and music approached as incorporating, domesticating, or resisting mainstream culture. For instance, Tara Browner's (2002) monograph, *Heartbeat of the people*, which explores the Northern powwow in a fully Americanist framework, is a felicitous example of this new, more explicitly "Americanist" approach. Browner's discussion of the emergence of the term and event "powwow" traces a complex history in dialogue with multiple streams of North American tradition; Browner traces encounters between Native peoples and German immigrants, including folk-healers of European descent, which gave rise to a series of travelling events ranging from the medicine show to the powwow:

> Among the first Indian people German immigrants encountered as they began to arrive in the Colonies during the mid-seventeenth century were the various Algonquian-speaking tribes of New England. Folk-healers from European societies gravitated toward Indian healing practices. They appropriated the term pau wau, used by Indians to describe specific ritual actions that took place during curing ceremonies, and adopted it to describe the settlers' general use of herbal remedies. Since that time, practitioners of Anglo-American and Pennsylvania German folk medicine (known as "powwow doctors") employed the word pow-wowing to denote charms, incantation, magic and laying on of hands for avoiding or curing disease or injury. (Browner 2002, 27)

Browner (2002, 28) goes on to show how the promotion of alleged Indian medical remedies through the travelling "medicine show," which toured the country accompanied by Indians who performed dances, resulted in the use of the term *powwow* being associated with Indians dancing, leading to, by the 1880s, travelling shows by Native Americans themselves. Here we have a Native American ethnomusicology with a clear and fully articulated Americanist frame. But once again, I am getting ahead of my story.

We can now return to what might be termed the "exoticization" of ethnomusicology—that is, ethnomusicology's emphasis on foreign fieldwork by the mid-twentieth century. It may be that the move abroad effec-

tively postponed the development of a North Americanist agenda in ethnomusicology until little more than a decade ago. The emphasis on ethnomusicological research abroad was fed by a number of factors, some
internal to the field, others more broadly social, political, and economic.
The move to the field at home and to local, urban field sites (Reyes
Schramm, 1979) also led many North American ethnomusicologists, on
both sides of the border to establish patterns shorter than the classical
year in the field. At the same time, a serious lack of funding for research
projects at home in North America surely discouraged domestic research.
In the US establishment of foreign studies area centres during the early Cold
War era post–World War II made substantial funding available for language and area studies, thus encouraging research abroad. Whether Canadian scholars responded to the same or different pressures is a question I
would raise here, wondering as well what different factors shaped Canadian ethnomusicology as situated within a self-governing country of the
British Commonwealth. But there is no doubt that economic factors shaped
emerging patterns of fieldwork among both Canadian and US ethnomusicologists. In the United States, one can only surmise if other factors
implicitly dampened nascent ethnomusicological tendencies to work closer
to home in non-Native America, such as the political witch hunts of the
1950s and the aura of suspicion directed at many aspects of difference in
American creative and cultural life.

By the 1960s, too, the counterculture and the US anti-war movement
had fuelled the move toward foreign fieldwork. It may not be coincidental that research on North American music traditions did not carry much
cultural capital in heavily Eurocentric schools of music; additionally, the
historical primacy of Native North American studies led those specializations to be regarded, whether rightfully or not, by many later twentieth-
century ethnomusicologists as somewhat retrospective.[3] Important, too,
were institutional currents that fed a desire to distinguish ethnomusicology and its agenda from that of historical musicology. It may be relevant
that many of the ethnomusicologists most active in Native American studies post–World War II were either trained in anthropology (here I would
include David McAllester, Charlotte Frisbie, and Bruno Nettl, as well as
[in South American studies] Anthony Seeger) or were outside the formal
boundaries of academia and its politics altogether (Judith Vander). The
generation of ethnomusicologists who came of age and carried out fieldwork in the late 1970s and 1980s, even those trained by the distinguished
colleagues just mentioned, perceived foreign fieldwork as the most valid
cross-cultural encounter. Ethnomusicologists were further encouraged in

their foreign pursuits by the emergence of strong schools of scholarship
by the mid-1960s in certain (soon to become) canonic areas: lineages of
ethnomusicologists studying Southeast Asian, East Asian, Middle Eastern, and West-African musics.[4] This in contrast to important European-
born scholars in Canadian and US ethnomusicology such as Kolinski and
Nettl, who both encouraged and were themselves active in Native American studies.

By the late 1970s and early 1980s, more ethnomusicologists began
tentatively to engage with American music beyond the boundaries of First
Nation communities—they came home to study what were perceived as
bounded, ethnic communities. While a few early pioneers such as Adelaida Reyes Schramm (1975) and Regula Qureshi (1972) were motivated
in part by methodological and theoretical concerns, most ethnomusicologists who did "come home to North America" in the 1970s simply transferred their ethnographic interests and field sites to the study of so-called
American ethnic communities. Canada was first in this venture, sponsor-
ing a special "Canadian issue" of *Ethnomusicology* (Katz 1972); in 1978
a volume of the UCLA Selected Reports, edited by James Porter, marked
an important milestone of the ethnomusicological move to "ethnic America." While the earliest of these studies sought less to relate ethnic communities to a North American context than to examine their relationship
to their various homelands, by the late 1980s a crucial shift had occurred.

Perusing ethnomusicological publications in North American musics
since the late 1970s and early 1980s, one is struck by the sudden proliferation of studies of two American communities in particular: African
Americans and Jews. The history of each was marked by strong factors of
descent ranging from race to religion, and by collective trauma; each of
these communities provided rich musical materials and active performance traditions still being actively transmitted. Ethnomusicological interests in the music of the African-American community were no doubt
sparked in part by the civil rights movement. Here we could cite a few
examples from the ethnomusicological literature on blues and jazz by individuals such as Charles Keil (1966), Jeff Todd Titon (1977, 1994), Paul
Berliner (1994), and Ingrid Monson (1996).

Jews and their music also attracted substantial scholarly attention
early on, with ethnomusicological work in this area expanding dramatically post-1970, no doubt in part as a response to the dramatic loss of
European Jews, their music, as well as a generation of scholars during
the Holocaust. Here we can acknowledge Mark Slobin (1982, 2000) as
a leader, with more recent contributions by Kay Kaufman Shelemay

(1998), Ellen Koskoff (2000), Jeffrey Summit (2002), Mark Kligman (2009), and Judah Cohen (2009).

It is interesting that while a few ethnomusicologists came home to work in areas of Black and Jewish musics in North America, both fields have remained on the margins of ethnomusicology until quite recently. One can only wonder if ethnomusicology was not yet sure *how* to institutionalize scholarship at home in North American locales, about peoples other than Native Americans, and how to engage with a broader swath of American history and culture. While scholars working on African-American and Jewish musics have shaped lively fields of research, both areas can still be said to continue to occupy borderlands between ethnomusicology and other disciplines, such as African-American studies and historical musicology. Both fields further include a wide range of participants who hang their disciplinary hats outside ethnomusicology and/or the academy altogether. Here one might point to journalists contributing to African-American musical studies and cantors publishing actively about Jewish musical traditions.

When many ethnomusicologists did finally "come home" to North America in the later 1980s, it was to a fluid, transnational America. This transition emerged in part from increasing interest in popular musics. However, ethnomusicological studies of ethnic America also resonated with emerging transnational studies and post-colonial theory, reinventing themselves within the framework of diaspora studies, as seen in recent work by Reyes (1999, 2005) and others. The ethnomusicological engagement with diaspora also opened the door for work with a much broader range of ethnic communities and made space for new questions. Since 1990, there have been a proliferation of such studies, including work on Mexican Americans in Los Angeles (Loza 1993), a biography of an immigrant Cuban *santero* (Velez 2000), and cross-cutting studies of other Caribbean musics in New York (Allen and Wilcken 2001), to cite only a few. All of these publications provide richly contextualized and creatively theorized approaches to the widest range of musical traditions explicitly posited within North American cultural and musical life. It is important to acknowledge, however, that many of these studies emerged from accidental encounters, not from a decision to construct a North Americanist ethnomusicology; indeed, one might label this move ethnomusicology's "accidental North Americanist agenda."

As an example, let's take the work of Gage Averill, whom, as we have already noted, transcends the Canadian–US divide in his teaching and administrative career. In the introduction to his prize-winning social history of American barbershop music, Averill writes that he started to work

on barbershop singing only when he urgently needed a local venue in
which to practise using his new recording equipment prior to a fieldtrip
to Haiti. Averill is quite frank about what he thought of a North Americanist research venture in 1987:

> Admittedly, this was not my idea of ethnomusicology, or of a good time.
> I expected that neither the music, nor the performers, nor their audience,
> nor the mall in which they were performing would be of any sustained
> interest to me, but it occurred to me that that just might be for the better.
> After all, I could practice some concert videography, snap some photos,
> maybe even tape a short interview, and leave with no lingering sense of obli-
> gation. (Averill 2003, vii)

Yet, Averill goes on to note that he quickly realized that he "might have
inadvertently stumbled on an ideal research topic: statistically important,
undertheorized (a so-called lacuna in academic studies), and a fount of
important issues and questions in cultural studies.... The more I discovered of this relatively hidden history, the more certain was I of its draw.
Here was a story from American musical history ..." (Averill 2003, viii–ix).
Averill goes on to detail the myriad connections of his barbershop case
study to public figures, institutions, and social upheavals of the twentieth-century US.

However, other North American ethnomusicologists have, since the
mid-1990s, quite intentionally engaged with the widest varieties of music
traditions in explorations that were clearly and carefully planned. Here
Theodore Levin's exploration of Central Asian music traditions in Central Asia as well as in Queens, New York (1996) provides a notable example. Although the title of Levin's book suggests that fieldwork in Queens
was an afterthought, Levin clearly gave thought and effort to the New
York–based climax to his Central Asian study:

> I saw Ilyas several times during his first year in Queens, but it wasn't until
> the fall of 1993, a year after his arrival, that we were able to arrange the
> first of several long visits. I told Ilyas that I wanted to write about his adap-
> tation to musical life in New York, that I'd like to spend several days talk-
> ing with him and perhaps accompanying him a performance or two. (Levin
> 1996, 262)

The sheer breadth of subject matter and topics entering into the North
American musical discourse are highlighted in essay collections such as
Canadian music: Issues of hegemony and identity, edited by Diamond and
Witmer (1994). The editors openly acknowledge the essays' departure
from the past:

Both the subjects and the approaches in the anthology vary widely. The former are not delimited to a specific historical frame, by any genre or type of musical practice, or by any social community or contexts. The latter include conventional historical documentation, textual analysis and structuralist approaches as well as newer paradigms (frameworks of thought) including recent reflections on "subjectivity," new assessments of nationalism, or feminist interpretations. Readers may be able to trace some significant shifts in approaches to similar issues over the past few decades. (Diamond and Witmer 1994, 2–3)

To move toward a conclusion, we can ask if ethnomusicology is at last "at home" in North America. Can we trace a new, North Americanist agenda that has emerged in ethnomusicology? I believe so, and see the beginnings of the institutional traces of this trend. Since the later 1990s, one finds:

- An increasing dialogue across the boundaries of the Society for American Music (SAM) and the Society for Ethnomusicology (SEM).
- A move to include the broadest range of American musics in ethnomusicological pedagogy. Here we find the beginning of a pedagogical literature that includes a wide swath of North American traditions, with recent titles such as Lornell and Rasmussen's (1997) collection of studies of twelve musical communities, *Musics of multicultural America*, Adelaida Reyes's (2005) *Music in America*, and my own *Soundscapes* (Shelemay 2006). For example, Lornell and Rasmussen assert that *Musics of multicultural America* responds to the growing need on college campuses to teach a "new American canon," one characterized by diversity as well as the continuing creation, interaction, and regeneration of multiple multicultural voices.
- Scholarly initiatives have increased, some from beyond ethnomusicology, to look at the borderlands between the Euro-American classical arena as well as interactions with a range of ethnic or world music traditions. Here one can cite Carol Oja's (1990) study of Colin McPhee's career, which documents aspects of the emergence of a transnational American compositional tradition; Judith Tick's (1997) broadly inclusive exploration of Ruth Crawford Seeger's work in American folk music; and, moving back to the first source cited here, Richard Crawford's (2001) *America's musical life.*
- New academic programs and publications series, underway for some time, have emerged. To note just one, music publishing, editor Judith McCulloh at University of Illinois Press has constructed a virtual monument to North American musical studies with the *Music in American life* series, with well over one hundred volumes now in print. Mark

Slobin has begun a series called American Musicspheres at Oxford University Press, which provides a new and congenial home for ethnomusicologists pursuing a North Americanist agenda.

In closing, if ethnomusicology is at last on the move in North America and constructing its own Americanist agenda, we should not neglect the task of charting the history and historiography of this process. Beverley Diamond has participated actively in this historical process and at the same time has taken a reflexive look at the course of this history. Here we can celebrate Diamond's role in constructing a North Americanist agenda, one that indeed transcends the Canada–US border.

Notes

1   I thank Gage Averill for supplying these personal particulars in correspondence dated 17 October 2007.
2   Beverley Diamond (2000, 55–56) has, in fact, questioned the narrative of Canadian diversity, writing that "While many critics claim that Canadians generally respect cultural difference and vigorously resist the melting pot ideology that we associate with the United States, several recent analyses are vigilant about strategies which have had the effect of 'managing' and controlling difference." I thank Robin Elliott for bringing this quotation to my attention.
3   The late-nineteenth- and early-twentieth-century evolutionary and primitivist paradigms embedded in early studies of Native North American traditions were surely a barrier to later twentieth-century ethnomusicologists engaged with structuralism and symbolic anthropology.
4   See Shelemay (1996, 14–16) for a more detailed discussion of this point.

References

Allen, Ray, and Lois Wilcken, ed. 2001. *Island sounds in the global city: Caribbean popular music and identity in New York*. Urbana: University of Illinois Press.

Averill, Gage. 2003. *Four parts, no waiting: A social history of American barbershop harmony*. New York: Oxford University Press.

Beckwith, John. 1982. "Kolinski: An Appreciation and List of Works." *In cross cultural perspectives on music*, edited by Robert Falck and Timothy Rice, xvii–xxiv. Toronto: University of Toronto Press.

Berliner, Paul. 1994. *Thinking in jazz: The infinite art of improvisation*. Chicago: University of Chicago Press.

Browner, Tara. 2002. *Heartbeat of the people: Music and dance of the northern powwow*. Urbana: University of Illinois Press.

Cavanagh (Diamond), Beverley. 1982. *Music of the Netsilik Eskimo: A study of stability and change*, 2 vols. Ottawa: National Museum of Canada.

Cohen, Judah. 2009. *The making of a Reform Jewish cantor: Musical authority, cultural investment*. Bloomington: Indiana University Press.

Crawford, Richard. 2001. *America's musical life: A history*. New York: W.W. Norton and Company.

Densmore, Frances. [1910–13] 1973. *Chippewa music*. Minneapolis: Ross and Haines.

Diamond, Beverley. 2000. "What's the Difference? Reflections on Discourses of Morality, Modernism, and Mosaics in the Study of Music in Canada." *Canadian University Music Review* 21, no. 1: 54–75.

———. 2006. "Canadian Reflections on Palindromes, Inversions, and other Challenges to Ethnomusicology's Coherence." *Ethnomusicology* 50, no. 2: 324–36.

Diamond, Beverley, and Robert Witmer, eds. 1994. *Canadian music: Issues of hegemony and identity*. Toronto: Canadian Scholars' Press.

Fletcher, Alice C. [1904] 1997. *The hako: Song, pipe, and unity in a Pawnee Calumet ceremony*. Lincoln: University of Nebraska Press.

Frisbie, Charlotte J., and David P. McAllester, eds. 1978. *Navajo Blessingway singer: The autobiography of Frank Mitchell, 1881–1967*. Tucson: University of Arizona Press.

Halpern, Ida. 1967. *Indian music of the Pacific Northwest coast*. Sound recording. FE 4523. New York: Folkways Records.

Hollinger, David. 1995. "Assimilation." In *A Companion to American Thought*, edited by Richard Wightman Fox and James T. Kloppenberg, 44–48. Oxford/Cambridge: Blackwell.

Howard, James Henri, and Victoria Lindsay Levine. 1990. *Choctaw music and dance*. Norman: University of Oklahoma Press.

Katz, Israel J., ed. 1972. *Ethnomusicology* (Canadian Issue) 16, no. 3.

Keil, Charles. 1966. *Urban blues*. Chicago: University of Chicago Press.

Kligman, Mark L. 2009. *Maqām and liturgy: Ritual, music, and aesthetics of Syrian Jews in Brooklyn*. Detroit: Wayne State University Press.

Koskoff, Ellen. 2001. *Music in Lubavitcher life*. Urbana: University of Illinois Press.

Levin, Theodore Craig. 1996. *The hundred thousand fools of God: Musical travels in Central Asia (and Queens, New York)*. Bloomington: Indiana University Press.

Levine, Victoria Lindsay, ed. 2002. *Writing American music: Historic transcriptions, notations, and arrangements*. Middleton, WI: A-R Editions, Inc.

Lornell, Kip, and Anne K. Rasmussen, eds. 1997. *Musics of multicultural America: A study of twelve musical communities*. New York: Schirmer Books.

Loza, Steven. 1993. *Barrio rhythms: Mexican American music in Los Angeles*. Urbana: University of Illinois Press.

McAllester, David Park. 1954. *Enemy way music: A study of social and esthetic values as seen in Navaho music*. Cambridge, MA: The Peabody Museum.

Monson, Ingrid T. 1996. *Saying something: Jazz improvisation and interaction*. Chicago: University of Chicago Press.

Nettl, Bruno. 1989. *Blackfoot musical thought: Comparative perspectives*. Kent, OH: Kent State University Press.

——, ed. 1997. *Excursions in world music*, 2nd ed. Upper Saddle River, NJ: Prentice-Hall.

Oja, Carol. 1990. *Colin McPhee: Composer in two worlds*. Washington, DC: Smithsonian Institution.

Porter, James, ed. 1978. *Selected reports in ethnomusicology* 3, no. 1. Los Angeles: University of California.

Potvin, Gilles. 1972. "The Canadian Broadcasting Corporation and Canadian Folk Cultures: The Preservation of Ethnic Identity." *Ethnomusicology* 16, no. 2: 512–15.

Qureshi, Regula. 1972. "Ethnomusicological Research among Canadian Communities of Arab and East Indian Origin." *Ethnomusicology* 16, no. 2: 381–96.

Reyes, Adelaida. 1999. *Songs of the caged, songs of the free: Music and the Vietnamese refugee experience*. Philadelphia: Temple University Press.

——. 2005. *Music in America: Experiencing music, expressing culture*. Oxford: Oxford University Press.

Reyes Schramm, Adelaida. 1975. The role of music in the interaction of Black Americans and Hispanos in New York City's East Harlem. Ph.D. dissertation, Columbia University.

——. 1979. "Ethnic Music, the Urban Area, and Ethnomusicology." *Sociologus* 29 new series: 1–18.

Seeger, Anthony. 1987. *Why Suyá sing: A musical anthropology of an Amazonian people*. Cambridge: Cambridge University Press.

Shelemay, Kay Kaufman. 1996. "Crossing Boundaries in Music and Musical Scholarship: A Perspective from Ethnomusicology." *The Musical Quarterly* 80, no. 1: 13–30.

——. 1998. *Let jasmine rain down: Song and remembrance among Syrian Jews*. Chicago: University of Chicago Press.

——. 2006. *Soundscapes: Exploring music in a changing world*, 2nd rev. ed. New York: Norton.

Slobin, Mark. 1982. *Tenement songs: The popular music of the Jewish immigrants*. Urbana: University of Illinois Press.

——. 2000. *Fiddler on the move: Exploring the Klezmer world*. New York: Oxford University Press.

Summit, Jeffrey A. 2002. *The Lord's song in a strange land: Music and identity in contemporary Jewish worship*. New York: Oxford University Press.

Tick, Judith. 1997. *Ruth Crawford Seeger: A composer's search for American music*. Oxford: Oxford University Press.

Titon, Jeff Todd. [1977] 1994. *Early downhome blues: A musical and cultural analysis*, 2nd ed. Chapel Hill: University of North Carolina Press.

——, ed. 2002. *Worlds of music*, 4th ed. Belmont, CA: Schirmer/Thomson Learning.

Vander, Judith. 1988. *Songprints: The musical experience of five Shoshone women.* Urbana: University of Illinois Press.

Velez, Maria Teresa Velez. 2000. *Drumming for the gods: The life and times of Felipe Garcia Villamil, Santero, Palero, and Abakua.* Philadelphia: Temple University Press.

SIX

Encountering Oral Performance as Total Musical Fact[1]

REGULA BURCKHARDT QURESHI

Oral Tradition

ORAL TRADITION IS COMMONLY USED to designate the creation, dissemination, transmission, and preservation of verbal and musical "texts" by means of oral-aural communication and its retention in memory. This process requires the co-presence and interaction of those who produce sonic messages and, equally important, of those who receive them, whether they are called "speakers" and "hearers" or performers and audience. Together, they create speech and music events that range widely in form, function, and configuration of participants' oral performances in the widest sense of the word.

This chapter posits that oral performances are more than enactments of already extant musical texts; they are total musical facts that encompass everything that makes the music happen. The event *is* the music; they both identify each other, and it is common that the name of one also names the other. Because in every performance, music is sonically created anew, it is inseparably linked to its human agents. How they interact is as much part of the performance process as is its purely sonic aspect and must be considered of musical, cultural and social importance.

With the primacy of music as a subject of contemplation deeply engrained in Western scholarship, early ethnomusicologists focused on all music as a sonic construct, with sound recordings providing their primary musical texts, to be transcribed and analyzed and compared. A parallel and still foundational approach has been to learn from musicians how to sing or play their music and thereby to acquire a culturally appropriate understanding of the musical language if not its use in performance (Hood's "bi-musicality," 1963). The focus on music as a performative process—rather than as an autonomous body of sound or a repertoire—is a recent development, advanced by anthropologically trained scholars (Asch 1975; McLeod and Herndon 1980; Seeger 1980) who drew on performance studies in socio-linguistics and folklore where the idea was pioneered that the contextual dimension of performance should be included in the study of verbal communications (Labov 1972; Baumann 1975; Ben-Amos and Goldstein 1975; Silverstein 1976). Singer's "cultural performance" concept contributed seminally to this development for India (Singer 1972).

Ethnomusicologists have encountered an astonishing variety of musical performances across the world. Most are associated or are expressly identified with designated contexts (e.g., religious, familial, agricultural, etc.), and they fit the designation of "oral tradition," even where the music is complex and the musicians are professional specialists. Remarkably, such oral performances include religious and art music where musical notation coexists with oral tradition, thus problematizing the oral–literate dichotomy (e.g., in South Asia, China, and Japan). Finally, most of these performances are vocal and include verbal texts, which are set to music or vice versa.

One of the most vivid and complex oral performance traditions is Qawwali, the predominant Sufi music of India and Pakistan. The Sufi assembly challenged me with a complex musical-verbal repertoire and the most elaborate interaction between performers and audiences I had ever dreamed of. This essay has its intellectual roots in my own study of Qawwali and its highly interactive performance of spiritual songs. Qawwali thus became a case study for a multi-dimensional analysis that encompasses both music as well as its relevant contexts, including musicians, patrons, and listeners (Qureshi 1987, 2006).

To describe Qawwali music briefly, a lead singer heads a small vocal group accompanied by a drum, harmonium, and rhythmic clapping in a continuous sequence of mystical poems, which are sung in a fluid responsorial style, characterized by repetition and improvisation. The Sufi assembly, the performance occasion for Qawwali, is a gathering held under a spiritual leader for the purpose of listening to this music in order to achieve a spiritual experience of ecstasy. The Sufi devotees respond spontaneously, but in accordance with religious and social convention, expressing states of mystical love. The musicians, on their part, structure their performance to activate and reinforce their listeners' emotions, while also attempting to elicit offerings, which represent their remuneration.

Consider entering a Sufi assembly held in Delhi at the anniversary of the Sufi Saint Nizamuddin Auliya:

At the beginning of the Qawwali performance: immediately the lead musician intones the obligatory Arabic hymn that introduces every Qawwali at Nizamuddin Auliya. A great stirring begins among the audience. One by one, most of them stand up and seek the assembly leader, bowing low with extended hands, to present him with an offering of money. Some Sufi disciples kneel before him or even put their head to the ground; others enlist a senior person to make their offering jointly; yet others offer instead to their own personal preceptor who then rises to present the offering to the leader. The leader himself accepts each offering by raising it to his forehead in deep respect. Then it is placed on the ground where it lies until one of the singers picks it up at suitable moments in the music. Indeed, this collection constitutes the musicians' monetary reward.

Throughout this intense offering activity the performers have been singing the opening line of the song over and over. Now they follow with the remainder of the brief hymn and immediately, without coming to an actual close, the lead singer introduces a second obligatory hymn, which celebrates spiritual discipleship. This is the moment for an even greater surge of offerings. Suddenly, the music changes, the drumming and clapping cease abruptly to let the leader's voice float high, sustained only by the reedy sound of the harmonium. As he shapes the first words of the new song in a slow recitative, every Sufi in the audience recognizes the cascading melody of the classical Persian masnavi and its message of the Sufi seeker's infinite longing:

"We, the supplicants of love, have come to your threshold...." A prominent Sheikh at the centre, draped in the orange colour of India's highest saintly lineage, bows in a gesture of deep humility and a hush has fallen over the assembly. Now the drum joins in a compelling pattern that perfectly articulates the verse rhythm, so that several Sufis begin to sway or tap. All eyes are drawn to the central Sheikh who is visibly moved to tears, his gestures bespeaking his intense emotion. When he suddenly falls on his knees to touch the feet of the assembly leader and then kisses the hallowed wall behind him, the gathering is suffused with a sense of fervor and devotion. Exclamations rise and one venerable old Sufi loudly repeats a phrase that has moved him greatly. Immersed in the message of the song, several listeners are swooning as if entranced.

A more effusive mood suddenly arises when, imperceptibly, the singers have moved on to a devotional Hindi song with a raga-like melody full of pathos. The words and the music of Khusrau, the saint's greatest disciple, is every devotee's call from the heart. Several Sufis are quick to rise and prostrate themselves before their Sheikh, as if unable to contain their emotion. Meanwhile, the performers repeat over and over the salient phrase of the song, emphasizing and embellishing it. At once, the lead singer breaks in with a recitative that profoundly expands the meaning of the repeated phrase. With this, the focus shifts once again to the orange-draped Sheikh whose expression and gestures demand a restatement of the entire recitative. The lead singer responds, skillfully returning to the salient phrase, which he embellishes with variations. Soon thereafter, he ends the song, in answer to the assembly leader's discreet signal. After a moment of silent prayer, all rise. (Qureshi 2006, 2–3)

Experiencing Qawwali means, above all, hearing music, a never-ceasing sequence of different songs performed many times, but never the same way twice. It also means observing a ritual built around this music where the mystical quest is pursued with proper form and under a Sufi leader who controls both audience and musicians. But in pursuing his personal spiritual quest, each listener responds to the music in his own way, according to his inner needs and the mood of the moment. Finally, experiencing Qawwali means charting a process of interaction between musicians and listeners, between musical sound and audience responses. What is the nature of this interaction, what does the music say to the audience, and how does the performance situation affect the music?

To chart the interactive process must begin with the music. Qawwali has a vast repertoire of strophic songs structured in an open-ended way of sequencing the musical units so that verses can be repeated, extended, and combined with different text segments. As a light music genre, Qawwali is musically accessible far beyond the bounds of its immediate constituency. But as the musical idiom of its particular performance practice, Qawwali music has unique musical traits linked to three religious functions: it must effectively impart mystical poetry through musical articulation of textual features (verbal sound, poetic metre, and structure); at the same time it must evoke the repeated sound of God's name and arouse spiritual emotion through metric stress (drumming accents and handclapping). Finally, and most elaborately, Qawwali music must serve the individual spiritual needs of diverse Sufi listeners to hear particular text segments reiterated; this is achieved through a uniquely flexible compositional format that renders possible the isolation and manipulation of text units without loss of continuity or coherence using directional melodic movement as a syntactic principle for sequencing and connecting such units through alternative endings. Figure 6.1 is a capsule outline of the Sufi hymn heard in the Qawwali performance sketched and transcribed in Figure 6.2.

FIGURE 6.1 Qawwali hymn in outline form

Transliteration	Translation
Muflisānem āmadā dar kūe to	The distraught supplicants of love, we have come to your threshold,
Shai 'ullah az jamāl-e-rūe to	To perceive God's substance from the beauty of your face
Ka'ba-e-dil qibla-e-man rūe to	The *ka'ba* of my heart, and the direction of my prayers is your face:
Sajdagāh-e-'āshiqāṅ abrūe to	For lovers the place of adoration is your presence.
Amir Khusrau verses:	*Amir Khusrau verses:*
Idgah-e-ma- gharībāṅ kūe to	We, the humble and poor, pray at the *ī'd* assembly of your threshold
Imbisāt-e ī'd dīdam kūe to	All the joy of *ī'd*, I see at your threshold

The Performance Context

Performer-audience interaction is more than a set of musical and gestural behaviours; it is informed by shared meanings that inform that surface. The primary source of these meanings is the Sufi belief system, which emphasizes *sama* ("listening") in order to attain closeness to God. Music is a means to this spiritual end, hence the subordination of the music-maker to the listeners. Ranging from a raised palm to the dance of ecstasy or *raqs*, the listeners' individual gestural and verbal/vocal responses represent stages and types of mystical arousal. A more formal response and its expressive variants is making an offering to a spiritual superior, thereby linking the expressive dimension of arousal with the spiritual hierarchy of Sufism.

FIGURE 6.2 Qawwali hymn executed in performance

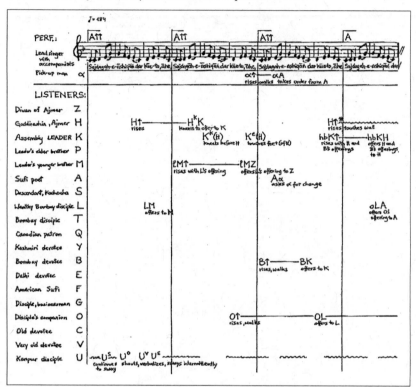

The performer's role in this complex contextual setting is tightly circumscribed, yet it also demands creativity. Within a loosely structured thematic sequence, he may choose and execute his songs freely on the basis of his own apperceptions. At the same time he is always subject to the assembly leader's censure, and his very presence in the assembly is at the leader's pleasure because as a musician, he acts as a functionary in a ritual that is ultimately controlled by spiritual leaders.

What actually evokes listeners' responses ranges widely from a diffuse composite of musical and non-musical factors to a very specific song phrase. Thus, a performer's knowledge of the listeners' gestural repertoire, his understanding of the spiritual state they represent, and the performance requirements that follow from that are as crucial as musical competence. Most important among these is the reinforcement and intensification of spiritual arousal. Concretely, this requires applying the principles of reiteration, amplification, and multiple repetition (takrar) to salient text units and thereby also to the music. In the case of a listener's ecstasy, the rule is categorical that a single phrase may have to be repeated for hours to sustain the ecstatic state of one person, while the remaining listeners stand in reverence, suspending their own responses. Here, spiritual and economic aims may clash most obviously, for during ecstasy, all possibility of offering is precluded, and while a shower of offerings may follow ecstasy, there may also be none.

Documenting the Interaction

How does a performer assess the spiritual states of his listeners, and how do these relate to the song being performed? Tracing their interaction in actual performances requires the use of video recordings, in order to document the complex interfacing of music and listeners' responses in visually and aurally accurate and repeatable detail. And the fleeting character of a moving picture necessitates some form of written transcription, a prerequisite for analysis. A comprehensive method of transcription called the Videograph is designed to capture the simultaneously ongoing responses of many listeners, along with the ongoing musical sound.

Figure 6.2 is a transcription excerpted from the performance described in the earlier part of this chapter. The Videograph traces the song as it is performed along a horizontal axis at the top of the page, each graph unit representing one metric unit of the song. Below the music notation all participants are listed vertically, starting with the performers. Then follows a list of all the listeners who can be identified on the video recording, arranged in order of decreasing spiritual status from the assembly leader on down. Along a horizontal line following each name, the individual's action or response can then be noted in a simple code, always vertically in line with the exact moment in the music at which it occurred and to which it lasted. The Videograph thus provides a blow-by-blow visual and auditory record of audience behaviour as it occurs in response to the ongoing song performance, which also supplies the temporal axis for plotting that behaviour. What can be seen is a variety of expressive gestures and exclamations along with offerings of spiritual devotion, with some spiritual leaders displaying intense emotional engagement with the spiritual message of the song.

How the performer deals with this situation musically is, however, based not only on his perception of the audience's responses, but also on his choice of focus on the listeners whom he considers most important. A second method of video transcription, the Videochart, is designed to

FIGURE 6.3 Qawwali performance and ecstasy

Performer	Interaction	Audience
Second line (A)		
3× A1	Expects to expand this → line to allow full meaning to sink in.	D moves with increasing intensity.
1/2× A2	Interrupts A2 to insert → Farsi verse as *girah*, to amplify meaning of line and impress sophisticated listeners.	D becomes still instantly.
Insert, line 1		
(1×) I	Begins *girah* in solo presentation. →	S immediately signals performers to stop Insert and continue repeating A2, giving priority to D's aroused state.
Second line		
(3×) A2	Instantly obeys S and → returns to repeating A2.	D instantly turns round to performers and breaks into loud weeping.
(3×) A1	Returns to beginning → of line to keep its message intact.	D, shaking head, searches pocket, stands up with a shout and makes offering to L, bowing low.
(3×) A2	Waits for offering to reach him, repeating A2. →	L passes offering to S who hands it on to performers. D, meanwhile, stands up, raises arm and shouts several times while starting to turn on the spot, having reached ecstasy. L and S rise in recognition of D's state.

follow the interactional dynamic that results from the performer's selective focus. Represented in three vertical columns that are connected with directional arrows, the musician's performance decisions are tracked in the central column, the audience responses on the right, and the resulting song segments (in notation) on the left, also providing a (vertical) temporal axis for the interactional process.

Figure 6.3 is a Videochart transcription of the sonic and gestural/vocal interaction between a performer and a Sufi listener who is entering an ecstatic state. The performer duly repeats verse segments that inspired the listener's ecstasy. Suddenly, he intones a new verse/tune to satisfy another, more prosperous listener, but instantly abandons it in response to a negative gesture by another senior Sufi.

Both recordings/transcriptions show how a predictable vocabulary of audience gestures and exclamations is necessary for the performer to provide his Sufi listeners with the textual/musical experience that matches their personal spiritual quest. Equally crucial is the performer's ability to "read" the subtle meanings conveyed by this vocabulary. But they also show that ultimate control over the performers rests with spiritual leaders, thereby attesting to the functional power that Sufis assign to the complex music of Qawwali.

Extending the Lessons from Qawwali

The study of Qawwali reveals how a musical performance emerges simultaneously as social and musical action created by all participants who use music as a language with extra-musical meaning built into the sound structure. These findings are a starting point for examining other musical performances from an interactive perspective, in order to include a range of musical or societal complexity in a range of musical cultures. Furthermore, performer–audience interaction comes in highly diverse constellations, ranging from complete separation between performer and listener to their total convergence. The following are three brief explorations of musical performance traditions situated in widely disparate musical cultures, social constellations, and geographic regions. I then turn to what appears to be the great exception to interactive performances: the Western art music concert.

Listener Interaction from Words to Vocal Drone: Staging Social Relations in Albanian Weddings

Jane Sugarman, in her differentiated account of Prespa Albanian wedding gatherings (Sugarman 1997), points to singing as a performance of social roles determined by gender and seniority. Men and women sing while sitting at separate tables at wedding celebrations, and elders take a prominent place in the informal singing. Individual guests make their place in society manifest by singing familiar songs to approving and teasing remarks from some listeners. But there is also an ethos of joining together as equals

and with mutual respect; this is expressed musically by other guests inton-
ing a drone to the songs being sung. Here, the very shift between solo and
audience, and the singer-listener interaction becomes subsumed under a unison umbrella that joins all listeners in a single note. Droning is considered the equivalent of attentive listening and a sonic means of eliminating
verbal comments on the song or the singer, in the interest of creating
"love" or social harmony (muabet).

Creating Community in the Dene Drum Dance

Michael Asch traces a unique interactive process in this Aboriginal drum
dance in northern Canada, a major event held to mark special occasions
in a hunting-trapping community of equals.[2] Dene Elders introduce the
event, and then sing drum songs while drumming; the goal is to motivate
the seated spectators or audience to become dancing participants (Asch
1988). If all present respond by joining the dancing line, the performing
elders introduce a different song genre and change from beating the drum
to tapping the frame of the instrument. They continue singing, but then
leave the drums altogether in order to join the dancing, linking arms and
facing the dancers. The dancing audience now begins to join the performers in a linked circle. The goal is unity among the community by performers and listeners merging in the dance. Music is used interactively to attract
people to join together in dance. If not everyone chooses to dance, the interaction is not complete and the social goal of the drum dance is not achieved.

The flexible patterns of interaction between both Albanian and Dene
performers and listeners render problematic any categorical distinction
between the roles of performers and listeners. Social goals govern both
musical and non-musical interaction, and social relevance determines who
speaks musically, how, and when. While social relevance can be seen even
in the music of stratified, professionalized societies exemplified by Qawwali,
studies of small-scale egalitarian societies offer the clearest instances of
how all musical activity effectively constitutes social activity in the sense
of governing social life itself.

Society as an Orchestra: Erasing the Performer–Audience Distinction in the Amazon

Anthony Seeger has pioneered what he calls a full account of an Amazon
ceremony where the Suyá people are totally embedded in music-making
within ten days of ritual activity and so multiply interactive that "the
euphoria of community participation" transcends any categorization of
performer and audience (Seeger 1987). Like members of an orchestra,

individuals variously sing or shout their own songs, alone or simultaneously with others, and they sing in groups or collectively in unison. Based not on musical criteria but on social groupings determined by age, sex, and name set, Suyá singing and the responses it evokes are seen as the practice of social life itself. Thus, men sing to their sisters, who in turn send their brothers food from their natal home, in a performer–audience interaction that activates a deep affective bond between siblings who must reside apart in the moiety system of Amazonian societies.

Oral Performance and the Western Classical Concert

If performer–audience interaction in oral traditions teaches us about the social dimensions of musical performances, is this any less the case for text-based art music? For Western art music, focusing on interaction between performers and audience as a topic of significance derives relevance from a question that has animated Western musical discourse since the nineteenth century. It is easy to believe that one's own music (and language) is fundamentally different from all other music. Yet Western concert performance, too, is an oral tradition and can be examined as an interactive process between performer and audience rather than only as an enactment of musical texts. Even in the universal presence of written music, a Western concert is more than the sonic realization of a composer's score by a performer, although the Western meaning of the term *performance practice* is limited to just that. A studied absence of interaction characterizes the actual musical performance, but this absence can also be seen as a deliberate stance that the audience adopts by means of a brief formalized interaction with the performers that precedes the performance of each work. Prompted by the appearance of the leading musician(s) on the stage, the audience claps a collective welcome, which signals the musicians to take their place; in response the audience adopts complete silence and stillness, which in turn elicits the start of the performance. Likewise, as soon as the performers conclude the work, the audience interrupts their silence and stillness with vigorous clapping, signalling their appreciation, whereupon the musicians rise and bow to accept the applause, and then exit. While clapping lasts they may exit and return for more bows, or for an encore, which once again elicits complete silence and stillness from the audience until the conclusion of the piece is greeted with the final and even more intense applause.

These interactional phases are expressly peripheral to the music being performed. All the more remarkable is the listeners' rigid conformity to their oral script of collective silence as well as collective noise, resulting in a remarkable acoustic solidarity among listeners. Clapping not only marks off the music performed, it creates a grotesque inversion of music into noise, a liminal sonic space that categorically separates the musical performance from the interactive sphere between (and among) concert participants.

Classical works are deemed canonical and beyond personal preference for performers as well as listeners. A performer is but a mediator enabling listeners to experience their impact by listening, but the listeners' experience of the work must be confined to the interior sphere; sharing the experience with others begins only after the performance. What ideology motivates this separation of the work from its performers? Is it to focus total listener attention on the authority of the composer as the creator of the work? How listeners derive meaning by abstracting the music from the performers who make it has been an interpretive project of both philosophy (Goehr 1992) and semiology (Nattiez 1990). Lydia Goehr theorizes the ideational and institutional conditions that have sustained and naturalized the autonomous work concept, while Jean-Jacques Nattiez has provided a compelling model of this estrangement between performer and listeners, showing how each invests the musical work with meaning, thereby implying an independent existence for the work both as text and ideation.

Performer–audience interaction in traditional societies teaches us about the social dimensions of musical performances. For Western art music, focusing on interaction between performers and audience as a topic of significance derives relevance from a question that has animated Western musical discourse since at least the nineteenth century: Is musical meaning immanent or is it constructed with reference to context, including verbal text, function, and social aspects of musical production? Philosophically, music has been aestheticized into a transcendental art (Kant) and conceptualized as a creation separate from its makers (composers, performers) as well as its listeners (Goehr 1992). The notated text of music becomes experiential evidence supporting this "separability," a concept that is elegantly articulated in Nattiez's (1990) semiotic scheme of musical meaning in which the music itself is seen as a sonic "trace" that becomes invested with meaning creatively by the composer as well as interpretively by the listener.

In terms of social goals, the concert audience shares bourgeois aspirations of respectability, connoisseurship as well as a sense of ownership and cultural responsibility. In concert this means sharing a commitment to aestheticized listening that prioritizes the work, reveres the composer, and maintains only a disinterested admiration of the performer as the work's interpreter (Bourdieu 1984). It is precisely the absence of behavioural (inter)action by listeners that most effectively signals both interiority and disinterest, contrasting significantly with opera and its highly interactive, performer-centred history (Feldman 1995).

The performers reciprocate, showing interest in nothing but their music; this is epitomized by the conductor's backside facing the audience in the interest of musical execution. They too have their rigid code of behaviour beyond the delivery of the musical work in the form of visual displays, of coordinated mass production (e.g., bow strokes) by sartorially marked ritual functionaries (Small 1998).

Seen as equally significant total musical facts, what do the diverse interactional patterns between performer and audience communicate beyond their immediate reference to diverse musical events? The Western concert articulates and is governed by depersonalized post-industrial relations, in stark contrast with the very personal relations of feudal patronage acted out in the Qawwali performance. Albanian weddings use songs to affirm and inculcate social norms of peasant society. Interaction in the Dene drum dance in Canada as well as the Suyá mouse ceremony both test and invite harmony within an egalitarian co-residential community to the point of erasing divisions between performing and listening. They also sonically enact lived social relationships. Performer–audience interaction varies greatly in extent and degree, but in all cases it becomes the significant locus of social-musical processes. Most of all, it effectively connects the musical event to its human agents and their creative input into the music through its social relations of musical production. This extends to the way performer–audience interaction shapes musical processes. In all cases, the music is subject to some degree of situational variability motivated by its social function, from choice of song (including the encore of classical concerts) to individual variations or improvisation of songs that variously shapes a variety of musical dimensions, from duration and melody, to accompaniment and texture, and structuring processes like repetition. Clearly, music as an art does not become degraded by being context-sensitive, functional, and meaningful outside of itself. On the contrary, recognizing these dimensions makes room for exploring all music as aesthetically coded social action revealed in performance regardless of cultural status, sonic complexity, or degree of acknowledged orality.

Notes

1   This evocative phrase, "encountering oral performance as total musical fact," originates
    with Jean Molino and is used by Jean-Jacques Nattiez in the context of musical semi-
    otics (Nattiez 1990, 42–43). Here I take the liberty of situating the concept within a
    broader socio-musical horizon.
2   The First Peoples of the Yukon, Northwest Territories, Nunavut, as well as northern
    portions of the western Canadian provinces of British Columbia, Alberta, and
    Saskatchewan, refer to themselves as Dene First Peoples, meaning "human being." Asch's
    work has focused on the Slavey drum dance (Mackenzie River), and later expanded to
    include the kinship system in his 1988 study.

References

Asch, Michael. 1975. "Social Context and the Musical Analysis of Slavey Drum
    Dance Songs." *Ethnomusicology* 19, no. 2: 245–57.
———. 1988. *Kinship and the drum dance in a northern Dene community*. Edmon-
    ton: Boreal Institute for Northern Studies Academic Printing and Publishing.
Baumann, Richard. 1975. "Verbal Art as Performance." *American Anthropologist*
    77: 290–311.
Béhague, Gerhard. 1984. "Introduction." In *Performance practice: Ethnomusico-
    logical perspectives*, edited by Gerhard Béhague, 3–12. Westport, CT: Green-
    wood Press.
Ben-Amos, D., and Goldstein, K., eds. 1975. *Folklore: Performance and commu-
    nication*. The Hague: Mouton.
Bourdieu, Pierre. 1984. *Distinction: A social critique of the judgment of taste*.
    Translated by Richard Nice. Cambridge, MA: Harvard University Press.
Feldman, Martha. 1995. "Magic Mirrors and the Seria Stage: Thoughts towards
    a Ritual View." *Journal of the American Musicological Society* 43, no. 3:
    423–84.
Goehr, Lydia. 1992. *The imaginary museum of musical works: An essay in the
    philosophy of music*. Oxford: Clarendon Press.
Hood, Mantle. 1963. "Music, the Unknown." In *Musicology*, edited by F.L. Har-
    rison, M. Wood, and C.V. Palisca, 215–36. Englewood Cliffs, NJ: Prentice-
    Hall.
Kapferer, Bruce. 1986. "Performance and the Structuring of Meaning and Expe-
    rience." In *The anthropology of experience*, edited by V. Turner and E.M.
    Bruner, 183–203. Urbana: University of Illinois Press.
Labov, William. 1972. *Sociolinguistic patterns*. Philadelphia: University of Penn-
    sylvania Press.
McLeod, Norma, and Marcia Herndon. 1980. *The ethnography of musical perform-
    ance*. Norwood, PA: Norwood Editions.
Nattiez, Jean-Jacques. 1990. *Music and discourse*. Princeton, NJ: Princeton Uni-
    versity Press.

Qureshi, Regula Burckhardt. 1987. "Music Sound and Contextual Input: A Performance Model for Musical Analysis." *Ethnomusicology* 33, no. 1: 55–86.

———. [1986, 1995] 2006. *Sufi music of India and Pakistan: Sound, context, and meaning in Qawwali.* New York: Cambridge University Press.

Seeger, Anthony. 1980. "Sing for Your Sister: The Structure and Performance of Suyá Akia." In *The ethnography of musical performance*, edited by Norma McLeod and Marcia Herndon, 7–42. Norwood, PA: Norwood Editions.

———. 1987. *Why Suyá sing: A musical anthropology of an Amazonian people.* Cambridge: Cambridge University Press.

———. 1992. "Ethnography of Music." In *Ethnomusicology: An introduction,* edited by H. Meyers, 88–109. New York: Norton.

Silverstein, Michael, 1976. "Shifters, Linguistic Categories, and Cultural Descriptions." In *Meaning in anthropology*, edited by Keith A. Basso and Henry A. Selby, 11–56. Albuquerque: School of American Research, University of New Mexico.

Singer, Milton. 1972. *When a great tradition modernizes: An anthropological approach to Indian civilization.* New York: Praeger.

Small, Christopher. 1987. "Performance as a Ritual: Sketch for the Enquiry into the Nature of a Symphony Concert." In *Lost in music: Culture, style, and the musical event,* edited by A.L. White, 6–32. London: Routledge and Kegan Paul.

———. 1998. *Musicking: The meaning of performing and listening.* Music/Culture Series. Hanover/London: Wesleyan University Press.

Sugarman, Jane C. 1997. *Engendering song: Singing and subjectivity at Prespa Albanian weddings.* Chicago: University of Chicago Press.

Turner, Victor W. 1969. "Liminality and Communitas." In *The ritual process: Structure and anti-structure,* 94–130. Ithaca, NY: Cornell Paperbacks.

You Also Work as a Church Organist? Whatever For?

CHARLOTTE J. FRISBIE

W hen invited to participate in this volume to honour Bev, one of my wonderful, longtime friends and colleagues in the Society for Ethnomusicology (SEM), I again became aware of concerns that have been bubbling inside of me, albeit beneath the surface of other interests.[1] My topic connects with Bev, who, besides being a scholar and educator, is herself extraordinarily talented as a musician and pianist. The link, however, lies only in performance, since here the focus is on my own work as a church organist. The stimuli for this chapter and its history are clarified below. It is offered with the sincere hope that Bev and others will find it enjoyable to read, fun to think about, and socially relevant. Given the issues with which it deals, and in a Dr. Seuss mode, "the Places You [Could] Go" with them, hopefully this essay will stimulate more work on church music in the future, and perhaps even influence some positive changes.

Background and Sources

In 1990, a group of anthropologists interested in the arts, including me, joined together and, with Steven Pastner as organizer, proposed a session for the 1991 American Anthropological Association meetings in Chicago. Entitled When Etic Becomes Emic: Anthropologists in the Arts, the session took place on 24 November. It was intended to be reflexive; all participants spoke from their personal experience as artists. Our original hope was that the session would be published in one of the more humanistically oriented anthropological journals, but this possibility was never pursued. We all returned to our individual campuses full of excitement, but with time, lost touch with each other and the symposium faded into memory.

When I started revisiting this topic for Bev's volume, I first contacted Steve Pastner to learn if anyone had pursued any of the questions we had raised in 1991. As far as we both knew, no one had. Then I located a copy of my 1991 paper, thanks to the files of an organist friend. When I reread it, it became clear that it could be a jumping-off point for this chapter, no more, no less. Fortunately, in the intervening fifteen years, my ideas have been enriched not only by the accumulation of more experiences as a church organist, but also by being one of ten invited consultants at a Religion and Music conference, held 20–21 March 1992 at the Louisville Institute for the Study of Protestantism and American Culture, in Louisville, Kentucky. Sponsored by the Lily Foundation and the institute, the conference revealed that we had yet to begin serious work on many of the issues under discussion.

Today, many members of SEM are performers, both of Western classical music and now of the musics they study. The current performative nature of ethnomusicology was not characteristic in earlier days. Those who know our history will recall the introduction of Mantle Hood's "bimusicality" model (Hood 1960), the ensuing arguments, and the eventual bifurcation between anthropologists and musicians. That hardly was the only bifurcation if one remembers arguments over fieldwork, lab work, transcription, analysis, music as part of culture, music in culture, and all of the rest. Yes, today participant observation fieldwork is accepted, and it is expected that fieldwork will include performance and study of the music as an "insider." The big interests now are in popular musics, even popular musics in our own cultures, how these relate to the historical and present-day features of every other aspect of the culture, and music as process, especially as illustrated by improvisation. Of course, other issues such as gender roles, gender expressions, sexual identity, race, economic issues, music and violence, and the need for more collaborative projects are also timely. The same can be said of the adoption of reflexivity from anthropology, and now even some initial work on what Laura Nader termed "studying up" or studying our own institutions, such as doing ethnographies of conservatories, music schools, or arts organizations (Atkinson 2005; Kingsbury 1988; Nettl 1995). Rather than pursue any of these issues, I want to summarize work I did while preparing to write this chapter.[2]

One of my first endeavours was to access data compiled during the anonymous 2002 SEM membership survey. I was especially interested in how many were involved in western European church music as performers, especially as organists. Data showed fourteen organists among the 566 respondents.[3] As Gray (2006b) noted, other data revealed thirteen members interested in hymns, twelve interested in church, two listed as Catholic, and four as Protestant.

Many of us know that finding anthropologists who are musicians in Western classical music is not unheard of. Within SEM, one prime example, of course, was David McAllester, whose beautiful voice was one of his trademarks. As Nettl (2002, 65) has reminded us, another example is his former colleague, Oscar Lewis, "a lifelong excellent amateur singer of opera," voice student at the University of Illinois, and "cantor in synagogues." Another is Philip Bock, a friend of mine after he arrived at the University of New Mexico during my graduate work there. In addition to teaching, publishing, and doing editorial and administrative work, Phil's artistic talents led him to join an early music group in Albuquerque and, most recently, to perform with and write for various local theatre groups.

Turning to ethnomusicologists more from the music side of the discipline, Nettl (2002, 72) notes that earlier it was common for those arriving at the University of Illinois as graduate students to come from classical music backgrounds, and sometimes to be performers in their own traditions. Now they are more apt to come from popular music ensemble backgrounds. Among the earlier group, he cites many individuals; to name just a few: Steve Blum and Phil Bohlman, both virtuoso pianists; Vicki Levine, a pianist and harpsichordist; Carol Babiracki, a flutist; Rich Haefer, a choral conductor, and Ron Riddle, a cruise ship pianist, all-round musician and composer.[4]

To round out the background information, it also helps to remember that at the fiftieth anniversary meeting of SEM in Atlanta, on 19 November 2005, there was a concert dedicated to Robert Stevenson entitled Pioneers of Ethnomusicology as Composers. Six compositions were performed, written by William Malm, J.H. Kwabena Nketia, Charles Seeger, Miecyzslaw Kolinski, John Blacking, and Mantle Hood. The performers included the Emory Woodwind Ensemble and the Georgia State University Percussion Ensemble groups, as well as Eric Nelson, baritone; Karen Freer, cello; Deborah Thoreson, piano; Judith Klassen, violin; and Beverley Diamond, piano. Bev and Judith played the Seeger and Kolinski pieces.[5] Interesting to me was the program note that John Blacking's piece was originally scored for SATB choir and organ; in Atlanta, it was

arranged for woodwinds, piano, and cello and played by the Emory Woodwind Ensemble.[6]

After considering performers of Western classical music who are ethnomusicologists, either as anthropologists or musicologists, I decided to
do some other research. Having taught our Anthropology and the Arts
class in the fall of 1999, right before retirement, I suspected I had at least
some work to do to update myself on developments in this area, especially
when adding music in American religious studies to the picture. Surprisingly, it turned out to be relatively minimal, although I did enjoy reread-
ing some earlier favourites and catching up on some new works (Becker
2004; Holzapfel 2006; Koskoff 2001; Levine and Gray 2001; Royce
2004; Saliers 2006; Turner 1987; Venbrux, Rosi, and Welsch 2006).

To date, in ethnomusicology very little work has been done on church
music and church musicians in western European cultural settings. Now,
with the advent of interest in popular music, we are slowly beginning to
see discussions of contemporary Christian music at our national meetings.[7] But to date, there are few publications about church music beyond
studies, albeit interesting and well done, and with a long history in ethnomusicology, of hymnody among various Native American groups.[8]
Hymnody is also a major concern in many issues of the *American Organist*, and in the Bohlman, Blumhofer, and Chow (2006) volume. Yes, there
is *much* to be said and done about hymns—their histories, transmissions,
introduction and disappearance, role in ethnic identity, the production of
hymnals in specific denominations, the stories of their revisions over time,
the struggles over change that ensued, the resulting hybridity, syncretism,
pluralism in textual and musical aspects; and successful techniques to use
when introducing new hymns in today's world where simpler times, when
church and social life were more coterminous, are gone. It's all fascinating and calls for field studies, documentation, deconstruction, thick description, or what have you. But there continues to be very little attention to
the performers of church music, beyond the studies of a few well-chosen
contemporary preachers, gospel groups, and the like.

The review of three years of *American Organist*[9] was both professionally stimulating and, at times, also a source of humour. For example, in a
2005 issue, an entry (Anonymous 2005) on "The Last Page" reminded
readers that most females in asylums in 1915 were organists; the link was
that devoting all of one's time to religious matters led to insanity.[10] Perhaps most important was the October 2004 report of the American Guild
of Organists (AGO) membership survey (American Organist 2004). Surveyors wanted to learn how many members worked full-time and how

many had other jobs. The results showed two groups. The high end, pure members were the full-time church musicians who were working in big churches with decent salaries for their work with choirs, ensembles, instrumentalists, handbells, liturgical drama, dance, as well as organ work and expected recitals, or all of that plus teaching organ and maybe one music history or theory class at a nearby college or university. The rest, by far most of those responding, were part-timers, "wannabes," or, perhaps, "have beens and don't want to be anymores." These were organists who did something else full-time and worked as organists on the side. AGO surveyors expected to find lawyers and educators at all levels in this group, which they did. But they also found organists who were health care workers, architects, installers of septic systems, cowgirls, professional engineers, accountants, MBAs, heads of Fortune 500 companies, embalmers, airline pilots, and long-haul truckers. The part-timers were said to be usually successful at technical pursuits, perhaps mirroring their attraction to the organ, a complex instrument itself. Today, most church organists are in the second group. Just how the AGO and other groups will address this reality and the problems it is already causing—reflected in fewer viable graduate degree programs in church music, organ performance, and so forth—remains to be seen.

As my reading came to an end, many of the articles in *American Organist* remained important, as did the edited Bohlman, Blumhofer, and Chow (2006) volume. Both Judith Gray[11] and Phil Bohlman, SEM colleagues, contributed to this volume, a work important for anyone interested in current work on music in the American religious experience. Other thought-provoking sources included Dissanayake's essay in Brown and Volgsten (2006), and two works by Richard Anderson (2000, 2004), an anthropologist interested in the arts in culture.

In addition to these resources, continuing conversations with colleagues and friends both in church music and SEM were also important sources of inspiration. Within SEM, I knew I could talk with at least three colleagues: Phil Bohlman, Judith Gray, and Rich Haefer. Conversations in spring 2006 with Phil, who is himself an organist, revealed that he was going to the Yale Institute for Sacred Music in the fall, and was already thinking about some of the questions I posed. He agreed that there had yet to be any concerted co-operation between ethnomusicologists and theologians, or any strong bibliographical work that would yield the kind of resource list I was hoping to have on hand as a guide when preparing to write this chapter.[12] Judith, who is a long-term choir member, said that probably many others in SEM were choir members, but chose not to report

that. Rich, who continues to direct a mixed choir and the men's scola for
the Traditional Latin mass at Mater Misericordiae Mission in Phoenix,
edits and arranges choral music, and has authored articles on chants of
Compline and Pentecost, and Gregorian chant; he is currently working
on a book on Latin hymns in postmodern hymnals (Haefer 2005–06).
Rich reported not knowing any other ethnomusicologists with church
jobs, perhaps because they were too busy, or perhaps because they were
not attuned to Western religions unless they were of the folksong type. He
also said that perhaps if there were, they felt they had to hide these interests from others in SEM. Those comments, like Judith's, are interesting
observations that are clearly worth pursuing.[13] The issues, of course, relate
to the fact that religious scholarship in the United States is sectarian and
denominationalist. In music scholarship, we separate religious music from
religious experience, and constantly tread lightly, carefully walking a
tightrope, worrying about the separation of church and state, while in
some cases, almost paralyzed by fears of not being politically correct. Perhaps these are among the reasons that religious music becomes just music
and, for many, fades from view. It is worth wondering whether the picture
will change in the near future, given the contemporary charismatic evan-
gelical Christian music movements that continue to gather steam in America. These movements involve "popular music," or "praise and worship
songs" composed and performed in pop-song styles, with electric guitars
and synthesizers, as well as much physical movement. Since students of
American popular culture have already started examining the movement's
associated materialism (McDannell 1995), perhaps ethnomusicologists
will follow their lead. Perkins's (2006) study of the commodification of the
praise and worship song movement may indicate that this has already
started.

Before turning to "my story," I should note that I have retained the
etic/emic frame used in our 1991 American Anthropological Association
session. I do so with reservations, most certainly. Since the original excitement in the early 1960s about doing anthropology by using this model,
borrowed from Kenneth Pike's 1954 linguistic concepts of phonetic and
phonemic, many of us jumped on the bandwagon of cognitive anthropology, ethnoscience, ethnography of speaking, or whatever else it was called.
Enthusiasm for culture as a mental map and a mental phenomenon continued into the 1980s, and in ethnomusicology, at least through some
1992 annual meeting panels. Then some started abandoning ship, turning to the French structuralism of Claude Lévi-Strauss, the symbolism of
Victor Turner and others, or to other directions, all of which were even-

tually consumed by postmodernism with its deconstruction, head bash-
ing, discussions of the right ways to write, and on and on. In the course
of it all, the constant binary opposites, dualistic thought, either/or
approaches, and all of the dichotomies we inherited from the Western
Enlightenment and used in our work, including: insider/outsider,
public/private, nature/nurture, stratified/non-stratified, oppressed/oppres-
sor, subjective/objective, self/other, emic/etic, and Native/non-Native
started to be dissected and re-examined. The same was true of static
boundaries on maps, given population flux, border crossings and re-cross-
ings, and all the other fluid realities in today's world. None of these
boundaries or binary opposites reflects the complexities of lived experience in today's world. They are overly reductive, limiting, simplistic, and
while useful for some purposes, overall serve as blinders on our thinking
and research efforts.

The anthropological literature in the past two decades has been full of
wonderful discussions about who is Native, when, why, and according to
whom. Then there are the discussions about the moral rights of insiders/out-
siders, the costs and gains of each set of views, and their connections to
the continuing need to decolonialize anthropology. For example, do cultural outsiders have any contribution to make, or should insiders be privileged because of their superior understandings, intuition, moral rights, or
knowledge of things that are clear only to insiders? If insiders are privileged, what roles should be left open to outsiders? Interpretation? Anything?
The spirit of some of those questions, and others such as: Is emic/etic a
dichotomy or really a continuum? Isn't etic a kind of emic? and so forth,
is reflected in Rice (1997, 104–19), who suggests that the researching and
researched selves are potentially interchangeable and capable of change
through dialogues that typify fieldwork experiences.[14] His solution, based
on his transformative experiences in Bulgaria while learning to play the
Bulgarian bagpipe, rests on the proposal of hermeneutical arcs to medi-
ate between the oppositions, such as field methods and field experience,
from pre-understandings to new understandings. Perhaps one of the most
attractive aspects of his suggestion is that the arcs recognize and under-
score an anthropological truism: like cultures, all individuals are always
changing. As people change, they give cultural practices new meanings,
and they evolve new senses of self, community, and the world, whether
they are from within or outside a particular place. The ideal approach to
understanding any aspect of the global world today and its people would,
of course, be through research methodologies that acknowledged and
accommodated the constant flux, required true collaboration in the entire

ethnographic enterprise, and incorporated the contributions possible from both points of view, be they emic or etic.

Whether we want to shed models based on dichotomies and binary opposites or not, they are deeply ingrained in the West, including in the arts. One of the consequences we need to remember is that here in the United States, we Westerners remain deeply ambivalent about the arts. As Anderson (2004) has shown, this positive/negative dialectic is an integrating theme in Western aesthetics, just as pervasive in vernacular aesthetics as in theories focused in so-called fine arts. As Nettl (2002, 69) has reminded us, it is typically American to be ambivalent toward music. For some anthropologists, historically this has meant avoiding music while studying other aspects of culture. For others, it means that music is both desired and feared; one doesn't discuss it unless one is a professional. The musician, as a person, is "simultaneously wanted and avoided." And, according to Nettl (2002, 69), that person "gets away with behavior not generally tolerated, perhaps as a person with unconventional dress, hair style, sexual mores, language."

In summary, this chapter draws from many sources as well as from my own personal experiences as a church organist and those of other organist friends. While I have not interviewed the latter group in any systematic way, they were asked to read and comment on an earlier version of the chapter. It is timely in that it deals with music in our own culture, one of the so-called new directions in ethnomusicology. More importantly, it is a response to Bohlman's (2006a, 239) call for information about the individual musician in the American religious experience, something he wants to emphasize to get at the "dialectics of selfness and otherness, private and public worship, individual beliefs and community cohesion" in American religious experience. Bohlman (2006a, 237) states that the individual and his or her musical voice is largely absent in the historiography of American religious experience, being replaced by congregational song and denominational experiences. However, Bohlman (2006a, 240) now finds that there is new interest among American church historians in the individual and personal practices of music. So, this is one voice beginning to speak. Yes, it's a woman's voice, but it makes no claim to represent all women organists, let alone all organists in all denominations in America. It also does nothing to address other aspects of "otherness," some of which have now become so problematic for a number of American churches.

My Own Story

Like many artists in Anderson's (2000) study, my interest in church music can be traced back to childhood. Growing up in a family that was both musical and regularly involved with a New England Congregational church, early on I started piano and then violin and flute lessons. At church, I began in the children's choir and then moved through the age-graded groups of youth choir, junior high, and high school choirs. Organ lessons began in junior high school as one of the benefits of my father's friendship with Ernest M. Skinner of the Skinner Organ company. Mr. Skinner came to our town to install a Skinner pipe organ in our church, and stayed with us during the times he needed to be on site. One of the consequences was my father's purchase of a used, parlor-size Skinner organ, which he installed in his study, with the understanding that I would learn to play it. I had become fascinated with the organ in our church once I began lessons, and the organist there had promised that once I was "good enough" and "knew what I was doing," he'd be glad to have me substitute for him on Sundays. Looking back now, I realize that he, of course, had no substitute. With this beginning, I started doing substitute work in high school, most often but not always in my own church. I continued those jobs, now and then, in college, but after high school, organ lessons did not resume until I was in graduate school at Wesleyan.

Since then, *excluding* stints as substitute organist and interim organist, to date, I have worked as a "real organist" four different times. The first was a two-year period as organist/choir director in a Methodist church in Portland, Connecticut, while working on my M.A. in ethnomusicology at Wesleyan. This was followed by an eight-year hiatus during which I played only for weddings and funerals in a variety of Catholic and Protestant churches in New Mexico, Arizona, and then Illinois. In that period I finished my Ph.D. in anthropology, got married, had one daughter, and moved twice. My second real organist experience was a six-year stint, again as organist/choir director, in a Lutheran church in Carpenter, Illinois, a church associated with the Missouri synod. When that job started, I had been teaching anthropology at Southern Illinois University, Edwardsville (SIUE), for two years, we had moved to a farm down the road from the church, and our second and last daughter had just been born. In 1978, I left that job for a variety of reasons; besides the change in clergy, I wanted our children in a different church setting, one that I shopped for according to its music program, among other things.

For the next four years, I participated in church music as a choir member (again), and as a substitute organist. When both key people left that music program, I began working as "interim organist" during the ensuing searches for replacements. From 1982 to 1986, I did this three times in this Edwardsville, Illinois, United Church of Christ (UCC) church with three-month, three-month, and eight-month jobs following the resignations of three more organists. Then I played handbells there for two years while continuing to do weddings, a few funerals, and some substitute work there and in other churches in the area, both Protestant and Catholic. In 1989, I accepted an organist job in another UCC church in Highland, Illinois, a large one with 1,500 members, where a good friend of mine was director of music ministries. I remained there until 1996, when I was eligible for what became my last sabbatical from SIUE and decided to take a whole year off at half pay in order to complete a book that had been "in process" for too long. Both the director of music ministries and I resigned from that church at the same time, and the reasons went beyond the timing of my approved sabbatical.

Upon returning, I went back to playing handbells and doing occasional weddings and funerals as an organist, as well as some substitute work in both Catholic and Protestant churches in the area. However, mentally it was clear to me that I needed a break from being tied down every Sunday and two nights a week for rehearsals. Thus, when I retired from teaching, I did not immediately think about finding another church job. I wasn't sure I wanted another one ever again. We wanted to travel, and I had some ongoing research projects that would necessitate more fieldwork. Neither meshed with having a church job. Then, too, almost immediately, I became a grandmother, and that also increased my interests in being free on weekends.

However, about two years into retirement, even though I was again playing handbells, it was clear to me in my soul that I missed church organist work. So, when I was called by a search committee from a small UCC church in Glen Carbon, Illinois, and told they were looking for someone who wanted a part-time job playing their new electronic organ, I said I would consider it. The part-time nature of the job was actually its main attraction. Like some other small churches these days, the congregation wanted to rotate between piano and organ music, and thus have both a pianist and an organist on staff. While ordinarily this would be a detriment to a church organist, to me, then, it was a blessing. I have now been there for seven years, and while it's far from the perfect job and is very frustrating to me musically, I will stay at least for the foreseeable future. For one thing, it helped me to complete my Social Security credits, which were close to being finished, but not done when I retired from SIUE, which is not a Social Security institution. Then too, I, enjoy most of the people in the congregation, and its laid-back atmosphere. In some ways, it's the opposite of my last job: there are no choirs of any kind and there is only one service most weeks. My biggest regret is that there is also no beautiful three-manual Wicks pipe organ to play. As usual, the job includes weddings and funerals upon request. The pianist and I arrange our own schedule since we both travel professionally. The guiding principle is that we play an equal number of regular and special services during the year, and we do not leave the congregation stranded on Sundays.

In June 2009, while this chapter was in press, I was approached by a larger UCC Church, Troy, Illinois, about another part-time organist job when one of their two organists resigned and moved. After observing a service and trying out their organ (another Wicks pipe organ), I submitted my resumé. An audition and interview followed, and then a job offer, which I accepted. On 19 July, I began working there as part of their musical staff. Job requirements and scheduling are the same but may change in the future, since the church has two bell choirs and an adult choir. Meanwhile, as per agreement, I also continue to play part-time in Glen Carbon until that congregation finds a replacement.

My case is *not* one of etic becoming emic. As noted above, I grew up with music, playing instruments, singing in church choirs all along, and starting organ lessons in junior high. In college I continued singing, was a music honours major, gave a senior recital on piano, and went to Europe during the summer of 1961 with a small, exclusive singing group. All of those experiences made up the emic base to which different organist job experiences have been added, each of which has caused me to expand and rethink my emic understandings and perspectives. Anthropology, the etic perspective, got added later. While it appears that I now have both emic and etic options, I don't think I can offer an etic view of church organists because I'm too involved in the job from the inside. Do I have the only emic view around? No, each organist has her or his own. Is it possible to study your own culture, your own job or profession? I think so. Do we also need perspectives from non-organists when trying to understand our jobs, roles, significance, and other questions? I would argue *yes*! But while you can find people who have never played the organ, one has to remember that even organists have varied experiences, participating in church music to varying degrees and at different times in their lives and careers. Would the level of participation and whether or not it was current affect how they answered potential questions? I don't know that we've tried to find out yet. In reference to any pool of etic views, I think in our culture, especially in a church congregation, one would be hard pressed to find people to talk with who had absolutely no experience with music, religious or otherwise. But then I would also argue that the emic/etic distinction, while interesting as a tool, is not particularly productive. People's understandings of "the truth," the "world," or first and second jobs are based on their own experiences and viewpoints. Like cultures, people change; nothing is static, and flux—the norm—is the challenge! Should we not be searching to understand each other through dialogues that empower all people, rather than perpetuating another Western either/or box, or dichotomy with emic/etic?

Why Do This?

Reflecting on why I have worked as an organist at different times of my life and career, and why I continue to do so has suggested that a few of Anderson's (1989, 84–155) ideas about what motivates artists apply to my case. The intangible motivators of prestige and potentially high social standing are non-existent, and only rarely have I been heir to the kind of emotional satisfaction that derives from connections between the arts and the supernatural realm. So then, why do it?

For me, part of it is an attraction to the instrument, the major voice of church music for over five centuries, and still the king of the instruments. I'm not personally attracted to church pipe organs according to church architecture, location of organ, or design and manner of installation in the sanctuary. What attracted me from the beginning was the unending variety of sounds, colours, and textures that one can create with it. For some, it's the power inherent in these sounds. For me, it's more of an association between the diversity of sounds and their metaphorical connection with hope, joy, praise, prayer, belief. As one organist said, the organ expresses "the songs in your heart that must be sung." And yes, sometimes, but only sometimes, performing on such an instrument enables you to transcend your normal, everyday existence, and connect with something higher. Call it a great spirit, God, the Ultimate, or whatever. It does happen, but I can never predict when. It certainly does *not* happen if you are worried about what you are playing for the Postlude, if your back hurts, or if your mind has been cluttered once again with church politics, choir problems, or necessarily focused on other details that frequently "hit the fan" on early Sunday mornings.

While the sixty-five artists Anderson (2000) interviewed during his work on the arts in America (13 percent of whom were associated with the sacred arts such as church music and preaching) saw their talent as coming from God, their families, or nature, I am among those organists who see God as responsible for the gift of any musical talents they possess. Such a gift requires development, as far as I have always been concerned. One is also obligated to share the talents and, as it were, give back the gift. With such a belief, it is not strange that like others, I feel a strong bond between working as a church organist and my own self; it's part of being me, and has been since junior high school.

I also love playing the organ because even practising gives me a chance to "unhook." Here, I am talking about an emotional escape, a release, a chance to find inner balance, peace, or sanity. Organ music can profoundly affect my emotions. And I have learned that if I am really disciplined, and master techniques required for pieces I love to play, performing them in church can actually bring about a sense of disconnect, or freedom from everything else. If all really goes well, I can achieve, in my soul, a feeling of closeness with Heaven or the Divine. Such a feeling becomes a goal; it does not depend on critiques of one's performance by the choir, other staff members, or the congregation. And for me, it is also both unpredictable and, sadly, rare.

There are many other reasons I enjoy being a church organist. Some include:

- the chance to continue participating in music-making, most often at the keyboard, but sometimes as a substitute singer for a cappella numbers, a bell ringer, instrumentalist, or even as a substitute choral director
- the chance to continue exploring musical literature, build repertoires, and discover other composers while continuing to learn and grow
- the chance to continue to be creative, to compose, and to improvise
- the mental stimulation and challenge of regular practising, learning, and rehearsing music; keeping technical problem-solving skills active; maintaining ambidexterity in both hands and feet, and constantly keeping all four coordinated with the brain
- the opportunities for expanding personal networks, both social and professional
- the chance to do something therapeutic that helps me keep the rest of my life in balance and a healthy perspective on jobs, employers, deadlines, or other sources of worry and tension. Many of my anthropological friends who play music, paint, sculpt, make jewelry, or work with

fabric talk about doing what they do, not because the result is art but because it is soothing, balancing, calming. I, too, sometimes "work things out" while practising, and when performances go well, I do feel the intangible that Anderson (1989, 100) calls "pleasure"

- opportunities for continuing adult education through summer classes, workshops, camps, seminars, concerts by well-known organists preceded or followed by discussion groups, and other formats; such larger, non-local groups give organists a chance to discuss internal issues, denominational issues, performance concerns, repertoire questions, and national issues, and provide other sources of support
- self-identity as not only an anthropologist, ethnomusicologist, teacher, researcher, author, wife, mother, sister, grandmother, aunt, sheep farmer, and community volunteer but also a music-maker and a church organist
- the chance to fulfill a life goal, which was to work where there was a very fine, well-maintained pipe organ, and a respectable music program directed by a good friend who was also an excellent musician, a sensitive human being, and who knew how to teach people to make excellent music
- a job that entails very few expenses; these might include a church calendar planning book, organist copy of the hymnals in use, and possibly new organ shoes and new music. But they definitely will include transportation to and from the job for practising, rehearsals, and services.

The Other Side of the Coin: The Frustrations

Since no job is perfect, it should be no surprise that being a church organist also brings its own problems. How unique these are I do not know. How denominationally specific these may be, I also do not know. Let me just list a few drawbacks that come readily to mind:

- The pay is always poor or, as some say, non-existent. Struggles over pay are common, with some congregations going so far as to suggest that you ought to be willing to use your talents to glorify God without charge. While the paycheque may give you Social Security credits, it will not put bread on the table for very long, nor will it make a dent in sending a daughter or son to college.
- In a full-time job, there are few or no free weekends. It is rare to have a readily available substitute with appropriate musical abilities within the congregation.

- The job is stressful. There is often a big workload coupled with even larger expectations. The peaks, of course, come during holidays, during Advent leading to Christmas, or during Lent through Holy Week and Easter. Other stressors may include performances of children's musicals and the like.
- It is not uncommon to have no teamwork among clerical people, music people, office individuals, or others. Often there are real staff communication problems; sometimes there are issues of power and game playing. Occasionally there is just plain disdain and nastiness on the part of "those of the cloth" toward those in music, especially the lowly organist.[15] You may be treated as if you are invisible. If the organ is out of sight of the congregation, you will also be physically invisible, which you may or may not find to be a good thing. There are many other things that can make working conditions oppressive besides actual personalities of co-workers. To name only two: denominational rules about participating in communion, and joining the church as an employee.
- Playing the organ is hard work. You are not born with the skills, and to acquire them takes years of lessons and dedicated, regular practice. Do not be surprised by congregational members who think anybody can play the organ because "it's just like the piano."
- Unlike other instruments, pipe organs are not portable and most people do not own one. Thus, you have to travel to practise sites, and using the organ, once you get there, can easily become a real problem. You will find yourself at the mercy of the schedule outlined in the church bulletin, and of the janitors, painters, youth groups, and others who need to be in the sanctuary. Even if you have a regularly scheduled practise time, it may be superseded by someone else's needs without notice or consultation. You may end up practising when others are asleep. Also, the conditions in the sanctuary may reflect the church budget, weather, both, or other factors. You may be in a freezing cold building or one that is overly hot. Hopefully you will have access to appropriate lighting and security if you practise at night.
- Frequently you have to fight to get approval for a service call for repairing, tuning, or other matters unless you are blessed with a caring, educated music committee or comparable group. Otherwise, it's typical to be told: "It sounds okay to me. We don't need to call anyone." "Nobody around here can tell the difference anyway, so why should we waste the money?" "It all sounds the same to me anyway." "Don't worry about it; it doesn't matter." "Nobody else hears anything wrong with it. Maybe it's just your ears."

- Often, there is next to no feedback, although you might be told that something was "too loud for my hearing aid" or "that piece you played in the beginning was too gloomy." When you know there are people in the congregation with musical knowledge and experience, lack of feedback can be very frustrating.
- The challenges of aging need to be mentioned. These may include: arthritis in your hands, neck, fingers, feet, or knees; changes in eyesight that require glasses for reading music from the organ bench; back and neck problems as discs disintegrate; and for some, but thankfully not for me yet, hearing loss or tinnitus. Some of these can be temporarily held at bay with creams, hot packs, special cushions, special shoes, and special glasses, but sooner or later, one may have to retire if one's body can no longer do what it has learned to do while playing the music correctly. When pain, stiff joints, and other concerns add more stress, it will be impossible to enjoy what you are doing or, I dare say, get anything out of the liturgical end of the service, either.

How Does Being an Anthropologist Enrich Being a Church Organist?

While there are many answers to this question, let me emphasize just a few. Over the years, I have found that certain anthropological skills can be particularly helpful in church jobs. The people skills are basic as they are in any job. Also useful are the abilities to observe analytically, what is going on, both verbally and non-verbally, to think holistically (beyond the particulars of music analysis), to listen effectively, to identify structural and other problems, and to participate in, or lead brainstorming sessions about, problem resolutions. Sometimes the ability to ask questions, especially in the beginning when new to a scene, can get festering issues out in the open and on the table. For example, are discussions underway about improving acoustics in the sanctuary? Would removal of carpet, curtains, or a relocation of the organ help? Do people in the congregation have favourite composers of organ music or, more generally, church music? (Do people see J.S. Bach as the only meaningful option, or are they interested in others, be these Widor, Wesley, or composers whose works may be less familiar?) Who chooses the hymns? Do people want a brief introduction to congregational responses to prayers, offerings, or scripture readings? What do people want in terms of introductions to the hymns to be sung? Are there any other musicians in the congregation? Would they be interested in being included in the music-making during the service? What is the role of the organist according to members of the congregation, the church council, the executive committee, the clergy, other musicians either on staff or participating as volunteers (e.g., in choirs)? How do people define their expectations of what happens during the three major places when an organist can contribute to the service—the Prelude, the Offertory, and the Postlude? Is there a special Thanksgiving service? Is current praxis satisfying the needs of the congregation for worship during special holidays in the church calendar, such as Holy Week, Good Friday, Easter, Thanksgiving, Advent, Christmas, Pentecost, or other times? Has the congregation ever been surveyed about these things? Recently? Are there any issues related to church music that the congregation would like to discuss with or hear discussed by the organist, with or without the clergy? Is there interest in discussing biblical references to why we sing? Is there any interest in exploring hymn settings of familiar, frequently used congregational responses? The questions, as you can tell, can go on and on.

What Is the Job All About?

To demonstrate the use of an anthropologist's analytical skills in a church organist's job, let's consider what the job is really all about. Particular expectations will be discussed in job interviews, and hopefully most, if not all, will be known before contracts are signed. But behind those discussions are other understandings, at least on the part of church organists, and it is those shared understandings in organist culture that I now want to examine.

Most organists, I am certain, expect to contribute to the overall experience of worship through music. They expect to support the message of the service through their choices of music, and the performance of that music. Most, I think, also expect to support the ecumenical interests of the denomination either openly, or more indirectly, such as by quietly showcasing works by women composers, new composers, composers from other countries, or music from other cultural traditions. Throughout the service, they hope to project a sense of welcome, encourage group singing, and foster what some would call a sense of awe, delight, and beauty, or what others call a sense of authentic worship. Many organists understand they have a unique role to play in affecting moods and shaping behaviours. Through their efforts, the overall experience of worship can become more effective. Music can and often does bring relief from pain and anxiety; it nurtures worshippers, promotes co-operation, feeds spirits, and nourishes souls. Music can also foster hope about enlightening humans and moving them toward actions that address world problems such as abuse, hunger, marginalization, discrimination, closed borders. As such, one could say that music is capable of bringing about changes in the world. Do church organists, like priests, pastors, or other religious leaders, convey social or political messages? I guess one would have to do an ethnography of church organists and their culture to know. Anderson's (2000, 2004) work with artists shows that what really moves you stays with you. It is quite clear that sacred music, as an example of the diversity of arts found in America, satisfies two of the four artistic paradigms Anderson identified in America: the instrumental one of being capable of making a place better; and the emotionalist one of affecting the emotions of individuals and audiences.

Our job focuses on three parts of the worship service most Sundays, in addition to the three or more hymns many churches use during worship, various responses, and whatever other music is expected during communion. The three are the Prelude, Offertory, and Postlude. For many of us, the Prelude is a time when the organist should draw the people in the congregation away from their worldly cares, out of their everyday worlds and experiences, and help them enter extraordinary states in preparation for worship. The music should encourage them to become prayerful and meditative. The Prelude is a time for reflection, quiet, and preparation for the group activity of worship that will follow—that of singing hymns, hearing scripture, praying together, reciting other statements of belief, hearing sermons, homilies, or messages, and sometimes also sharing in communion. It is the time to be drawn into thoughts about the larger world and how it could become a better place, thoughts about peace and the Divine. As one writer said, it should enable individuals to locate themselves on the sacred landscape. The Prelude should not have to compete with loud talking in the sanctuary, or attempt to cover up or accompany conversations.

The Offertory should continue the mood established for the service, providing continuity during the collection and presentation of gifts. The Postlude should be uplifting, signifying the end of worship, and the return to the world once again. Some churches encourage those attending to stay and listen to the Postlude to complete their worship experience. In any case, throughout, the organist should be leading the people in worship and ministering to the congregation, nurturing all who are there, including the clergy. Church organists can help people receive that much needed grace that empowers them to do unselfish acts. Their music can feed spirits and nourish souls while ultimately bringing worshippers closer to direct contact with the Divine, the transcendent.

The other main part of the job is *hymn playing*.[16] In today's American culture, where many are afraid to sing, or are timid about their abilities, it is even more important than before, when lusty hymn singing was common, that the organist plays the hymns in ways that encourage people to participate. Hymns need to be introduced so that the people who are present can grasp the tune or its setting. They need to be played slowly enough so the words can be understood and, hopefully, also contemplated. But at the same time, they need to be played with energy, projecting the metre while breathing with the singers (which automatically enhances the text), and promoting confidence and a warm welcome to one and all to join in the group singing. As hymns are introduced, the organist should make it clear that she will be leading enjoyable, metrical singing by the corporate group.

Hymns, as well as other church music, can be viewed as metaphors for hope, longing, prayer, loving, and belief. They are the songs in your heart to be sung, and the atmosphere created by the organist should make people want to release those songs. In Protestant churches, I think it's safe to say they are songs of faith to be sung wholeheartedly, but they are also songs of an individual, self-reflective faith. Hymns are also viewed by many as sung prayers and sources of unification. As St. Augustine reportedly said, "Those who sing pray twice."[17]

Another way in which anthropology enriches work as a church organist derives from the diversity of anthropological knowledge. A socio-cultural anthropologist has acquired a broad, cross-cultural perspective on religion in culture, religious personages, proselytizing religions, denominational differences in commitments to global ecumenical interests, sexism in religion, gender issues in religion, broader questions about the future of the species and the planet, the biology of music-making, aging and its effect on the bodies of singers, bell ringers, choral directors, and organists, and all kinds of other things, including the constancy of cultural change. You can use this knowledge in countless ways in staff discussions about the use of inclusive language in worship, in choosing to perform works by women composers to combat the idea that Bach's music is all there is for the organ, and to add humour to rehearsals or difficult working conditions. If you are also trained as an ethnomusicologist, you can do a lot, either overtly or covertly, to remind people of the multicultural world in which we live.

At present, perhaps the most pressing problem in many congregations is what is often labelled "contemporary versus traditional Christian music." As some churches add contemporary services in an attempt to maintain and

expand memberships in this increasingly secular world, the music associated with worship also changes. The organ, hymnals, and old traditional
songs vanish and are replaced by praise and worship (P & W) songs, mod-
elled on spiritual-pop influences and associated with individual "stars."
Proponents see the new scene as "participatory music." Believers stand in
huge auditoriums reading lyrics from multiple overhead screens, swaying
and clapping to amplified sounds, mainly percussive accompaniments for
star vocals. Sometimes participants focus on humming or lip synching, as
electric guitars and synthesizers reign supreme. Their physical movements,
usually labelled "spontaneous," are often viewed as proof and demonstration of their deep devotion. Obviously, this movement, with its wide appeal
to the masses, gives rise to material pop religious art items that can be
marketed, rock star charts, and a huge P & W industry. And, unless organists can adapt and play "keyboard" or something else now relevant, their
services are no longer needed.[18]

In addition to the anthropological skills and knowledge that an organist possesses and can apply to discussions of the praise and worship movement, you can also contribute an understanding of effective interdisciplinary
dialogue. As an artist, you already have interdisciplinary experience; you
know the problems that get in the way of effective dialogue such as stereotypes, personal and historical baggage, or the use of jargon to exclude others. In church settings, as in many others, you are dealing with bureaucracies
filled with specialized experts who have different agendas such as saving
souls, expanding memberships, getting new buildings and parking lots,
getting into big business through nursing and retirement homes or child
and/or adult daycare operations, comforting the sick and bereaved, making worship meaningful to all age groups, getting out of the red, or building empires. Financial managers, pastors, directors of music and arts
programs, ministers of music, directors of Christian education, and so
forth don't always do a good job of talking with each other. Sometimes you
can help.

As an anthropologist, you probably can contribute many other, more
specific skills. For example, you know something about linguistics, the
differences between sung and spoken speech, different dialects, and how
to pronounce words in Latin, Spanish, French, German, and possibly other
languages. You know how to write program notes of varying lengths, present information to audiences during concerts with a microphone while
instrumentalists, choral groups, soloists, or others are rearranging themselves. You are acutely aware of the importance of thanking donors and
supporters in public ways that satisfy human needs for recognition. As a

"people watcher," you also know how to "read" audience behaviours, including restlessness, children's boredom, and the like, and how to get everyone back on the same page.

How Does Being a Church Organist Enrich Being an Anthropologist?

To reverse the question, let me briefly consider how being a church organist enriches being an anthropologist. Two, very direct, fieldwork-related examples are available from my own experience. On two different occasions, being an organist helped me find accommodations while working in parts of the Navajo reservation where I had not yet established contacts. Of course, there were trade-offs for room and board, and yes, they included fulfilling the usual performance expectations of church organists, in one case during the week as well as on Sundays. But among the positive results both times was gaining access to a place I could use as a base of operations, a problem I needed to solve in order to proceed with fieldwork.[19]

In addition to those situations, my organist jobs have enriched my professional anthropological work in a number of other ways. First, they provide me with unending data to use in professional conversations. While teaching, the examples provided rich material in a variety of socio-cultural classes. In language and culture, for instance, you have: church-based battles over inclusive language, the use of titles and other forms of address among staff, the whole phenomenon of ritual talk—sermonese, the role of joking and storytelling in ritual settings, and so forth. In classes dealing with gender studies or contemporary American culture, among the major, perhaps most divisive issues now, especially if a congregation is not caught up in the contemporary versus traditional Christian music battle mentioned earlier, is that of homosexual church leaders, be these priests, pastors, ministers, youth directors, organists, choir leaders, or others. Discussions are heated in many so-called mainline denominations, and some old, well-established congregations, dioceses, or parishes, always part of national umbrella groups, are debating splits or have already left these groups because of disagreements with decisions made by their national leaders during assemblies, diocesan conventions, or conferences. Besides potential splits, the issue has already affected church employees, and yes, often those in music. Even locally, examples abound, and during the past three years, our newspapers, like others, have been filled with reports of these traumas (see, for example, Associated Press 2006a, 2006b; *Belleville*

News Democrat 2006, *New York Times* 2007). Now it has become almost predictable, at least in some denominations, that anyone who reveals a gay identity will have their employment in the church terminated. This has already included ministers of music, organists, choir directors, artistic directors, and others, in many cases individuals who have been working in church music for years before they revealed or acknowledged their sexual orientation. While many of the reports have focused on the Catholic Church, which views homosexuality as a "disorder" and whose priests are expected to take a vow of celibacy and publicly agree with the Church's position, Catholicism is not alone. The issue has many names, from same-sex marriage resolutions to gender equality, gay relationships, or equal marriage rights for all couples. As an observer, I thought the earlier heated arguments about including women in church leadership roles represented the worst nastiness possible in church politics, but the current wars about sexual orientation and legitimacy of same-sex marriages sadly have proven me wrong.[20]

In introductory, cultural, and political anthropology classes, churches can give you examples of people communicating, struggling for power, attempting to control and manipulate, using and abusing power, joining social groups, all in addition to examples of religion, magic, ritual, and the arts in religious settings. In anthropology and the arts classes, you have examples of dancing, liturgical drama, and ritual clowning, if any of these are "allowed" as ways to make religious messages more accessible to different groups. You also may have examples of vocal and instrumental music in addition to the predictable ones of ritual clothing, architecture, symbolic paraphernalia, and so forth. You have examples of artists and, as Anderson (2000) has demonstrated, you can ask many questions, such as: What are the religious arts and who are the artists? Where do they come from, and why? As Gray (2006a) and others clearly illustrate, there is much to be learned about behind-the-scenes decision making, and the process of judging and evaluating performances.

In anthropological theory classes, where many are still dealing with postmodernism, critical reflection, dissection, and decolonializing our discipline, there are unending possibilities, not the least of which is writing chapters like this one, or considering the roles of mainline religions in colonialistic imperialism and continuing neo-colonialism. For students needing research opportunities, activities in church settings may offer rich potential. Interesting questions could include: What is really going on in handbells rehearsal, choir rehearsal, or congregational quarterly meetings? How do choir members talk about singing? What do they have to say about decision making concerning music in their church? And there are many other possibilities, such as the archaeology of a church bulletin, if you really wanted to have some fun!

Of course, among the settings ripe for deconstruction are *weddings*, as all organists know. This topic is an age-old favourite of organists, or rather, I should say, discussing weddings and swapping wedding horror stories is part of the "organist culture." Wedding jokes abound and travel around on the Internet among organists.[21] Organists save wedding bulletins to remind us of the unending quagmires we can step into with wedding music, be it pre-service, during the service, while lighting the unity candle, escorting the mothers, or what have you. Is there a policy to guide the bridal couple's choices and move them away from music heard on non-organ wedding CDs? Who wrote the policy and when? Who had input into its construction? Do you have any input into its content now that you work there? Is there anything that is deemed inappropriate when using the church, chapel, or synagogue for a wedding? Is that specific to a particular congregation, or is it broader, more denominational in nature? Among the latest additions to wedding stories that I heard from local weddings in July (2006) that, thankfully, I did not play or attend are two in which a bride's dog was in the wedding party as the ring bearer in one, and as the flower girl in the other. How can we have arrived at this point, and why is it that people can and do purchase tuxedos and flower girl outfits for their dogs? Will we ever see an end to this in American culture? Evidently not. According to Adams (2006, 10), "incorporating pets into wedding ceremonies has become this year's hottest wedding trend."

Anderson (2000, 41–58), of course, has great fun with American weddings, reminding us that as major rites of passage, our weddings potentially involve diverse and abundant arts. Studying websites, bridal magazines, services of wedding planners and consultants, and interviewing many couples engaged, newly married, married for the second time, reaffirming their vows, or whatever, he walks us through the big business of weddings in America. Among the most fascinating aspects of this rite of passage for him is that it potentially involves all art media in America: body decoration, music, theatre, oratory, architecture, dance (at receptions), and so forth.

Being a church organist while you are also an anthropologist opens the door to many potential areas of research inquiry for yourself, too, if you are attuned to studying your own culture (Laura Nader's "studying up" as it were), and even studying yourself and your colleagues. There is so much we don't know, and not just because, as Bohlman (2006a) indicates, the individual has been slighted in serious studies of American religious experiences. I dare say that most organists are aware of what they'd like to know about the congregations, the religious leadership, and the governing bodies and music committees in the churches they presently serve. All undoubtedly have lists of things they'd like to pursue when conditions make it possible. If, in the future, church organists who are also anthropologists could be identified and asked to participate in a long-term research project that would address some of the issues raised in this chapter, it might be possible to reach a better understanding of questions about the roles and expectations of organists, organists' own definitions of their jobs, the relationship between statistical information about congregations and attitudes toward the kinds and amounts of music during worship services, potential changes in church music, and all the rest. Eventually better understandings of the culture of church organists might emerge. Whether denominational differences would also become apparent is unknown, but that, too, is an interesting question.

If you are an anthropologist, especially one committed to lifelong participation in the religious arts, church organist jobs can heighten your awareness of others' talents, creativity, and needs to express themselves in the arts. You can encourage students, members of a particular congregation, other congregations, or no congregation in this direction, thereby attacking pervasive cultural ideas that champion only the stars, the greats, and the professionals. These ideas shut down creativity in others because the "I'm just not good enough" attitude becomes prevalent, which makes most people passive consumers at best. Should you discover instrumentalists in a setting in which you are working, with appropriate discussions you can usually get them included in the music-making end of the service. You may have to do some detective work to identify these people, but remember that age and actual place of residence should not exclude potential performers. Participating in the service, beyond the level of singing the hymns and congregational responses, allows people to share their own musical talents or abilities. It can also lead to improved self-esteem and feelings of self-worth, and create reasons for families to get together again, this time around the event, in church. It might lead to recruiting new members, and if you, as the instigator, see recruitment as part of your job, fine, but it doesn't have to be done with that in mind. For some, if that motive were suspected, their willingness to co-operate and contribute would vanish overnight. It may involve other requirements and extra efforts that may not be apparent at first. For example, if they insist on playing with organ accompaniment, you may need to practise one or more times before performing with such individuals. You may discover that while they do play, they don't read music, they can only play in the key of C, or they can play only a set number of religious songs with fixed personal interpretations. You may need to transpose songs, or compose interludes to weave their contributions together in a meaningful way. You may also need to provide transportation to or from rehearsal and performance sites, and spend time visiting their families, and so on. Of course, a social bond is being established; it's all part of the picture, but one that's easily forgotten when, as the organist, you are mainly focused on implementing something different during a worship service.

Finally, work as an organist, especially when you may also be composing and improvising, deepens your own understanding of the creative process, which continues to be an anthropological enigma. If all of us continue both introspection and dialogue, perhaps with time we will have something more to contribute to professional understandings of creativity. Work as a church organist can also serve as a recruitment device, not just to your university but also to your discipline. It's another way of explaining your discipline to the public, to let people know, of course, that college teachers are human beings, but also that anthropologists don't "study rocks," and that there are places in anthropology for music-makers, sculptors, weavers, potters, painter, quilters, and the like. It's also a way of demonstrating issues of professional concern, be these issues about peace, survival of the planet, parity, multiculturalism, or now, finally, multiple voices engaged in conversations from the heart as well as from the mind.

Final Thoughts

At present, being on the organ bench still works for me. I continue to be deeply interested in all of the issues connected to working and surviving in church music. Beyond those already mentioned, at present it is clear to me that the number of organists available to fill church jobs is rapidly dwindling. This is acknowledged nationally, and discussed at the American Guild of Organists and other forums, but now, even local pastors are asking their congregations for recruitment help. Just how damaging this trend will be in the future remains to be seen.[22] Part of the issue, of course, is the ever-changing nature of some of the mainline religions as they scramble to survive in our secular culture, stay culturally relevant, and meet everyone's needs. In the latter group may be people seeking contemporary worship formats however these are defined. For some, maybe the format entails Christian rock music bands. For others, it might be praise and shout choirs, praise and worship artists. Maybe it means all song or mainly song-filled services with severe reductions of "the word." In any case, in such settings, the organ is almost always absent. Personally, I hope that there continues to be a place for the glorious church music of earlier centuries as well as for new compositions for both choirs and organists. But that's my bias, and I have no crystal ball.

I've been at this long enough to know that music is part of me, has been almost since my earliest memories, and that music, especially church music, enriches my life. I am happiest when I am part of church music-making, and obviously, my favourite role is that of a church organist. Serving in a variety of church settings over the years has made me a more perceptive and, I hope, a more effective anthropologist. Simultaneously, bringing the viewpoints and knowledge acquired in that discipline to my church jobs has increased my fascination not only with life as a church organist or church music as one of the religious arts in America, but also with the arts and the lives of musicians and other artists around the world.

Notes

1   I would like to thank the following colleagues for their willingness to read and critique one or more earlier versions of this chapter, or to discuss some of the topics it addresses: Joann W. Kealiinohomoku (2005–06), J. Richard Haefer (2005–06), Philip Bohlman (2006b), Stephen Wild (2006), Richard Anderson (2006), Judith Gray (2006b, John Coghill (2005–08), Audrey Deeren (2005–08), and Patricia Newman (2005–08). After submitting this chapter in 2006, I had the opportunity to present a different and shorter version as the 2006 Bruno and Wanda Nettl Lecture at the School of Music, University of Illinois on 9 October 2006. My understanding is that Beverley was the second lecturer in this series, and I was the sixth. I set the mood at the outset by playing a recording of the "Final" from Louis Vierne's Organ Symphony no. 1 (1899), and illustrated the presentation by using overheads of some of my favourite organist cartoons. My sincere thanks to the School of Music for the invitation, to those who helped with the arrangements, and to all who participated in the lively discussion that followed the presentation. I have incorporated some of the comments into these endnotes. Currently (2008), I continue to work as an organist, to remain interested in the topic, and to follow developments in all of the numerous related areas. For examples, see WashingtonPost.com (2007), *Belleville News Democrat* (2006), and the *New York Times* (2007).

2   After the fiftieth anniversary conference of SEM in Atlanta (November 2005), some of us raised questions about anthropologists in ethnomusicology, and Dan Neuman and I, later in November 2005, decided (via round robin emails) to construct a master list thereof. I soon discovered that the 2002 membership survey had not included this question. Dan and I constructed a partial list, but then had to table the issue because of other commitments. We plan to give it attention in the future. Nettl (2002, 62) has suggested

that the number of socio-cultural anthropologists who also call themselves ethnomusicologists is small and always has been, accounting for less than one-fifth of all ethnomusicologists. In addition to pursuing this question briefly, I also read and reread a variety of works in anthropology and ethnomusicology before writing this chapter; these are listed in the References.

3 My queries were processed through the SEM business office; I am grateful to Kimberly Marshall-Bohannon, a graduate student in anthropology and ethnomusicology at Indiana University, for her help in answering my questions.

4 Nettl's (2002, 72) list is focused on his advisees and includes Daniel Neuman, "a long-time student of violin." Dan, of course, is among anthropologists who are also ethnomusicologists.

5 The Kolinski piece was "Little Suite" (published in 1974 by Harmuse Publishers). It is worth remembering that during her doctoral work at the University of Toronto in the 1970s, Bev studied with Kolinski, among others.

6 The title of the Blacking piece is "Laat ons 'n Nuwe Loflied Sing" (Let us sing a new song of praise), with text by Faan Aucamp (dated Johannesburg, 3 January 1965).

7 For example, at the 2006 Atlanta SEM meetings, Section 1J was entitled Christian Music in Changing Societies. Section 1H, on Native Cultures in North America, included a paper on Creek and Seminole Indian Christian Hymnody (Taborn 2006); Section 2C: Music in a Variety of Christian Contexts included Selling the Sacred: Contemporary Christian Worship Music as General Market Commodity by David Horace Perkins, and finally, Section 7C was entitled Music and Dance in Christian Worship in African and African-American Societies. At the 2007 SEM meetings in Honolulu, Section 13H was entitled Negotiating Faith and Belief/Scholarship and Pedagogy: The Emerging Presence of Ethnomusicology in the Southern California Christian Academy.

8 See, for example, Kurath (1957), Cavanagh (1987, 1988), Diamond (1992), Gray (2001), and McNally (2000).

9 The magazine has become a very diverse publication, now going beyond the expected news about churches, recitals, festivals, graduate programs, summer workshops, job opportunities, organ-building companies, and credentialing requirements to queries and comments columns, announcements about organ installations, and reviews of books and recordings. At times, from 2003 to 2006, the journal also carried continuing discussions on learning to improvise, easy service music, roles of the choir, and body mapping for organists.

10 The article reports a paper given by a noted female neurologist at a Chicago convention. Two quotes are worth repeating. The doctor noted that "the woman whose mind most frequently gives way is one whose work is amid the most uplifting music and whose thoughts dwell on all that is noble and good in this life and the next—the church organist." The last paragraph sums it up: "It has been noted frequently that the young woman organist, a model in a community, reserved and modest, retiring and active in church and Sunday school work, becomes suddenly careless in her habits and a menace to the community. She begins to show hatred to her friends, who try to reason with her. Also, she displays aversion to good habit" (Anonymous 2005, 128).

11 Judith's essay (Gray 2006a) is a model for some of the work needed in the future. It is a "thick description" of one UCC (United Church of Christ) church's hymnody practises over a five-year period, and is fascinating, especially if you are a church organist!

12 Continuing discussions with Phil, while he was at Yale, covered many topics. For example, Phil readily identified four organists within SEM, but didn't know if they were among the fourteen who self-identified as such during the survey. He also spoke of an increase in work on religious music among younger ethnomusicologists, and of backgrounds in sacred music, and other music disciplines that many are bringing to the graduate program at Chicago. Whether some of the links that he, Blumhofer, and Chow were calling for in their 2006 volume are already happening remains unclear; as he noted, the trends he is seeing may or may not be Chicago-specific phenomena (Bohlman 2006b).

13 The discussions with Rich, Phil, Judith, and Steve Wild led me to others in SEM who formerly worked or currently work as church organists. However, with two exceptions, I have not yet been able to have detailed conversations with them. One potential problem, hinted at earlier by Judith and Rich, is already clear: inquiring about one's religious beliefs and involvement may be taboo. This sentiment was expressed by two organists who said immediately and very directly that information about their own religious beliefs and involvement in religious practices was personal, private, and not open to discussion or publication. But both did comment, albeit in different ways, that for them, organized religion was associated with childhood; church was important in their families and in their communities as a social activity that one "just did as a kid without question." They suggested that such attitudes "might be a generational thing," no longer true of today's young or middle-aged adults.

14 There is now a huge literature on writing culture, self/other, speaking for others, moving out of dialogic anthropology through post-colonial anthropology into collaborative projects. Some of the resources include: Abu-Lughod (1990); Aguilar (1981); Appadurai (1991); Barz and Cooley (1997/2008); Behar and Gordon (1995); Bernard and Pedraza (1989); Clifford (1988); Clifford and Marcus (1986); Domiquez (1994); Fabian (1983); Fluehr-Lobban (1991); Herndon (1993); Lassiter (2001, 2005); Lavie, Narayan, and Rosaldo (1993); Lawless (1992, 2000); Marcus and Fischer (1986); Minh-ha (1989); Narayan (1993); Ohnuki-Tierney (1984); Salmon (1997); Smith (1999); Stocking (1983, 1992); Tedlock (1991); Tedlock and Mannheim (1995); Turner (1997), and Valandra (2005).

15 During the discussion after my lecture at the University of Illinois, a male pastor who did not identify himself or his church took issue with my reference to some preachers' feelings of disdain toward organists. He noted that in his experience, it has "always been hard to work with people in church music." They are "set in their ways and make lots of impossible demands." These remarks made me wonder if maybe we shouldn't also try to investigate the backgrounds of church leaders themselves and what they learn about organists in seminary.

Another audience member, herself an organist, jumped in and asked him if he felt that organists were a threat. Someone else pointed out that it might really be an issue of perceived power, with pastors feeling they were competing with the organist's voice since in many services, the organist is actually more often in charge than the pastor.

Another person felt that we need to investigate American ideas about social hierarchy and the social standing of church employees; she believed that organists are viewed "purely as service people" and thus, "like secretaries, they are low on the totem pole."

16 Here I am, of course, assuming that one is working in a church that uses organ music. It is worth remembering that without observation and participation, you may *not* know

what actually transpires during the service. This is particularly true given the practice in some parishes of using the bulletin, the only daily handout, solely as a vehicle for announcements, reminders, and identification of who is in charge of today's doughnut hospitality. I have found that in some denominations, the bulletins tell you nothing about the day's scripture, hymns, or the topic of the homily, message, or sermon. About the only musical information they might convey is the identity of those working in music at the church.

It is also important to remember that if we are to become serious about research in church music, at some point we need to make room for traditions that do things differently. For example, in the Amana Church Society, Middle Amana, Iowa, the undated church bulletin available during a visit in May 2006 stated that "our hymns are sung a cappella with only the aid of song leaders." Two hymns are used during the service. The bulletin says, beside the place announcing the closing one, the "Congregation stands to lift voices of praise during the last verse." Among other sources, a brief discussion of Mennonite hymns; unaccompanied, monophonic Amish church service hymns; and faster, newer Amish hymns used on Sunday evenings and weekday meetings can be found in the religious music part of the chapter by Rahkonen, Goertzen, Post, and Levy (2005, 176–78) in Koskoff (2005).

17 Other definitions view hymns as: the breath of the congregation; songs of faith sung by a group that unify singers in fellowship and faith; sung statements of faith, hope, seeking, and praise; corporate acts that express faith and empowerment; vehicles for the voice of the individual, and, as Erik Routley said, "folksongs of the church" since so many come from the ranks of the faithful rather than from famous composers (Newman 2005–06). If the denomination and its clergy are open to new music and interested in introducing new hymns, new songs from other sources, new responses, or new hymn books, part of the organist's job will be to educate the congregation by helping with the teaching and learning. There are many ways to facilitate such endeavours, such as offering extra practice sessions before or after services, holding group hymn sings once a month, featuring the new hymn tunes as Preludes in conjunction with their use on specific Sundays, or starting "hymn of the month" programs. If the music also entails learning a singing style different from the congregation's own, some broader education and discussions about diverse styles of singing may very well be appropriate and necessary.

18 This movement, which started in the late 1980s, now deserves its own studies. Anderson (2000) includes contemporary Christian music in his study of the sacred arts in America; also see Anonymous (2006), McDannell (1995), and Perkins (2006). Opinions about the movement expressed during the post-lecture discussion at the University of Illinois in October 2006 ran the gamut. Some people believed it appealed to the masses because "it's like what they hear on the radio," "it has pop stars," "it's easily accessible and anyone can fit right in." Others said: "No, this isn't religion"; "The music is trashy, not church, not sacred"; "The songs are too loud"; "The lyrics are too confusing, always changing"; "They're impossible to learn."

19 Both cases happened during my first two years of fieldwork when my contacts on the reservation were still limited. In both situations I needed to be located near the interpreter with whom I was working. In one case, I was involved in a reservation-wide survey of ceremonialists, and was using a different interpreter for each quadrant. We were on the road a lot, but I still needed to pick up the interpreter early in the morning and

bring him back late at night to his family. In each case, the interpreter was male, and in one quadrant, totally new to me, the man's family had no room for an additional person. I had no friends in that part of the reservation then, there were no motel options, and I had not brought camping gear with me, so I approached a mission relatively near his home and asked about room and board possibilities. These were successfully negotiated in exchange for use of my organist's skills on Sundays.

In the other case, I was working with an interpreter on a translation job for Leland C. Wyman. This was in the early 1960s and Wyman had hired me to translate the untranslated portions of the Blessingway manuscript located in Father Berard Haile's materials at the University of Arizona (see Frisbie 2007). In 1970, as editor, Wyman published all three versions that Father Berard had collected as *Blessingway: With three versions of the myth recorded and translated from the Navajo by Father Berard Haile, OFM* (Tucson: University of Arizona Press). While I started working on the job during the school year, Wyman knew that I wanted to do much of the work in conjunction with Navajo linguist, William (Willie) Morgan, who had served earlier as one of the Navajo Nation's official interpreters (Frisbie 2008). Since Wyman wanted both "word for word" and "a free translation" of all the sections of the manuscript in question, I knew it would take a while and that I would need a quiet place in which Willie and I could work. Morgan insisted on staying near his home and family, but had no access to suitable work sites. Once again, I thought of contacting one of the missions in the area, and once again, I was able to negotiate room and board in exchange for working as their organist, both on Sundays and during the week on evenings as needed. I also helped in the kitchen cooking, serving, and cleaning up since they were running a well-attended Bible school program. While the room I was given in the dorm worked well as a place where Willie and I could work and safely leave materials, not everyone on site was hospitable to us, either individually or collectively. Several of the teachers told me flat out that if I were based there, I should be helping with missionizing instead of doing anthropology, pursuing things that might help preserve Navajo culture.

20 Some musicians are even jumping the gun and resigning as soon as it becomes clear that their congregations oppose supportive, national level, denominational statements. As one gay musician friend told me, "As much as I knew the people loved me, after all my years there and everything we had built together, I *had* to leave that job. It was clear that given their attitudes, they could've fired me at any time and I would've had no recourse." (See Thumma and Gray 2004 for one study of gay religion.)

21 On weddings, among my current favourites is "If organists wrote wedding columns" at http://home.ease.lsoft.com/scripts/wa.exe?A2=indo105&L=classical &O=D&P=14541. For other kinds of organists jokes, one can Google "organist jokes" and have fun. Among some of the more creative is www.jeffgoldgraphics.com, which includes "Get organ-ized."

22 One person at the University of Illinois lecture pointed out that the dwindling number of trained organists may not matter. "P & W-style services are going to supplant traditional Christian religion anyway, and in those, you don't need organists."

References

Abu-Lughod, Lila. 1990. "Can There Be a Feminist Ethnography?" *Women and Performance: A Journal of Feminist Theory* 5, no. 1: 7–27.

Adams, William Lee. 2006. "Weddings: You, Me, and Poochy." *Newsweek*, 11 September, 10.

Aguilar, John. 1981. "Insider Research: An Ethnography of a Debate." In *Anthropologists at home in North America*, edited by D. Messerschmidt, 15–26. Cambridge: Cambridge University Press.

American Organist. 2003–06. All issues (published monthly).

———. 2004. "Vox Humana: What's My Line?" October, 40, 42, 44.

Anderson, Richard L. 1989. *Art in small-scale societies*, 2nd ed. Englewood Cliffs, NJ: Prentice-Hall.

———. 2000. *American muse: Anthropological excursions into art and aesthetics.* Upper Saddle River, NJ: Prentice Hall.

———. 2004. *Calliope's sisters: A comparative study of philosophies of art*, 2nd ed. Upper Saddle River, NJ: Prentice Hall.

———. 2006. Discussions by email of this chapter and issues related to it.

Anonymous. 2005. "Organists Often Insane?" The last page. *American Organist*, September, 128.

———. 2006. "Worship Songs Grow, Change with Times." *Edwardsville Intelligencer*, 15–16 April, B-3. Article is from Franklin, TN.

Appadurai, Arjun. 1991. "Global Ethnoscapes: Notes and Queries for a Transnational Anthropology." In *Recapturing anthropology: Working in the present*, edited by Richard G. Fox. Santa Fe: School of American Research Press.

Associated Press. 2006a. "Parish Fires Gay Music Director: Issue Stirs More Debate." *Belleville News-Democrat*, 28 May, A-10.

———. 2006b. "Dallas Episcopalians Mulling Split." *Edwardsville Intelligencer*, 2–3 September, B-3. Article is from Dallas, TX.

Atkinson, Paul. 2005. *Everyday arias: An operatic ethnography.* Lanham, MD: Altamira Press.

Barz, Gregory F., and Timothy J. Cooley, eds. 1997. *Shadows in the field: New perspectives for fieldwork in ethnomusicology.* New York/Oxford: Oxford University Press. 2nd edition, 2008.

Becker, Judith. 2004. *Deep listeners: Music, emotion, and trancing.* Bloomington: Indiana University Press.

Behar, Ruth, and Deborah A. Gordon, eds. 1995. *Women writing culture.* Berkeley: University of California Press.

Belleville News Democrat. 2006. "Episcopalians Take Steps to Secede," 3 December, A-9.

Bernard, H. Russell, and Jesus S. Pedraza. 1989. *Native ethnography: A Mexican Indian describes his culture.* Walnut Creek, CA: Altamira Press.

Bohlman, Philip V. 2006a. "Prayer on the Panorama: Music and Individualism in American Religious Experience." In *Music in American religious experience,* edited by Philip V. Bohlman, Edith L. Blumhofer, and Maria M. Chow, 233–53. New York: Oxford University Press.

———. 2006b. Continuing email conversations about the earlier conference at the Louisville Institute in Kentucky, co-operation between ethnomusicologists and theologians, and other relevant topics.

Bohlman, Philip V., Edith L. Blumhofer, and Maria M. Chow, eds. 2006. *Music in American religious experience.* New York: Oxford University Press.

Brown, Steven, and Ulrik Volgsten, eds. 2006. *Music and manipulation: On the social uses and social control of music.* New York: Berghahn Books.

Cavanagh, Beverley (Diamond). 1987. "The Performance of Hymns in Eastern Woodland Indian Communities." In *Sing out the glad news: Hymn tunes in Canada,* edited by John Beckwith, 45–56. Canadian Musical Documents 1. Toronto: Institute for Canadian Music.

———. 1988. "The Transmission of Algonkian Indian Hymns: Between Orality and Literacy." In *Musical Canada: Words and music honouring Helmut Kallmann,* edited by J. Beckwith and F. Hall, 3–28. Toronto: University of Toronto Press.

Clifford, James. 1988. *Predicament of culture: Twentieth-century ethnography, literature, and art.* Cambridge, MA: Harvard University Press.

Clifford, James, and George E. Marcus, eds. 1986. *Writing culture: The poetics and politics of ethnography.* Berkeley: University of California Press.

Coghill, John. 2005–08. Continuing email discussions about organist culture and issues.

Deeren, Audrey. 2005–08. Continuing discussion in person about numerous issues in church music.

Diamond Cavanagh, Beverley. 1992. "Christian Hymns in Eastern Woodlands Communities: Performance Contexts." In *Musical repercussions of 1492: Explorations, encounters, and identities,* edited by Carol E. Robertson, 381–94. Washington, DC: Smithsonian Institution.

Dissanayake, Ellen. 2006. "Ritual and Ritualization: Musical Means of Conveying and Shaping Emotion in Humans and Other Animals." In *Music and manipulation: On the social uses and social control of music,* edited by Steven Brown and Ulrik Volgsten, 31–56. New York: Berghahn Books.

Dominquez, Virginia R. 1994. "A Taste for the 'Other': Intellectual Complicity in Racializing Practices." *Current Anthropology* 35, no. 4: 333–48.

Fabian, Johannes. 1983. *Time and the other: How anthropology makes its object.* New York: Columbia University Press.

Fluehr-Lobban, Carolyn. 1991. *Ethics and the profession of anthropology: Dialogue for a new era.* Philadelphia: University of Pennsylvania Press.

Frisbie, Charlotte J. 2007. "Fr. Berard Haile, OFM, Anthropologist and Franciscan Missionary." In *Anthropology's debt to missionaries,* edited by Leonard Plotnicov, Paula Brown, and Vinson Sutlive, 46–63. Ethnography Monographs 20. Pittsburgh: University of Pittsburgh Press.

————. 2008. "On Two William Morgans in Navajo Studies." *New Mexico Historical Review* 83, no. 4: 495–500.

Gray, Judith A. 2001. "Christian Hymnody." In "Musical Interactions" by Victoria Lindsay Levine and Judith A. Gray, 484–96. In *Garland encyclopedia of world music, vol. 3: The United States and Canada,* edited by Ellen Koskoff, 480–90. New York: Garland Publishing.

————. 2006a. "When in Our Music God Is Glorified: Singing and Singing about Singing in a Congregational Church." In *Music in American religious experience,* edited by Philip V. Bohlman, Edith L. Blumhofer, and Maria M. Chow, 195–214. New York: Oxford University Press.

————. 2006b. Personal communications via email, August.

Haefer, J. Richard. 2005–06. Personal communications about topics related to this chapter via email.

Herndon, Marcia. 1993. "Insiders, Outsides, Knowing Our Limits, Limiting Our Knowledge (Emics and Etics in Ethnomusicology)." *Worlds of Music* 35, no. 1: 63–80.

Holzapfel, Otto. 2006. "Singing from the Right Songbook: Ethnic Identity and Language Transformation in German American Hymnals." In *Music in American religious experience,* edited by Philip V. Bohlman, Edith L. Blumhofer, and Maria M. Chow, 175–94. New York: Oxford University Press. .

Hood, Mantle. 1960. "The Challenge of Bi-musicality." *Ethnomusicology* 4, no. 20: 55–59.

Kealiinohomoku, Joann. 2005–06. Discussions by email of issues related to this chapter.

Kingsbury, Henry. 1988. *Music, talent, and performance.* Philadelphia: Temple University Press.

Koskoff, Ellen, ed. 2001. *Garland encyclopedia of world music, vol. 3: The United States and Canada.* New York: Garland Publishing.

————. 2005. *Music cultures in the United States: An introduction.* New York: Routledge.

Kurath, Gertrude. 1957. "Catholic Hymns of Michigan Indians." *Anthropological Quarterly* 30, no. 2: 31–44.

Lassiter, Luke Eric. 2001. "From 'Reading over the Shoulders of Natives' to 'Reading alongside Natives,' Literally, toward a Collaborative and Reciprocal Ethnography." *Journal of Anthropological Research* 57, no. 2: 137–49.

————. 2005. *The Chicago guide to collaborative ethnography.* Chicago: University of Chicago Press.

Lavie, Smadar, Kirin Narayan, and Renato Rosaldo, eds. 1993. *Creative/anthropology.* Ithaca, NY: Cornell University Press.

Lawless, Elaine. 1992. "'I Was Afraid Someone Like You … an Outsider … Would Misunderstand': Negotiating Interpretive Differences between Ethnographers and Subjects." *Journal of American Folklore* 105: 301–14.

————. 2000. "'Reciprocal Ethnography': No One Said It Was Easy." *Journal of Folklore Research* 37, no. 23: 197–205.

Levine, Victoria Lindsay, and Judith A. Gray. 2001. "Musical Interactions." In *Garland encyclopedia of world music, vol. 3: The United States and Canada*, edited by Ellen Koskoff, 480–90. New York: Garland Publishing.

Marcus, George E., and Michael M.J. Fisher. 1986. *Anthropology and cultural critique: An experimental moment in the human sciences*. Chicago: University of Chicago Press.

McDannell, Colleen. 1995. *Material Christianity: Religion and popular culture in America*. New Haven, CT: Yale University Press.

McNally, Michael D. 2000. *Ojibwe singers: Hymns, grief, and a Native culture in motion*. New York: Oxford University Press.

Minh-ha, Trinh T. 1989. *Woman, Native, other: Writing postcoloniality and feminism*. Bloomington: University of Indiana Press.

Narayan, Kirin. 1993. "How Native Is a 'Native' Anthropologist?" *American Anthropologist* 95: 671–86.

Nettl, Bruno. 1995. *Heartland excursions*. Urbana: University of Illinois Press.

———. 2002. *Encounters in ethnomusicology: A memoir*. Detroit Monographs in Musicology. Studies in Music 36. Warren, MI: Harmonie Park Press.

Newman, Patricia. 2005–08. Personal communications and ongoing discussions about all of the issues, both by email and in person.

New York Times. 2007. "US Church Rebuked on Same-Sex Unions." *New York Times Digest*, 20 February, 1.

Ohnuki-Tierney. Emiko. 1984. "'Native' Anthropologists." *American Ethnologist* 11, no. 3: 584–86.

Pastner, Steven L. 2006. March and April email discussions about anthropology and the arts. These included his sharing of his syllabi and course packet materials for a 2004 University of Michigan class, Anthropology 458: Art and the Anthropological Imagination.

Perkins, David Horace. 2006. "Selling the Sacred: Contemporary Christian Worship Music as General Market Commodity:" Paper presented in Session 2C, Music in a Variety of Christian Contexts, at the fiftieth annual meeting of the Society for Ethnomusicology, Atlanta, Georgia, 17 November.

Rahkonen, Carl, Christopher Goertzen, Jennifer C. Post, and Mark Levy. 2005. "European American Musical Cultures." In *Music cultures in the United States: An introduction*, edited by Ellen Koskoff, 161–84. New York: Routledge.

Rice, Timothy. 1997. "Toward a Mediation of Field Methods and Field Experience in Ethnomusicology." In *Shadows in the field: New perspectives for fieldwork in ethnomusicology*, 1st edition, edited by Gregory F. Barz and Timothy J. Cooley, 101–20. New York: Oxford University Press. 2nd edition, 2008.

Royce, Anya Peterson. 2004. *Anthropology of the performing arts: Artistry, virtuosity, and interpretation in a cross-cultural perspective*. Walnut Creek, CA: Altimira Press.

Saliers, Don E. 2006. "Aesthetics and Theology in Congregational Song: A Hymnal Intervenes." In *Music in American religious experience*, edited by Philip V.

Bohlman, Edith L. Blumhofer, and Maria M. Chow, 335–43. New York: Oxford University Press.

Salmon, Merrilee H. 1997. "Ethnical Considerations in Anthropology and Archaeology, or Relativism and Justice for All." *Journal of Anthropological Research* 53, no. 1: 47–63.

SEM Business Office. 2006. Data from 2002 survey sent by Kimberly (Jenkins) Marshall-Bohannon.

Smith, Linda Tuhiwai. 1999. *Decolonizing methodologies: Research and Indigenous peoples*. London: Zed Books.

Stocking, George, Jr., ed. 1983. *Observers observed: Essays on ethnographic fieldwork*. History of Anthropology, vol. 1. Madison, WI: University of Wisconsin Press.

———. ed. 1992. *The ethnographer's magic and other essays in the history of anthropology*. Madison: University of Wisconsin Press.

Taborn, Karen. 2006. "Hybridity in Creek and Seminole Indian Christian hymnody." Paper presented in Session 1H, Native Cultures of the North American Continent, at the fiftieth annual meeting of the Society for Ethnomusicology, Atlanta, Georgia, 17 November.

Tedlock, Barbara. 1991. "From Participant Observation to the Observation of the Participant: The Emergence of Narrative Ethnography." *Journal of Anthropological Research* 47, no. 1: 69–94.

Tedlock, Dennis, and Bruce Mannheim, eds. 1995. *The dialogic emergence of culture*. Urbana: University of Illinois Press.

Thumma, Scott, and Edward R. Gray, eds. 2004. *Gay religion*. Lanham, MD: Altamira Press.

Turner, Terence. 1997. "Human Rights, Human Difference: Anthropology's Contribution to an Emancipatory Cultural Politics." *Journal of Anthropological Research* 53, no. 3: 273–91.

Turner, Victor. 1987. *The anthropology of performance*. New York: PAJ Publications.

Valandra, Edward. 2005. "The As-Told-To Native [Auto]biography: Whose Voice Is Speaking?" *Wicazo Sa Review* 20, no. 2: 103–19.

Venbrux, Eric, Pamela Sheffield Rosi, and Robert L. Welsch. 2006. *Exploring world art*. Long Grove, IL: Waveland Press.

WashingtonPost.com. 2007. "In US, Hispanics Bring Catholicism to Its Feet," 6 May. http://www.WashingtonPost.com/AR2007050601082.

Wild, Stephen. 2006. Discussions in person of issues related to this chapter.

Wyman, Leland C., ed. 1970. *Blessingway: With three versions of the myth recorded and translated from the Navajo by Father Berard Haile, OFM*. Tucson: University of Arizona Press.

EIGHT

The Politics of Organology and the Nova Scotia Banjo

An Essay in Honour of Beverley Diamond

NEIL V. ROSENBERG

National Romance

I AM PLEASED TO CONTRIBUTE TO THIS collection of writings in honour of Beverley Diamond. I have known her since 1971, and am pleased that she is now my colleague at Memorial University. No one has worked harder to advance the discipline of ethnomusicology in Canada. Bev makes things happen. She gives those around her tremendous support. She has thought and written about topics that matter very much to me. Her recent article in the fiftieth anniversary edition of *Ethnomusicology*, "Canadian Reflections on Palindromes, Inversions, and Other Challenges to Ethnomusicology's Coherence," addresses all who study vernacular music in Canada: "I suppose I speak from the margins of North America, but is that position distinct or different from that of my US colleagues?" (Diamond 2006, 324). My chapter focuses on that question. I draw from my own experiences as a Canadian, immigrant, academic scholar, and bluegrass musician.

My short answer to Bev's question is: You have given us a question we must pose ourselves whenever we engage in dialogue across boundaries. Is ours a distinct or different position? Should it be?

Every nation tells itself stories about its cultural history. As Bev points out in her article's telling parable of Mieczyslaw Kolinski, we who study vernacular music must work very hard to avoid becoming involved in the projects of nationalism.

It is easy to overlook this fact because we study music-making as vernacular practice from the bottom up. In theory, we begin our research by looking for individual examples of the vernacular practice in which we are interested.

But our interests are shaped by the stories of national cultural history told to us early in life. Though I've lived in Canada for nearly four decades, I still view things with the immigrant's bifurcated vision. And as all Canadians know, the culture of our American neighbours is always nearby and accessible.

By the time I began graduate studies in folklore, American studies, and ethnomusicology at Indiana University, I'd been fully schooled in the New Directions beat orthodoxy of the 1950s in which African-American music was given pride of place.[1] In the San Francisco Bay Area, where I grew up in the 1950s, jazz ruled with the adults, and R & B with the kids. By the time I found out about folk music, Alan Lomax had moved Black music to centre stage in his construction of North American folk music. His sidekick Pete Seeger gentrified the five-string banjo while making a point of its exotic African ancestry. The property of people sold as slaves in the New World, this instrument had various names and shapes among the first generations of slaves, but by the late 1700s when Thomas Jefferson wrote about it in his *Notes on Virginia*, it was being called "banjar" in English.

In the second half of the twentieth century research began in Africa aimed at discovering more about the banjo's origins. The results are still unfolding, but perhaps it is really beside the point to look for physical or linguistic similarities. What matters is the music produced.

My perspective on this comes from a stint as a graduate assistant in Indiana University's Archives of Traditional Music, then known as the Archives of Folk and Primitive Music. The first task that director George List assigned to me was in the recording studio. I was to dub the Tracey Collection from LP to tape. Hugh Tracey, a South African ethnomusicologist, was in the field early with sound recording equipment, documenting local music in many parts of Africa from the late 1920s into the 1950s. Now, in the early 1960s, his International Library of African Music had produced a massive 210 LP archival set, *Sound of Africa*. There were no liner notes, just a printed four-by-six-inch file card for each band. These cards—there were thousands of them—came in duplicate sets.

My task was not just to dub but also to check the contents of the LPs against the cards. This was easy to do because at that time, part of the dubbing process at the archives entailed recording of announcements on the tape for each item. A leisurely pace was guaranteed. One set of Tracey's cards was stapled to blank pages in a loose-leaf binder. I followed that and annotated as per Dr. List's instructions, noting anything I found remarkable.

For a period in the fall of 1964 I was paid to spend hours every week listening to this music. I heard a variety of drums, voices, stringed instruments, melodic percussion instruments, and whistles. Did I say voices? The previous year I'd taken two ethnomusicology courses with Alan Merriam, and he'd spoken often of African music and African music in the New World. At the time he was writing *The anthropology of music* (Merriam 1964). His lectures reflected his work on the book.

I came away from that year of coursework with Merriam with the idea that two important principles informed African musicality. The first was that all voices are instruments, and vice versa. An ardent fan of African-American vernacular music, I felt I knew what he was talking about for it described to me perfectly the music of Blind Willie Johnson and Blind Gary Davis, whose voices and guitars wove a musical tapestry.

The second Merriam called "the percussive principle." He meant that melody was accented by sounds that conveyed rhythmic pulse. "Shake and roll" was not enough; you had to have that "rattle." It could be Johnson's raspy voice, or the slap of the bass strings, or those cheap tube amps that, along with fret noise, made blues guitars buzz. Behind the percussive principle is the idea that all instruments/voices are not just producers of melody but also of rhythm.

Now I heard music informed by these principles in unimagined diversity and variety. Among the sounds were many of instruments that reminded me of the sound of the banjo as I knew it: sanzas, lutes, lyres, guitars.

What I heard was tone quality—the same mix of melody and percussion that can come from banjo strings plucked or brushed. And I heard rhythmic sophistication from syncopation to polyrhythm in the same way I heard the thumb string of the banjo.

The banjo differs from European stringed instruments in that its strings are not arranged in a hierarchy that follows the scale from the lowest note on one side of the fingerboard to the highest on the other as with the guitar, which, when conventionally tuned, runs from highest to lowest as follows:

1	2	3	4	5	6
E^2	B^2	G^1	D	A	E

As it developed in America, the banjo took on a standardized form. It came to have five strings, and one of the most common tunings, again from highest to lowest on the fretboard, is:

1	2	3	4	5
D^2	B^2	G^1	C	G^2

The banjo's fifth string, the string that is (like the sixth string on a guitar) closest to the face of the musician, is the highest pitched. It is next to the lowest pitched string, the fourth.

Not only was the fifth string tuned in this unusual way; it was also shorter than the other four strings. It was attached to a tuning peg located on the side of the fingerboard at the fifth fret. Because it was not fingered, it was often called a "drone string." Sometimes, because it was generally plucked with the thumb, it was the "thumb string."

Throughout its many developments since the 1840s, the five-string banjo has kept this distinctive feature. Early in the twentieth century four-string banjos were developed that use tunings derived from the guitar ("plectrum banjo") or viola ("tenor banjo"). Then came mandolin, bass, and cello-tuned versions. All these lacked the thumb string. Why is the thumb string so important? Because it is used as part of a percussion system, it automatically lends an African rhythm to the music it makes whether it is plucked or brushed. This is the perspective on the banjo that I had when I entered Canada.

The Immigrant Experience

I moved to St. John's, Newfoundland, in 1968. In the early 1970s I began research in the Maritimes that focused on discovering how country music, a popular vernacular form with strong American associations, grew in what I, as an immigrant, first thought of as foreign soil. I soon realized that country music everywhere was shaped in part by indigenous culture (see Rosenberg 1986). This led me to a number of studies on aspects of this topic (Rosenberg 1976a, 1978, 1980, 1994b).

I argued about this for over a decade with the leading historian of country music, Bill Malone, whose *Country music USA* (2002a) was first published in 1968 (see also Malone 2002b). So did Simon Bronner (see Bronner 1987). Malone and most other American scholars who studied country music saw it as distinctly southern, carrying values of the region abroad. Well, that's their story. I not only wanted—I felt I needed—a Canadian story. I've written in detail about my experience in Bruce Jackson and Sandy Ives's book on the fieldwork process, *The world observed* (Rosenberg 1996).

There I tell how I felt encouraged to study the amazing folk culture of Newfoundland, but that it was a stretch for me to study in the Maritimes. Most of my colleagues viewed it as another nation. And it was. In Nova

Scotia I found five-string banjo music. That challenged me. It was similar to the music I'd studied in southern Indiana and Ohio. Was this the Canada I needed to find? It presented a mystery I wanted to solve: How are these things different in Canada?[2]

One difference I found in Canada was the presence of Black country musicians at the local level (Rosenberg 1994b). Another difference came to me when I met some five-string banjo pickers on the south coast of Nova Scotia. They'd grown up in a local fishing/farming culture populated largely by descendants of political refugees who resettled there following the American Revolution. They first saw the five-string banjo in the hands of local Black musicians in the nineteenth century. This sounded to me a lot like the history of the five-string banjo in the American South. Among the pickers were several who'd played on the very first recordings of Canada's Don Messer, a figure who dominated the music I was studying, just as Bill Monroe dominated bluegrass.

But there were differences too. As soon as I'd learned enough to talk for twenty minutes about it, I proposed a paper on my findings for the American Folklore Society. I presented it orally several times. The first came on 24 October 1975, at the annual meeting of the American Folklore Society at the Hotel Monteleone in New Orleans, Louisiana, when I read a paper titled "'I never heard anything like that in my life': The five-string banjo in Nova Scotia."[3]

The American Folklore Society (hereafter AFS) was booming. In the previous decade Indiana's lone folklore graduate degree program had been joined by others, some using the recently introduced European name, "folklife."[4] The bill to establish the American Folklife Center was being shepherded through Congress by folklorist Archie Green. Behind it was what people were beginning to call the public sector folklore movement. A few years earlier it had been "applied folklore," but that had become contentious (see Byington 1989). Its legacy today can be seen in the American work on the UNESCO-led Intangible Cultural Heritage initiative.

Fierce battles about the propriety of academic participation in government activities took place at every AFS business meeting from the late 1960s until 1976, when President Carter signed the bill creating the American Folklife Center at the Library of Congress. Opposition was led by Richard M. Dorson, head of Indiana University's Folklore Institute and leading champion for folklore as a free-standing academic discipline. Dorson spoke proudly of his battles against popularizers.[5]

He was concerned about the way public folklore activity was spreading to federal and state arts agencies across the nation.[6] Ironically, as such activity—like the Smithsonian's annual (since 1967) Festival of American Folklife—grew, folklorists were finding new jobs as ethnographers, archivists, and technicians. They moved between graduate school and grant-funded public sector jobs, hoping that something more permanent was down the road (a representative narrative is Belanus 1994).

In these early years of American public folklore activity, the folk festival was the predominant model for bringing the ideas of folklore and folklife to the public arena (see Camp and Lloyd 1980). Music loomed large in this mass entertainment context. That was not surprising, given that many of those entering the discipline of folklore had come to it from the folksong revival. Most of the prime movers in the public folklore movement were from those ranks (see Jackson 1993). A paper about banjos for this audience seemed to me a good fit. After all, one of the folksong revival's biggest stars, Pete Seeger, had transformed the five-string banjo from a minstrel show stereotype into an African-American icon.

I presented the paper at a session titled Folk Music. Held in a crowded room at a prime time—Friday morning—it was chaired by Joe Hickerson, head of the Library of Congress's Archive of American Folk Song. My presentation followed Robert Baron's paper on salsa and preceded those of Bob Doyle on Pennsylvania fiddling and Nick Spitzer's on Western swing pioneer Bob Wills.

I was a familiar figure at AFS meetings then. I hadn't missed one in ten years. I'd presented papers, acted as a discussant, and organized a panel. My first paper there, in 1966, on bluegrass was published in the Society's *Journal of American Folklore* (*JAF*) in 1967. In 1974 my first book, *Bill Monroe and his blue grass boys*, had been published (Rosenberg 1974). I'd also published articles and liner notes on bluegrass.

At the Memorial University of Newfoundland, where I'd been teaching since September 1968, I'd just returned from my first year-long sabbatical. Newly promoted to associate professor, I was head of the Department of Folklore. Now it had four faculty members, a publication series, and graduate students from Canada, the US, and England.

During my sabbatical I'd conducted research on the relations between country and folk music in the Maritimes. I recall describing my decision to move to New Brunswick for a year to former classmate Elliot Oring, a specialist in humour. He responded to my description of the region in the ironic Yiddish-inflected style of stand-up comedians: "This is *different* from Newfoundland?"[7] My reasons for going to the Maritimes grew in part from my immigrant status. I wanted to live for a while in another part of Canada, and learn more about my new home. Also, after studying bluegrass, which I conceived of as a popular music that had grown out of regional folk traditions, I wanted to examine the folk-popular boundaries in another region.

Since moving to Newfoundland, I'd been studying local musics in Atlantic Canada. I was working to develop models of musical systems so that I could speculate with students and colleagues about issues of theory. Teaching a yearly folk music course, I sought examples that would be familiar to my students.[8]

I didn't want to be an old-fashioned folksong collector—an A & R ("artists and repertoire," a recording company term) man or talent scout for the intelligentsia who bought folksong publications and booked folk festivals. I wanted to know how things worked so I could explain them to students with romantic notions about such things. I was interested in issues like repertoire, status, and regionalism. My first report from the field was a survey of what I'd studied (Rosenberg 1976b; reprinted in Rosenberg 1976a). After that I presented my findings in case studies as papers at meetings like the AFS. Most of these were subsequently published, but not this, my first case study. Why?

To answer that question I now present the text of my paper as I first read it. I've interspersed my comments, which are in italics. When one writes a paper to be read in fifteen to twenty minutes, there's little time for explanation. Every facet of the paper has to be polished. In this case I was acutely aware of my audience—the largest gathering of folklorists in the world at that time. That fall we were just getting started at establishing a Canadian folklore society. I was excited by my new findings in Canada and wanted to share them.

New Orleans, 1975

"'I never heard anything like that in my life': The five-string banjo in Nova Scotia" —Paper read by Neil V. Rosenberg at the Annual Meeting of the American Folklore Society, New Orleans, Louisiana, 24 October 1975, Working Paper: Not to Be Quoted

In 1968, when I first watched Don Messer's popular national television show, Messer, the patriarch of Canadian fiddlers, included in his band a bluegrass-style five-string banjo player. I assumed that banjoist Vic Mullen represented a concession to popular taste, but Mullen later told me that Messer had hired him because during the thirties he'd had in his band two brothers from Shelburne County, Nova Scotia, one of whom played five-string banjo. Messer liked the five-string banjo, but had not been able to

find another until the mid-1960s when he hired Mullen. Although Mullen
is from Nova Scotia, he had not met the two brothers.[9]

*I watched the show on the TV in an Antigonish, Nova Scotia, motel
room on my second night as a landed immigrant. I'd been living in Bloomington, Indiana, for seven years, but had spent the summer teaching in
Austin, Texas. Deeply immersed in bluegrass music, only a few weeks earlier I'd been at a fiddle contest at the Richland Hills Mall near Fort Worth,
performing on stage with fiddler Byron Berline and jamming offstage with
him, Sam Bush, Alan Munde, and other stalwarts of the southwestern
bluegrass world. I was elated to see a bluegrass banjo picker on this show.*

*I knew little about Vic beyond having seen him on Messer's TV show
until four years later—June 1972—when he came to St. John's for a tap-
ing of his own CBC show, Country Time.[10] By then Vic was leading a
country band, the Hickorys. In my paper I equivocate in talking about "a
concession to popular taste," for what I really thought was that Messer was
folding bluegrass banjo into his music. That's what I wanted to see!*

*By 1975 I'd seen Messer in performance (just months before he died),
had begun buying his records, and was working on a Messer discography.[11]*

About a year ago a Nova Scotia country music collector who had
heard about these brothers visited one while on vacation in Shelburne.
His letter, describing the visit with Sheriff Vernon Doane of Gunning
Cove, prompted me to go to Shelburne County.[12] There I learned of a
small but vigorous indigenous tradition of five-string banjo music dating
at least as far back as 1895. In the following paper I will outline and discuss my preliminary findings.[13]

*How did I meet the collector? In 1969 RCA Victor hired me to edit a
bluegrass album in their Vintage Series. This was the first publication that
listed my affiliation with Memorial University. Sold widely, this first
major-label bluegrass anthology reissue in a prestigious series introduced
me to a lot of people. Mike Kolonel, a record collector in central Newfoundland, got it and put me in touch with Fred Isenor of Lantz, Nova Scotia,
a small community near the Halifax airport.*

*Fred is a deejay, record collector, musician, and passionate historian
of country music in the Maritimes. In the summer of 1972 I joined Fred
and Vic Mullen in helping to organize and host the first annual Nova
Scotia bluegrass festival, the first of its kind in Canada. Fred and Vic
knew a lot about the history of old-time country music in the Maritimes.
They gave me good advice and introduced me to the people they knew.*

Neither had met these Doane brothers, but they were eager to do so. Fred, who worked for many years running the stockroom at Shaw Brick in Lantz, took vacation time to drive down the South shore and look up Vernon Doane. Afterwards, Fred wrote to me:

COUNTRY MUSIC SALES LTD. NEW & USED INSTRUMENTS & SUPPLIES MUSICAL INSTRUCTION LANTZ, NOVA SCOTIA BON 1RO PHONE (902) 883-2085	OVATION MARTIN DOBRO SHO-BUD GRETSCH BALDWIN HARMONY GIBSON LUDWIG FENDER

Lantz, N. S.
October 20, 1974

Dear Neil,

     Spent Friday in Shelburne Co. and located Vernon Doane who played 5-string with Don Messer. This was during the late 30s, just before the move to Charlottetown in 1939. He lives in a little place called Gunning Cove. By asking questions I located his house and saw his banjo which turned out to be a Vega Whyte Laydie and not a Gibson as I presumed it was. According to serial number it was built between 1910-1915. He is presently the sheriff of Shelburne Co. His wife then called his office and he invited me over. After I got there I learned that his brother who lives just two houses away has the old Mastertone but I didn't have time to go back to see it. Played me a tape of him and his brother who plays the old style. Vernon now plays three finger and prefers bluegrass.

     Asked about the old recordings and learned that they did not go to Montreal to record in those days. They had this coast to coast radio show out of St. John and Compo (Can. Decca) would record them off the radio program in Montreal. If you have the original Messer cut of "Billy Wilson's Clog" you will hear his banjo on a prominent break. The sidemen's pay at that time for the half hour show was $6.00

     While talking about instruments he told me that 5-string banjos were plentiful in the pawn shops in those days. Said when he bought the Vega they were stacked on top of each other on the floor. At the time he was not familar with names and doesn't recall what makes were there but played several and liked the tone of the Vega. His brother got the old Mastertone from a lady who loaned someone $25. on it and they never came back.

     Another brother, Maxwell Doane, who played the Martin guitar with Messer at the same time is still living in Saint John and still has the old Martin. You may meet up with him on your travels. Vernon told me he hadn't heard of our bluegrass & old time music festival but made a note of the weekend and said if they could be free at that time next summer they would play some numbers. They still play music for their own enjoyment or an occasional party or benifit. Made several notes for my scrapbook but really should have taken my casette recorder. Asked me to come back again and let him know in advance so he can get the brother with the Mastertone and play a few tunes. Will not get back until next year.

FIGURE 8.1 Letter from Fred Isenor

I replied a few days later saying I'd like to meet Doane and asked if Fred thought he would mind my dropping in. He wrote back saying: "Vernon Doane is Shelburne County High Sheriff and can be reached at home or at the courthouse during the day. Think it would be okay to call him at work as I visited him at the courthouse and the only call he had was from a fellow musician who had just bought a new J-45."[14] Fred's letters told me about the Doanes—especially their instruments—and encouraged me to travel to visit them.

In reporting my findings, I began by constructing a theoretical framework. Were I doing this today, I would be able to avail myself of the much more comprehensive discussion by Diamond, Cronk, and von Rosen in the first chapter of their study of First Nations musical instruments (1994). But in speaking to folklorists in 1975 I kept things simple, emphasizing the novelty of this project, which married a relatively new branch of folkloristics—material culture studies—with one of the oldest: music.

The study of traditions involving musical instruments combines two aspects of folkloristics rarely studied together: material culture and music. The central question in such a study is: What in fact constitutes an instrumental tradition? There are at least four parameters that must be taken into account: The instrument, the style in which the instrument is played; the repertoire associated with the instrument, and the performance contexts in which the instrument is used.

Before discussing the tradition in terms of these dimensions, here is a brief setting of scene: The region I am talking about is Shelburne Bay, on the south coast of Nova Scotia, and the settlements that constitute the hinterlands of the county seat town of Shelburne. The region was settled in the last quarter of the eighteenth century by Loyalists, who brought with them their Black "servants," most of whom were actually slaves. The people I will be talking about are descendants of either the New Englanders[15] or the Afro-Americans who settled at that time. In the nineteenth century Shelburne was an important fishing port and shipbuilding centre. Today its economic mainstays are the fishery and tourism.

Five-string banjo music was and is performed in Shelburne County by members of at least four White families, mainly among the men of the generation born in the first two decades of this century. There are also reports of Black banjo players in the region in the preceding two generations. Today several younger men play the banjo. I will confine my discussion to the Doane brothers: Mac, born in 1906; Ben, born in 1908; and Vernon, born in 1918.

On 11 November, A few days after receiving my second letter from Fred Isenor, I wrote to Vernon Doane, telling him I hoped to visit him on Friday of the following week. That Tuesday I called to see if he'd gotten my letter. Vernon was very cordial over the phone and invited me to stay with him and his wife at his home in Gunning Cove. I spent two days, recording a house party on Friday night and an interview with Vernon on Saturday. The following April (1975) I went to Saint John, New Brunswick, to interview Mac Doane, and in May I spent another two days visiting Vernon. At the end of May Mac visited me in Pleasant Villa, New Brunswick, where I was living during my sabbatical. As usual, I took extensive notes in addition to doing the interviews, and then typed up those notes for my field journal. These field notes, taped events, and interviews were my data sources for the paper.

Their father, John Doane, was born in 1880 in Gunning Cove, a small community on the west side of Shelburne Bay. Like everyone in the community, he did some inshore fishing, but he also ran a general store and was the local blacksmith, undertaker, and square dance fiddler. The Doane home was the centre for music in the little community. Neighbours would visit regularly in the evenings to hear Mr. Doane's fiddle tunes and Mrs. Doane playing the organ and leading the family in hymns and popular songs.

Instrument

The first five-string banjo John Doane saw was in 1895 when he was fifteen; a "coloured man" in the home of a "coloured woman" played it. About twenty years later, Doane's second son, Ben, saw the banjo for the first time when two "coloured men," a fiddler and a banjo-picker named Tom Jacklyn, played for a dance in the family's home community. Ben recalls his excitement—"I never heard anything like that in my life"—and since that time, when he was less than ten years old, he has been a banjo connoisseur.

At this point in my paper I summarized the history of banjo scholarship as it then existed. Since then much more has been done. Dena J. Epstein surveyed the early colonial literature to find descriptions from the slavery era (Epstein 1977). Robert Winans analyzed the early minstrel music to begin a focused dialogue on techniques of composition and performance (Winans 1976). Cecilia Conway studied contemporary African-American banjo players in Appalachia (Conway 1995). Karen

Linn documented the banjo in American popular culture (Linn 1991).
That's just the tip of the iceberg. A recent summary of the scholarship is
Peter Szego's two-part series in The Old-Time Herald *(Szego 2006a and*
2006b). Much of this scholarship is driven by several factors. A majority
of the researchers collect or play banjos, or both. There is a focus on the
earliest connections—what Melville J. Herskovits called "Africanisms"—
of the banjo. This approach privileges the five-string banjo over later adap-
tations like the plectrum, tenor, and mandolin banjos, all of which have
in their tuning and tonality European rather than African origins. Indeed,
Szego shows that recently considerable research has been done on track-
ing down the African connections.

The banjo is a North American descendant of African chordophones
with gourd resonators. In the early part of the nineteenth century it was
adapted from slave culture as part of the minstrel show. Just as the minstrel show and subsequent White borrowings from Afro-American culture
tended to fix fluid Black folk expression—dance, song, speech, or dress—
into a stereotype, so the minstrel musicians took the African instrument
and regularized it.

The introduction of the banjo to European-based North American culture led to its standardization as a factory-made instrument; by the 1870s
it was being used not only by minstrel troupes but many other types of musicians from longhairs to buskers (see Adler 1972). A relatively light and
cheap instrument, it was available throughout North America and in many
parts of Europe, when John Doane first saw one in 1895.

On the morning of Sunday, 11 May 1975, Vernon took me on a
leisurely tour of the back roads of Shelburne County, introducing me to
people who owned banjos old and new, and pointing out the homes of
those who'd had banjos in the past. From what he told me then and on
my other visits, and from similar experiences elsewhere, I mused on the
archaeology of instruments at this point in the paper.

Factory-made musical instruments are often impulsively purchased
luxury items in our culture. Relatively easily pawned or sold in times of
need, they may sit in the home or the attic unplayed for years. They are
tools that people purchase, meaning to use, and then, for one reason or
another, do not use. Hence, the existence of a banjo—especially a factory-
made one—in a home does not necessarily indicate the existence of an
indigenous tradition in the region.

Today I don't agree with that conclusion. Surely the impulse to buy an instrument reflects some kind of interest in using it to make music! Isn't that part of a tradition? Moreover, I did get plenty of information from the Doanes about the prevalence of indigenous banjo players in the region.

After young Ben Doane saw the Black banjo-player Tom Jacklyn, he began imitating him, using a stick as a banjo, whenever his father played the fiddle. In 1919, when Ben was eleven years old, his father purchased a used banjo from a stable owner in Shelburne who had received it in payment for a debt. The cost was two dollars. Ben and his older brother Mac both began playing this instrument, but Mac soon switched to guitar.

In Newfoundland, where, as in the Maritimes, many people had family connections in New England, it is still common to speak of "the Boston states." I turned next to a brief description of this phenomenon as lived by the Doane family.

Like their father before them, the Doane brothers all went to high school in the Boston area, boarding with relatives. The two older brothers lived and worked in the US during the 1920s and between this time and 1935, Ben owned several open-back five-string banjos. In 1935 he lost a finger in an accident and stopped playing for three or four years. Then, while working in Montreal, he was lonely and purchased an English Clifford-Essex banjo in a pawnshop. In the early 1950s he purchased his present banjo, a 1920s Gibson Mastertone, in Toronto, from a friend who had taken it in payment for a debt of thirty-five dollars. He sold the Clifford-Essex to his brother-in-law.

Meanwhile the youngest brother, Vernon, had been learning on the original family banjo. While living during the 1930s with his brother Mac in Saint John, New Brunswick, Vernon found a Vega Whyte Ladie number 7 in a pawnshop for twenty-five dollars. He still owns it. The Doanes have never built their own banjos. They are proud of their nice, old factory-made banjos, but are not instrument collectors.

As I read this paper I assumed that many in my audience would be familiar with the brand names and model numbers of the various fancy old factory-built instruments that the Doanes came to own. Indeed, many musicians tell their life histories using their instruments as markers (see Glassie 1970).

Playing Style

Here I mean the way the instrument is tuned, fretted, and plucked. John Doane did not know how to tune, fret, or pluck the banjo he bought in 1919. A cousin showed Ben Doane how to tune the instrument's fifth string to the A string of the fiddle. Eventually Ben Doane came to use two tunings: one called "high bass" in which the strings are in an open A major chord, and the other called "low bass" in which the instrument, when chorded, is played in the key of D. These are the two most commonly encountered banjo tunings, although in contemporary practice, they are a whole tone lower, in G and C, respectively. The A and D tunings enable Ben to play with most of his father's fiddle tunes.[16]

Ben Doane taught himself how to fret the banjo, and synthesized his own plucking style from local models. The earliest was Tom Jacklyn, who played simple melodies alternating the thumb and index finger. A second influence was Emory Amirault, a blind Acadian from Yarmouth, Nova Scotia, who travelled widely in the region as a Fuller Brush salesman. He used the thumb and index finger to pick out the basic pulse notes and the index finger was used also to brush upwards on the higher strings, producing a series of triplets. This fit well with the local fiddle tunes, which have a typical ornamentation pattern of triplets within duple metre tunes. From these two styles and the few tunes that he learned from other musicians, Ben Doane developed his personal style, using the thumb and two fingers for the playing of melody on foxtrots, clogs, and other songs, and Amirault's thumb and index finger style for backing up duple metre fiddle tunes. He also invented a homemade finger pick, which he used to keep his index finger from blistering when playing this style at dances. He now uses plastic picks. Although he was familiar with vaudeville banjo players and the recordings of Fred Van Eps and the early hillbilly performers, he rarely strove to copy the style of these rather more distant models. When Ben lost his left middle finger, he ceased playing. He later began playing again, but his stylistic development seems to have stopped at about this point.

Ben was the first to tell me about Amirault. He was blind, Ben said, but he rode a bicycle. Go figure! Later I mentioned this to Vic Mullen, who recalled seeing Amirault playing the banjo at a pool hall in Yarmouth. Clearly Amirault was well known to the region's banjoists.

So I was surprised when, in 1988, Helen Creighton published in her final book a song she'd collected from Amirault in 1947, "Les jeunes gens de Chéticamp" (Creighton and Labelle 1988, 179). Creighton's note to the

*song told only that the song was sung by Amirault in Yarmouth in 1947,
and that the words were written down, but not the tune. Recently, with
the substantial help of Clary Croft, I learned more of Creighton's experience with Amirault through her 1947 diary.*[17] *She was doing fieldwork with
Joe Raben, an American linguist and literary scholar who had an interest
in traditional music.*[18]

In her diary for 11 September 1947, she wrote:

> *Frustrated at every turn. Drove to poor farm for Blind Emery, only to be
> told he was in Yarmouth. At Yarmouth couldn't find people he stays with,
> and learned he has no fixed abode but may be anywhere. Everybody seemed
> to have seen him at one time or another, but nobody knew where he was.
> It was thought he had gone to Hebron, so we went there. He wasn't....*

The next day's entry reads:

> *Drove to Exhibition to see handcrafts and listed them. Looked up Blind
> Emery who wasn't there.... We stopped again at Blind Emery's, and found
> he had been trying to get in touch with us. So we arranged to call for him
> in the morning and bring him out to the cabin as the place he lives is a hovel.
> Then we saw him on Main St. and got out and talked to him.*

The next day, she got a song from him:

> *Yarmouth. We picked Blind Emery up at ten. He said he could sing bet-
> ter with a banjo, so we got one from Mr. Muise who hesitated at first
> because the last time he had loaned him one he'd pawned it. He sings all
> right, but no milk white steeds or early in the morning in that lovely
> month of May. Mostly comic songs for entertainment. We took down a few
> and Joe and I alternated the lines which was a very workable scheme.
> One song of West Pubnico was good and a French song of Cheticamp. At
> one we took him to a canteen for lunch and I gave him two dollars and
> we drove him home.*

*Creighton's disappointment of the lack of milk-white steeds and the
like to accompany Amirault's banjo reflects her national romantic vision.
Consequently, we now know only that he was an important figure in his
time, a travelling professional. The Acadian involvement with the banjo
in country music and bluegrass continued throughout the twentieth century with figures like Maurice Bolyer and Eddie Poirier. Today the flour-
ishing Maritimes bluegrass scene is dominated by Acadian bands and
musicians. In 2007 J.P. Cormier's banjo album won the East Coast Music
Association's "Best Bluegrass Recording of the Year" award.*

Returning now to Ben, I note that in this paper I glossed over the effect of the hiatus in his musical career, which, I came to understand, was quite significant. When he resumed his music-making in the 1950s, he retained his musical habits of two decades earlier. Hence I was able to contrast his playing with that of his younger brother.

The youngest brother, Vernon, who played and recorded with Don Messer, learned Ben's style. Later, he was taught the "correct" lower tuning for the banjo by one of Messer's sidemen. During the 1950s he became aware of bluegrass-style banjo recordings, and began to study that right-hand technique. His sister's husband, who had purchased Ben's English banjo, also began playing in that style. At this time Vernon learned an open D chord tuning associated with the bluegrass version of "Home Sweet Home."

I met Vern first at his office in the Shelburne County courthouse. Here's what I wrote in my field notes for 22 November 1974 after describing an evening of music and drinks at Vernon's home across the harbour in Gunning Cove:

> when I first arrived, Vern had me come up and play the banjo in his office while he called his brother-in-law, Danny Bowers. He had me play "Home Sweet Home," using the Scruggs tuners. He told me that when a record of that first came out (probably Don Reno's 1955 hit; see Rosenberg 2005, 105–6), he'd listened and finally figured out the tuning, but couldn't figure out how the fellow was getting the slurred notes. Eventually he devised a system of stretching the strings using a bevelled toothbrush handle. He called up his brother-in-law and played the result for him; the brother-in-law asked him how he did it and Vernon wouldn't tell. So Danny called up Vernon's brother Ben, who lives a few houses away, and asked him to sneak over and peek in the window. This story was retold with laughter several times that night.

"That night" was a good old-fashioned house party in Gunning Cove. With the phone call and the party I was introduced to the Doane family as a musician. Vernon was still working to develop his banjo picking (he was a good fiddler and guitarist, too) and insisted that I play banjo with him. As Posen (2005) has shown, in circumstances such as this, coaxing is an essential aspect of the social transactions that take place when music is, in his terms, "accomplished." I recorded much of our evening's music, and Vernon made recordings too. Next morning I woke up hung over to the sound of our music as he played it back over speakers outside on his deck for his family members who lived nearby.

At this and subsequent sessions, my goal was to find out as much as I could about their repertoire.

Repertoire

I have divided the Doanes' banjo repertoire into five categories: Black tunes, fiddle tunes, songs of the day, banjo show tunes, and bluegrass tunes. These analytic categories reflect differing musical structures, which have parallels in both style and performance contexts. The first tunes that Ben learned were associated with Tom Jacklyn and with a "coloured lady" in Liverpool named "Old Aunt Kate." These are characterized as "simple," involving one chord and one or two short phrases repeated in a litany-like form. It is tempting to compare these with African melodies, but it should be pointed out that the local Black musicians, including Jacklyn, gave minstrel shows in the Shelburne area and were probably influenced by these and other popular traditions.

I've recounted my subsequent work on Black musicians in Atlantic Canada in several articles; there's good evidence in the printed record that people of African descent—whom George Elliott Clarke (1991) calls "Africadians"—played an important role in spreading the banjo in the region and abroad. This story reaches back to the middle of the nineteenth century (Rosenberg 1988).

Fiddle tunes came mostly from musicians within the community, and from New Brunswick and Cape Breton fiddlers. A few were learned from radio and records. These tunes are in the keys of A, D, and G; strophic in form with an A/B or AA/BB structure; and in a number of different time signatures: 2/4, 4/4, 6/8, 3/4.

Popular songs, which the Doanes call "songs of the day," ranged from "coon" songs through music hall material to foxtrots and hillbilly songs. The entire family was continually immersed in recorded popular music of the times, from cylinders to LPs. Another source of songs was the sheet music sent regularly by relatives in the Boston area for Mrs. Doane to play on the organ. In this context the banjo was used primarily as an accompaniment for singing.

The banjo show tunes emphasize dexterity and the performer's command of the instrument. Typical tunes in this category include "The World Is Waiting for the Sunrise," which Ben learned from watching a plectrum banjo player in a vaudeville show, and "The Juggler," a piece learned from Emory Amirault, which involved spinning the instrument, swinging it like a pendulum, passing it over the head, between the legs, and so forth, while keeping a tune going the whole time. The ubiquitous "Spanish Fandango" was another such tune.

Finally, the bluegrass repertoire has been recently introduced via records and, in recent years, younger local musicians. Vernon now plays the older "tunes of the day" in this style, as well as a few banjo show tunes. Ben's repertoire does not include these tunes.

Performance Contexts

Three categories of performance situation can be described for the Doanes: the house party, the dance, and the radio broadcast.

Music was important in the Doane household. Their grandfather had considered music "damned foolishness," so their father felt compelled to redress the balance by immersing his children in music. The musical evenings of that era served as a model for the house parties, which constitute the only performance context in which the brothers are still active. Dancing, singing, drinking, and conversation are all part of this performance context.

The house party was the Doane métier. When I saw Vern and Ben in May 1975, Vern recalled how, on one of Messer's last visits, he had arrived with a case of Scotch. He brought it into Vern's family room where they always made music, plopped it down, and told them "Here, boys, you entertain me for a change." In my field notes I wrote that Vern told me:

> They had quite a party. Again Vern said he liked Don Messer's fiddling, but not his band, and felt he played better informally "in the kitchen." And, Vern added, he had a pretty good "back-step" that he danced. One of Vernon's cousins [Del] Doane who fiddles ... once fiddled for Messer's step dancing, an event which he told about with great amusement to his friends—"Messer Danced to My Music" story.[19]

Mac affirmed Messer's love of house party music. He told me that "Messer preferred playing all night at a party to playing on the radio or for a dance."[20] But Mac admired the way Messer had provided for his family even after his death. The Doanes were proud to be associated with such a successful musician.

As soon as they were able, the boys were expected to help their father provide music at dances. When they were older, they played on a number of occasions with Don Messer as paid dance musicians at rural country dances in New Brunswick. However, for the most part, their dance music was played around their home community, during holidays, and the various times when they held seasonal jobs in the area.

When Mac Doane moved to New Brunswick, he met Don Messer, who eventually asked him to play on his radio program. Over a period of about five years, all three Doane brothers played with Messer on radio. Several of these broadcasts were recorded by Compo Records in Montreal and six songs from these recordings were issued as Don Messer and His New Brunswick Lumberjacks, with Vernon's banjo playing audible in the backup, and on "Billy Wilson's Clog," as a lead instrument. These were the only radio broadcasting experiences the brothers had. For different reasons, they rejected musical professionalism, preferring the context of the house party and the local dance to the financial risk and rigour of a musician's life on the road.

What follows is based on my later research on the Don Messer discography. The Compo Recording Company logs, on file in Canada's National Library, show that the company recorded twenty performances of Messer's Saturday night broadcasts over seven weeks in 1937, starting on 26 June and ending on 14 August. Six tunes recorded in early July appeared simultaneously in 1937 and 1938 on three 78 rpm singles under the Melotone label in English Canada and the Starr label in French Canada, credited to "Don Messer's New Brunswick Lumberjacks." Issued after 1942 on Apex label 78s, the same recordings were credited to "Don Messer and His Islanders." From the 1950s to 1970s they were reissued on LPs. Today one track, "Lamplighter's Hornpipe," can be heard on MCA Records' CD MCAD 4047, The Very Best of Don Messer. It's mislabelled there (half of the tunes on the CD are mislabelled!) as "Atlantic Polka, 3rd Change."[21]

In reviewing the various elements in the banjo music of the Doanes, one is struck by the way in which folk and popular culture are intertwined, starting with instruments: they have always used factory-made rather than home-made instruments. Strictly speaking, then, these are not folk instruments.

This comment drew a hoot of derision from someone in the audience when I read it. In 1975 the impact of folklife studies, with the then-new emphasis on material culture studies, was just beginning. I said this because I wanted to be provocative, and I succeeded.

When we turn to style, just the opposite is the case. Virtually all the models came from immediate oral tradition, from relatives and travelling musicians who were members of adjacent ethnic groups in the region. Vernon Doane eventually did learn a "correct" way to tune the banjo, but this too came from oral tradition. And while his recent performances have been influenced by the bluegrass model, those of his brother have not; Ben has consciously rejected this style and has maintained his older tunings and the terminology associated with them. Hence in this parameter we seem to be dealing with a folk style.

I was arguing here for my vision of the vernacular, which was evolving as I studied local folk and country music in the region.

In repertoire, there is a mixture of folk and popular musics from many sources. The oral/aural inputs were the Black tunes, some of the show pieces, and the fiddle tunes, although a few of the latter came from recordings. Singing at house parties involved new and comparatively popular tunes from outside, while dances called for old tunes from the community traditions. Today the family repertoire is relatively fixed: the "songs of the day" are mostly the favourites from the period between 1915 and 1940 when the Doanes were most active musically, while the old dance tunes remain as instrumentals. Today they consider their repertoire "old-time," in the sense that it contains aged songs and tunes, whatever the source. Incidentally, each brother has a different set of repertoire favourites.

In my work in Atlantic Canada, "old-time" came up again and again as a native term. It referred not to the American southern music, but to music that in some way or another had a tie with the past; music that was not trying to be modern (see my comments in Rosenberg 1991, 46).

All three brothers have preferred face-to-face small group performance contexts to those of radio and stage. This preference for intimate contexts continues to the present. In the summer of 1975 they were the most popular group in the parking lot jam sessions at the Nova Scotia Bluegrass Festival, but refused to appear on stage. I have just described a folk tradition in which factory-made tools and popular-market materials have been fitted into folkloric performance situations through the use of orally, aurally, and visually learned styles. Obviously this is little more than an outline, but hopefully it serves to point out some of the dimensions and problems in the study of folk instrumental traditions.

Here my paper ended. I don't recall the questions asked, although there were some. I also don't recall anyone asking if I wanted to send it to his or her journal for consideration. No one approached me about publishing a recording. I left New Orleans thinking that this needs more work.

Nationalism and the Politics of Organology

I return now to Diamond's question: "I suppose I speak from the margins of North America, but is that position distinct or different from that of my US colleagues?" (2006, 324). My answer, like my paper, is multidimensional. Let's take "different" first. My theoretical position was not, I think, very different from that of the other folklorists in the room. Folklore studies was, like ethnomusicology, introduced to me as a discipline that thinks of itself as "international." I saw my paper as part of the international dialogue of the discipline: folk instruments exist in many cultures, and in theory, universal principles of description and analysis can be suggested. The music/material culture nexus remains challenging for folklorists since it involves potentially conflicting perspectives about oral and aural traditions.

When we come to "distinct," a term with strong cultural connotations in Canada, the picture changes. The Doanes' cultural milieu was both similar and different from the one described by my US colleagues. Vernon and Ben had much in common with Snuffy Jenkins, the southern White banjo player whose style inspired Earl Scruggs, the first banjoist in bluegrass. All were playing state-of-the-art, three-finger, five-string, old-time banjo music. In July 1937 when Vernon took his break on "Billy Wilson's Clog" on Messer's New Brunswick Lumberjacks recording, he was one of the first, perhaps *the* first, to record a banjo solo in his generation's version of that style, beating Jenkins out by a month.[22] Both Snuffy and Vernon played music based on styles learned earlier from older Whites and Blacks. Their style had connections with the stage, in particular the minstrel show, as well as with local social rituals: dancing and house parties. Ben's "The Juggler," learned from Amirault, was contemporaneous with similar performances by American country pioneer Uncle Dave Macon and African-American jug band leader Gus Cannon.

But Vernon's recording with Don Messer is a document in the Canadian fiddle music story. Even though Messer liked the banjo in his music to the extent that he hired Vic Mullen in the early 1960s, the banjo never had the exotic cachet in Canadian vernacular music that it gained with Scruggs in bluegrass. "Billy Wilson's Clog," with its unique three-finger break, did not lead to a new banjo-centric genre. When I gave this paper, there seemed no easy place for me to fit my banjo story into the Canadian folk music picture.

The banjo seems to come into this picture only with Americans. The 2006 Canada Day edition of the *Globe and Mail* focused on Canada's northern-ness, with many pieces on the topic in its different sections. In section T, "Globe Travel," titled "The Arctic Issue," I read that there are more Americans and other foreigners than Canadians as tourists in the region.[23] This brought to mind Ken Perlman's CD, *Northern Banjo* (2001). Its cover painting plays with the American tourist vision of Canada, depicting New Englander Perlman in a birchbark canoe. He's dressed as a modern voyageur, with his tent and bedroll in front of him on the floor of the boat, paddling along, not in the Arctic, but in a very eastern-Canadian-looking stream or maybe a Maritimes inlet—perhaps the confluence of the two. His paddle is a five-string banjo.

In its introductory notes he explains that he is using the repertoire of fiddle tunes that he collected and studied on Prince Edward Island (Perlman 1996) to advance a banjo performance technique, "melodic clawhammer," at which he is one of the most acclaimed performers. He uses this technique to perform intricate pieces associated with the Celtic movement—tunes played mainly on the fiddle but also on accordion, pipes, whistles, etc. But his argument for the technique also holds that it is linked to "the mid-19th century minstrel-banjo tradition ... itself as much a Northern as a Southern phenomenon" (Perlman 2001, liner notes, 3).

Perlman took the banjo to Canada as an American tool to explore the region's vernacular fiddle music, which, with its strong European connections, he sees as an extension of the American North. His album was constructed with the help of Ontario's best-known young acoustic musicians. It introduces a new repertoire for the banjo.

When I first came to Canada, I experienced something like what Perlman's cover depicts. Then I ran across Canadian banjo players. My banjo became a tool to explore the banjo music of people who had developed their own performance techniques for their own repertoire.

In my research I wanted to know how things worked. In 1977 I videotaped Ben doing "The Juggler," and Ben and Vernon playing banjo and guitar backup to their cousin Del Doane, the one who had played for Messer's back-step dancing. Except for this videotaping I generally played with them when the tape recorder was running. This was what they wanted. My connections with southern banjo music appealed to them, and fieldwork etiquette demanded that I help them create a document that lent prestige to their story as they wanted to tell it. That meant that I didn't have much in the way of recordings that I felt comfortable publishing, for I couldn't leave myself out of the picture. Indeed, I was glad to be a welcomed immigrant.

I might have had more success at telling their story if I'd followed the folk talent scout system. But that wasn't what interested me and I have not been adept at working in the youth and pop-oriented Canadian folk festival system. The Doanes enjoyed playing music at parties; they came to Nova Scotia bluegrass festivals to jam. But there seemed no way to get them on stage in the folk revival as icons of Canadian music.

These are my ongoing thoughts about the issues Bev raises in "Canadian Reflections." I'm thankful for her continuing work to keep us focused on the essential question of how individual, local, national, and international perspectives intersect and overlap. It has helped me tell my story about Canadian banjo music.

A Postscript

Since 2007, when I completed work on this chapter, national recognition has come to two Canadian five-string banjoists in the form of Juno Awards. In 1975 the Canadian Academy of Recording Arts and Sciences (CARAS) began hosting these annual awards, "created specifically and solely to enhance our music industry through an annual, nationally televised awards show."[24]

In 2008, the Juno for "Instrumental Album of the Year" went to the Ontario banjoist Jayme Stone for his self-published album *The Utmost*. In 2009, Stone was co-winner of "World Music Album of the Year" with African griot singer and kora player Mansa Sissoko for their album *Africa to Appalachia*. Also winning a 2009 Juno with the five-string banjo was Old Man Luedecke (the recording name of Chris Luedecke) from Chester, Nova Scotia, whose album *Proof of Love* was named "Solo Roots & Traditional Album of the Year."

It gives me pleasure, and fills me with hope, that Stone and Luedecke have taken my favourite instrument to new heights of recognition in Canada.

Notes

1 See Lovelace and Narváez (2001); for a more informal account, see Rosenberg (2001).

2 I address this question from a different perspective in Rosenberg (1998).

3 I presented the paper again at the Queen's University Department of Music in November 1981 as one of three lectures under the title "Folk music traditions in Canada" that Beverley invited me to give. I built another lecture on it as "Collecting banjo music in Nova Scotia," which I gave to the Atlantic Canada Institute at the University of Prince Edward Island on 2 August 1983.

4 Interestingly, this came as European scholars were abandoning "folklife" in favour of "ethnology" to describe their discipline, a name shift reflected in the French language version of the name of the Folklore Studies Association of Canada: "Association canadienne d'ethnologie et de folklore."

5 Generally speaking, Dorson represented the older, the more conservative, and those ensconced in the most prestigious universities.

6 A recent account of this struggle is given in Bulger (2003).

7 Had we been conducting this exchange onstage at a Canadian stand-up comedy venue, I would have turned to the audience, shrugged my shoulders, and said: "What do *they* know?"

8 I wrote about my folksong course in Rosenberg 1989.

9 Interview with Vic Mullen, St. John's, Newfoundland, 15 June 1972.

10 Mullen's relationship with Messer, which had some difficult periods, is described in Robbins (2005, 49, 70, 77–78, 90).

11 To date I've written two articles based on this research: Rosenberg 1994a and 2002.

12 Letter from Fred Isenor, 20 October 1974.

13 The information presented here derives from tape-recorded interviews and notes taken during visits to the Doanes of Gunning Cove, Nova Scotia, in November 1974, May 1975, and July 1975, as well as from visits with Mac Doane in Saint John and Pleasant Villa, New Brunswick, in April and May 1975. This research was done during the tenure of Canada Council Leave Fellowship W74–0346.

14 Letter from Fred Isenor, 4 November 1974. The J-45 is a popular Gibson guitar model that has been in production since 1942.

15 I oversimplified the history in this statement: some of the Loyalists came from the central and southern American colonies.

16 Clyde Dykes, a three-finger-style banjo player from East Tennessee, used the same tunings: "he would tune up a whole step higher in order to play in the keys of A and D rather than using a capo, which did not become common until the mid-1950s as a result of the increasing influence of bluegrass stylists" (Stafford and Blaustein 1989, 3).

17 The diary is part of the Nova Scotia Archives and Records Management's Helen Creighton Fonds, MG1 vol. 2830 #3.

18 A biography from a review published by Craven in 2000 on the website of the Resource Center for Cyberculture Studies (http://rccs.usfca.edu/bookinfo.asp?BookID=86& ReviewID=89) describes him: "Joseph Raben, professor emeritus of English at the City University of New York, is the founding editor of *Computers and the Humanities* and the founding president of the Association for Computers and the Humanities." In addition to his extensive work in this field, early in his career Raben collaborated in collecting music in Canada with several scholars. Rahn mentions "the Gertrude Kurath and

Joseph Raben collection made at the Six Nations Reserve in 1950 and deposited at the National Museum in Ottawa" (1977, 49).

19 Field notes, Gunning Cove, Nova Scotia, 10 May 1975.

20 Field notes, Saint John, New Brunswick, 17 April 1975.

21 The track titled "Lamplighter's Hornpipe" on this 1994 CD is, in fact, "Atlantic Polka, 3rd Change." The same error occurs on *The Best of Don Messer: Twentieth-Century Masters, the Millennium Collection* (Universal 0249829389, 2005).

22 DeWitt "Snuffy" Jenkins recorded twelve sides for RCA's Bluebird label as a member of Mainer's Mountaineers at a session in Charlotte, North Carolina, on 5 August 1937 (Russell 2004, 582).

23 Buhasz (2006, T5) writes of German-speaking visitors, Japanese "aurora tourists," and "mainly rich Americans" who come for hunting and fishing.

24 From the website http://www.carasonline.ca/CAR_about.php. The awards predate the creation of CARAS. Initiated in 1970 by the music trade weekly *RPM* as the Gold Leaf Awards, they became the Junos in 1971.

> The name was changed to the Juno Awards in honour of Pierre Juneau, then head of the CRTC and responsible for the implementation of the Canadian Content Regulations in 1971. When it was discovered that Juno had been the chief Goddess of the Roman Pantheon, the spelling was changed and the awards permanently named. (http://www.junoawards.ca/archive_about.php)

References

Adler, Thomas. 1972. "The Physical Development of the Banjo." *New York Folklore Quarterly* 28 (1972): 187–208.

Belanus, Betty J. 1994. "Serving the Public: An Assessment of Work in Public Sector Folklore." In *Putting folklore to use*, edited by Michael Owen Jones, 201–13. Lexington: University Press of Kentucky.

Bronner, Simon. 1987. *Old-time music makers of New York State.* Syracuse: Syracuse University Press.

Buhasz, Laszlo. 2006. "Northern Exposure." *Globe and Mail*, 1 July, T1, T5.

Bulger, Peggy A. 2003. "Looking Back, Moving Forward: The Development of Folklore as a Public Profession." *Journal of American Folklore* 116 (2003): 377–90.

Byington, Robert H. 1989. "What Happened to Applied Folklore?" In *Time and temperature*, edited by Charles Camp, 77–79. Washington, DC: American Folklore Society.

Camp, Charles, and Timothy Lloyd. 1990. "Six Reasons Not to Produce Folklife Festivals." *Kentucky Folklore Record* 26 (1980): 67–74.

Clarke, George Elliott. 1991. "Editor's introduction." In *Fire on the water: An anthology of Black Nova Scotian writing*, vol. 1, 11–29. Lawrencetown Beach, NS: Pottersfield Press.

Conway, Cecelia. 1995. *African banjo echoes in Appalachia.* Knoxville: University of Tennessee Press.

Creighton, Helen, and Ronald Labelle. 1988. *La fleur du rosier.* Sydney, NS: University College of Cape Breton Press.

Diamond, Beverley. 2006. "Canadian Reflections on Palindromes, Inversions, and Other Challenges to Ethnomusicology's Coherence." *Ethnomusicology* 50, no. 2: 324–36.

Diamond, Beverley, M. Sam Cronk, and Franziska von Rosen. 1994. "Cultural Knowledge: Searching at the Boundaries." In *Visions of sound: Musical instruments of First Nations communities in northeastern America*, edited by Beverley Diamond, M. Sam Cronk, and Franziska von Rosen, 1–16. Waterloo: Wilfrid Laurier University Press.

Epstein, Dena J. 1977. *Sinful tunes and spirituals: Black folk music to the Civil War.* Urbana: University of Illinois Press.

Glassie, Henry. 1970. "'Take that night train to Selma': An Excursion to the Outskirts of Scholarship." In *Folksongs and their makers*, edited by Henry Glassie, Edward D. Ives, and John F. Szwed, 4–6. Bowling Green, OH: Popular Press.

Jackson, Bruce. 1993. "The Folksong Revival." In *Transforming tradition*, edited by Neil V. Rosenberg, 73–83. Urbana: University of Illinois Press.

Linn, Karen. 1991. *That half-barbaric twang.* Urbana: University of Illinois Press.

Lovelace, Martin, and Peter Narváez. 2001. "Neil V. Rosenberg: Odyssey of a Folklorist." In *Bean blossom to bannerman, odyssey of a folklorist*, edited by Martin Lovelace, Peter Narváez, and Diane Tye, 1–20. St. John's: Memorial University of Newfoundland Folklore and Language Publications.

Malone, Bill C. 2002a. *Country music USA*, 2nd rev. ed. Austin: University of Texas Press.

———. 2002b. *Don't get above your raisin': Country music and the southern working class.* Urbana: University of Illinois Press.

Merriam, Alan. 1964. *The anthropology of music.* Evanston, IL: Northwestern University Press.

Perlman, Ken. 1996. *Mel Bay presents the fiddle music of Prince Edward Island: Celtic and Acadian tunes in living tradition.* Pacific, MO: Mel Bay Publications.

———. 2001. *Northern banjo.* Copper Creek CCCD-0191.

Posen, I. Sheldon. 2000. "Coaxing." In *Northeast folklore*, edited by Pauleena MacDougall and David Taylor, 137–51. Orono: University of Maine Press.

Rahn, Jay. 1977. "Canadian Folk Music Holdings at Columbia University." *Canadian Folk Music Journal* 5: 46–49.

Robbins, Li. 2005. *Don Messer's violin: Canada's fiddle.* Toronto: Canadian Broadcasting Corporation.

Rosenberg, Neil V. 1974. *Bill Monroe and his blue grass boys.* Nashville: Country Music Foundation.

———. 1976a. *Country music in the Maritimes: Two studies.* Department of Folklore Reprint Series no. 2. St. John's: Memorial University of Newfoundland.

———. 1976b. "Studying Country Music and Contemporary Folk Music Traditions in the Maritimes: Theory, Techniques, and the Archivist." *Phonographic Bulletin* 14: 18–21.

———. 1978. "Goodtime Charlie and the Bricklin: A Satirical Song in Context." *Journal of the Canadian Oral History Association* 3: 27–46.

———. 1980. "'It was a kind of hobby': A Manuscript Song Book and Its Place in Tradition." In *Folklore studies in honour of Herbert Halpert*, edited by Kenneth S. Goldstein and Neil V. Rosenberg, 315–33. St. John's: Memorial University of Newfoundland Folklore and Language Publications.

———. 1986. "Big Fish, Small Pond: Country Musicians and Their Markets." In *Media sense: The folklore-popular culture continuum*, edited by Peter Narváez and Martin Laba, 148–66. Bowling Green, OH: Bowling Green State University Popular Press.

———. 1988. "Canadian Newspapers as Source Material: Further Notes on James Douglass Bohee (1844–1897)." *Black Music Research Bulletin* 10, no. 2 (Fall): 15–17.

———. 1989. "Introduction to Folksong." In *Teaching folklore*, edited by Bruce Jackson, 118–28. Buffalo, NY: New South Moulton Press.

———. 1991. "The Gerald S. Doyle Songsters and the Politics of Newfoundland Folksong." *Canadian Folklore Canadien* 13, no. 1: 45–47.

———. 1994a. "Don Messer's Modern Canadian Fiddle Canon." *Canadian Folk Music Journal* 22: 23–35.

———. 1994b. "Ethnicity and Class: Black Country Musicians in the Maritimes." In *Canadian music: Issues of hegemony and identity*, edited by Beverley Diamond and Robert Witmer, 415–46. Toronto: Canadian Scholars' Press.

———. 1996. "Strategy and Tactics in Fieldwork: The Whole Don Messer Show." In *The world observed*, edited by Edward D. Ives and Bruce Jackson, 144–58. Urbana: University of Illinois Press.

———. 1998. "Notebook/Carnet: *The Anthology of American Folk Music* and Working-Class Music." *Labour/Le Travail* 42: 327–32.

———. 2001. "George Lyon Talks to Neil Rosenberg." *Canadian Folk Music Bulletin* 35, no. 1 (May): 1–10.

———. 2002. "Repetition, Innovation, and Representation in Don Messer's Media Repertoire." *Journal of American Folklore* 115: 191–208.

———. 2005. *Bluegrass: A history*. Urbana: University of Illinois Press.

Russell, Tony. 2004. *Country music records: A discography, 1921–1942*. New York: Oxford University Press.

Stafford, Tim, and Richard Blaustein. 1989. Notes to *Down around Bowmantown*. Now and Then Records 1001. Johnson City, TN: Center for Appalachian Studies and Services.

Szego, Peter. 2006a. "Searching for the Roots of the Banjo—Part I." *The Old-Time Herald* 10, no. 4 (April–May): 14–23.

———. 2006b. "Searching for the Roots of the Banjo—Part II." *The Old-Time Herald* 10, no. 5 (June–July): 10–20.

Winans, Robert. 1976. "The Folk, the Stage, and the Five-String Banjo in the Nineteenth Century." *Journal of American Folklore* 89: 407–37.

NINE

Strategies of Survival
Traditional Music, Politics, and Music Education among Two Minorities of Finland

PIRKKO MOISALA

HIS CHAPTER EXAMINES THE FACTORS and strategies involved in the process of incorporating traditionally orally transmitted music into formal and established educational programs.[1] The emphasis lies on the discursive and material aspects of this process, not on the examination of the changes in the music-making, which in itself would also make an interesting subject of study. The examples for this study are drawn from among the oldest minorities, the Sámi people[2] and the Finland-Swedes,[3] of present-day Finland. The natural oral transmission of their traditional musics, such as the *joiku* (in English, yoik) tradition of the Sámi and fiddling (*spelmansmusik*) of the Finland-Swedes, no longer ensures the continuation of these traditions because the major part of the traditional functions of these musics vanished decades ago. Today, there are only a few tradition-bearers left and only an occasional youngster takes an interest in learning music by heart. This situation worries people who value these musics either for their musical or their political and cultural value. Among both the Sámi and Finland-Swedes, traditional music is seen as a medium for sustaining cultural identity and local economics.

To analyze the factors involved in the process of drawing oral music transmission into a form of music education, I combine the theory of social movements developed by Sidney Tarrows (1999) with the concept of "assemblage" put forward by Gilles Deleuze and Félix Guattari (1987). Even though the strategies for supporting traditional music can hardly be claimed to reach the level of a social movement, the three dimensions that

"move" a social movement as defined by Tarrows—motives (what motivates people), means (what means and resources they have at hand), and
opportunities (what various situations provide)—provide useful models
for the analysis. They are not enough, however, to identify the discursive
and material dimensions of the process. For that purpose I turn to the
concept of "assemblage," defined by Deleuze and Guattari (1987, 406)
as the "very constellation of singularities and traits deduced from the
flow—selected, organized, stratified in such a way as to converge ... arti-
ficially and naturally." Thus, in the following I will examine the assemblage
of discursive and material factors that motivate the Sámi and the Finland-
Swedes to find strategies to maintain musical traditions and that provide
them with means and opportunities to seek and establish methods of musical education.

Finnish Music Education and Minority Musics

Music has always had a high status in the construction of Finnish cultural
identity, at first during the process of nation-building at the turn of the nineteenth century and again during World War I, when particularly the works
of Jean Sibelius served the purposes of national unification. When Finland became a part of the European Union in 1995, the importance of
Finnish music in developing and sustaining Finnish cultural identity in an
increasingly integrated Europe was again emphasized (Heiniö and Moisala
1999). The national Finnish music education system, which primarily
builds on Western art music and its theory, is well organized, it is pervasive throughout the country, and, due to the internationally successful
conductors and performers it has produced, it is highly valued. In addition
to art music made by Finnish composers, traditional Finnish music has
also been an important element in Finnish cultural identity. Both Finnish
art and folk musics have enjoyed strong financial support from the state
for decades.

As a result of the revival of folk music in the 1970s traditional Finnish
music became gradually integrated into the national education system.
For the past two decades traditional music has been taught even at the
foremost school of music, the Sibelius Academy (see, among others, Ramnarine 2003 and Hill 2005). Teaching of folk music is done both by oral
transmission and supported by notation. Students learn with the help of
archival recordings and from older performers how to play, sing, or compose in the style in question. They are also encouraged to improvise freely,
as well as to pick up musical influences from whatever source is available:

from media, CDs, and from music of various kinds of cultural backgrounds. The underlying idea is that folk musicians have always been free to adopt influences from whatever sources are available for them; thus, today's musicians should have the same freedom to receive and assimilate influences and change the tradition (Laitinen 1994). The core of the musical material and styles taught at the folk music department of the Sibelius Academy nevertheless consists of Finnish folk music repertoires and instruments, such as *kantele, jouhikko*, fiddle and accordion. Although it can be said that Finnish folk music education is relatively well organized, this education system does not provide equal opportunities for different ethnic and language minorities to promote their own musical traditions, nor does it provide equal opportunities for minorities to gain an education in their own language, even though short courses on minority musics are occasionally added to the course program and a student coming from a minority culture may, in the course of his or her studies, use the archival materials of his or her own musical heritage.

In this educational and political context, the oldest ethno-language minorities of Finland—the Sámi (who are the indigenous people of the country) and the Finland-Swedes—are striving to maintain their traditional music on their own terms. They have begun to seek means and methods of music education for their orally transmitted musical traditions, looking for ways to combine resources and methods of mainstream music education supported by the state with local interests and means of music transmission. This requires careful balancing between different kinds of conceptualizations of music as well as the consideration of many-sided— both local and national—political and economic aspects. This chapter examines these attempts, aimed at identifying material and discursive factors involved in the process when an oral music system is rearticulated into a formalized music education.

Spelmansmusik and Joiku/Yoik

The Finland-Swedish identity was constructed over roughly the same decades of the nineteenth century as the formation of Finnish cultural identity.[4] Among other cultural emblems, "authentic" traditional music of the rural Swedish-speaking Finns was chosen as a criterion for the promotion of language-based minority cultural identity. The Swedish-speaking population also consisted, however, of upper classes, nobles, and inhabitants of the bigger cities who did not share the same culture with the fishers and peasants of the countryside, from whom the emblems of cultural identity were collected. Finland was established in 1917 as a bilingual country, Finnish and Swedish being its *lingua francas*, official languages. Today, 5.6 percent of the whole population of Finland, about 290,000 people, are Swedish-speaking. There are no restrictions on who may declare himself or herself to be a Swedish-speaking person. The majority of Finland-Swedes live in the islands of Åland,[5] in the Turku archipelago, by the west coast of Finland, as well as in the bilingual cities of Helsinki/Helsingfors and Turku/Åbo.

The idea of a commonly shared Finland-Swedish music was constructed in the early stages of nation-building (Nyqvist 2007). The traditional fiddle music among the Finland-Swedes relates to Finnish *pelimanni* and Swedish *spelmans* traditions; it has been seen as a style somewhere between these two, although the borders between these styles are like lines drawn on water: tunes, as well as musical and stylistic influences, have been exchanged in both directions. If very roughly generalized, Finland-Swedish traditional fiddling possibly includes more ornamentation than Finnish fiddling of the same regions, and is rhythmically more complex than Finnish fiddling.[6]

Sámis are the indigenous people of Finland who nevertheless have been treated until the last decades only as a linguistic minority without the same kind of official status as the Swedish. Even though the rights of the Sámi have recently improved, the Sámis are still struggling to secure rights to their lands. Today 8,600 people are considered Sámi in Finland. Language is an important criterion of Sáminess, although only slightly more than half of the Sámi population speaks one of the three Sámi languages spoken in Finland. The Sámi people consist of three language and cultural groups: the Northern Sámi, Inari Sámi, and Scolt Sámi. They live in Finnish Lapland, bordering on Sweden, Norway, and Russia, and they constitute a third of the total population in this region.[7]

The Finnish word *joiku* as well as the pan-Sámi word *juoiggas*, refer to the traditional Sámi vocal style in general; the standard English word for *juoiggas* is yoik. The several regional traditions of yoik share some general characteristics: yoik is at one with its subject; it represents the person, the animal, or the place it presents (Järvinen 1999; Jouste 2006). A yoik is made for a child and it develops with the child. Many Sámis consider it improper to yoik (in Finnish, *joikua*) a person without the permission of his or her family. Yoik is also bound up with time and place; places produce different improvised versions of yoik. In addition to regional, family, and personal yoiks, there are also yoiks that have become commonly owned. The complete yoik is formed from melodic, rhythmic, stylistic, textual, and performative elements (Jouste 2006, 276). Language used is also an important ingredient of yoik. Different languages and traditions have their own yoik traditions: *luohti* of the Northern Sámi, *leu'dd* of the Scolts, and *livde* of the Inari Sámi. Modern times have also produced a variety of yoiks, from world music yoiks to yoik schlagers, jazzy yoiks, yoik-raps, and yoik-songs, to name just a few.

It is important to recognize the many-sidedness of what is called "the Sámi" and "the Finland-Swedes": they both are more like multi-faceted discourses than real-life social realities. The political and statistical representations of these peoples correspond only modestly to their many-sidedness. Despite the relative functional autonomy of the Swedish-speaking culture with its schools, newspapers, radio channels, TV, church, and military service, and despite the growing number of cultural and political institutions supporting some kind of pan-Sáminess, there are several regional and cultural variations. This multiplicity can be examined as an "assemblage" of resonating effects. In addition to regional differences, the several different kinds of "flows" (in the Deleuzian sense) encourage a view of the Sámi or the Finland-Swedes as a discursive and "imagined nationhood" (Anderson 1982). The "flows" at work in the assemblages of the Sámi and the Finland-Swedes reveal geographies of discourse, commodities, bodies, and infrastructures. I admit that it is hard to approach any reality in a specific context without assuming in advance that a particular set of logics determines its form because the official numbers and stereotypical representations tend to cloud the sight.

Despite the distinct histories of the Sámi and the Finland-Swedes, their differing official status in present-day Finland, and their internal many-sidedness, there are interesting similarities in their attempts to support their traditional musics in current circumstances. Assimilation into the mainstream culture and language is seen as the biggest threat to distinctive cultural identities at the same time as internal differences within the minority culture make it difficult to set common goals. It is particularly challenging to create favourable conditions for the survival of minority music cultures, which do not have a clearly differentiated geographical region.

Toward *Joiku*/Yoik Education

When you ask older Sámi people how they learned to yoik, they reply "I just learned it," without being able to describe the process of learning in greater detail. They may recall people whom they heard yoiking in their childhood environment, and name places and occasions where yoiking took place; often it was a family member, grandparent, a parent, or uncles who yoiked at home, on special occasions, and also during work and everyday activities. On the other hand, if yoiking was regarded as sinful in the region, which was often the case, it was done alone in the woods, *tunturilla* (on the mountains) or with a trusted group of friends. Since the 1950s, yoiksongs (in other words, notated yoik-melodies maintaining some structural features of yoik) were included in school songbooks. However, their effectiveness in promoting the learning of yoik was limited due to the variety of yoiking techniques and improvisation. In the 1970s, the situation changed. The example of Nils-Aslak Valkeapää, who was the driving force for the emerging Sámi cultural identity, inspired many other yoikers to produce records, LPs, and, later on, cassettes and CDs (see also Jones-Bamman 2006). They became "stars" and their music was played at home. Since then many people have learned yoiks from recordings. Thanks to the records, they learned the yoiks of families from far away and yoiks representing people they did not know.

Today all these kinds of learning processes of the yoik—enculturation into the yoik tradition, learning from the elders in the family as well as from the notated versions, songbooks, and recordings—still continue in the Finnish region of Sámiland, although to a much lesser degree than before. Yoik has lost its traditional uses and functions in Sámi society, partly as a consequence of the Lutheran Laestadius sect, which regards it as sinful, but also due to general modernization. For instance, there is no longer any yoiking while herding reindeers when motorized snow ski vehicles (skidoos) are used. Therefore, there are many who worry about the transmission of yoik to new generations: many "yoik-aware" people no longer trust the "natural" ways of learning to be effective enough to keep yoik alive. The first steps have consequently been taken in Finland to formalize yoik transmission into yoik education. It is important to note that the situation of yoik transmission and education varies depending on the country. In the Norwegian region of Sámiland, the survival of the yoik (in Norwegian and in Swedish, *joik*) is guaranteed by music schools and the professional yoiker training in Kautokeino, as well as, more recently, through educational books compiled by Frode Fjellheim (2004). The other extreme can be found in the Russian side of Sámiland.

Today, a considerable number of diverse projects have been undertaken for the maintenance and transmission of yoik in Finland. Together with collaborative partners from different Sámi organizations, Ulla Pirtti-järvi, a yoiker who has worked for three years as the provincial artist of Lapland, has taken on the task of promoting yoik at schools. She has tried to find local yoikers who would join her in teaching the pupils yoik at schools. In the school, her role was also to make a "pedagogical translation" of the yoiks performed by the visiting yoikers: she simplified the yoik if the voice formation of the yoiker was too foreign for the children, pointed out the essential features of the yoiks, and changed the register in order to make it easier for the children to follow the example. Pirttijärvi emphasizes yoik as a local tradition, the importance of family yoik traditions, and the consideration of yoik ownership. In her opinion, the area and family bonds should be carefully acknowledged in yoik education. In addition to Pirttijärvi, there have also been other active Sámi working for the promotion of yoik traditions, such as Tiina Aikio from the village of Vuotso.

In 2003, the Sámi Parliament initiated a project to promote Sámi music education, financed by the European Union. The planning proceeded from an investigation of the present state and current issues regarding traditional Sámi music to a primary project plan in 2004. The planning was initiated by the Sámi Parliament in Finland and undertaken by the ethnomusicologist and Sámi musician Annukka Hirvasvuopio together with Annukka Näkkäläjärvi, in collaboration with *Juoigiid Searvi* (The Yoik Association), Lapland's Music Institute, the Polytechnic of the Sámi region, the municipality of Inari, and the Union of Music Institutes in Finland. The plan suggested that a music institute be established, the study plan of which would combine Sámi music education with the Finnish national music education system. In this way, Sámi music education had become guided by the national study program for music constructed on the basis of the Western art music system. In the application for further financing directed to the European Social Fund within the European Union, the promotion of Sámi music education was, among other things, motivated by tourism and employment.

Attempts to adjust the improvisational and performative yoik into the music education system based on Western art music theory raised many problematic issues. It turned out to be extremely difficult to explain to music educators and administrators that yoik is not a song like any other song, but instead it needs a pedagogical approach that emphasizes socially grounded teaching methods and imitative learning. At the end of the discussions some of the music educators stated that the Sámis should decide whether they wished to have an "excellent bassoonist or to promote traditional music." In other words, did the Sámi want to provide educational possibilities for their children to make a professional career in the Finnish music culture or did they want to support their own musical traditions?

These two musical systems seemed irreconcilable. Questions of power as well as regional and economic interests have also played a part in the process. The planning of Sámi music education has included discussions about which societies or institutions will carry the main responsibility for the project, which and whose yoik repertoire will be taught at schools, where the project will be placed, what the benefits of this project will be and to whom.

By August 2006, the planning of the project had proceeded to the second stage, the report of which suggests that emphasis be put on bringing Sámi music education to the villages, where the teaching should be given by local yoikers, and organizing yoik teaching at primary schools and establishing a centre for Sámi music under the Sámi Parliament in Finland. The Canadian method developed for the Learning from the Elders project and Ulla Pirttijärvi's activities are mentioned as positive precedents. The planning group also organized two successful Sámi music seminars for teachers and daycare workers. The objective is to compile teaching materials in Northern, Inari, and Scolt Sámi languages on the basis of the songs, plays, and yoiks presented in the course of the seminar.

The project was finished by the end of March 2007.[8] The final report includes a suggestion for organizing music education of Sámi traditions (*Saamelaisten musiikkiperinteiden opetuksen toimintaidea*, 2007) written by Annukka Näkkäläjärvi, who based the suggestion on interviews with Sámi musicians and the models of music education used in Finland and at *Sámi Allaskuvla* (the Sámi high school) of Kautokeino in Norway. The plan is grounded in the "learning from the elders" method referred to above: the basis of Sámi music education should lie in Sámi and other indigenous musical traditions, and their music theories augmented with transcription and note-reading, as well as with knowledge of music technology and studio work. The aesthetics, performance styles, vocabulary, and the variety of local and other styles of traditional Sámi musics are presented as important elements of teaching materials, which are sought both from local tradition-bearers as well as from archives. The teachers should also try to seek teaching environments that correspond with the traditional musical context. Sámi music education is regarded as a tool to enliven musical traditions, to teach the pupils elements of Sámi culture and its models of thinking, and as a tool to strengthen their cultural identity.

Spelmansmusik and Music Education in Kökar

During the first years of this new millennium, the Finland-Swedes also established a planning group, the so-called KRUM (*Konstnärliga rådet för finlandssvenska utbildningsfrågor i musik*), for coordinating and organizing music education in Swedish in Finland. The main goal of this group was to make plans for providing equal opportunities for music education at all levels to Swedish-speaking youth in their mother tongue. The group has also discussed the possibility of providing education in traditional Finland-Swedish music. Musical life in three Swedish-speaking communities—Kökar, Korsholm, and Espoo—was studied in order to gain information for the planning. The following detailed example is taken from the island of Kökar in the Baltic Sea, where the issue of *spelmansmusik* is more prominent than in many other Finland-Swedish communities (see also Moisala 2007).

Kökar has a relatively well-documented folk music tradition; the earliest documentation is from the early nineteenth century (see Högnäs 1991). The island was, for decades, known for its lively tradition of fiddle playing and folk songs (*vissång*). In the 1930s and 1940s there was an instrument in every house; almost everyone tried to play the fiddle. The fiddle was used mainly to accompany dance, and when first the accordion and later recordings gradually replaced it as the dance instrument, aging fiddlers had fewer opportunities to play their walzes, polkas, schottises, and mazurkas in public. The exception is weddings, which still today are often done with fiddlers. In the 1950s, the islanders began to invite dance bands from the mainland Åland or even from Sweden.

The folk music revival reached Scandinavia and the island of Kökar in the late 1970s (see Ronström 1996). The new primary schoolteacher of the island, Per-Ove Högnäs, who originally came from the mainland Åland, wished to revitalize the old fiddle tradition of the island. He took a serious interest in documenting the local fiddle repertoire (close to sixty tunes), and called the old fiddle players to form an ensemble, *Kökar spelmansgrupp*, in 1977. The fiddlers who used to be "dance musicians" became "folk musicians," who played Kökar tunes on stage and on records. This kind of group playing was not customary, although two fiddlers may have occasionally played together for a wedding. As ensemble playing occasions were rare, the playing styles of the fiddlers were highly individual. Högnäs did not standardize these individual playing styles, but he coordinated the weekly meetings during which everyone could learn the same tunes. Many of the fiddlers had their own tunes, which were then shared and taught to others at the weekly rehearsals. Several fiddlers playing the same tune together in their own style with individual embellishments gave birth to a special sound, rich in nuances and variations. The popularity of *Kökar spelmanslag* became more widespread through performances at folk music festivals outside the home island. The audiences enjoyed the liveliness, speed, and swing, "*livet, farten och fläkten,*" of its performance style. Once the ensemble was even invited to perform for King Carl XVII Gustaf of Sweden. In the early 1990s Kökar had the greatest number of fiddlers in relation to the population among the islands of Åland. Over the years, the permanent population of the island diminished greatly; in the 1960s it was only half of what it had been forty years before. The economics of the island changed: the traditional occupations of small-scale farmers, sailors, and fishers no longer offered the same economic security as they had previously. Young people left the island for opportunities of higher education and work; many never returned to live on the island. Today, the winter population of only three hundred inhabitants is doubled during the summer months; people come to spend their vacation back on their home island, and the isolated and beautiful island attracts a number of tourists.

Two decades ago Gunnar Sundström, who had lived in the mainland Åland, returned to live on the home island of his parents. In his childhood and during his summer vacations he had often heard fiddlers playing, but finally he wished to learn to play it himself. He joined the group in the mid-1990s when *Kökar spelmanslag* still had close to fifteen members. However, the fiddlers got older and the younger islanders were not interested in learning the repertoire. Today, there are only four fiddlers left, two of whom are no longer capable of playing the fiddle. At weddings, Gunnar Sundström's playing companion is now a female fiddle player, Oili Jansson, who moved to Kökar when she married a local man and learned the local repertoire and playing styles from the old fiddlers. Oili Jansson had spent her childhood on the mainland of Finland, studying violin and classical music. Marriage brought her to Kökar in the early 1980s. When her children were young, Jansson's violin hung on the wall, but she regained her interest in music when she was persuaded to join *Kökar spelmanslag*. Even though her background was in classical violin music, she became enthusiastic about the old tunes: if she did not have a chance to visit older fiddlers because of the demands of caring for her children, she learned from them by phone.

In the beginning of the millennium when his own children reached the right age, Sundström began to teach folk fiddling and the Kökar repertoire to a group of children. Some of them also participate in a fiddle group on mainland Åland; the trip there takes nine hours. The islanders have also organized folk music summer camps for which the teachers have come from the neighbouring islands or even from the mainland. The music taught in these camps originates outside of Kökar, in the Finland-Swedish folk music tradition.

The future of the music of Kökar has been of concern to local cultural activists. Despite political differences between the various participants involved, the islanders have gathered their "troops" to raise the status of music in the local school as well as to apply lessons of folk music from the Åland music institute, both without success. One of the cultural actors is Gunnar Sundström's mother Sylvia Sundström, who has worked in tourism and established the local museum. Together with the local cultural society, *Kökar Hembygsförening*, authorities of the municipality, as well as tourist entrepreneurs, she compiled an application to the European Union. They gained funding for a three-year project, *Kulturturism på Kökar* (cultural tourism on Kökar), the objective of which is to promote cultural life, tourism, and local economics. The project has heightened the discussion about the value of local traditional music and about the most effective ways it can be transmitted, taught, and supported. The aim is to establish instrumental and dance groups that would perform for the summer visitors; so far, traditional song (*vissång*) and folk dancing are not included in these plans. The hope is that, in addition to encouraging tourism, the enlivening of cultural and economic life would entice those who migrated decades ago back to the island.

The financial support received from the European Union has made it possible to organize weekly folk music sessions for children between the ages of twelve and sixteen. The teaching is done partly orally, after Gunnar Sundström's example, and partly by notes taught by the local school music teacher, Philip Hällund. In fact, Sundström has taken on the task of carefully weaning the children from the notation. Oili Jansson also occasionally attends the sessions (see Figure 9.1). The repertoire taught is based on transcriptions of archival recordings; Per-Ove Högnäs is also invited to come and show his films of the old fiddlers.

The problems in Kökar have been largely the same as in Sámiland: the national network of music institutions builds on the Western art music model and, therefore, other organizational constructions and teaching methods are needed. Even though Finland-Swedish fiddling is closer to Western art music theory than yoik, it is hard to apply the conventional methods of art music education without losing some of the central characteristics, such

FIGURE 9.1 Gunnar Sundström and Oili Jansson playing together with the children of Kökar.

as variations and embellishments, of the orally transmitted music. Furthermore, it has not been easy to make children and youth interested in local music traditions in the era of global music markets.

Assemblage of Motives, Means, and Opportunities

The strategies of survival among the Sámi and the Finland-Swedes build on the same elements as a social movement: on motives, means, and opportunities. The motives for organizing traditional music education are obvious: the importance of traditional music for the cultural identity of the ethnic/language group in general, as well as the positive effect that an active musical life has on people and their locality, including its tourism and economics. The means to promote the education of traditional music are derived both from the oral methods of music transmission and, in part, from the formalized music education system. The resources needed include financial support and archival sources of traditional musical repertoires. Finally, the European Union, with its cultural politics, provides new opportunities in addition to the opportunities arising from the tourist industry.

The discursive dimensions, which overlap each other, involved in the strategies to maintain traditional music are about music, ethnic and cultural identity, as well as language and minority politics. The essential subject matter within the music discourse is about the "music" (which features of the sound phenomenon are regarded as central and which repertoire is to be taught) and about teaching methods (if the music should be taught orally, through imitation, or based on the score or as a combination of these two). For instance, does the "Sámi music" chosen to be taught mean all songs in the Sámi language; only yoiks; only the oldest yoik traditions; yoiks of a certain language group; music done by Sámi people in general? Or should only the very local repertoire to be taught? The current discourses of ethnic and cultural identity deal with questions about desired kinds of representations of ethnic and cultural identity: which musics are the most suitable for these ends and which are preferable musical icons and representations of Sáminess and Finland-Swedishness? Both music and identity discourses include different kinds of understanding of what is regarded as "traditional," "local," and "authentic," as well as about their value in today's world. One of the central questions has also been if music education should aim at supporting local ethnicity or providing the pupils with basic competence as preparation for musical careers in the majority music culture (that is, education in Western art and popular music theory and practice), or if these aims could be combined.

Political discourses address both minority and language politics, both within the language group in question, within the particular location as well as in the context of language and minority politics of the state of Finland. Language plays an essential role in music education, not only as the texts of singing, such as in yoik, but also as the teaching language. It is important for the minorities to provide music education in children's mother tongues because both language and music reinforce their cultural identity.

The central political discourses are about power and status. The local and national cultural politics compete, for instance, about who is to be granted the power to organize traditional music education: should the traditional music education relate to national education systems and, if so, in which ways? Due to the financial support provided by the European Union, even European cultural politics play a role because only certain kinds of cultural projects will attract support from the EU.

The material factors include the human resources available: educators, yoikers, fiddlers, and pupils; different localities with their geographies and distances (including discourses on what is regarded as the "centre" and "periphery"); regional musical styles; local repertoires. Multi-faceted economic considerations complicate the material factors further: who pays, from which funds, how the financial support is received from outside sources (national or European funds), and how these factors will dictate the form and aim of musical education.

Within this assemblage of several material and discursive effects, it is difficult to see what the future of these traditional musics will be.

Nevertheless, I am tempted to conclude with a couple of insights provided by the theory of assemblage. By producing homogeneity and stereotypical images of yoik, the planning of traditional music education may force these traditions into models that do not acknowledge personal, local, or regional differences. On another level, however, the planning may promote both a new kind of creativity and new processes of becoming. It will at least open up new paths of thinking about yoik of the Sámi in Finland and fiddle traditions of the islanders of Kökar.

Unpublished Material

I am grateful for the information and time provided particularly by Katarina Gäddnäs, Greta Dahlblom, Annukka Hirvasvuopio, Philip Hällund, Margareta Jorpes-Friman, Oili Jansson, Oula Näkkäläjärvi, Ulla Pirttijärvi, Gunnar Sundström, Sylvia Sundström, and Virpi Veskoniemi.

Delrapport för KRUM. Compiled by Ros-Marie Djupsund, 12 December 2004.
Kulturturism på Kökar. Lägesrapport. Compiled by Kökar hembygdsförening, January 2006.
Projektisuunnitelma. Saamelaisen musiikin opetuksen organisointi. Compiled by Annukka Hirvasvuopio and Annukka Näkkäläjärvi, August 2004.
Saamelaisen musiikkiopiston musiikkikoulutuksen järjestäminen. Esiselvitys. Suomen musiikkioppilaitosten liitto, Saamelaiskäräjien toimeksiannosta, March 2004.
Saamelaisten musiikkiperinteiden opetuksen toimintaidea, written by Annukka Näkkäläjärvi. Sámediggi, The Sámi Parliament of Finland, 2006 http://www .samediggi.fi/projektit/muspro.htm.
Väliraportti saamelaismusiikin opetuksen kehittämishankkeesta saamelaiskäräjien hallitukselle. Compiled by Annukka Hirvasvuopio and Annukka Näkkäläjärvi. Sámediggi, The Sámi Parliament of Finland, November 2005. http://www .samediggi.fi/projektit/muspro.htm.
Vuosiraportti, saamelaismusiikin opetuksen kehittämishanke. Compiled by Annukka Hirvasvuopio and Annukka Näkkäläjärvi. Sámediggi, The Sámi Parliament of Finland, 2006. http://www.samediggi.fi/projektit/muspro.htm.

Notes

1   Ethnomusicological research has paid surprisingly little attention to changes in music transmission. An interesting exception is an article by Niall Keegan (1996), which examines the way traditional Irish music has shaped notational systems to its own needs and sees notation as just another result of larger changes in the music culture. Oral music learning systems, particularly those of non-Western origin, have been of interest to scholars working in the area of music education as well, although mostly only from the standpoint of pedagogical objectives. For instance, the cross-cultural comparative survey of

musical transmission and of the methods of delivery and acquisition of music conducted by Patricia Campbell (2001) provides useful information about the various forms of oral-aural transmission.

2 I have had the pleasure of conducting a couple of short fieldwork trips to Finnish and Norwegian Lapland with Beverley Diamond. Some of the interviews used as the material for this chapter were conducted with her. I dedicate this chapter to her with these dear memories in mind.

3 The terms *Finland-Swedish* or *Finland-Swedes* refer to the Swedish minority in Finland rather than the two countries.

4 A section of the Finnish population has always spoken Swedish as its mother tongue: Finland was a part of Sweden when the state of Sweden was founded. When Finland was part of Sweden (ca. 1150–1809), the Swedish language was promoted as the official language of the country. However, when Finland was seeking independence from Russia in the early nineteenth century, the language of the majority of the population, Finnish, was promoted for the purposes of Finnish nation-building. This led to language struggles and eventually to two *lingua francas*. The construction of Finland-Swedishness has been thoroughly researched (for instance, see Ståhlberg 1995; Åström et al. 2001; Vilstrand 2001).

5 Åland, a group of islands in the Baltic Sea between Sweden and Finland, has military and political autonomy within Finland.

6 There is no comparative research on the playing styles and, in fact, surprisingly little has been written about the fiddling styles among the Finland-Swedes. The most outstanding of the pioneering researchers, Otto Andersson (among others, 1909 and 1912), conducted comparative melody analyses on Finland-Swedish dance tunes. His crucial role in the construction of Finland-Swedish musical tradition has been analyzed by Niklas Nyqvist (2007). An anthology compiled by Marianne Maans (2006) includes an illuminating CD of one local Finland-Swedish music tradition.

7 Sapme/Sámiland also reaches across the northern parts of Norway, Sweden, Finland, and Russia, with the greatest number of the Sámis living in Norway. Even though the idea of Sapme is functional, the cultural and ethnic unity of people speaking different Sámi languages is strong. Nevertheless, the Sámis live in different kinds of cultural and political conditions depending on their country of habitation. The Sámi rights and cultural conditions have been most improved in Norway.

8 This article was written in 2007, and so does not describe later developments regarding minority music eduaction in Finland.

References

Anderson, Benedict. 1982. *Imagined communities: Reflections on the origin and rise of nationalism*. London: Verso.

Andersson, Otto. 1909. "Bidrag till kännedom om polskemelodiernas byggnad." *Brages årsskrift* 4: 170–76.

———. 1912. "Djävulspolskan," finländska varianter. *Brages årsskrift* 7:133–59.

Åström, Anna-Maria, with Bo Lönnqvist and Yrsa Lindqvist. 2001. *Gränsfolkets barn. Finlandssvensk marginalitet och självhävdelse i kulturanalytiskt perspektiv*. Helsingfors: Svenska Litteratursällskapet.

Campbell, Patricia. 2001. "Unsafe Suppositions? Cutting across Cultures in Questions of Music's Transmission." *Music Education Research* 3, no. 2: 215–26.

Deleuze, Gilles, and Félix Guattari. 1987. *A thousand plateaus: Capitalism and schizophrenia*. Translation and Foreword by Brian Massumi. Minneapolis: University of Minnesota Press.

Fjellheim, Frode. 2004. *En laerebok i musikk—med joik som utgangspunkt*. Trondheim: Vuelie forlag.

Heiniö, Mikko, and Pirkko Moisala. 1999. "Musiikki nykysuomalaisuuden konstruoijana." *Musiikki* 4: 363–68. Helsinki: Hakapaino.

Hill, Juniper. 2005. From ancient to avant-garde to global: Creative processes and institutionalization in Finnish contemporary folk music. Ph.D. dissertation, Department of Ethnomusicology, University of California, Los Angeles.

Högnäs, Per-Ove. 1991. *Låtar från Kökar. Uppteckningar och historik över spel-och danstraditioner i en skärgådsbygd*. Mariehamn: Ålands folkminnesförbund r.f.

Järvinen, Minna Riikka. 1999. *Maailma äänessä. Tutkimus pohjoissaamelaisesta joikuperinteestä*. Helsinki: Suomalaisen Kirjallisuuden Seura.

Jones-Bamman, Richard. 2006. "From 'I'm a Lapp' to 'I'm a Saami': Popular Music and Changing Images of Indigenous Ethnicity in Scandinavia." In *Ethnomusicology: A contemporary reader*, edited by Jennifer Post, 351–67. New York: Routledge.

Jouste, Marko. 2006. "Suomen saamelaisten musiikkiperinteet." In *Kansanmusiikki*, edited by Anneli Asplund et al., 272–307. Helsinki: Werner Söderström Osakeyhtiö.

Keegan, Niall. 1996. "Literacy as a Transmission Tool in Irish Traditional Music." *Irish Musical Studies* 4, edited by Patrick F. Devine and Harry White, 335–52. Dublin: Four Courts Press.

Laitinen, Heikki. 1994. "Music-Making as Research Method." *Ethnomusicology* 38, no. 3: 408–10.

Maans, Marianne, ed. 2006. *Musik och människor, folkmusik från Kristinestadsnejden* [with CD]. Vasa: Finlands svenska folkmusikinstitut.

Moisala, Pirkko. 2007. "Kökarmusiken inför morgondagens nya utmaningar." *Musiikin Suunta* 2: 3–14.

Nyqvist, Niklas. 2007. *En spelmans väg från bondson till folkmusikikon. Otto Andersson och den finlandssvenska folkmusikens kanon*. Åbo: Åbo Akademi tryckeri.

Ramnarine, Tina K. 2003. *Ilmatar's inspirations: Nationalism, globalization, and the changing soundscapes of Finnish music*. Chicago: University of Chicago Press.

Ronström, Owe. 1996. "Revival Reconsidered." *The World of Music* 38, no. 3: 5–20.

Ståhlberg, Krister, ed. 1995. *Finlandssvensk identitet och kultur*. Åbo: Åbo Akademi, Institutet för offentlig förvaltning.

Tarrow, Sidney. 1999. *Power in movement: Social movements and contentious politics*. Cambridge: Cambridge University Press.

Villstrand, Nils Erik. 2001. "Språket långt—finlandssvenskheten kort." *Finsk Tidskrift*: 8–20.

Wiley, Stephen B. 2003. "Nation as Transnational Assemblage: Three Moments in Chilean Media History." In *Animations (of Deleuze and Guattari)*, edited by Jennifer Daryl Slack, 129–63. New York: Peter Lang Publishing.

TEN

Father of Romance, Vagabond of Glory

Two Canadian Composers as Stage Heroes

JOHN BECKWITH

OW OFTEN IN THE ANNALS of lyric theatre has the real or imaginary life story of a composer served as the inspiration? Faced with this trivia question, an opera buff or a fan of musical comedy might reach for Rimsky-Korsakov's *Mozart and Salieri* (1898), Pfitzner's *Palestrina* (1917), or Sigmund Romberg's *Blossom Time* (1921), with an unhappy Franz Schubert as its hero. Hans Sachs was an actual sixteenth-century lyricist-composer before he became the key character in Wagner's *Die Meistersinger*. Other examples that come to mind depend on artistic invention rather than biography: in *Ariadne auf Naxos* and again in *Capriccio*, Strauss and Hofmannsthal depict a fictional composer; and Virgil T. is the male chorus in Virgil Thomson's *The Mother of Us All*, his female counterpart being Gertrude S., obviously the opera's librettist, Gertrude Stein. In early 2007, the Metropolitan Opera in New York gave the first production of Tan Dun's *The First Emperor*, a work it had commissioned. One of the main characters is a fictitious composer, and the main plot line is Emperor Qin's demand that he write an anthem to celebrate the unity of China. The first act ends with an emphatic curtain-line, sung by the Emperor (Plácido Domingo): "Finish the anthem!"

In the annals of *Canadian* lyric theatre, surprisingly, two examples emerge: *Le Père des amours* (Montreal, 1942) and *Le Vagabond de la gloire* (Montreal, 1947). In the former, the central figure is the French-born composer and writer Joseph Quesnel (1746–1809), active in Canada from his emigration in 1779, while the latter features Calixa Lavallée (1842–91), the outstanding musical personality of nineteenth-century Canada, best known as the composer of "O Canada." The stage works recount their careers with little regard for the known historical facts, an approach familiar from the Rimsky, Pfitzner, and Romberg items mentioned, and from many a Hollywood biopic.

The composer of both works is Eugène Lapierre (1899–1970), a prominent Montreal critic, teacher, and church musician. He was educated in the generation of Abbé Lionel Groulx's *L'Action catholique* (later *L'Action française*), and as a student at the Université de Montréal he came under the influence of the noted exponent of "cultural economics," Édouard Montpetit. After studies in Paris in the mid-1920s he became the director of an independent Montreal music school, the Conservatoire national, a post he held until 1951. Apart from his two operettas, he composed a body of sacred choral pieces and works for organ. His published writings of the 1930s include a book, *Pourquoi la musique?* (1933a), and several pamphlets with titles like "Le rôle social de la musique," "Les vedettes de la musique canadienne," "Un style canadien de musique," and "La question du Conservatoire." They range from broad questions of musical aesthetics to the special place of music in Canadian society, the accomplishments of its main exponents, and specific issues such as the need for a state-supported music school. He is best remembered, however, for the first (and until recently the only) biography of Lavallée, *Calixa Lavallée, musicien national du Canada*, published in 1936 with further editions in 1950 and 1966. Lapierre was a forefront instigator of the 1933 ceremonies reinterring Lavallée's remains in Montreal from the original burial site in Boston. His writings align with the conservative Roman Catholic teachings of his time and uphold a patriotic view founded on a sense of French culture transplanted in francophone North America. To judge from his work, Lapierre stands as a Quebec nationalist before the decline of clerical authority, before the *révolution tranquille* of the 1960s, and before the term "Québécois" came into common use.[1]

One of the earliest researchers to argue for the serious study of Canada's musical past,[2] Lapierre, however, often surrounds his findings with a romantic idealism that transcends scholarly objectivity. Later cultural and historical commentators contrast him with other figures in his generation of wider perspective, such as the progressive composer Rodolphe Mathieu and the pianist, critic, and composer Léo-Pol Morin.[3] Indeed, Lapierre's recipe for an authentic Canadian musical style was held up to ridicule by a musicologist of a later generation, Yves Chartier:

"Our music will be serene and melancholic," somewhat like Russian or Finnish music. (The force of geography!) "Canadian music will be rhythmically virile"—as befits a "strong and devout" people. This music "will be mystical, like Russian music." (The force of Catholicism, this time!) Canadian music "will be systematically melodic," meaning neither "futurist" nor modern—by which one gathers that our music will be the opposite of that composed by "decadents" such as Richard Strauss or Max Reger. (Chartier 1973, 76)[4]

On the other hand, Morin, in Chartier's view, "made an effort ... to see in Canadian music something other than an echo of racial traditions or ancestral faith" (1973, 77). Lucien Poirier similarly contrasts the opinions of Lapierre to those of Mathieu and Morin: noting Lapierre's frequent approving references to Groulx, he concludes: "the corpus of terms and ideas behind [Lapierre's] discourse is borrowed from the official ideology of the Quebec church" (1984, 253).

Lapierre's two stage works of the 1940s could be called patriotic tracts disguised as entertainment. His brief account of Quesnel in *Pourquoi la musique?* (1933a, 166ff.) gives a fanciful summary of this composer's output—songs, string quartets, symphonies, church music—without mentioning specific titles, for the good reason that no such works survive, if in fact they ever existed.[5] At the same time it omits all reference to Quesnel's two major compositions, written in the late-eighteenth-century genre of *comédie mêlée d'ariettes*, *Colas et Colinette* and *Lucas et Cécile*; both of these works *have* survived, albeit only in partial form, and in recent years have been successfully restored and performed (see the articles on each work in Kallmann 1992/3). The Lavallée biography (Lapierre 1966) singles out his "chant national," since 1980 Canada's official national anthem, for extended analysis and commentary, but gives the same treatment to none of the other, larger works by this composer.[6] The librettos of *Le Père des amours* and *Le Vagabond de la gloire* employ severely edited versions of the known life stories of the two musicians, invent wholly imaginary accounts of their love lives, and ignore their extant creative repertoires. Quesnel and Lavallée appear before us to enact two different fables of Franco-Canadian history: Quesnel becomes a troubadour akin to those of medieval France, singing his way into the hearts of settlers in early Quebec, and Lavallée a North American "vagabond" and a perpetual loser, his talent crushed over and over by people and circumstances mainly, we're led to suppose, because of his *Canadien* origins.

Joseph Quesnel, "Father of Romance"

Le Père des amours was first mounted at the Monument national, one of Montreal's best-known cultural centres, on 10, 12, and 13 December 1942, in a production co-sponsored by the Montreal Tercentenary Commission and the National Saint-Jean-Baptiste Federation. The printed program describes the work as the "premier opéra-comique canadien"—the "first Canadian comic opera"—although Lapierre was surely aware that both Quesnel and Lavallée composed works that could be termed comic operas, as did other composers in Canada prior to 1942.[7] He wrote both the libretto and the music. There are references to Quesnel's best-known poem, "L'Épître à M. Labadie," and to the character of the bailiff in Quesnel's *Colas et Colinette*, but no borrowings from Quesnel's own music.[8] The musical component is substantial, amounting to more than thirty orchestral, choral, ensemble, and solo numbers. Judging from the typescript of the libretto,[9] the five-act piece probably occupied more than three hours in performance, not counting intermissions.

The "amours" of the title refer to the concept of courtly love, the *Minne* of the German aristocratic singer-poets of the late Middle Ages, whose romances address idealized patronesses rather than lovers. In Lapierre's story, the young Joseph Quesnel earns the title "Père des amours" through his success in poetry competitions in his native Brittany, rather like an eighteenth-century French Walther von Stolzing. The title derives, Lapierre tells us, from an obscure medieval tradition. An appropriate English equivalent might be "Father of romance."[10]

Lapierre's notes in the program for the 1942 production describe the historical Quesnel and suggest reasons for adopting him as a stage hero:[11]

> In 1779, at the end of summer, an elegant French frigate sailed to America, under the command of a twenty-nine-year-old captain, Joseph Quesnel de La Rivaudais. He had been entrusted with the mission of relieving Lafayette at New York. Born in Saint-Malo, like Jacques Cartier, this sailor was destined to play a role in the history of our country. Where Cartier discovered our lovely land and gave it to France, Quesnel was the first to apply energy here in fostering the arts, song, and the fine French spirit.

A "reality check" reveals that the ship was a privateer carrying munitions, and that Quesnel was thirty-three, not twenty-nine.[12] The quasi-aristocratic second surname "de La Rivaudais" was employed in Brittany by his father, Isaac Quesnel, but not in Canada by Joseph Quesnel. Though undoubtedly an important pioneer in theatre and music, Quesnel was not "the first." Further "reality checks" to Lapierre's program note are interspersed below in parentheses.

> Arriving within view of Newfoundland, the ship, the *Espoir*, became encircled by fog, and stark phantom figures surged slowly alongside. English ships patrolling the sea seized it and towed it to Halifax along with its entire crew. Instead of facing a gloomy hulk such as at that time was usual for prisoners of war, Quesnel found himself welcomed with letters of domicile by [Governor Frederick] Haldimand, who had known his family in France. Decidedly, Providence protected our hero.

(Haldimand, born in Switzerland, was indeed acquainted with the Quesnels. During his period of service in Canada, 1778–84, his capital was Quebec City, not Halifax, although his authority extended over the Maritime colonies.)

> Having had in Brittany a solid upbringing in literature, poetry, and music, but unable to cultivate his talents owing to the troubled times, Joseph Quesnel set out to visit our Canadian country houses, reciting verses, performing delightful comedies, and dedicating French songs to the leading lights of the age. These leaders were often our great military men, our storied soldiers, now a leisure class comparable to the nobility at the time of the Crusades. In our homeland, Quesnel became a kind of troubadour to that life of song so very attractive for the historically curious. As such, our ancestors found him immensely to their liking. They rapidly dubbed him the "father of romance."

(Quesnel passed his formative years in Bordeaux, where he pursued his artistic interests while working in his uncle's business, and from where he set out on a number of commercial voyages. After capture and release in 1779, he settled first in Montreal and later in Boucherville, a short distance away on the south shore of the St Lawrence. He was a man of enterprise— a merchant, an importer of wines and exporter of furs, and in his prosperous later years a poet, playwright, and composer. Of his two known musical comedies, the first was written in 1789 in Montreal and produced there early the following year, while the second is undated, and, though completed, was apparently left unperformed at his death. His 1780 marriage to Marie-Josephte Deslandes produced thirteen children, six of whom survived to adulthood. Not all army officers active in the Indian and Revolutionary wars of those decades joined a seigneural "leisure class" on their retirement.)

> [T]he contemporary historian Bibaud depicts Quesnel as the "father of stage acting" in Canada. This expression is undoubtedly a reminder of the

traditional "father of romance." Musical-theatre forms in France at this period concentrated on allegory and a type of mythological fantasy where nymphs, zephyrs, spirits of pleasure and laughter, were given the general name of "les amours." Assuredly, therefore, the term "père des amours" is appropriate for Canada's "father of musical theatre."

(The historian cited is Michel Bibaud [1782–1857]. Quesnel was an active member, as playwright-composer and also as performer, in the Montreal production of *Colas et Colinette* in 1790 and he likely also attended the revivals of this work in Quebec City in 1805 and 1807. Neither *Colas et Colinette* nor *Lucas et Cécile* includes the fantasy figures enumerated by Lapierre.)

Calixa Lavallée, "Vagabond of Glory"

Le Vagabond de la gloire is conceived on a more modest scale than *Le Père des amours*. There are two acts, each consisting of five scenes. The libretto is by a Montreal lawyer, Aimé Plamondon. The typescript runs to a total of fifty-four pages.[13] Spoken dialogue and action occupy more playing time than the musical numbers, of which there are seventeen: nine in Act 1 and eight in Act 2.[14] There are several reprises, notably four occurrences (in whole or in part) of "O Canada." Apart from this inevitable inclusion, one of the other numbers is a version of Lavallée's song "L'Absence," but there appear to be no further citations from his extensive compositional output.

In his introductory notes,[15] Plamondon refers to the work as a "comédie musicale," and offers alternative titles: *O Canada*, *Un Canadien errant*, and *Le Fou à Gustin*. ("Un Canadien errant" is a well-known song inspired by the Lower Canada Rebellion of 1837; Gustin was the nickname of Lavallée's father, an abbreviation of Augustin.) The libretto typescript calls the play a "comédie dramatique et musicale"; in the program of the first production it receives yet another designation, "comédie-opérette." A synopsis in the program is introduced by Lapierre and Plamondon as follows:

> The vagabond in question is Calixa Lavallée, the composer of "O Canada." All his life, he looked for recognition from his own countrymen. It was owed him both through his talents and through his cultural efforts. But his countrymen haggled over his glory. Fifty-six years after his death, he still had no memorial apart from his tombstone. If he sometimes knew fame, it was far from his homeland, in a foreign environment and by chance, like a vagabond [he was] always on the move to earn his daily bread.

Dear Public: the authors of this lyric piece present you with a modest attempt, a little expression of posthumous thanks to the composer of the national anthem of Canada.

Le Vagabond de la gloire ran for two performances, 27 and 30 November 1947, at the Auditorium St-Alphonse. This hall, adjacent to the Église Saint-Alphonse-d'Youville, where Lapierre was organist, was renamed the Chapelle Sainte-Anne in the 1970s. In Lapierre's time, it enjoyed a busy and varied schedule, not only for church events but also as a movie theatre, a centre for amateur theatricals, and a radio studio.[16] Its modest location in a north-central neighbourhood of the city presents a contrast to the downtown venue of *Le Père des amours* five years previously.

Synopsis, *Le Père des amours*

(Indented portions are abbreviated quotations from the synopsis in the printed program of 1942.)

Act 1. Halifax, 1779. To the crowd mingling in the marketplace, the town crier reads a decree forbidding commerce with the American rebels. He declares there need be no fear of famine: a French ship has been seized, with an important load of supplies. Governor Frederick Haldimand inquires after the commander of the vessel, and recognizes the name: Quesnel de la Rivaudais is a talented poet he met some years before in Brittany. He arranges to give this captive his freedom, and Louis de la Haie, a Canadian landowner, undertakes to lodge Quesnel at his country estate. Quesnel appears, and informs his mates that he is liberated with them and plans to settle in New France so as to realize a long-felt wish, to be a troubadour. During a contest, years before, he earned the title "father of romance."

Introductory numbers include a general chorus, a solo "Complainte" by a beggarwoman whose sons are serving in the army, a chorus of girls introducing the Baroness de Repentigny, and a chorus ("chœur triomphal") of returning soldiers. At his entrance, the Governor tells de la Haie and the Baroness (de la Haie's cousin) about Quesnel: "At the Jeux floraux de Bretagne et de Normandie, he even received, one day, in a memorable contest, a curious title (but much treasured in that area) of bard-minstrel or 'Père des amours.' You'll see shortly, de la Haie, your estate turning into a sort of olden-time castle with a minstrel hired to teach poems to the lady of the house." He also mentions Labadie and his encounter with the Duke of Kent. (This is contrary to actual historical chronology: Edward, Duke of Kent, was twelve years old in 1779; his period of

service at Quebec and Halifax belongs to the 1790s.) The governor's
extensive solo lauds "la femme Canadienne-Française." There follows a
comic exchange between a sentinel, Zéphyr, and a naval officer, centring
on the former's inability to spell. They also speak of Quesnel.

> z. "Your Captain favors romance? What a touching idea! But I don't know that
>   that is a career."
> o. "And then he writes poetry and plays the violin."
> z. "Hey! Music too?"

Quesnel enters with the sailors. He tells them "it will not be displeas-
ing to settle in this great country of Canada." His solo cavatina recounts
his dream of New France. "That world that our kings lost with scarcely a
fight: our arts and our songs may regain it." (As a fugitive from the French
Revolution, he appears to appreciate living once again under a monarchy,
even if the monarch is British.)

> *Act 2.* Harvest season in the Richelieu valley—a time when the Canadian
> peasants render feudal homage to their seigneur. During the festivities, de
> la Haie presents to his tenants Joseph Quesnel, "bard of Brittany, minstrel
> of France, and father of romance." The gesture neatly foils the intrigues
> of public informers bent on arresting peasants. However, Quesnel becomes
> a mysterious suspect. The celebration continues and we meet Généreux
> Labadie, a schoolmaster with four jobs and two obsessions: he sings at
> mass, rings the church bells, teaches grammar, and grows melons; in addi-
> tion, he writes flowery verses flattering those in high places, and begs
> repeatedly for a pension in compensation for his French translation of
> "God save the King."

The Act opens with the chorus of harvesters. Jeannot and Labadie doze
by the mill. The latter sings in his sleep, some fragments of his song referring to the Baroness, others quoting the folksong "Les trois beaux canards."
The peasants comment further about him, noting that he has translated
"God Save the King." A young peasant, Marthe, gossips with the women.
Following a trio sung by Des Épinettes (de la Haie's partner), his son
Célestin, and the town constable, they meet with Labadie. He is off to the
church to stand as godfather to a newly born infant, a duty he has performed many times, he tells them; he will also be asked to ring the church
bells. *Des É.:* "It appears you have no shortage of jobs, my dear Labadie."
In a series of stanzas, Labadie outlines his various functions in the community, and continues with his views of poetry. Perhaps he will compose
a "bouquet" honouring Des Épinettes. He recites one he has written for
de la Haie, and then a second one for Célestin to address to the seigneur's

niece, Josette des Landes.[17] Célestin pockets the two manuscripts. His father, ambitious for their marriage, wants him to memorize the love poem; he is nervous, but agrees to read it. When Josette appears, he inevitably becomes flustered and recites the wrong poem. She says she will marry no one but Quesnel.

A change of scene takes us to the hall of the seigneurie for the "Fête de la Grosse Gerbe." The Baroness sings Quesnel's praises. *B.:* "I always thought that minstrels, troubadours, and romanesque bards were fiction. But here we have one in flesh and blood." A choral episode, with dancing, includes a song of homage to the seigneur, during which Labadie recites his "bouquet." This is interrupted by Des Épinettes, who wants de la Haie to arrest a suspected revolutionary agent. Quesnel enters, dressed in medieval garb as "Blondel," and performs the "Chanson du petit bonhomme." (The text is based on Quesnel's poem.) Des Épinettes quarrels with Quesnel, who in defence quotes Corneille. Des Épinettes' motive in reporting the agent is to get de la Haie to rescind Haldimand's leniency toward strangers such as Quesnel, but de la Haie opts for delay and everyone dances a cotillion. Des Épinettes is arrested by the constable, whose promotion to bailiff is announced. Josette and Célestin lead a flirtatious party-game involving a spinning top, and the busy Act concludes with a chorus and dancing (the "Valse de la Gerbe").

Act 3. The "father of romance" gives a poetry lesson to Josette. He looks for a chance to talk of love. She herself provides it by asking how the poets in earlier times expressed themselves when addressing their ladies. At Quesnel's impassioned response, she runs away in agitation. While this exchange is graceful and well-mannered, the succeeding one is clumsy and ridiculous: here Labadie, grammar-book in hand, declares his affection for the Baroness. A sheet of love-verses, incorrectly addressed, sends the four lovers into confusion.

Quesnel contemplates nature in an "air romantique." He gives Josette a sung lecture on the poetic vocation. The ideal poet is depicted as a fantasist. A "ballet des amours" brings the images to life: one of the dancers shoots an arrow in the lovers' direction. After their duet, Quesnel sings "Les Lilas," whose ardour Josette finds alarming. The parody love-duet by the Baroness and Labadie follows, at the end of which Labadie reads his "bouquet."[18] The Baroness, in a solo, finds Labadie's advances ridiculous, and again praises Quesnel. She reads Labadie a note that Quesnel had written to Josette. She believes it is intended for her; they are both confused.

Act 4. The love between Josette and Quesnel upsets the plans of the seigneur's partner, Des Épinettes, who is expecting to marry his son to the wealthy young heiress. He swears to have Quesnel deported—this fake poet and interloper. With the constable, now bailiff, and Labadie, he conspires in a forest retreat, unaware that their schemes are overheard by the Baroness. She hurries to tell Quesnel of the plot which threatens him. Weary of these deceitful goings-on, Quesnel longs for his homeland, France, which crowns its poets rather than banishing them. He exaggerates the misunderstanding that has arisen between himself and Josette.

The woodsmen ("bûcherons") sing as they are about to fell a huge pine. With the chorus, Quesnel conjures an earlier age of chivalrous love, in a "Chanson de Charlemagne." He characterizes the woodsmen as inheritors of the coureurs de bois, with a similar style of dress. Josette sings a "complainte" and Quesnel a "villanelle," to conventional love verses. The Baroness, overhearing, wonders if the verses are for her. The bailiff (a reference to the unsuccessful suitor in *Colas et Colinette*—the subtitle of that drama is *Le Bailli dupé*, "the bailiff tricked")—argues that Quesnel's play *L'Anglomanie* is seditious, and that Quesnel is under the influence of the "revolutionary" Marivaux. The Baroness alerts Quesnel to his danger. The mix-up regarding the love verses is revealed. Quesnel resigns to his fate of deportation.

Act 5. Josette weeps for her beloved poet as she watches the last ship of the season sailing away down the river—the ship that is meant to deport him. As the last sail disappears, Quesnel suddenly presents himself at the seigneurie. She regains her *joie de vivre* and Quesnel his fighting courage. His enemies close in; they attempt to stop him for good with a warrant from the military authorities. But—a dramatic turn of events!—the Baroness has defused the plot: she has gone to Fort Sorel along with de la Haie, and now returns with orders from the Governor putting an end to the intrigue. Des Épinettes is sent to prison for having sabotaged a royal workparty; the bailiff receives his comeuppance and becomes a subject for satire; the Baroness shows her caring nature; everything is resolved. Even Labadie foresees immortality as Quesnel dedicates to him his *Epistle*.

A "Prayer to the Virgin" is played by the orchestra, while Josette halfsings. She reads part of Quesnel's letter to Labadie and reflects that Quesnel was "too great for us." Her song addresses the ship as it sails away. Quesnel's voice is heard offstage under the final phrases. They are reunited. Des Épinettes and his cronies enter with a warrant for Quesnel's arrest. The Baroness produces a rescinding document, preventing them. The bailiff reads the rescinding document, which not only exonerates Quesnel but also hands out a two-year prison sentence for Des Épinettes. Quesnel announces his plan to put the bailiff in his next play. The final chorus addresses Quesnel as the "father of romance" and pays tribute to "our ancestors" who "watched over our pride, our language and freedom" ("nos pères / Nous ont gardé notre fierté / Notre langue et la liberté").

Synopsis, *Le Vagabond de la gloire*

Act 1. Scene 1. As a child in Verchères, Calixa Lavallée is already haunted by the magic of music, obsessed by fragments of tunes from which one day will burst the sublime chant which our anglophone fellow citizens have translated so as to sing along with us.

Aged six, Calixa responds to notes resembling "O Canada," played by his father on the anvil, and teaches the phrase to the peasants.

Scene 2. Ten years later, in Montreal, the young Lavallée meets three blackface performers at the Theatre Royal before a show. He is thrilled to hear them sing a popular minstrel-show number, and runs away with them to the United States.

The trio—Black Bill, Ned West, and Al Taylor, of Primrose and West's Minstrels—sing "Ma petite amie, ma Rose chérie," in minstrel style.

Scene 3. The Civil War is in progress. Lavallée returns home and becomes a music teacher. In Montreal he finds the people have little enthusiasm for musical training.

The pupil and the pupil's mother are depicted in a broad *joual*. Lavallée's idealistic definition of music proves beyond their comprehension.

Scene 4. This scene bears the title, "Lessons continue, no two alike." The pupil is the teenaged Rosita del Vecchio. She sings part of an opera aria [by Gounod?]. The other numbers are a popular romance, "Lina, te souviens-tu?," and a [supposed?] composition by Lavallée, "Quand je vois passer la Canadienne."

Scene 5. The Grand Opera House, New York, where Lavallée has been hired as music director. We hear excerpts from his operetta *Lou-lou*: the rehearsal goes badly, but tomorrow there will be a triumph! But this very day the owner of the theatre, Jim Fiske [*sic*], is assassinated in the street, and the house is closed down. Lavallée must go back to Montreal, denied his première, a vagabond once more.

Lavallée plays the piano accompaniment for a pas de deux. The vocal duet "Mari vaudage" represents the lost score of *Lou-lou*.

Act 2. Scene 1. Returning from studies in Europe, Lavallée tries again to make a career in Montreal, opening a studio in Cathcart Street. He prepares a collaborative concert introducing the Belgian violinist Frantz Jehin-Prume and the singer Rosita del Vecchio, formerly Lavallée's talented pupil, who has lately become this virtuoso's wife. (Lavallée had however cherished a rather different dream.)

Rosita's solo, "La Luciole," is described as a dialogue for voice and flute. There is a reprise of "Lina," now described as the theme from the composer's lost Cello Concerto.

Scene 2. The tiny music room at Laval University in Quebec City, an evening in June 1880. It is here that one of the most beautiful national songs of the world is sung for the first time.

Tancrède Trudel, tenor, sings "O Canada" with Lavallée at the piano. His fellow composer, Arthur Lavigne, looks on.

Scene 3. A hospital room in Hartford, Connecticut. Lavallée is ill and faces financial ruin: following an election, he has not been reimbursed for his work with the previous government. Adding to his misfortune, he learns that Rosita del Vecchio, his dear pupil and the star of his artistic hopes, has just met with a tragic end.

"Solitude" (by Lavallée?) is followed by another reprise of "Lina." After he reads of her death (of complications after childbirth), Rosita appears in a vision.

Scene 4. At the height of his fame, Lavallée attends a world congress of music teachers in London, and is honoured by the Lord Mayor. When his host asks him to perform one of his compositions, Lavallée sings his song "L'Absence," a work infused with sad nostalgic memories of love betrayed.

Lavallée's work is appreciated by all but his own countrymen. But he refuses to consider the Lord Mayor's suggestion of a concert of his music. The libretto calls for an "improvised" piano part in this scene.

Scene 5. Boston: Lavallée's home in Tremont Street. A publisher comes to offer him ten thousand dollars for exclusive rights to his music; but it is too late. The Bishop of Boston, Mgr. Williams, bestows a final blessing on the organist and choirmaster of his cathedral. A silhouetted chorus gives out with a triumphal "O Canada."

Before the entry of the Bishop, another character appears—Lavallée's loyal Montreal friend and patron, Derome. There is a scene change to 1930s Montreal, where an old man of eighty and his grandson watch from their window the procession for the reinterment of Calixa Lavallée. The man recounts his memories of 1880 and weeps, the youngster applauds as Lavallée's anthem swells up.

In 1933, amid the reinterment observances and subsequent renewal of public interest in Lavallée, Lapierre wrote a play entitled *Le Traversier de Boston*. There is no evidence of its having been staged, but the text survives in two forms, a one-act typescript with the author's pencil annotations, and a published version expanding this to three acts.[19] The title-page of the latter, interestingly, is headed by the motto from the Quebec coat-of-arms, "Je me souviens," familiar since the 1970s on all vehicle licence plates in Quebec. The play, called a "tragi-comedy," centres on an episode of Lavallée's versatile musical life when for a couple of summers he was pianist on a steamer of the Colonial Line between New York and Fall River, Massachusetts. (The preface to the script depicts this as a miserable comedown for the musician: "He encountered there a time of unspeakable mortification.") The three-act version includes further episodes from his US career, ending with a deathbed visit by the Bishop, similar to that in *Le Vagabond de la gloire*. Indeed, the play may have served as a preliminary draft for Plamondon's libretto. Writing to Plamondon in 1943, the composer already describes his study of Lavallée's repertoire, aimed at exploring its dramatic potential further.[20]

As the 1936 publication of *Calixa Lavallée, musicien national du Canada* had already demonstrated, he viewed the composer as an icon of Franco-Canadian cultural aspirations. The biography indeed had elicited a congratulatory letter from the Abbé Groulx himself, the dominant personality of the nationalist movement at the time. Groulx appeared not only convinced but deeply affected by the account of Lavallée's restless career and recurrent professional disappointments vis-à-vis the Canadian musical establishment:

> [T]he life of poor Lavallée stands as a symbol. To be aware of one's spark of talent, perhaps genius, but to be obliged to realize one's goal all alone, without anyone's help; at the same time ... to protect that spark and guard it against ... extinguishers, and ... against the atmosphere of the country, an atmosphere ... where every light is flickering or snuffed out; to manage, however, by force of energy and endless effort, to bring forth a glimmer, to create something living and beautiful; but then to die in misery, doubting one's fate, the fate of one's work, of one's role of torchbearer....[21]

(Amid these fulminations one awaits the completion of the sentence, but it never comes.)

Running a "reality check" on the libretto of *Le Vagabond de la gloire*, one may readily expect to refer to Lapierre's biography of Lavallée. However—disappointingly, though perhaps not surprisingly—it presents a heavily biased account of his life, rather than a factual one. Tracing his hero's ancestry to seventeenth-century settlers in the Île d'Orléans, who "possédaient les traits distinctifs de 'nos gens' de l'ancien régime," the author follows them in their resettlement in the Richelieu Valley in the eighteenth century, where they became "d'excellents miliciens, des politiques habiles, des patriotes ardentes" (Lapierre 1966, 12–13). He paints an idealized picture, in which Lavallée's character merges the qualities of the pre-Revolutionary French and the "Patriotes," to become a "martyr" for "us"— "nous pourtant qui sommes des Français." The frequent use of the first-person plural together with glowing images from the culture of the mother country may well echo a song that Lavallée composed in the 1880s for the Ligue des Patriotes, a francophone society in New England. The title is "Restons Français!" and the text argues for a political reunion with France.[22] Lavallée's friend and sponsor, Léon Derome, is described (confusingly to outsiders) as "un Canadien digne de son nom de Français" (1966, 40). Other sympathetic figures in the biography are often depicted as "brave": for example, the young Lavallée "retournera souvent faire de l'orchestre avec [les] braves villageois de son enfance," and the parish priest who supports Lavallée in his mounting of Gounod's *Jeanne d'Arc* becomes "le brave curé" (1966, 24, 127).

Before his 1867 marriage to Josephine Gentilly in Lowell, Massachusetts, Lavallée required his bride and her mother to convert to the Roman Catholic faith. Whatever this meant for the two women, Lapierre tells us it represented a risk for the groom, who was, however, "en tout cela bien digne de nos pères" (1966, 109). Little is said (it seems little is known) of Mme Lavallée. The couple had four children, only one of whom survived to adulthood. She does not appear in the libretto. On the other hand, the libretto stresses in several scenes a sentimental attraction of Lavallée for Rosita del Vecchio. Del Vecchio, her husband Frantz Jehin-Prume, and Lavallée did appear together in joint recitals, and some of their programs are described in detail in the biography. Lapierre accuses the singer of having seduced Jehin-Prume into marrying her, but offers no evidence for this (1966, 103–4).

The author covers Lavallée's years as a touring minstrel-show performer only briefly. He distorts the history of this genre by mistakenly tracing it to slave songs of the US South, inventing an explanation for its syncopated character ("the weak beat will be the master"), and identifying French-speaking Canadians with Black slaves: "Nos gens aussi étaient des souffrants et des opprimés."[23]

Regarding "O Canada," Lapierre suggests that it was composed in or near Lavallée's boyhood home of Saint-Hyacinthe, and that the central phrases ("ton bras sait porter l'épée, …") were inspired in the melody by a waterfall on the Yamaska River and in the bass rhythm by his father's hammering on the anvil. He dismisses Arthur Sullivan's "Dominion Hymn," written around the same time, perhaps as a rival national song, and quotes a later governor-general, Earl Grey, as preferring "O Canada" to Alexander Muir's "The Maple Leaf Forever" (Lapierre 1966, 188, 244). Both are secure judgments: "O Canada" is stronger both in music and in text than the two songs mentioned, and has proved more durable than either. The account of the Quebec City première of "O Canada" finds Lapierre in full descriptive heat:

> Everybody stood, not out of politeness, but electrified by an irresistible impulse. French Canadians have never since felt such a flood of patriotic fervor coursing through their veins. And these emotions were roused by a poor little village musician whose art had been disdained! Oh, such a sweet and noble moment, as if on eagle's wings, for our misunderstood compatriot! He could delude himself, perfectly happy with the thought that, surely, now he was going to be recognized. (1966, 173–74)

This vivid scene is based on no known eyewitness version.

For reality and factuality, luckily, there is another source, Brian C. Thompson's doctoral dissertation, "Calixa Lavallée (1842–1891): A critical biography." Thompson, a musicologist educated in Montreal and currently with the Chinese University of Hong Kong, is the first researcher to examine Lavallée's US "exile" in depth. He observes that "during his thirty-year career, Lavallée spent roughly two years in Europe, seven in Canada, and twenty-one in the United States" (2007, 7n). Though a Montreal newspaper article of 1873 already called Lavallée "Canada's national musician," thus inspiring the subtitle of Lapierre's biography, Thompson shows that his patriotic ardour was just as strong for the musical scene of the United States as for that of his native Canada. A striking feature of his activities with the (US) Music Teachers' National Association (MTNA) in the 1880s was his championing of US composers: he performed a putative historic first in Cleveland on 3 July 1884 by giving a full solo recital of their music.[24] As Thompson puts it,

> Nationalism was a pervasive social force throughout [Lavallée's] life: as a child in the Richelieu Valley in the aftermath of the Rebellions of 1837 and

1838, with his republican teacher [Charles W.] Sabatier in the 1850s, during the American Civil War, and in Paris after the Franco-Prussian War. He had projected nationalist views in subtle ways, such as organizing and participating in benefit concerts ..., and in the major efforts of his career: attempting to establish a conservatory in Canada, and promoting American music. (2000, 276–77)

In Lapierre's drama, Lavallée points these nationalist feelings primarily toward francophone Canada, and the creation of a national hymn.

To focus on events depicted, or conspicuously *not* depicted, in *Le Vagabond de la gloire*, Thompson reveals in detail Lavallée's youthful adventures as pianist, violinist, and music director with Duprez and Green's blackface minstrel company just before the outbreak of the Civil War, tours that took him to many cities of the northeastern US, the Ohio Valley, and the South. This is a passage of his hero's life to which Lapierre refers only obliquely (Act 1, Scene 2), perhaps because he was reluctant to demonstrate that Lavallée's musical versatility extended to popular entertainment and was not exclusively confined to the "higher" forms of concert fare. It was not Ned West but more probably the Franco-Canadian Charles Duprez who recruited him in Montreal (Thompson 2000, 37ff.). In Act 1, Scene 3, Lavallée's service as a bandsman in one of the Northern regiments during the Civil War is dealt with even more cursorily. Like other commentators, Thompson finds irony in the fact that, in a favourite youthful photo, "Canada's national musician" is shown in his US bandsman's uniform (2006, 2).

Turning to Act 1, Scene 5, the correspondence between history and fantasy becomes tenuous in the extreme. The Grand Opera House in New York—while in no sense "the predecessor of the Metropolitan Opera" as Lapierre has it—did exist. The repertoire consisted only occasionally of grand operas; more usual were seasons of light opera, plays, and (sometimes) minstrel shows. The proprietor, James Fisk, Jr., was murdered in January 1872. Lavallée was not the "musical director" of the house, and in fact is listed only once in its annals, in an appearance with the San Francisco Minstrels on 29 August 1870.[25] Around that time he was working on an operetta, *Peacocks in Difficulties*; this work, referred to in French as *Lou-lou*, is evidently lost. Though announced in 1871 for production in New York (not by Fisk), it has apparently never been produced, and may not have been completed. Fisk was shot on 6 January 1872 (in a local hotel, not "on the street"), and died on 17 January; from Thompson's evidence, Lavallée not only was not associated with the Grand Opera House at the time, but was not even in New York, having moved to Boston to work with another minstrel troupe there (Thompson 2000, 107ff.).

Events of the final decade of Lavallée's life are only slightly reflected in the libretto. The factual basis of Act 2, scenes 2 and 3, is well enough established: Trudel and Lavigne were friends and fellow musicians who assisted in the promotion of "O Canada" at its première; Lavallée, in Hartford, was ill with the first signs of tuberculosis, and heavily in debt after the performance of his cantata in Quebec City the same year. Act 2, Scene 4, has Lavallée honoured in London without noting that this was the climax of his work with the MTNA, which included a term as its president. The hero's self-accompanied vocal solo seems inserted to accommodate the versatile performer, Albert Viau, rather than to re-enact a known detail of the Lord Mayor's party.[26] Lavallée's wife, Josephine, and surviving teenage son, Raoul, do not appear in the deathbed scene (Act 2, Scene 5), although they were with him in Boston. Lavallée died in poverty (a subscription was mounted for the family's support shortly afterwards), but not in obscurity: there was an imposing funeral at the cathedral where he had served as music director, and significant obituaries in both the Canadian and American press (Thompson 2000, 271). Lapierre prefers to ignore these upbeat aspects of the composer's passing; in his version, Lavallée dies "far from his homeland, in a foreign environment" and receives just recognition only on his posthumous return to Montreal in 1933.

Reception History

The première of Le Père des amours was announced in a display advertisement in the Montreal daily La Presse: the "first Canadian comic opera" comprises "5 acts, 6 scenes, and a period minuet [Menuet d'époque]." The main soloists are listed, and we learn there will be "a mixed chorus of 70" and an "Orchestra of 20 musicians conducted by M. Eugène Chartier of the Orchestre Symphonique [de Montréal]."[27] Clearly the paper's anonymous reviewer the next day is accurate in claiming that "a considerable effort has been applied to ensure the success of M. Lapierre's work." This short notice adds mention of the choir of the Conservatoire national, which sang "with much precision," and the dancers from the École de danse Gérard Crevier, who performed the minuet. But there is no further description of the work, and no reference to its historical sources and patriotic intentions.[28]

In Le Devoir, the critic Frédéric Pelletier tendered a brief notice, beginning ominously: "A première [création] is always what the word implies: bringing something out of chaos.... M. Lapierre, to whom I spoke in an intermission, acknowledges that trimming certain scenes and reducing the length of certain numbers would not harm his work in the least." But "[the performance] ended so late that I am unable to give it today the review it deserves…. Early next week I will give a more detailed review."[29]

True to his promise, Pelletier followed with a two-column essay dealing with the text, the score, and the performance in considerable detail. Here he again notes the excessive length of the piece, and offers advice on how to cut it:

> Thursday's performance began at 8.45, the intermissions were the shortest ever experienced at the Monument national, and the curtain did not fall on the final act until 1 a.m. I said to M. Lapierre—and he appeared to agree—that he could cut the whole scene of Haldimand and that of the fool [Zéphyr] in Act One, a good portion of the dialogue in the other acts, and reduce almost all the songs to two verses only (many have three or more) … without damaging what he has to say.

Pelletier judges the leading role of Quesnel to be "amorphous": "he is neither fish nor flesh, but a mere puppet." By contrast, Labadie is "the most successful portrait":

> This schoolmaster, who makes his declarations of love with the aid of a notebook, like a German tourist consulting his conversation book in ordering an omelette, is a happy invention … I know not whether [the historical Labadie] resembled the author's portrait of him, but M. Lapierre gives him a vividly sketched personality.

The critic's reservations regarding the drama do not apply to the musical score. It is indeed "in the music that one finds the theatrical appropriateness that the libretto lacks." The Gavotte and three of the choruses come in for special praise. In general, the musical style "avoids rooting itself in the dryness of olden days, but relies just as seldom on effects borrowed from modern harmony and rhythm," a stylistic path midway between faux-antique and avant-garde, clearly the correct one in this critic's estimation. Referring to the opening chorus of Act 2, Pelletier says:

> M. Lapierre draws on various folksongs of French origin, preserved here— suggesting them rather than emphasizing them. [This] chorus of harvesters is the most interesting illustration of his method…. A less able composer might have quoted the entire chanson, but M. Lapierre does better than that: "Meunier tu dors" is accompanied by the orchestra,[30] with, here and there, some phrases taken over by the chorus…. [T]he persistent rhythm in the instruments gives an almost visual impression of flails threshing the grain. Bravo!

Unlike his *La Presse* colleague, Pelletier seems somewhat aware of the historical Quesnel: "M. Lapierre has used some of Quesnel's own poetry and music. There is nothing extraordinary about them, but they help establish the historical setting." With proper revision, Pelletier suggests, the work could "enter the regular repertoire of the Variétés lyriques" (Montreal's light-opera company). He ends his review with the hope "that M. Lapierre, having seen this realization of his work, will give it further thought. He worked on it for six years, an example one cannot but admire. It is unthinkable that such a work will not have a future."[31]

The more modest circumstances of the 1947 première of *Le Vagabond de la gloire* may be symbolized in the brief listing in the "Events" column of *Le Devoir*, in lieu of a paid display advertisement. The work is announced as a "comedy-operetta in 2 acts, on the life of Calixa Lavallée."[32] The next day a succinct review, unsigned, appears in almost identical form in both *La Presse* and *Le Devoir*. The anonymous writer extends generous praise to the authors and the cast, and mentions a few highlights, among them "the hilarious Minstrel Trio," without mentioning "O Canada" or Lavallée or the patriotic themes of the story as told by Lapierre and Plamondon. "La Luciole," sung by Marthe Létourneau (Rosita), had to be encored. "In sum, a delightful comedy, sometimes light, sometimes dramatic, to which M. Lapierre's music adds great charm and vitality."[33]

Montreal's two English-language newspapers apparently ignored both Lapierre productions. Further research may reveal coverage in the periodical press. Neither work has been remounted since the 1940s.

The Music

Regarding both of Eugène Lapierre's musical comedies, it is possible to gain a clear picture of the books and the lyrics by consulting the typescripts of the librettos and the printed program synopses. It is far more difficult to assess the music. The Fonds Lapierre of the Bibliothèque national du Québec contains, for *Le Père des amours*, a piano/vocal score and fourteen numbers in various other formats, some resembling incomplete sketches, and, for *Le Vagabond de la gloire*, a fragment of just one number, in vocal parts only. There is evidently no preserved full score of either work. The "Menuet d'époque" and four or five separate songs from the earlier piece were issued in sheet-music format, adding to the resources on hand, though only in a limited way.

The extent and order of musical numbers in *Le Père des amours* are hard to reconstruct. Consider the following:

- The libretto indicates approximately thirty-five musical numbers.
- A typewritten list of titles gives a total of thirty-four numbers, combining two from the libretto into a single heading, adding two, and ignoring two.
- Ink emendations and circled numbering in the same list produce a new total of thirty-three numbers, crossing out three, and adding two.
- A penciled copy of the list rearranges several items, retitles others, and provides two alternative numberings, totalling respectively thirty-two and thirty-three numbers.
- Frédéric Pelletier's Le Devoir review mentions eight numbers, six for admiration and two as suitable for deletion.
- The piano/vocal score contains thirty-three numbers, arranged in four acts, corresponding to Acts 2 through 5 of the libretto; among these, five numbers from the libretto's Act 1 reappear out of sequence. During and after the production in 1942, there was apparently a good deal of shuffling of the material.

The choral numbers employ symmetrical shapes, simple diatonic lines, and the minimal harmonic vocabulary of tonic and dominant, with enhancement of the dominant by its leading note as the only contrast. The "Chœur triomphal" of Act 1 is typical (Figure 10.1). The "Chœur des moissoneurs" in Act 2 is based on a droning pattern that eventually accommodates a quoted tune, "Meunier, tu dors" (figures 10.2a, 10.2b). The final chorus in Act 5, more ambitiously, projects the title phrase, "le Père des Amours," and expands in a rising harmonic sequence (Figure 10.3).

Most rounded of the vocal solos is the song "Charlemagne," sung by Quesnel in Act 4 (Figure 10.4). "Le P'tit bonhomme," from Act 2, achieves melodic vitality with its pickup rhythm; while the vocal line is largely diatonic, the accompaniment lends it a chromatic flavour (Figure 10.5). Quesnel's martial air, "Je choisis de rester," at the end of Act 1, attempts "operatic" depths with more variety of harmonic motion, and asks a heroic high C from the soloist at the end. The squareness of the "Romance" (alternatively called "Air romantique") in Act 3 belies its tempo marking, "Avec abandon" (Figure 10.6). The comic patter songs may suggest models from the nineteenth-century opéra-comique repertoire: consider Marthe's "Les Cancans" and Des Épinettes' "C'est légal," both from Act 2 (figures 10.7a, 10.7b). Labadie's lines have a similar tone, crisp and syllabic within a small range, as in his Act 2 "Arioso" (Figure 10.8). His "Couplets," also in Act 2, incorporate a reference to the British anthem (Figure 10.9).

FIGURE 10.1 *Le Père des amours*, Act 1: "Chœur triomphal," soprano line only

FIGURE 10.2 (a): do., Act 2: "Chœur des moissoneurs"

FIGURE 10.2 (b): do., Act 2: "Meunier, du dors"

FIGURE 10.3 do., Act 5: "Grand chœur final," chorus parts only

Often the voice parts lean toward modality, for example, in the obvious device of the flattened seventh degree of the scale. In Josette's "Complainte" from Act 4, the trait is clear (Figure 10.10). Similarly, the lower
of the two male-voice parts in the "Chœur des bûcherons" in the same
act has the flat seventh; the final cadence, bar 27, is "open," i.e., it
employs no seventh (figures 10.11a, 10.11b). A recurrent cadence in
the instrumental gavotte (Act 2) also illustrates avoidance of the seventh

FIGURE 10.4 do., Act 4: "Charlemagne," solo line only

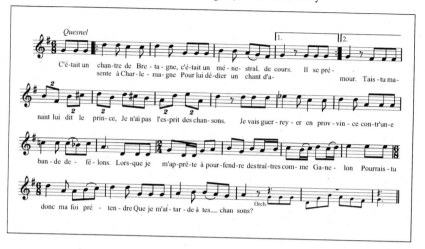

(Figure 10.12). By these devices Lapierre evidently aimed to suggest a period flavour. The question arises: What period? The late eighteenth century of the events enacted, or the imaginary medieval period they were thought to evoke? The few citations from early Quebec folk music have a similar character: "Les trois beaux canards," quoted near the start of Act 2, is among the half-dozen best-known songs in the folk repertoire (under various titles), and the version found in Ernest Gagnon's *Chansons populaires du Canada* is in a natural-minor mode with a flat seventh degree (1955, 21).[34] But there is little consistency in all this: the "Valse de la gerbe" from the end of Act 2 has chromatic embellishments and added sixths recalling Offenbach or Messager rather than antiquity (Figure 10.13).

The minuet seems to have been a highlight, mentioned in the advance notice as a special attraction, and singled out for favourable comment in the reviews. The music, based on an undistinguished stepwise tune, hardly typifies the traditional minuet (Figure 10.14). The choreography must have been outstanding. Neither this dance nor the gavotte is mentioned in the libretto. Among the miscellaneous holdings in the Fonds are fragments of *two* gavottes, one in A and the other in g; the second, corresponding to the copy in the piano/vocal score, derives from an earlier "Gavotte et musette" by Lapierre, dedicated to Vincent D'Indy and characterized as "de genre clavecin." The dance component of *Le Père des amours* is confused by the inclusion of that "Valse" as the second-act finale: the waltz is a nineteenth-century dance, and this one concludes with solo coloraturas reminiscent of Arditi's "Il bacio" or the "Jewel Song" from

FIGURE 10.5 do., Act 2: "Le P'tit bonhomme"

FIGURE 10.6 do., Act 3: "Romance," solo line only

FIGURE 10.7 (a): do., Act 2: "Cancans"

FIGURE 10.7 (b): do., Act 2: "C'est légal," solo lines only

FIGURE 10.8 do., Act 2: "Arioso de Labadie," solo line only

FIGURE 10.9 do., Act 2: "Couplets de Labadie," solo line only

FIGURE 10.10 do., Act 4: "Complainte de Josette," solo line only

FIGURE 10.11 (a): do., Act 4: "Chœur des bûcherons," opening, chorus
parts only

FIGURE 10.11 (b): do., Act 4: "Chœur des bûcherons," ending

FIGURE 10.12 do., Act 2: "Gavotte," main melody (oboe) of musette
section

FIGURE 10.13 do., Act 2: "Valse de la gerbe"

FIGURE 10.14 do., Act 2: "Menuet," opening melody (violin)

FIGURE 10.15 *Le Vagabond de la gloire*, Act 1, Scene 2: "Trio des ménestrels," voice parts only

Faust. The "cotillion" mentioned earlier in the same act has no corresponding music in any of the sources.

Pelletier says Lapierre employs "some of Quesnel's own poetry and music."[35] While passages of the poetry are identifiable, there is, as noted already, no evidence that Lapierre was acquainted with the music of either *Colas et Colinette* or *Lucas et Cécile*.

The Bibliothèque national du Québec files containing sets of orchestral parts present a mysterious aspect: recto and verso of the pages show numbers in an evidently haphazard sequence. Moreover, for some numbers only a few instruments have the second item on verso pages. (Although the players at the première were unlikely to have been all anglophones, conceivably some of them were, and the copyist of the parts evidently was: in almost every set, the instruments are named in English: "oboe, trumpet, viola," and so on, rather than "hautbois, trompette, alto.") The program of the première credits the conductor, but gives no list of the orchestral musicians. From parts and a few full-score pages in the *Fonds*, one gathers the instrumentation was for single winds (flute, oboe, clarinet, bassoon, horn, trumpet), timpani, and strings; in two numbers only, second players are called for on flute, clarinet, and trumpet, and in one number a trombone appears.

From materials surviving for *Le Père des amours* a fair impression of the work's musical qualities emerges. No such evaluation is possible for *Le Vagabond de la gloire*. The two known borrowings from Lavallée, "O Canada" and "L'Absence," can be located elsewhere (Poirier 1987, 59, 142), although one is curious as to how they were employed by Lapierre. Whether there are further borrowings it is impossible to say for certain. One file in the *Fonds* contains an a-cappella "Trio des Ménestrels," with a missing middle section.[36] The text "Un peu, beaucoup," is that of the refrain (only) of the song in Act 1, Scene 2, "Ma petite amie"; the music is only faintly imitative of the minstrel-show idiom (Figure 10.15). There is no indication, either in the program of the première or in the archival collection, of the orchestration for *Le Vagabond de la gloire*. The performance may in fact have been accompanied only on one or two pianos.

Conclusion

On examination, aside from the curiosity of their composer-heroes, the two Lapierre works have little to recommend them, and do not encourage revival, either for their romantic and propagandistic scripts or for their surviving musical materials, adequate in the one case, practically nil in the other. They may, however, have the positive value of reminding us that the stage works of Quesnel and Lavallée are themselves decidedly worthy of the occasional production. Vinyl recordings of Quesnel's *Colas et Colinette* and Lavallée's *The Widow* from the 1960s have not so far been transferred to compact disc.[37] Concert performances and stagings of *Colas et Colinette* in the 1960s, of Quesnel's other comedy, *Lucas et Cécile*, in the 1990s, and of *The Widow* at regular intervals over the years have confirmed the vitality of these pieces. *The Widow* is overdue for publication in a performing edition similar to those of the two Quesnel works. Musical excerpts from all three, and also from Lavallée's *TIQ (Settled at last)* are available on various compact discs.[38]

Whatever future plans Lapierre may have had in 1947 for his two musical plays, his career around that time was headed for decline, and in 1951 he was dismissed from the directorship of the Conservatoire national. The reason? He had presented over a decade a large number of non-resident candidates (many of them from the US) for doctorates at the Université de Montréal (the Conservatoire was a U. of M. affiliate) without requiring proper qualifications. The provincially supported Conservatoire du Québec had meanwhile come into existence (1942), and the U. of M. was in the process of strengthening its own music faculty when this shoddy practice was exposed.[39] Lapierre's views of Conservatoire curricula centred on education for sacred music. In his writings on this topic, if not in his direction of the program, he may be interpreted as repeating the efforts of Calixa Lavallée in the 1870s toward a national music school. As he watched others (notably Claude Champagne) take the fight successfully to a different sort of goal, he may have identified with Lavallée's feelings of frustration and disappointment.

Less than a year after the first production of *Le Vagabond de la gloire*, a young group of Montreal artists and intellectuals, led by Paul-Émile Borduas, issued the manifesto *Refus global*, a loud signal that the days of Church dominance of education and culture in French-speaking Canada were numbered. A prominent musical associate of the signers of the document was the twenty-year-old composer Pierre Mercure. Mercure's secular *Cantate pour une joie* (1955), a cosmopolitan and literate modern score, is a resounding *refus* to the narrow-minded world of Eugène Lapierre.

Notes

1 On the evolution of the noun and adjective applied to the French-speaking population of Canada from 1759 to the present (Canadien/Canadian, Franco-Canadien/French-Canadian, Québéçois/Quebecker), see Hayne (1994).

2 He once declared, "Notre musique a une histoire" (Lapierre 1933a, 92). This sense was rare among professional musicians in Canada prior to the 1950s. In his efforts in support of his convictions, he comes across as part historian and part tale-spinner.

3 See, for example, Lefebvre (2004, 50 ff., 65–66, etc.).

4 The quotations are from Lapierre's (1942) essay "Un style canadien de musique." This and all subsequent translations from French in this article are by the author, unless otherwise noted.

5 Quesnel's own writings, and various sources concerning his career, mention a number of compositions that are presumed lost.

6 The two chapters dealing with "O Canada" occupy twenty-four pages (169–93), while the chapter entitled "Les autres œuvres" occupies six pages (195–201).

7 The entry "Théâtre musical," by Ross Stuart, in the *EMC* (Kallmann 1992–93), under a subheading "Opéras légers et opérettes," cites sixteen locally produced works prior to the 1940s, in addition to others produced abroad. A dozen works in this genre are excerpted in Cooper (1991).

8 Of the two Quesnel musical comedies, the libretto of *Colas et Colinette* was published in 1808, but that of *Lucas et Cécile* not until 1984. Their extant musical materials (vocal parts and one orchestral part for the former, vocal parts only for the latter) were accessible only in manuscript in the Archives du Séminaire, Quebec City, prior to their restorations (in 1967 and 1992, respectively), and it appears doubtful that Lapierre examined them. His score not only contains no musical references to Quesnel but bears little similarity to Quesnel's style.

9 Bibliothèque nationale du Québec, *Fonds Eugène Lapierre*, A.1.7.

10 Quesnel's writings were widely cultivated in early nineteenth-century Canada. Roy (1909) quotes the following, in a periodical of 1825, attributed to "un admirateur de *Colas et Colinette*": "Quesnel, le père des amours, / Semblable à son petit bonhomme, / Vit encore et vivra toujours." This is the probable prime source for Lapierre's title. The phrase "petit bonhomme," from the refrain of a Quesnel poem, occurs several times in the libretto.

11 Sincere thanks to Marie-Thérèse Lefebvre for providing photocopies of the house programs from the premières of *Le Père des amours* and *Le Vagabond de la gloire*.

12 For these and other citations regarding Quesnel's career, see John E. Hare, "Quesnel, Joseph," in the *Dictionary of Canadian Biography* (Brown et al. 1983, 700–3).

13 *Fonds*, A.1.22.

14 Twelve numbers are listed in the printed program of the première. Another five are indicated in the libretto, but appear to be short interpolations rather than developed numbers.

15 *Fonds*, A.1.21.

16 Information kindly obtained by Marie-Thérèse Lefebvre from the present church secretary, Colette St-Pierre, 13 January 2006.

17 Josette is the nickname of Josephte, the woman who married Quesnel in 1780.

18 Curiously, Labadie's comical song about studying grammar bears a certain textual kinship to the entrance song of the pedant DuSotin in *Lucas et Cécile*, at this date known only in the manuscript. Since the Quesnel work is otherwise not reflected in *Le Père des amours*, this is probably coincidental.

19 *Fonds*, A.1.48 and A.4.3; Lapierre (1933b).

20 Lapierre to Plamondon, 25 March 1943, *Fonds*, A.2.33.

21 Groulx to Lapierre, 5 April 1937, *Fonds*, 041.008.005.

22 The song, composed in 1881 to words by Rémi Tremblay, is reproduced in Poirier (1987, 142).

23 This foreshadows *Nègres blancs de l'Amérique* by the FLQ activist Pierre Vallières (Paris: François Maspero, 1969), published in English as *White niggers of America*, trans. Joan Pinkham (Toronto: McClelland and Stewart, 1971).

24 Lapierre (1966, 219–20); Thompson (2000, 215–16). At Lavallée's death, the *Musical courier* (28 January 1891, 75) called him an "ardent champion of the cause of the American composer" (quoted in Thompson 2000, 269).

25 Odell (1937, 74). This source is mentioned in Lapierre's biography, but he appears not to have consulted it.

26 Viau is described in the opening-night reviews as "pianist, singer, and actor." *La Presse* and *Le Devoir*, 29 November 1947. He was also known as a songwriter.

27 *La Presse*, 10 December 1942.

28 *La Presse*, 11 December 1942.

29 *Le Devoir*, 11 December 1942.

30 Laforte (1987, item F-137) gives fifty citations of this chanson, twenty-two of them from Canada. See Conrad Laforte, *Le Catalogue de la chanson folklorique française*, V (*Les Archives de folklore*, 22), (Quebec: Les Presses de l'Université Laval, 1987), item F-137. It appears in *Chante, rossignolet!* (Quebec: Les Éditions Ferland du Conseil de la vie française, n.d. [1964?]), 69, in a version slightly different from Lapierre's.

31 *Le Devoir*, 14 December 1942.

32 *Le Devoir*, 28 November 1947.

33 *La Presse*, 29 November 1947; *Le Devoir*, same date.

34 The collection includes at least six other songs with related texts and tunes. See also Barbeau (1947).

35 Frédéric Pelletier, review in *Le Devoir*, 14 December 1942.

36 *Fonds*, A.1.20.

37 *Colas et Colinette*, Radio Canada International RCI 234/Select CC 15.001 and SSC 24.160 (1968); *The Widow*, Radio Canada International RCI 231/RCA LSC 2981 (1967).

38 For example, *Le Souvenir*, Centrediscs CMC CD 5696; *À la claire fontaine*, Opening Day ODR 9321; *Songs of Canada*, Carleton Sound CSCD 1003.

39 Lapierre was charged with "having distributed university [doctoral] diplomas without sufficient preparation, without a proper thesis, without assessment of the thesis by a competent jury, and without a public defense" (Lefebvre 1984, 47).

References

Barbeau, Marius. 1947. "Trois beaux canards (92 versions canadiennes)." *Les Archives de folklore* 2: 97–138.

Brown, George W., et al, eds. 1983. *Dictionary of Canadian biography/Dictionnaire de la biographie canadienne*, vol. 5. Toronto: University of Toronto Press / Quebec City: Presses de l'Université Laval.

Chartier, Yves. 1973. "Musique et critique au Canada français aux XIXe et XXe siècles." *Les Cahiers canadiens de musique* 7: 75–77.

Cooper, Dorith R., ed. 1991. *The Canadian musical heritage/Le Patrimoine musical canadien*, vol. 10. Ottawa: Canadian Musical Heritage Society.

Gagnon, Ernest. 1955. *Chansons populaires du Canada*. Montreal: Éditions Beauchemin; original, 1865.

Hayne, David M. 1994. "'By any Other Word ...': The Designations of Canadian Literature in French." *University of Toronto Quarterly* 63, no. 4: 481–87.

Laforte, Conrad. 1987. *Le Catalogue de la chanson folklorique française*, vol. 5 (*Les Archives de folklore*, vol. 22). Quebec City: Presses de l'Université Laval.

Lapierre, Eugène. 1966. *Calixa Lavallée, musicien national du Canada*. 3rd edn., Montreal: Éditions Fides.

———. 1933a. *Pourquoi la musique?* Montreal: Éditions Albert Lévesque.

———. 1933b. *Le Traversier de Boston*. Montreal: Éditions Albert Lévesque.

Lefebvre, Marie-Thérèse. 1984. "Histoire du Conservatoire national de musique," *Les Cahiers de l'ARMUQ* 4: 37–51.

———. 2004. *Rodolphe Mathieu, 1890–1962*. Montreal: Septentrion.

Kallmann, Helmut et al, eds. 1992/3. *Encyclopedia of music in Canada / Encyclopédie de la musique au Canada*, 2nd ed. Toronto: University of Toronto Press / Montreal: Fides.

Odell, George C. 1937. *Annals of the New York stage*, vol. 9. New York: Columbia University Press.

Poirier, Lucien, ed. 1987. *The Canadian musical heritage / Le Patrimoine musical canadien*, vol. 7. Ottawa: Canadian Musical Heritage Society.

———. 1984. "Les vues de quelques auteurs canadien-français de la première moitié du XXe siècle sur le sujet du style musical au Canada: compte rendu et analyse," *Les Cahiers de l'ARMUQ* 4: 6–32; reissued in Beverley Diamond and Robert Witmer, eds., *Canadian music: Issues of hegemony and identity* (Toronto: Canadian Scholars' Press, 1994, 244–68), trans., M. Benjamin Waterhouse and Beverley Diamond.

Roy, Camille. 1909. *Nos origines littéraires*. Quebec City: Imprimerie de l'Action sociale.

Thompson, Brian C. 2000. Calixa Lavallée (1842–1891): a critical biography. Ph.D. diss., University of Hong Kong.

———. 2006. "Lavallée Portraits: Images of the 'Musicien National'." Institute for Canadian Music *Newsletter* 4, no. 1: 2–7.

Funk and James Brown
Re-Africanization, the Interlocked Groove, and the Articulation of Community

ROB BOWMAN

T IS INTERESTING TO NOTE THAT the three dominant styles of African-American popular music in the early and mid-1960s—Motown, Stax, and Chicago soul—were all in their own individual ways products of the central social/political facts of integration and the civil rights movement. The story of Motown and Berry Gordy Jr., for example, was predicated on the rise of large-scale Black capitalism partially inspired and made possible by the momentous changes of the times, while Stax and southern soul, on the other hand, can be seen as a product of the civil rights movement, as it was founded squarely on the collaboration of Black and White musicians. To paraphrase Peter Guralnick, southern soul music, purely and simply, grew out of the impulse toward integration (Guralnick 1986, 5). (In the South at the time, this was a political gesture, whether conceived of as such or not.) Finally, much Chicago soul in the mid-1960s, such as the Impressions' "We're a Winner" and "People Get Ready," tied directly to the civil rights movement via both lyric content and mode of performance.

The civil rights movement clearly brought about substantial and profound legal and social changes for Black and White Americans. For many, the tenor of the time was optimistic—A New Day Was Dawning. It was easy to believe that very soon all people would be free and equal, and most of the garbage that had infected American life for close to four hundred years would shortly be a distant, half-remembered relic of an earlier, less civilized place and time.

Such a dream had a lot of resonance, but proved ultimately to be naive. By 1967 there may not have been legally segregated washrooms and drinking fountains, Blacks may not have had to ride at the back of the bus, and, theoretically, the same schools were open to all, but the reality for the vast majority of African-American people was that their lives remained basically the same. They lived in segregated housing in areas of cities with the least social amenities, the schooling their children received was markedly inferior to what White children received, and they continued to be the last hired and the first fired in the job market, earning wages substantially lower than their White counterparts. In other words, equality wasn't even remotely at hand.

Ironically, in some unforeseen ways, legal desegregation affected the majority of Black Americans negatively. Once the opportunity presented itself, large numbers of Black Americans with money moved out of so-called "ghetto" areas, in the process denuding the community of economic resources, leadership, political influence, and role models of achievement. Similarly, a number of the most intelligent minds within the community could now take their ideas and talent to whoever was willing to pay the highest price rather than having to employ these skills within the community. To some degree, the civil rights movement unintentionally created a brain and money drain for the African-American community. This process continues to this day. A small percentage of African Americans achieve great financial success, but, that said, all leading economic indices indicate that the position of the majority of Black Americans vis-à-vis White and Latin Americans has steadily gotten worse over the last thirty years.

As this reality slowly made itself manifest, the tenor of parts of Black America began to change. In 1966, during the James Meredith march in Mississippi, the former Stokely Carmichael coined the phrase "Black power." A year earlier Watts had burned in the first of the modern-day so-called "race riots." In 1967 Newark and Detroit would also burn. This new militancy no longer asked for equality and strove to achieve it by adopting mainstream (read "White middle-class") standards of deportment. Instead equality was assumed and demanded, and Black Americans were encouraged to celebrate and embrace everything Black. Phrases such as "Black is beautiful" emerged at this point in time. Africa was taken up psychologically as the motherland. African garb and African names achieved cultural currency, as did the "Afro" or "natural" haircut.

Not surprisingly, these changes in beliefs and ideals, this re-Africanization of Black culture, were reflected musically. In popular music the most radical example of these impulses was the development of funk by James Brown. In the simplest terms, Brown, beginning in 1967 with a record called "Cold Sweat," de-emphasized melody and harmony (i.e., no chord changes within sections of a song, near spoken lyrics) while privileging rhythm (both in qualitative and quantitative terms—i.e., employing more complex syncopated figures and using several different rhythm patterns at once, creating what I refer to as interlocked grooves). This reconstruction of Brown's music could be interpreted as de-emphasizing parameters favoured by Euro-American society while privileging sub-Saharan African characteristics, in effect re-Africanizing the music, thus paralleling the re-Africanization of African-American society at large at the time.

Those knowledgeable with regard to the richness and variety of sub-Saharan African musical practices might object to what may seem to be my invocation of the stereotype of African music as being rhythmically complex but melodically simple. I contend that such a stereotype, as erroneous as it is, had cultural currency in the late 1960s and early 1970s with many, if not most, White and Black North Americans. It is likely that this stereotype was understood as a "truism" by the majority of Brown's audience as well as by Brown and his musicians. As such, its cultural meaning, its value as a semiotic sign connoting African-ness, holds.

I should also state that in some ways the grooves found in all African-American and African-American-influenced musics could be argued to be interlocked. Here, though, due to the de-privileging of melodic and harmonic content, there is a greater focus brought to bear on rhythm. This, combined with what could be argued to be an intensification of syncopation, meant that, for many, funk automatically connoted Africa.

It might be worth noting that Brown himself has never connected funk to African musical practices. He saw funk as the development of something wholly new. I'm not sure that this particularly matters with regard to the argument that I am trying to advance. The re-Africanization of Black culture was a loose concept that tied most meaningfully to a general sense of a newly emergent pro-Black consciousness-at-large, which could be expressed in a variety of ways. Some of these ways tied directly to Africa, while others simply connoted a strong sense of Blackness that automatically resonated with the larger affinity of Blackness and Africa on a general ideological level. Brown and everyone else intrinsically understood funk to be manifestly "Blacker" than the music he had been creating up to this point as well as most other forms of contemporaneous rhythm and blues and that would include Motown, Stax, and Chicago soul.

At this point in my presentation I played the introduction, first verse and first chorus of "Cold Sweat" and pointed out the two interlocked grooves that the performance is constructed around. I also played an excerpt from the middle of the performance which included a fifty-four bar alto sax solo, a four-bar drum break and the beginning of the bass solo. In this latter excerpt Brown can be heard calling out to a variety of performers by name as well as uttering a variety of vocables that he inserts at various places in the sonic matrix. I also gave the following factual contextual information:

"Cold Sweat," recorded May 1967, released July 1967—no. 1 R & B, no. 7 pop. Performing force: two trumpets, trombone, alto, two tenors, baritone, two guitars, bass drum

What values can we ascribe to this performance and these patterns of interlocked grooves? I contend that the rhythmically interlocking parts of "Cold Sweat" could be interpreted to parallel the musicological and the sociological formations of African drum ensembles. All of the instrumental parts gain full meaning only in the context of the whole, and that meaning is primarily articulated through rhythmic relationships, secondarily through pitch relationships. The correlation between this type of rhythmic organization and a societal ideal tending toward pluralistic, yet interpersonal, and communal values, I think, is quite manifest. Everyone and every part is dependent, in a positive sense, on the individual contribution of everyone else. According to a number of scholars, including Richard Waterman, Kwabena Nketia, Robert Farris Thompson, and John Chernoff, interlocked drum patterns, or multi-part rhythmic structures as Nketia refers to them (Nketia 1974, 133) reflect this very same societal ideal in African drum ensembles. To my mind, then, in "Cold Sweat" the employment of interlocked grooves feeds into the concept of re-Africanization already discussed, both on the musical level of the interlocked groove itself and on the social level of communal codependent gestures combining for a greater whole. In other words, re-Africanization is manifested on the concrete level in the musical gesture itself and on the symbolical level in the very fact that the musical whole replicates a particular societal ideal.

Richard Middleton, in his book *Studying Popular Music*, discusses two modes of repetition that he refers to as musematic and discursive (Middleton 1990, 269–84). The former denotes the repetition of relatively short gestures (i.e., the two-bar interlocked grooves of "Cold Sweat"), while the latter refers to the repetition of longer units such as phrases or sections. Middleton correlates the two types of repetition with a number of things, but salient for this chapter is his contention that discursive repetition tends toward a hierarchically ordered discourse that reinforces a capitalist economy. Musematic repetition, on the other hand, tends toward a one-levelled structural effect that Middleton finds homologous with *collective variative* forms of social organization typical of pre-capitalist societies. In light of this last point, Middleton is careful to stress that musematic repetition in the form of a riff generally serves as a framework for vocal and instrumental variative elaboration thereby paralleling the concept of collective variative forms of social organization.

According to Middleton's definition, "Cold Sweat" clearly is organized around musematic thinking. The underlying rhythmic interlocking grooves are harmonic and rhythmic examples of musematic repetition. The relationship between this riff/groove framework and the variative detail of Brown's vocal and the sax, bass, and drum solos is extremely important, paralleling what Chernoff has stated is the African norm of a collective variative form of social organization (i.e., communal and personal yet pluralistic) (Chernoff 1981, 154–55). Middleton's theory of the relationship between musical repetition and societal organization provides yet one more avenue to interpret "Cold Sweat" as manifesting an aesthetic that invokes both the notions of community and re-Africanization.

In the late 1960s many Black militants began to understand that a large part of the problems facing African-American people in the United States were inherent in capitalism, period. If Middleton is correct in his assertion of the relationship between discursive repetition and capitalism, and musematic repetition and collective variative forms of social organization, then it would make sense that the appropriate soundtrack for a critique or challenge to the existing capitalist hegemony would employ musematic repetition.

The notions of community and solidarity are also connoted in this record in a number of ways outside of the explicit concept of re-Africanization. Throughout the performance Brown utters any number of vocables that are judiciously placed within the rhythmic matrix. In doing so Brown is projecting himself as being part of the band rather than presenting himself as a separate, somehow special, more important front man. Similarly, he can be heard calling out a number of things during the performance, including "Maceo, Maceo," "give the drummer some," "Bernard, come on and help him out, play that thing."[1] What are all these utterances about? I think the answer is that Brown is conveying a sense of community. He explicitly *names* those who are contributing, projecting their intrinsic value as individuals and their implicit equality with him in *collectively* unleashing the spiritual magic of the performance. It is significant to note here that "naming" is a long-standing practice within all sorts of African and African-American expressive forms.

"Cold Sweat" ends after seven and a half minutes with an extraordinary section where Brown appears to be shredding his larynx, singing "I can't, I can't, I can't, I can't stop, I can't stop, I can't stop singing." The effect is extremely cathartic and I am sure that that is the explicitly intended effect, but I also think that more is going on. By such a performance Brown is demonstrating an exceptional level of commitment that is not lost on his audience. Brown is explicitly stating that he has no *choice* in the matter. I contend that such a commitment to the cultural moment and to the audience also strongly evinces the articulation of the notion of community.

Cynthia Rose, in her book *Living in America: The Soul Saga of James Brown*, argues that while European cultures tend toward linearity with gestures having clear beginnings, middles and ends, sub-Saharan African cultures tend toward an aesthetic of circularity where a process is continually repeated in a cyclic manner. Beginnings and endings are not as important as the fact of the *process itself*. Funk music, as manifested by "Cold Sweat," is obviously predicated on the latter aesthetic. I maintain that this is yet one more way that funk manifests the notion of re-Africanization.

Within a year Brown had connected funk lyrically to the newly emergent Black consciousness, specifically with the song "Say It Loud, I'm Black and I'm Proud." Significantly, this would be his last Top Ten pop hit until 1985's "Living in America." Conversely, this was the beginning of his greatest success on the R & B charts. Between 1968 and 1974 Brown had 41 R & B hits, thirty-two of which went Top Ten. This is extraordinary testimony to the meaning he held for the Black community in the United States at the time. It would appear that as Brown's music became understood as more African, it was encoded or at least decoded by Blacks and Whites as having a value and aesthetic system that was largely outside of the experience of most Euro-Americans. Consequently, most White Americans found little they could relate to, while, in direct contrast, Black Americans embraced funk as one of the most meaningful expressive forms of the time.

Given the adoption over the last twenty-five years, via the influence of Brown, of the aesthetics of both the interlocked groove and circularity in rap and the unparalleled acceptance of rap by White America, perhaps much of America and, for that matter, much of the world has become, in a certain sense, Africanized.

Note

1   Referring to alto sax player Maceo Parker, drummer Jabo Starks, and bassist Bernard
    Odum, respectively.

References

Brown, James. 1991. "Cold Sweat." *Startime*. Los Angeles: Universal Music.

Chernoff, John. 1981. *African rhythm and African sensibility: Aesthetics and social action in African musical idioms*. Chicago: University of Chicago Press.

Guralnick, Peter. 1986. *Sweet soul music: Rhythm and blues and the Southern dream of freedom*. New York: Harper & Row.

Middleton, Richard. 1990. *Studying popular music*. Buckingham, UK: Open University Press.

Nketia, Kwabena. 1974. *The music of Africa*. New York: Norton.

Rose, Cynthia. 1990. *Living in America: The soul saga of James Brown*. London: Serpent's Tail.

TWELVE

On the One

Parliament/Funkadelic, the Mothership, and Transformation

ROB BOWMAN

N "TOWARDS A POETICS OF PERFORMANCE," Richard Schechner locates the "essential drama" of performance "in transformation—in how people use theatre as a way to experiment with, act out, and ratify change." Schechner goes on to suggest that transformation in theatre occurs "in three different places, and at three different levels": (1) in the drama or story itself; (2) in the performers who "undergo a temporary *rearrangement* of their body/mind"; and (3) in the audience "where changes may be either temporary (entertainment) or permanent (ritual)" (Schechner 2002, 170).

This chapter will attempt to investigate Schechner's theoretical ideas as they apply to performances by the funk ensemble led by George Clinton, alternately known as Parliament, Funkadelic, and P-Funk in the years 1976–78.

The Funk Mob, as they are often referred to, has its roots in a barbershop in Plainfield, New Jersey, in the late 1950s. Originally a doo-wop vocal group, the Parliaments, as they were first known, recorded two singles for local independent New Jersey labels in 1957 and 1959. In the 1960s the group's style changed with the times and they recorded eight singles in Detroit for Golden World and Revilot Records, manifesting a substantial Temptations influence. (On Revilot, they enjoyed a Top Five R & B and Top Twenty pop hit with "(I Wanna) Testify" in 1967.)

In what turned out to be a successful attempt to circumvent then-cur-
rent contractual obligations, in 1969 Clinton decided that the group would
cease functioning under the name the Parliaments. He proceeded to sign
the group's backup musicians to Westbound Records under the name
Funkadelic. The five vocalists who collectively were the Parliaments would
"guest" on Funkadelic albums. A few years later, Clinton legally won back
the rights to the group's original name. Dropping the s, he signed the
vocalists, now known as Parliament, first to Invictus and then to Casablanca
Records. Funkadelic would "guest" on Parliament albums.

Necessity being the mother of invention, Clinton had stumbled into a
situation where the same group of people recorded for two different labels
under two different names simultaneously. At the height of the Funk Mob's
popularity in the late 1970s, besides Parliament and Funkadelic, the same
basic set of musicians recorded as Bootsy's Rubber Band, Fred Wesley and
the Horny Horns, Parlet, and the Brides of Funkenstein. In addition, a
number of members (Eddie Hazel, Fuzzy Haskins, Bernie Worrell, Junie
Morrison, and Philippe Wynne), signed solo contracts with a variety of
labels, recording still more product with the same basic set of musicians.

In 1973 the group's career began to take on commercial significance.
With an album by Funkadelic entitled *Cosmic Slop*, George Clinton began
to articulate a funk cosmology that included such mythic characters as
Dr. Funkenstein, Starchild, and Sir Nose D'Voidoffunk. To be part of what
became known as the "maggot" subculture, one had to become conversant
with, and psychologically embrace, this cosmology. At the same time,
the collective entity variously known as a Parliafunkadelicment thang, the
P-Funk All-Stars and the Funk Mob began to mount elaborate two-and-a-
half-hour stage shows that were high-tech spectacles involving spaceships,
pyramids, and the like, and that were metaphorically light years beyond
anything previously experienced in the world of rhythm and blues.

Their clothing at this time also stood in sharp contrast to the rhythm
and blues norm. With the exception of the hippie garb favoured by Sly and
the Family Stone, R & B bands had traditionally dressed in matching uni-
forms that, more often than not, were one or another variation of a dress
suit. In marked contrast, the Funk Mob appeared onstage in fur, cowboy
and Indian gear, diapers, painted bedsheets, mopheads, Arab djellabas,
bridal gowns, Martian suits, and so on.

By virtually any standards of arena rock and roll or rhythm and blues,
Parliament/Funkadelic was anything but an ordered, predictable, smoothly
running ship. On the contrary, the group's stage shows were chaos person-
ified. Such a presentation turns each night into an adventure of sorts for

the musicians and consequently serves the needs of inspiration and creativity, counteracting the ennui of multiple nights on the road, playing the same set in the same order, with nary a hair out of place, which is the reality for artists as diverse as Pink Floyd, Salt-n-Pepa, Blur, and Metallica. I think that the Parliament/Funkadelic mode of presentation, in addition to functioning as a creative tool, also has ideological significance. Parliament/Funkadelic's stage presentation communicated at least four values on the visual and organizational level: (1) value is placed in the notion of a rainbow nation comprised of a myriad number of personas; (2) African Americans are imaged as capable of being anything/anyone they want to be; (3) being different is projected as something to be celebrated, not scorned; and (4) craziness, play, and imagination are all posited as part of the celebration of life.

Between 1976 and 1978 Clinton mounted extraordinary tours whose performances culminated with the landing of the symbolically loaded "Mothership," a spaceship that brought the character Dr. Funkenstein (played by Clinton) back to Earth, carrying the secret of the funk, which had been buried in the Pyramids 5,000 years earlier. Funkenstein's mission was simply to make the Earth funky once again. In addition to Dr. Funkenstein, a number of other characters also appeared in these performances, representing various aspects of Clinton's complex funk cosmology.

Clinton first began to articulate funk as an ideological framework through which one could understand the world and thereby live one's life in 1973 on the Funkadelic album *Cosmic Slop*. The Parliament albums, *Mothership Connection* and *The Clones of Dr. Funkenstein*, released in 1975 and 1976, respectively, provided the already established ideology of funk with both a creation myth and a complex cosmology that became the focus of the P-Funk Earth Tour. It is this tour and specifically a show that is available on DVD from Houston, Texas, on October 31, 1976, that is the focus of this chapter.

Let me briefly outline the structure of the performance. With the house lights down and the audience filled with anticipation, an unseen MC declares, "I want you to know that the Mothership has landed. It's time to tear the roof off the sucker. Direct to you from Chocolate City, may I present Parliament/Funkadelic." While in some ways this is a typical concert introduction that simply states "the show is beginning, get your sensory antenna up, here are the stars," this particular introduction has further meanings. Chocolate City was the name of a Parliament album from 1974. The actual title refers to Washington, D.C., as a Chocolate City surrounded by vanilla suburbs, and the album puts Black people in the White House (renamed the Brown House), in charge of all media and all important institutions. The reference to Chocolate City in the introduction, therefore, frames the performance that is about to ensue within a specifically African-American world view, clearly separate and distinct from the hegemonic world that all participants will return to after the show is finished. The phrase "Tear the roof off the sucker" refers to a huge Parliament hit single from the *Mothership Connection* album, which largely consists of the chants: "We want the funk/Give up the funk" and "We're gonna turn this mother out" that, in effect, pledge allegiance to the ideology of funk. The reference to the Mothership itself serves notice that this is no ordinary concert. This event involves the landing of the Mothership, a spectacle totally unique at that time within the confines of Black popular music.[1]

The introduction by the MC is followed by keyboardist Bernie Worrell playing solemn church-like music, while a single Super Trouper spotlight lights up a pyramid on stage. In mere seconds, religion, Africa, ancient Black civilizations, and, for those who already have the albums, the story of the funk have been referenced and inextricably connected. A disembodied narrator then intones the historical context for the event that is about to occur: "Funk upon a time in the days of the funkopus, the concept of specially designed afronauts, capable of funkatizing galaxies, was first laid on man child, but was later repossessed and placed among the secrets of the pyramids until a more positive attitude toward this most sacred phenomenon, the cloning of the funk, could be acquired."

The narrator goes on to articulate the cloning principle whereby funkateers could multiply in the image of the chosen one, Dr. Funkenstein, upon his return to Earth. The religious references are obvious. Funk is referred to as a sacred phenomenon and Dr. Funkenstein is the chosen one who will return to Earth in what is, in effect, a second coming.

After the narration, the spotlights ebb and flow in their intensity as they light up the pyramid, while the band creates an incredibly loud cacophonous crescendo, which eventually gives way to the opening song, "Cosmic Slop." With the stage lights finally on full, the audience sees a disparate group of performers wearing diapers, fur, tie-dyed long johns, spacesuits, wizard hats, bathing suits, and so on. Visually, lyrically, musically, and psychologically, an alternate reality has been constructed.

While I would love to continue with a thick description of the entire performance, space does not permit. Suffice it to say that a sense of chaos and spontaneity pervades the show with performers coming and going (the number of musicians and singers on stage ranges from five or six up to nearly thirty), most of whom sport an incredibly bizarre array of unconnected or thematized costumes.

The emotional core of the performance occurs about halfway through when, in near total darkness, the band performs "Children of Productions" (about the cloning of Dr. Funkenstein) and "Mothership Connection" (about the Mothership itself) before segueing into "Swing Down, Sweet Chariot." The latter of course signifies on the nineteenth-century spiritual "Swing Low, Sweet Chariot." In the Earth Tour shows the song is used to bring the spaceship down with lead singer Glen Goins gazing up at the ceiling, hands extended to the sky in jubilation, wonder, and supplication. When the Mothership actually lands, the music stops, all members of the band put the P-Funk sign up in the air, and the audience emits a deafening roar. It is a powerful moment, loaded with symbolism on a number of levels.

In attempting to understand if and how the P-Funk Earth Tour had transformative effects on either audience or band members, I put postings on several funk and soul listservs, asking people who saw these shows to contact me. I surveyed as many contemporary print reviews of the show as I could access, and I interviewed a number of band members.

The results of my interviews and surveys were incredibly rich. Schechner (1988, 166) states that one of the purposes of transformational theatre is that within the theatre space itself, events take place that could not occur anywhere else. In the P-Funk Earth Tour, Parliament/Funkadelic place African Americans at the centre of the universe in a way that they virtually never were in the 1970s in public spaces in the United States. As one of my consultants stated,

> As a Black child growing up in the 1970s, you didn't see Black folks as astronauts or as superheroes. Then along came P-Funk, and all of a sudden we had Black folks in space and with ties to the Pyramids in Egypt. It was my exposure to P-Funk that had me entertaining the idea that I could be an astronaut (or afronaut) or one day could travel in space. Even though all the kids that were into P-Funk like I was knew that all of that space stuff was make-believe, there was still something unexplainably *real* about it to me.

This was a recurring trope. Many fans, reviewers, and audience members pointed out the power that the image of P-Funk as Black heroes had for them, stating that such representations ultimately helped to transform their own self-image and suggested possibilities in their lives that previously they had never imagined.

With the Mothership tours, George Clinton was signifying on contemporary science fiction, taking a mainstream genre, and making it oppositional. At the time there was only one African-American science fiction writer of note, Samuel Delaney, and most science fiction stories were populated exclusively by Caucasians. As Robert Elliot Fox (1995) has pointed out, Blacks have an especially critical stake in future worlds. They have long had to struggle to find the core of possibility within fantasy and to transform dreams into realities. With the Mothership, Clinton engaged in implicit critique of White versions of the future and, at the same time, offered a prophetic vision of African-American possibility. The mere act of dreaming and fantasizing can be empowering. The Mothership tours presented such dreams visually, lyrically, and sonically.

The Earth Tour performances were emotionally and psychologically framed by the notion of funk as religion. As referred to above, earlier P-Funk albums and concerts had articulated a cosmology, and had already constructed a sense of an alternate reality with an alternative logic system and multiple in-group references, verbal, musical, and gestural. All involved in the performances had well-understood roles that parallel those of ministers, choir members, church band, and congregation. Everything was in place except for a holy book; in time, that would appear as well. As such, the P-Funk concert space became a sacred space. More than one member of the band described the moment of crossing the threshold from backstage to front of house as akin to entering the pulpit in a church. (Several, as well, brought up connections between the Mothership and the bible, and the Mothership and the teachings of the Black Muslims.) Virtually everyone who sent me an email or did interviews referred to the spiritual aspect of the shows.

With that as a context, the ritualized performances of the Mothership tours became highly charged sacred/secular events where, at one level, the landing of the Mothership represented the descent to Earth of God, or at least the God of Funk, Dr. Funkenstein.

Particularly rich in this regard was the following statement offered by bass player Cordell "Boogie" Mosson:

> Back in the bible it says Ezekiel saw the wheel way up in the middle of the sky, but nothing flew then, so how could you see a wheel in the sky and what does that mean? I know what a wheel is: A wheel is like a car wheel or a bicycle wheel which is in a disc form if you turn it sideways. If it's way up in the middle of the sky and it's in the bible ... a lot of us was raised believing in God, believing in church, so ... I want to ride. It connected.

At the same time, the Mothership represented for various audience members deliverance from present-day suffering. It also made explicit, vis-à-vis the use of "Swing Down, Sweet Chariot," a connection with the notion of deliverance from slavery and thereby communicated strong and powerful connections to the African-American historical past. The invocation of the Pyramids suggested an even deeper connection to an African past, one of great, highly developed, and glorious civilizations. One commentator saw the Mothership as symbolizing repatriation back to Africa. For many, the Mothership landing symbolized in a general sense the *spirit* descending, people getting happy as they do in Pentecostal churches. For virtually everyone, the Mothership was, in some sense, a symbol of hope and connected at a deep-seated level to racial pride.

Mosson interpreted the descent of the Mothership as connecting human beings to vibrating beings in other galaxies, and thereby exposing the lie of governments in the West that continue to deny the existence of UFOs and extraterrestrial beings. This particular interpretation resonates strongly with what many respondents saw as the central articulation throughout the whole performance of cosmic oneness.

According to Schechner (2002, 176), it is the unfolding of an event that can be measured against a predictable script that gathers and holds people. For the first several months of the P-Funk Earth Tour, audiences did not know exactly what to expect. While there were obviously news reports and reviews that mentioned the Mothership prop and many fans would have been familiar through the albums with the broad outlines of the "story," the theatre piece was still new and had yet to become a ritually repeated experience for the audience. As band members remember it, for the first several months of the tour, the audience was simply stunned by what they saw, offering little in the way of participation. The band actually felt that perhaps the performance simply wasn't communicating. Such fears were allayed when they would return to a given city a half year later. At this point, returning audience members were aware of what Schechner terms the "predictable script." The story was now ritual and it was the unfolding of the predictable within the ritual that provided the audience with a framework in which they could freely insert themselves.

So much of Clinton's vision as manifested in song lyrics and audience chants centre on the notion of being "on the one." This obviously refers to the rhythmic organization of the performance (of funk), but, within a larger frame of reference, it also evokes what I referred to a few seconds ago as cosmic oneness. The connection between band and audience night after night was the material actualization of this oneness. This occurred in a variety of ways.

To this day P-Funk performances involve a substantial number of participatory chants. Immediately following the first actual song of the show in Houston, Clinton gets the audience roaring the chant "Shit! Goddamn! Get off your ass and jam." He only has to say it once before the audience picks up on it en masse. From then on he merely has to intone "Everybody say" or "Let me hear you say" between each reiteration of the chant by the audience. The bonding of thousands of bodies moving together and, as one, vocalizing the chant quickly cements what Victor Turner refers to as communitas, and, of course, also parallels the church experience, but in terms of much larger numbers.

Throughout the performance Clinton and other band members ask rhetorical questions of the audience such as "Can I get an amen?" which clearly invoke the pastor/congregation relationship. In fact, vocalist Mallia Franklin referred to the audience as "ameners": "They weren't the audience. They were part of us. They were the ameners in the church. A good pastor, if he can rouse that church, do they keep coming back? That's what it was to me. Dr. Funkenstein was able to do that." Other members of the band also stated that the audience and band fused over the course of the performance, their roles becoming virtually interchangeable, further articulating the notions of cosmic oneness and communitas.

"We were probably the first ones to let the audience become part of us," states guitarist and singer Gary Shider. "They were just as much the group as we were. I believe the man upstairs willed it that way. Different cities had a different vibe, but it was all spiritual. It was universal, one big church."

Just before the Mothership lands, Clinton asks the audience "Do you *believe* in the Mothership? Are you hip to the Mothership? Do you want to ride? Do you want the Mothership to land here?" He also commands the audience: "Prepare for the second coming of Dr. Funkenstein." As the Mothership is about to descend, he requests that the audience rise and put their hands in the air. All of these rhetorical questions and commands are obviously invitations to the audience to participate, but here they are also tied to lyrics and concepts that invoke Funk/P-Funk as a belief system. As such they take on a heightened significance when compared to standard concert clichés such as "Wave your hands in the air/wave them like you just don't care" or "Houston, do you want to party?" After the Mothership actually lands, Clinton proceeds with a chant about Dr. Funkenstein ("We'd love to funk you, Funkenstein/Your funk is the best/Take my body and give it a mind/To funk with the rest"). This chant is, in effect, a hymn to the supreme being and the religion of funk itself, yet further connecting audience and band and cementing the feeling of communitas and oneness. As one Internet poster put it,

> Many of us were able to experience [thanks to the civil rights movement], a kind of freedom that our parents had never enjoyed. And the FUNK was at the heart of it all.... One of the best parts about this is that it was a common shared experience of pure joy. For many people of that era the biggest "shared experience" that was available was a P-Funk show. You had to sorta be there to understand what I'm about to say now.... To be honest, in some ways those concerts weren't really very far from being like going to a *Funk church* to worship at the altar of a "Mothership." ... In fact, there are some people that I know who even today will tell you that seeing the Mothership land in Detroit, [for example], is one of the high points in their lives. Add to that a set of lyrics to go with the music that sounded like code words for Black Power, and what you have got here is a *seriously* powerful program to influence people.

Intensity was a common theme that came up in several of my interviews. Bernie Worrell spoke of the "Swing Down, Sweet Chariot" section as heightening his "sensory molecules." Other band members spoke of goosebumps and adrenaline rushes. Saxophonist Greg Thomas told me that when he looked out across the stage at this point every night, several band members had their eyes rolled way back up in their head. Other band members spoke of a feeling of being high during these shows that went beyond any drug experience they had ever had; many of them also attesting to the fact that they regularly had out-of-body experiences during the show.

To conclude, according to Schechner, theatre is a means to actualize virtual alternatives. In turning possibilities into action, whole worlds that previously didn't exist are born. Band members spoke of the Earth Tour performances as giving them a sense of just how powerful music could be. Bernie Worrell told me that it made him realize just how great a responsibility it was to use the gift of music wisely and positively.

For the audience, the transformative effect of these shows was perhaps even deeper. One respondent attested that "My P-Funk experience has been life lasting. [These shows] made childhood worthwhile for me." Several respondents simply said that the performances had a "permanent impact" on them, but declined or were unable to state specifically what the nature of the transformation was. For some it was quite general, but no less powerful. Let me close with the words of one such audience member:

It was like being preached to, and the message was trust your body, trust your instincts, it's okay to groove, you ain't hurtin' nobody! The power of the Funk. I have carried this feeling with me ever since.

Note

1   The stage was created by noted Broadway set designer Jules Fisher. Although Fisher has worked with a few rock artists engaged in large-scale theatrically imbued presentations such as Kiss, the Rolling Stones, and David Bowie, this was the first time he had ever worked with a soul or funk group. The cost of the production in 1976 dollars was $270,000. Most band members that I spoke with had a sense that the mounting of the Mothership tours was historic.

References

Clinton, George. 1998. *The Mothership connection*. DVD. Long Beach, CA: Pioneer Artists.

Fox, Robert Elliot. 1995. *Masters of the drum: Black literatures across the continuum*. Westport: Greenwood Press.

Schechner, Richard. 1988. *Performance theory*. New York: Routledge.

———. 2002. *Performance studies: An introduction*. New York: Routledge.

Politics through Pleasure
Party Music in Trinidad

JOCELYNE GUILBAULT

INCE THE 1990S, THE COMMERCIAL value of soca has been widely recognized.[1] Soca's socio-cultural and musical accomplishments, however, remain contentious and contested.[2] Since the 1990s, soca's performance of so-called "light" lyrics and its emphasis on sexualized bodies and pleasures have contributed to its dismissal by many. Judged against calypso's socio-political commentaries, soca has been criticized by numerous journalists, academics, calypsonians, politicians, and listeners for not engaging the political. At a time of escalating rates of crime and violence, and growing fears about personal and public safety in Trinidad, soca is regularly condemned for failing to address the country's social ills. Yet over the past decade soca has repeatedly succeeded in gathering large crowds numbering over 20,000 people at shows and fêtes.

As a participant in these audiences, I want to offer an ethnographic perspective on the cultural work that live soca performs. In this chapter, I focus on live performances of soca to highlight their transformative capabilities. As Natasha Barnes (2000, 98) puts it, "Live performance, as recent theorization in performance studies reminds us, has transformative capabilities that can exist independent of capitalist reproduction and co-option when experienced in live encounters." In particular, I want to address how soca enacts a politics of pleasure by highlighting the social intimacies and antagonisms it has helped produce. But before I do so, I would like to situate the premises on which the political dismissal of soca has been based.

I

The dismissal of musics such as soca that focus on pleasure and bodily expression *as a legitimate critical public discourse* is not unique to Trinidad and can be related to Enlightenment ideas and European colonial legacies.[3] Colonial plantation slavery was at once a crucial political technology of modernity and a Caribbean crucible in which musical expressions were invented and practised. The time and place when slaves could assemble, play music, and dance were heavily controlled for at least two reasons: although the colonial authorities and plantation owners recognized the necessity for the slaves to rest and relax from their harsh work in order to return to it the next day, they also feared that too much dancing could become counterproductive—leading slaves to become lazy—and that the large crowd it attracted could easily help foment organized rebellion. So if dancing and pleasure among slaves were allowed through a rationality of labour productivity,[4] it was carefully measured in order to avoid the slaves becoming out of control. This connection made by colonial administrators and plantation owners between dance and pleasure among slaves on the one hand, and laziness and the threat of unruliness on the other hand, took a strong hold in colonial and post-colonial countries. It has arguably encouraged many members of the middle and upper classes to view dancing, particularly by Black bodies, as suspicious and threatening.[5]

In addition to holding such views vis-à-vis dancing, European colonial administrations, drawing on Enlightenment ideas, upheld a Cartesian divide between mind and body as the guiding principle of their governing technologies in the Caribbean, Latin America, and Africa.[6] Viewing the mind and, by extension, reason as what distinguishes humans from lower forms of life, they privileged what they considered the mind's most direct expression—the word—over the body. In this perspective, expressions of sexuality in dancing were not only disparaged but also racialized and associated with slaves. In Trinidad, numerous travellers, along with administrators, decried slaves' dances as barbarous and lascivious, and depicted them as proof of the slaves' racial inferiority.

In turn, the Christian churches also policed slaves' bodies in the service of moral values. Viewed against spiritual attainment, musical practices focusing on pleasure and sexualized bodies were condemned for celebrating the flesh and leading people away from God. After Trinidad's independence, these views changed only slightly. Although non-White bodies are officially no longer viewed as racially inferior, many local cultural critics still consider lyrics to be more edifying than dance. For many

church members, musical practices focusing on pleasure are still conceived as dangerously leading people away from spirituality and religious
moral values.[7] These notions about dancing derived from institutionalized racism,
European epistemologies, and Christian beliefs were central to the articulation of colonial projects. Such understanding continued to have a strong
hold after independence in Trinidad. However, they were simultaneously
contested and viewed with ambivalence by many. It is well documented that
several members of both the colonial administration and the Creole middle class, while publicly criticizing the exuberant expressions of pleasure
through sexual dancing by the slaves and their descendants, in private
enjoyed them both for being enticing and for demonstrating great dancing skills.[8] In their turn, while some of the slaves' descendants adopted the
values imposed onto them by the colonial administrations and the Christian churches, many rejected these same values and continued to favour
musics emphasizing sexualized expression not only for their own pleasure,
but also as a means of defiance against the oppressive conditions in which
they lived. Since the 1990s (or what I have referred to elsewhere as
Trinidad's *neo-liberal era*),[9] several critics from middle- and upper-class and
religious associations have continued to disparage soca because of its
emphasis on sexualized dancing and light lyrics.[10] At the same time, a
growing portion of the population has been giving its support, as demonstrated by massive crowds of as many as 20,000 people attending soca
concerts and parties.

   Instead of dismissing soca as a legitimate critical public discourse
because of its focus on embodied pleasure, in this chapter I want to show
how such pleasure in soca is not experienced at the exclusion of other
projects. In this sense, I want to speak not about pleasure per se, but about
the *politics of pleasure* and highlight how the pleasure that soca fosters nurtures distinct skills, knowledges, and civic values that have efficacy in other
domains.

II

I want to examine here a significant part of the cultural work that live
soca performances achieve through the creation of what I refer to as *intimacies*. I use the word *intimacy* not in terms of "the more common one
of privacy, often figured as conjugal and familial relations in the bourgeois home" (Lowe 2006, 195). Drawing on Lisa Lowe's critical insights,
I use the word in two other ways: to speak about the spatial proximity that

soca helps create, and to address the variety of contacts among people that it makes possible.[11] These two different types of intimacies enabled by live performances of soca could be referred to as *public intimacies* as they unfold among artists on stage, between the artists on stage and their audiences, and among audience members during the performance. I want to stress that public intimacies at live soca performances are necessarily performative—that is, embodied practices that reiterate identities and produce discursive effects that articulate cultural understandings of race, class, gender, and sexuality.[12] To focus on the public intimacies enabled at live soca is thus useful to highlight how new points of connections are being developed (for example, among artists and audience members of different ethnicities, nationalities, and generations and across musical genres), and how the lines between the private and the public are being reworked (for example, what can and cannot be publicly shared or exposed).

Here a clarification of the terms I am using is important. Instead of speaking of regional or North American collaborations enacted through live soca, following James Ferguson's insights, I prefer to speak more specifically about the points of connection that soca enables. Echoing his argument about the way that financial capital travels, a musical practice such as soca may criss-cross the Caribbean region and North America, but it does not encompass or cover them. Challenging common understandings of globalization, Ferguson (2006, 37–38) writes: "The movements of capital [read, soca] cross national borders, but they jump from point to point, and huge regions [read, Caribbean nation-states and many parts of North America] are simply bypassed." In other words, the points of connection that soca helps create, to use Ferguson's words, "hop" over "unusable" Caribbean nation-states and parts of North America as well as distinct ethnic, religious, and linguistic communities, to name only a few. The significance of this social fact is, in my view, crucial for understanding the politics of inclusion and exclusion deployed by and through soca.

To focus on public intimacies as governing technologies further helps to address both their emancipatory and repressive potentials—that is, their politics of inclusion and exclusion of distinct musical sensibilities and sexual orientations. Nevertheless, the public intimacies performed at live soca shows need to be acknowledged as productive of pleasure and, as Sylvia Yanagisako (2002) argues in relation to sentiment in general, pleasure in turn needs to be recognized as a productive force.[13] As will be shown, pleasure is indeed not just central to soca music-making. It is also a vital force in soca community formation and consumer loyalty.

Soca artists on stage have produced what *Trinidad Express* columnist Keith Smith (2007) calls "a flood of collaborations." These collaborations on stage greatly contrast with the practice of calypsonians, who rarely ever share the stage during their presentations, except when performing what is called *picong*, the competitive satirical or taunting verbal exchange in song with other calypsonians.[14] Based on the local normative conception in the calypso milieu of an artist as one who combines expressive skills in poetry, dance, and singing, "true, true" calypsonians, to use a local expression, are expected not only to produce their own material but also to be judged on their own merits as solo artists in calypso competitions. Inspired by the musics that soca artists of the 1990s onward listened to (most particularly Jamaican dancehall, rock, pop, and hip hop from the Anglo-American mainstream), soca artists have transgressed several calypso conventions. A great majority, in fact, acknowledge composing songs in collaboration, and their songs often feature several singers to perform different sections of one song, a practice that challenges calypso competitions' prior judging of solo artists only. Machel Montano, one of the chief exponents of new trends in soca, explains that these changes enact a notion of authenticity profoundly different from the ways in which calypso has been traditionally defined. It is more a matter of resonating with soca artists' particular experience than being faithful to an established tradition. In his view, what makes soca songs "authentic" is that they are a "reflection of us," a reflection of the new visual and sonic environments that soca artists experience on a daily basis.

Based on this perspective, Smith points out that collaborations in soca entail a variety of contacts: for example, between younger soca artists and veterans of calypso (Shurwayne Winchester and Calypso Rose), between male and female artists (Machel Montano and Destra Garcia), between two artists of different ethnicities (Rikki Jai and Black Stalin), between artists from different islands (Machel Montano from Trinidad and Alison Hinds from Barbados), between artists from different musical genres (Machel Montano associated with soca and Shaggy with dancehall), and between artists living on the island and in diaspora (Bunji Garlin in Trinidad and David Rudder, a Trinidadian living in Toronto; Machel Montano in Trinidad and Wyclef Jean, a Haitian living in New York). The collaborations also revel in mixing linguistic accents and sounds as well as rhythms and clothing from different countries and musical genres.

These various kinds of collaborations—or what I call "intimacies" performed in and for the public—as Smith remarks, combine different talents and knowledges that, to the delight of all the artists involved as well as their audiences, have produced hits, great shows and parties, and musically, to use Smith's own words, "impressive results." When the *Collectors Riddim* appeared in 2003, the CD created a sensation. Based on a Jamaican technique called *riddim* (which involves the production of a pre-recorded rhythm section track over which several singers are invited to compose their own tunes), the *Collectors Riddim,* produced by Xtatik Ltd & Xtatik 5.0, featured a pre-recorded soca rhythmic track with a hint of ska played by a short riff on the synthesizer over which Trinidadian guest artists performed their original compositions. In so doing, the soca-based *Collectors Riddim* assembled musical techniques, rhythmic patterns, musical creativities, and voices that arguably contributed to the originality of the CD and the great amount of airplay it received. In relation to spatial proximity—the other type of intimacy to which I referred above—soca collaborations in live performances bring together bodies that have rarely ever performed together in the same space, let alone on the same stage. Here are other examples: Afro-Trinidadian Bunji Garlin and East Indian Sarika Mahabir, and Jamaican Red Rat and Trinidadian Machel Montano. Such performances thus combine on the same stage artists with differing ethnicities who share a common nationality, and artists with different nationalities who share a common racialization. In so doing, soca artists confirm and help reinforce in both sound and sight "the essential and increasing inter-connectedness of this thing called Trinidad music" (Smith 2007). In many interviews I conducted, soca artists speak of the joy and satisfaction they derive from bringing together the familiar and the less familiar face and sound, the brother and the sister, the elder and the neighbour, and also musical memories and new musical know-how.

Although performing togetherness on stage, soca has nonetheless excluded certain interconnections. Soca artists reinforce heteronormative relations and so far have excluded homosexual expression.[15] In other words, not all pleasures are permissible on the soca stage. "Wining"—a local term referring to the gyration of the waist—is still performed alone or usually between a man and a woman.[16] In the same vein, the hypersexualization of female and also of male bodies through outfits and performance gestures amplifies socially gendered prescribed looks and performances of women as feminine and of men as masculine. Women wear tight outfits that follow the contours of their figures, cut low to highlight the breasts, and short tops to reveal the buttocks in a style that conforms to widely shared heterosexual aesthetic values in the Caribbean. Men perform *djouk* movements (pelvic thrusts) on women invited to come on stage or touch their crotch à la hip hop to assert their masculinity.[17] In so doing, both soca male and female artists embody and (re)produce salient aspects of the conventions that inform how femininity and masculinity are construed by a vast majority of Afro-Trinidadians of the "oil boom generation" born in the 1970s.[18] These conventions draw not only from past Afro-Trinidadian gender politics, but also from the ways they are currently articulated by their peers in other African diasporas, most particularly in Jamaican dancehall and US hip hop.[19]

While performers may adopt conventional gendered outfits and dispositions, they can also challenge normative expressions of sexuality and of secularity. For instance, when Denyse Belfon demands that a man "wine" on her on stage to fulfill her sexual desires, she transgresses the normative notion of woman's sexual agency in its appropriate expression. And when Machel Montano invokes Krishna in his song "Harry Krishna" (1998), he transgresses a highly policed divide between the religious and the secular.

Soca performances produce public intimacies that are sources of pleasure not only among the artists performing on stage, but also between the artists and their audiences. Soca greatly relies on an *aesthetic of participation*.[20] From 1993—when Superblue launched his "Bacchanal Time" song in which he urged the crowd to jump up and wave their rags[21]—until now, soca singers "contact" their audiences through call-and-response: "Anybody from Trinidad? Anybody from Antigua? Anybody from Grenada?" They coordinate the crowd's body movements with theirs, creating a sea of bodies in motion: "move to the right, move to the left; start to wine; go down low," to name only a few actions performed during soca songs. Soca artists urge members of the audience to find a partner and wine. Following all of that, they often stop the music and keep simply the skeleton of the rhythm section accompaniment to relax together and "breathe" (as Machel Montano puts it in his 2005 song "You"). Someone in the crowd waves a huge Trinidadian flag; several audience members press themselves against the fence that separates them from the space reserved for the security guards and journalists and the stage where their favourite artists now speak and address them. Others just stand nearly still until their song leader unleashes the pulsating rhythm animating the song, the backup singers come in, and the entire band exults playing the chorus at full volume, sonically calling everyone to join in, feel the beat, and jump up and wave together with the soca artists and other dancers on stage.

For soca artists as well for their audiences, the focus of live performances is "interaction"—sensual, emotional, and physical. It is about sharing the experience of a moment, a pulse, a movement. The variety of contacts or public intimacies that soca artists establish with the crowds range from expressing together one's sense of national belonging ("Anybody from Trinidad?") to establishing "affective alliances" through the sharing of feelings—exuberance, joy, and exhaustion (by jumping up, waving your rag, and holding on to your partner).[22] Importantly, it also includes showing signs of reciprocal loyalty among artists and audience members and of solidarity with one another. When, in her 2006 song "Max It up," Destra sings to her audience, "Together we jumping/No racist no color define/Soca is we energy baby," and when she adds, "We chippin in file in one harmony/We defying poverty," she is not just sharing her world vision. She is fostering a sense of community together with her audience members. In her line, "is all ah we, so support yuh soca music, Yes yuh IDENTITY," she includes herself as part of the community and simultaneously calls on the audience members to support soca because, as she puts it, it enacts who we are, our "identity" (note her use of the singular).

While the call-and-response and dance movements performed by the artists on stage and the audience members create a shared knowledge of lyrics and tunes, and an aesthetic appreciation of sexualized bodies and moves—a kind of intimacy through shared knowledge that helps create a sense of "we"—they simultaneously produce the outsider, the "Stranger." Kezia Page (2005) takes up this issue by addressing the winning 2001 road-march song, "Stranger," by Shadow, one of the most acknowledged Trinidadian artists among both calypsonians and soca performers since the mid-1970s. She explains "how he, Shadow, a kind Trinidadian man, teaches a white Australian woman how to dance and how to enjoy Carnival" (Page 2005, paragraph 6). As she remarks, "Shadow's 'Stranger' is ironically not for strangers, but is a first place mobilizer for insiders who already know what to do when he shouts 'rag' and 'flag,' and find in his narrative a kind of power and pleasure, as revelers dance along with the fictional stranger—only better." She adds, "In effect, Shadow, by making a spectacle of the outsider strengthens the bonds of the insider community, for here, knowing the dance is the way one indicates her/his place in the community" (Page 2005, paragraph 7). Significantly, it should be noted, this is one of the privileged moments when returnees who came back to resettle permanently in Trinidad, as well as Trinidadian and other Caribbean emigrants back to the island for Carnival, experience a sense of belonging in an environment that is otherwise often hostile to them.[23]

As Page indicates, "Stranger" echoes many other songs in the Trinidadian Carnival music repertoire.[24] And, like them, it does more than just reinforce a sense of community "by drawing borders through what might be termed a choreographic map." It also effects "a power shift between tourist and local." Implicit in the "Stranger" is an evocation of tourism and sex. As she explains, "While these women might have expected to take advantage of friendly and easy access into Caribbean entertainment, they are in fact the ones who are exploited as they are made into spectacle, and perhaps worse." So while "the follow-along lyrics, with dance instructions included, on one hand seem to extend the dance community and thus the consumer community in an ingeniously welcoming gesture ... these same lyrics by making fun of outsiders and making unsuspecting insiders of people along just for the dance are clearly more than just welcoming" (Page 2005, paragraph 19). So, it can be concluded, pleasure in live performance of soca songs like Shadow's "Stranger" is not innocent. It transforms audience members "in the know" into subjects of community and, simultaneously, it constitutes the outsider as the necessary, even welcome—even though not fully accepted—counterpart of its formation.[25] In so doing, pleasure then becomes a productive force of power.

Live soca permits a variety of contacts and spatial proximity among audience members that produce visceral exuberance and intense delight. As mentioned above, typically soca competitions, shows, and parties during Carnival draw massive crowds, including often more than 20,000 people. Jumping up and down in close physical proximity to one another, people in the audience take pleasure in moving together and sharing the high volume of sounds pulsing from the speakers. It is a time not so much for conversation as one for co-action. As I have experienced as an audience member in soca parties and competitions over the past fourteen years, and as many soca fans in Trinidad shared with me, waving your rag together, singing along, and rolling your waist in time and in tune with others gives a sense of closeness. Wining alone or on a man or on another woman—a much emphasized dance movement in soca—is part of the sensual pleasures—public intimacies—enabled through soca. Moving to the right or moving to the left along with the person standing next to you and the one in front of or behind you in effect gathers together people who are often unrelated, in synchrony, and for that moment, in intense awareness of each other. Participation in such events literally embodies a viscerally experienced sense of collective belonging.

That live soca performances create spaces that invite sociality and encourage public intimacies, as I have just described, has been widely acknowledged in the press and in academic publications. What has been less often addressed is the price that audience members must pay, both literally and metaphorically, to access and engage in these spaces. In other words, pleasure does not come free. In Trinidad, it is linked to several other realities—socio-economic, gender politics, and state-related—that have a direct impact on who can participate in soca fêtes and how different audience members experience them.

While live soca aims to assemble as many people as possible and, to use Machel Montano's words, "to bring back the love," the cost of tickets makes many of these performances inaccessible to some.[26] While many popular fêtes may cost only TT$45 (around CA$7.50 at the time of this writing) to attend, during 2007 Carnival some of the most sought-after fêtes had ticket prices ranging from TT$80 to TT$250, an amount of money many cannot afford. These prices are prohibitively expensive for the most marginalized lower-class subjects, who themselves are often excluded from hegemonic constructions of the public. From the outset, soca fêtes thus include only those people who can afford them. In turn, the several thousand people who can attend soca competitions, shows, or fêtes are confronted with a reality of another sort that is state-related rather than economic, and concerns the issues of traffic jams and safety on the road (related to speed and drunk driving). The worsening of such problems every year has caused many participants—ironically, on their way to experience the public intimacies and pleasures enabled by soca—to feel deep resentment at the state's incapacity to address these issues. So, in an uncanny way, live soca performances lead their audiences to address state politics in relation to personal and public safety by voicing critiques on at least three matters: the lack of material infrastructure for improved roadways; the lack of police reinforcement of driving regulations; and, thus, the overall lack of delivery of social services and state planning.

There are other realities that mark the ways the expression of sexual dancing and pleasure enabled by the dynamic performance of soca songs is controlled. Although everyone in attendance is encouraged to jump up and wine, many people in the audience are not entirely free to really let go and "break away." Norms of propriety for many middle- and upper-class members of the audience—including both men and women, but even more so for women—do not entirely disappear, and these norms condition much of the ways that their bodies can move in dancing. Similarly, couple relationships can place limits on how close one of the partners can be to other people in the crowd. Fights at times erupt when a man is seen as wining too closely on what calypsonian the Mighty Duke once called another man's "property"—that is, a wife or girlfriend.[27] So class values and affective relationships intervene in how and how much soca audience members experience pleasure.

Over the past few years, the escalating rate of crime and violence in Trinidad, combined with the massive and rowdy crowds attending live soca performances, have in turn heightened how class differences have influenced the ways some people now experience those performances. Inadvertently, both crimes and crowds have created new opportunities for the organizers of live soca performances to make more money, and for members of the middle and upper classes, as well as tourists with money, to assert their privileged position. The "VIP Treatment," as it is called, refers to the special treatment that people paying high entrance fees receive. This includes access to protected spaces with their own facilities, food, and drink services where well-to-do guests can enjoy the fête with—and, at the same time, at a distance from—the masses. A crucial desire here is to be immersed within, but safely insulated from, rowdy crowds. As this last instance demonstrates, the energetic tempo of soca songs, the full-throat call-and-response of the song leader and crowd, the high volume of the musical accompaniment, and the sexual moves performed by the artists on stage and audience members produce distinct kinds of public intimacies and, by extension, different kinds of pleasure that are, for some, more "safe" than others.

By way of conclusion, I want to revisit what constitutes a legitimate critical public discourse about Trinidadian popular music. What is at stake here, I believe, are arguments over what projects and practices are deemed to engage the political. In this chapter, I have argued that the political can be articulated not only through words or by being related to state politics, as it has often been conceived in Trinidad as in many other countries. I have shown that through sound, sight, sexualized bodies, and movement, live soca performances articulate a variety of contacts and spatial proximities. I have highlighted how, in so doing, these contacts and spatial proximities provide a great source of pleasure for soca artists and audience members, and how through pleasure critical cultural politics are performed.

New musical sensibilities, knowledges, and practices emerge from soca artists' numerous collaborations. The physical proximity of people and the moving of bodies together engage interactions and co-actions that, for many participants, give a sense of closeness and belonging. The songs that soca artists perform call for and invite loyalty and solidarity. In addition, they also cultivate an effusive sense of national pride.

Simultaneously, power relations in terms of class and gender politics are deployed and negotiated through live soca performances. Expressions of heterosexuality on stage and among audience members dominate to the exclusion of any other expression of sexuality. The production of the "we"—based on a shared knowledge of the artists, their songs, typical body movements, and permissible spatial proximities and sensual/sexual expressions—makes at once those "in the know" the subjects of a community and makes the others the outsiders.[28] As I have shown, the "choreographic mapping" of this community, to use Page's expression, is managed through several other realities. I described those related to economic capital, class values, state politics, affective relationships, and class-based privileges and access.

Soca should not be dismissed as a political force by labelling it as a music only about and for pleasure. Rather than endorsing the normative opposition between pleasure and politics, my analysis underscores the productive political force of pleasure in soca performances.[29] On stages, soca artists enjoy crossing entrenched divides of ethnicity, race, and nation. Audience members revel in the new musical creations emerging from the numerous collaborations engaged in by soca artists as they help redefine the audience's own politics of belonging within multiple constituencies on an international stage. Virulent critiques of state incapacities to control traffic emerge from the assemblage of crowds at soca fêtes. By appreciating how pleasure in live soca is a political productive force, we can better understand the popular aspirations, affinities, and identities that are emerging through contemporary cultural politics in Trinidad's music scene.

Notes

This is a revised version of a paper presented at the annual conference of the Caribbean Studies Association in Salvador da Bahia, Brazil, in May 2007.

 1 With appearance fees in the range of TT\$5,000–\$10,000 (CA\$835–\$1,670 at the time of this writing), top Trinidadian artists like Machel Montano HD, Bunji Garlin, Destra Garcia, Shurwayne Winchester, and Rikki Jai earn substantial incomes, often performing twice in one night during Carnival weekends. With over 300 fêtes in Carnival 2007, bands and lesser-known artists earning, respectively, around \$15,000 and \$2,000, a performance can also boast earning important revenues during Carnival. In his article entitled "Carniomics: The New Economics of Carnival," Clarence Jagroopsing (2007) further describes how not only artists but also sponsors, cultural promoters, associations, and small traders all benefit from these fêtes, which, it should be noted, feature nearly exclusively soca, ragga soca, and chutney soca. Combined with the nearly year-round touring of top soca artists and bands in overseas Carnivals and other celebrations organized by members of Trinidad's diasporas, soca-related performances during and outside Carnival have thus been recognized as playing a vital role in Trinidad and Tobago's music industry and GNP.

2   For further information on the subject, see Grant (2004).

3   I use the expression "critical public discourse," associated with Jürgen Habermas (1989), in reference to the Trinidadian context not to connect it to a bourgeois idea as Habermas did, but rather to highlight how (similar to another aspect of his definition) in Trinidad, critical public discourse has also been conceived as representing a public's interests within civil society against the state. Following Lauren Berlant (1998), I want to show that this focus on the public's interests, as defined nearly exclusively in relation to the state and the legitimacy granted to the discourses articulating such interests, has foreclosed many other processes and practices of critiques dealing with power relations.

4   As Achille Mbembé (2001, 128) explains, while the colonial mode of domination was deployed through coercion, it also involved conviviality, "even connivance," as governing technologies.

5   For further information on how colonial administrations and members of middle and upper class dealt with dancing and the social gatherings it encouraged, see Rohlehr (1990), Liverpool (1993), and Cowley (1996), whose writings eloquently describe the many bans and edicts that were promulgated during the colonial period.

6   See, for example, Moore (2006, 107–34), Fryer (2000), Comaroff and Comaroff (1991, 213–43), and Copland (1985, 8–55).

7   See, for example, Rommen's (2007) illuminating account of how music and dance are heavily controlled in Trinidad's Full Gospel Pentecostal churches.

8   For an elaboration on the subject, see Brereton ([1979] 2002), Rohlehr (1990), and Liverpool (1993).

9   See Guilbault (2007).

10 It is important to note that since the early 1990s, while a great majority of soca songs feature "light" lyrics (i.e., lyrics that focus on affect and affinities and favour spontaneous expression and repetition in contrast with the carefully crafted humorous and socio-political commentaries of calypso), some soca songs occasionally include a storyline in the traditional alternation between verse and chorus associated in Trinidad with what has been viewed since the 1960s as the calypso form. Examples of this latter tendency from Machel Montano and Xtatik's catalogue alone include "Harry Krishna" in Machel and Xtatik's *Charge* (1998); "Doh Tell Meh" in *The Xtatik Parade* (2004); and "You" in *The Xtatik Experience* (2005).

11 For further elaboration on these understandings of "intimacies," see Ann Laura Stoler's (2002) insightful study of what she calls "the intimate" during colonial rule in Indonesia.

12 Even though Elizabeth A. Povinelli (2006) writes about love, her remarks about what intimacy means for many people apply equally well here. As she puts it, "intimacy is, among other things: an intensification of enduring social relations of kinship, geontology [sic], and ritual, themselves anchoring and anchored by institutions of everyday life; a means of building collectively oriented and materially anchored socialities; and [as will be shown below in this study of live soca] a manner of securing the *self-evident* social roles of men and women" (Povinelli 2006, 179; my emphasis).

13 As Yanagisako (2002, 10) explains, "Under particular conditions, sentiments generate particular desires and incite particular social actions." In addition, she adds, "sentiments, themselves the products of historically contingent cultural processes … influence and shape material production" (Yanagisako 2002, 11). For an elaboration of these points in relation to soca, see Guilbault (2007), in particular Chapter 7 and the Coda.

14 The text that follows in this paragraph is based on Guilbault (2007), in particular chapters 4 and 7.

15 For further information on the subject, see Rahim (2005). Although the author refers to calypso, her remarks well apply here.

16 While I have seen some women occasionally wine on each other, I have never seen a similar public performance between men.

17 For further elaboration on the subject, see the transformative collection of essays in Reddock (2004).

18 I owe this expression to Robin Balliger (2000), who, following local usage, employs it to refer to the generation born during the economic boost provided by Trinidad's oil industry during the 1970s.

19 For further information on Jamaican dancehall and American hip hop in relation to gender politics, see Cooper (2004), Hope (2006), and Norfleet (2006).

20 I borrow the expression "aesthetic of participation" from Packman (2007).

21 The expression "wave your rag" refers to waving something in the air, which can be any piece of cloth or a flag. Such motion represents a way to mark one's active participation in the show and one's support and loyalty to the artist.

22 I owe this expression to Lawrence Grossberg (1984).

23 For further information, see Plaza and Henry (2006).

24 Page (2005) refers to Lord Kitchener's "Miss Tourist" (1968) and Colin Luca's "Dolla Wine" (1991) as further examples of songs that, like "Stranger," explore the theme of easy dance instruction for tourists. According to her, such themes have been popularized again over the last five years.

25 Here I draw on Jean-François Bayart's (2004) insightful discussion of Michel Foucault's problematic of *assujetissement*.

26 Machel Montano in an interview with Cordielle Street (2007).

27 For an elaboration on the subject, see Dikobe (2003) and Miller (1991).

28 In that sense, one could speak about "pleasure-knowledge," an expression coined by Lauren Berlant (1998, 284), whose evocation of Foucault's famous expression "power-knowledge" produces significant links among pleasure, knowledge, and power.

29 In the editorial of the *New Left Review*'s first publication, Stuart Hall writes about the danger of conceiving politics in terms that are too narrow. In his view, this was "a main cause of the decline of socialism in this country [Britain]" (Hall 1960, 1). As he explains, the socialist rhetoric was too stodgy; it needed to reach out to popular culture and therefore to contemporary forms of public pleasure. I thank Donald Moore for sharing this insight with me.

References

Balliger, Robin. 2000. Noisy spaces: Popular music consumption, social fragmentation, and the cultural politics of globalization in Trinidad. Ph.D. dissertation, Stanford University.

Barnes, Natasha. 2000. "Body Talk: Notes on Women and Spectacle in Contemporary Trinidad Carnival." *Small Axe: a Journal of Criticism* 7: 93–105.

Bayart, Jean-François. 2004. "Total Subjectivation." In *Matière à politique: Le pouvoir, les corps et les choses*, edited by Jean-François Bayart and Jean-Pierre Warnier, 215–53. Paris: Karthala.

Berlant, Lauren. 1998. "Intimacy: A Special Issue." *Critical Inquiry* 24, no. 2: 281–88.

Brereton, Bridget. [1979] 2002. *Race relations in colonial Trinidad 1879–1900.* Cambridge: Cambridge University Press.

Comaroff, Jean, and John Comaroff. 1991. *Of revelation and revolution: Christianity, colonialism, and consciousness in South Africa*, vol. 1. Chicago: University of Chicago Press.

Cooper, Carolyn. 2004. *Sound clash: Jamaican dancehall culture at large.* New York: Palgrave Macmillan.

Copland, David. 1985. *In township tonight! South Africa's Black city music and theatre.* London: Longman.

Cowley, John. 1996. *Carnival, canboulay, and calypso: Traditions in the making.* Cambridge: Cambridge University Press.

Dikobe, Maude. 2003. Doing she own thing: Gender, performance and subversion in Trinidad calypso. Ph.D. dissertation, University of California, Berkeley.

Ferguson, James. 2006. *Global shadows: Africa in the neoliberal world order.* Durham: Duke University Press.

Fryer, Peter. 2000. *Rhythms of resistance: African musical heritage in Brazil.* Hanover: Wesleyan University Press.

Grant, L. Trevor. 2004. *Carnivalitis: The conflicting discourse of Carnival.* Jamaica/New York: Yacos Publications.

Grossberg, Lawrence. 1984. "Another Boring Day in Paradise: Rock and Roll and the Empowerment of Everyday Life." In *Popular music 4: Performers and audiences*, edited by Richard Middleton and David Horn, 225–58. Cambridge: Cambridge University Press.

Guilbault, Jocelyne. 2007. *Governing sound: The cultural politics of Trinidad's Carnival musics.* Chicago: University of Chicago Press.

Habermas, Jürgen. 1989. *The structural transformation of the public sphere: An inquiry into a category of bourgeois society*, trans. Thomas Burger and Frederick Lawrence. Cambridge, Mass.: MIT Press.

Hall, Stuart. 1960. "Editorial." *New Left Review* 1, no. 1: 1–3.

Hope, Donna. 2006. *Inna di dancehall: Popular culture and the politics of identity in Jamaica.* Mona, Jamaica: University of the West Indies Press.

Jagroopsing, Clarence. 2007. "Carniomics: The New Economics of Carnival." *Trinidad Express*, http://www.trinidadexpress.com/index.pl/article?id=161098649.

Liverpool, Hollis Urban Lester. 1993. Rituals of power and rebellion: The Carnival tradition in Trinidad and Tobago. Ph.D. dissertation, University of Michigan.

Lowe, Lisa. 2006. "The Intimacies of Four Continents." In *Haunted by empire: Geographies of intimacy in North American history*, edited by Ann Laura Stoler, 191–212. Durham: Duke University Press.

Mbembe, Achille. 2001. *On the postcolony.* Berkeley: University of California Press.

Miller, Daniel. 1991. "Absolute Freedom in Trinidad." *Man* (N.S.) 26: 323–41.

Montano, Machel, and Xtatik. 1998. "Harry Krishna." *Charge*. Mad Bull Music X24–11-74–23.

Moore, Robin D. 2006. *Music and revolution: Cultural change in socialist Cuba*. Berkeley: University of California.

Norfleet, Dawn M. 2006. "Hip-Hop and Rap." In *African American music: An introduction*, edited by Mellone V. Burnim and Portia K. Maultsby, 253–91. New York: Routledge.

Packman, Jeff. 2007. "We work hard at entertainment": Performance and professionalism in the popular music scenes of Salvador da Bahia, Brazil. Ph.D. dissertation, University of California, Berkeley.

Page, Kezia. 2005. "'Everybody Do the Dance': The Politics of Uniformity in Dancehall and Calypso." *Anthurium: A Caribbean Studies Journal* 3, no. 2 (Fall), http://anthurium.miami.edu/home.htm.

Plaza, Dwaine E., and Frances Henry, eds. 2006. *Returning to the source: The final stage of the Caribbean migration circuit*. Mona, Jamaica: University of the West Indies Press.

Povinelli, Elizabeth A. 2006. *The empire of love: Toward a theory of intimacy, genealogy, and carnality*. Durham: Duke University Press.

Rahim, Jennifer. 2005. "(Not)Knowing the Difference: Calypso Overseas and the Sound of Belonging in Selected Narratives of Migration." *Anthurium: A Caribbean Studies Journal* 3, no. 2 (Fall), http://anthurium.miami.edu/home.htm.

Reddock, Rhoda E., ed. 2004. *Interrogating Caribbean masculinities: Theoretical and empirical analyses*. Mona, Jamaica: University of the West Indies Press.

Rohlehr, Gordon. 1990. *Calypso and society in pre-independence Trinidad*. Port of Spain, Trinidad: Published by the author.

Rommen, Timothy. 2007. *"Mek some noise": Gospel music and the ethics of style in Trinidad*. Berkeley: University of California Press.

Smith, Keith. 2007. "A Flood of Collaborations." *Trinidad Express*, http://www.trinidadexpress.com/index.pl/article?id=161085192.

Stoler, Ann Laura. 2002. *Carnal knowledge and imperial power: Race and the intimate in colonial rule*. Berkeley: University of California Press.

Street, Cordielle. 2007. "HD." *The Guardian* [Trinidad], 5 February, http://www.guardian.co.tt/archives/2007–02–05/features2.html.

Yanagisako, Sylvia Junko. 2002. *Producing culture and capital: Family firms in Italy*. Princeton: Princeton University Press.

FOURTEEN

A Festschrift for the Twenty-First Century
Student Voices

KIP PEGLEY

VIRGINIA CAPUTO

N THE FALL OF 2006, A GROUP of Beverley Diamond's former students came together to contribute to this Festschrift. As an educator, mentor, supervisor, researcher, fieldworker, collaborator, and friend, Bev's impact has been widely felt, evidenced by the enthusiastic response from students hoping to contribute. Her ideas have guided us as researchers and teachers, and, most importantly, they have shaped us as people. For these reasons, among others, we embraced this opportunity to reflect on what we have learned from her about the collaborative and ethical dimensions of the process of producing knowledge, about sharing space, and about how to pose a thoughtful question and how to really listen to an answer. In our correspondences we explored many topics that are close to our hearts as well as Bev's, including gender, mentoring, pedagogy, technology, multiculturalism, and the future of Canadian ethnomusicology, to name a few.

Some who participated in these discussions took classes together at York or at Memorial. Others never met. Yet we all cultivated professional and personal relationships through the communities at both institutions that Bev played a pivotal role in fostering over two decades. Most of us have had the opportunity to work with Bev on ideas in her offices in Winters College and at MMaP, at the Absinthe Pub and Bitters, or at one of many dinner parties that she generously hosted at her home. Our time with Bev is the singular link that brings us all together in this place.

The purpose in coming together initially seemed quite clear to all of us. What was not so clear was the most appropriate way to go about accomplishing our goal given that we are all situated in various locations across several countries. This is when the idea of transforming the Festschrift into an online exchange first emerged. The editors realized at the outset of the project that using electronic mediation as a primary mode of communication to run ideas across continents and time zones meant that the group could face steep challenges and intellectually and emotionally costly decisions. Nevertheless, our previous experiences with one form of online exchange—blogs—suggested that this medium might be highly useful. Blogs can be efficient, allow for easy reference to previous discussions, and enable participants to leapfrog over one another in discussions to follow up on ideas that interested them. We decided to use this format and launched our effort with a set of key questions around themes intended to spark discussion.

In practice, however, the blog format posed challenges. Many contributors experienced this forum as too impersonal and unfriendly, especially given that we were not only communicating ideas, but also sharing private emotions about someone for whom we care deeply. Many reported privately that the blog felt as though it was cavernous, impersonal, and "out there." We decided that what was needed was an electronic *place* where sharing could be conducted in ways that might foster this feeling of closeness and intimate proximity. Out of these discussions, questions of process, identity, and community began to emerge.

To bridge the distance articulated by blog participants, we moved into an email discussion format, and we sensed immediately a change in the group's energy. Postings began to circulate, followed by an exchange of ideas and emotional tributes. To help facilitate our feeling of connectedness, contributors' names and addresses were left in the recipient list. Even if a contributor had not posted to the list for some time, his or her presence on the list was noted. In a sense, the list created a portal through which we were all visible to one another, at least in name. As one contributor stated, it was good to have one another "in each other's inboxes." We felt closer and back on track.

The online discussions then unfolded in multi-faceted ways. Some contributors clearly were more comfortable with this medium than others; some preferred to initiate ideas while others would sooner wait until ideas were generated before they would engage publicly. In some discussions, contributors chose to work with excerpts from Bev's publications on a variety of topics while others chose to discuss her pedagogical strategies and how these shaped their own approaches to teaching. While the project initially was designed as an online discussion, we pushed at its edges over time and often crossed over into "e-fieldwork," revealing ourselves to our colleagues through discussions of our work, our education, our varied histories, desires, challenges, frustrations, and successes. Despite the sometimes sensitive nature of these discussions, we held an advantage in our electronic setting over more traditional fieldwork venues: we were sharing emotions and ideas with old acquaintances, many of whom are qualitative researchers who engage with technology on a daily basis. In theory, our discussions should have gone smoothly, yet as we endeavoured to facilitate a successful virtual space into which people could enter, new challenges emerged.

One critical issue that underscored our contributions and may be useful to think about in contemplating some of the challenges we encountered in creating an online interaction is a conceptual one. What became clear to us as we moved through the process of this online group is that to construe community as a kind of static entity is a simplification that does not address questions of what communities are, how they are formed, how they are maintained, and to make sense of challenges and/or their dissolution. In an online space, a particularly pointed question arises: How is community envisaged and maintained to fully account for the subjects whose associations are not demarcated geographically or spatially? As we progressed through the process of writing this contribution, the collectivity of contributors was always fluctuating and never automatic or given. We called ourselves an "online" writing community, but what did this mean? As a conceptual tool that ethnomusicology, following anthropology, has relied on for some time, invoking community provides a way to locate research and, in turn, to help legitimate and make viable ethnographic subjects by delimiting and justifying a field of social relations that otherwise seems unbounded. In viewing our online interactions as a community, we drew upon concomitant ideas about belonging and affiliation that we tested over time. Our expectation was that through our exchanges we could create a "place of belonging" in this less formalized space through sharing our experiences about Bev's influence in our academic and personal lives. To a certain degree, therefore, the concept of community offered, as Vered Amit and Nigel Rapport (2002, 17) have noted, "a convenient conceptual haven, a location from which to safely circumscribe potentially infinite webs of connection." Indeed community became a haven for some, and a partial solution for the editors. However, what happened in practice in the field exceeded the boundaries of this framing.

FIGURE 14.1   Recollecting in Diamonds by former student Andra McCartney, who based the text on excerpts from the student online discussions

at **B**ox

to h**E**aring

[from **V**irginia

Caputo] h**E**llo all

of the fou**R** topic areas

for this b**L**og—gender

in particular B**E**verley's influence

of ordinary ever**Y**day life as it is

of sounding a bit od**D** I thought I would

year for my tenure appl**I**cation file part of the teach-

-ing philosophy and I w**A**nted to speak to the

here is an excerpt one for**M**ative experience during my grad

light what each individual br**O**ught to the table most of the

feel that they could contribute u**N**iquely to discussions there were

they were not as relevant to the **D**iscussion because they spoke from of this post

help us recognize and analyze our su**B**ject positions and identity constructs particularly how

expression barriers to such und**E**rstanding and analysis came tumbling

the compassion with which Be**V** taught her students to accept

or lack thereof so that on**E**'s expression can fully

as they interlaced in p**R**ocesses of artistic express

elation I was reading Ce**L**iz Haig-Brown's essay on

the play conveyed wom**E**n's experience of Van

categories the communit**Y**'s multicultural and

certainly espouse**D** communities of learn

already are **I**nspiring teaching

our profession**A**l work and

as been to **M**eet many won

rite a sh**O**rt note a

somethi**N**g that

extraor**D**inary

crediBle
studEnts
be a Voicing
blatantly askEd are you
values from patRiarchal China
act transfrom Lives studying
this wonderful mEntor in a way
on teaches thank You Bev Margaret

voices once again i'D like to echo your
my life and work I have certainly been
affected me the most is thAt she allowed even
understanding of why it was iMportant for me to do so
work she has done in Native cOmmunities and for Native
approach to studying differeNce more later as i think through
I hope many of you weigh in on this topic after reaDing Bev's article there's no going

these interact Wong raise and the questions asked By Kip are indeed pressing ones
of transition which is markEd by both excitement and
departments in the old conserVatory mould given the shaky
in some quarters an Ethnomusicology bearing
welcome ghettoized and peRceived as doubly threat
what degree they feeL they are politically
not tenured or arE politically vulnerable
and address waYs of learning and

to pick up with Deborah Wong's
education to recapItulate Bev
relativist Arguments
and perforMance into
years Often at
ethNomusic
regarDs

Far from any idealized vision of community, the groups of people who interacted online were distinguished by age, gender, interest, and power, among other differences. Moreover, community did not necessarily operate solely on principles of co-operation, but included exclusion and conflicting moments in some instances. Nor did our e-lists exist in a social, political, or economic vacuum. As members of families, as workers, as academics at various points in our careers, contributors to the online discussions were affected by various issues pertaining to the workforce, family relations, personal challenges, etc., that sometimes remained invisible in this space. In other words, the encounters online were embedded in multi-dimensional communities, yet it was our association with Bev, our shared interest in honouring her, and our common experience as her students that connected us without clearly defined boundaries. This is what defined this "community." And these boundaries were never defined once and for all. Rather, the webs of connection through which this collective of social actors configured community were tenuous at best, but highly important, nonetheless.

A second critical challenge was the question of how to create an equitable forum within our newly defined community. When the invitation was extended, the editors decided, in an attempt to share power as equitably as possible, that an online medium would be implemented. Indeed, as Stephen and Harrison (1994, 768–69) have argued, mailing lists seem to be highly successful in facilitating democratic exchanges, while "placing stress" upon established hierarchical roles. Yet we learned through this process that the abolishment of hierarchical structure may sound theoretically desirable, but its practice may not necessarily be the most beneficial: new tensions may arise *because* we are working antithetically to our academic training. Although many of us struggle deeply with the academic model, we at least understand how its power works: certain voices carry more cultural capital than others; we know that there is a price of admission to conferences and anthologies, and those people we deem important are often up on stage giving a keynote or plenary. In short, academia is a hierarchical meritocracy within which individuals become privileged through individual accomplishment. Is it possible, as Jill Walker asks (2006, 129), that engaging on listservs disrupts hierarchies that now clearly *serve* us, rendering our relationship to them more ambivalent? Is it possible to even conceive of a blog or listserv that openly shares vulnerable, budding ideas among equals, thus working against the academic model within which we are trained? What happens within electronic spaces when we can no longer rely upon the safety of a podium or the gentle nudge of an audible inhalation?

In addition to the lack of corporeality and familiar hierarchies, we were also grappling with the challenges of temporality: because our interactions were not in real time, messages were distributed to the list when the contributors' lives would allow. This resulted occasionally in a sparser quantity of mail, and sometimes in a slew of messages. As John Marshall (2001, 87) explains, the volume of mail is critical to creating and maintaining a successful online space: if a critical volume is not created, then a sense of place will not develop. Similarly, too much mail can create an overwhelming feeling to which people might respond by leaving the space or by controlling it. While no one left the space, certainly some voices were heard more than others and some quieter contributors reported privately that they found it difficult to figure out where to "jump in."

Thus it became important to validate the silences that sometimes lingered on the list. As Jean-Luc Nancy (1991, 30–31) wrote, "Speech, including silence, is not a means of communication, but communication itself, an exposure." In other words, as Bev told many of us in our fieldwork training, if we attend only to the content of what our informants tell us, we will miss the communication that is the actual revealing. Listening to the silences became a useful tool as we moved through topics and ideas with one another; they revealed and communicated much to our friends and colleagues on the list.

The question many quiet contributors faced, however, extended beyond *when* to "jump in" to *with what* and *with how much?* It became apparent that the electronic format adopted here was incongruent with our preconceived assumptions of what constitutes a traditional musicological/ethnomusicological Festschrift, or, for that matter, legitimate scholarly engagement altogether. While students have been trained to engage informally in seminar discussions—perhaps most related to the style encountered on written blogs—and compose articles and conference papers (more formal and sometimes lengthy articulations), can we say we are similarly familiar writing a scholarly mid-length form consisting of only a few paragraphs? Such postings can, on occasion, be nothing short of perplexing: If I write a succinct idea that I'm not yet comfortable openly developing (again placing oneself in a vulnerable academic position), can I post such an "unbaked" idea to the list? Should the entire "community" be burdened with yet one more email if it's just a quick thought? What is the minimum weight of a post?

If, as Jill Walker argues (2006, 135), scholars work in the genres of their time—Socrates, after all, disseminated many of his ideas through dialogues with his students—then are blogs and listservs the fora with which we must become familiar? Will collaborative listserv discussions like this one become the norm by 2040, becoming the basis of a new format that might even replace hard-copy articles? If so, how do we best train our students to electronically engage with one another and with their research informants? What might the post-print academic community look like?

There is a growing literature that explores questions of future electronic formats; too often this focuses on the fears surrounding mass amateurization in blog discussions. It is not surprising that the publishing market has an interest in undervaluing online publishing, depicting it as uninformed, and even quickly and haphazardly produced. This is a perspective enthusiastically purported in the realm of the academic, where online publishing of any sort is still not as heavily weighted as that in hard copy. Increasingly, however, we are compelled to consider the ethical implications of availability to public knowledge. John Willinsky, of the Public Knowledge Project, estimates that in 2006 only 15 percent of all academic research was available to open access.[1] Scholarly journal prices have risen considerably over the last few years, making it more difficult for smaller libraries to maintain even their current holdings. The University of Toronto libraries, for instance, had to manage a strangulating $13 million journal bill for the 2006 academic year. Compounding this scenario is that the public must now show a University of Toronto library card not only to access the stacks at Robarts Library, but even look at the computer holdings on site. So while online discussions and publishing do not *necessarily* diminish the cost of disseminating knowledge and facilitate access to it, they are an important place to start.

We have learned through this reflective exercise about various struggles inherent within the shift to the post-print era, from the generation of material to its presentation. It has been particularly compelling to do this while relinquishing the perceived capital of the print Festschrift—arguably *the* signifier of respect within the Western academic tradition—in favour of a student web Festschrift. We believe Bev would approve: In her presentation at the 2006 Canadian Society for Traditional Annual Meeting, Bev spoke about the process of establishing the MacEdward Leach Gaelic song website and emphasized the importance of approaching this text not as a completed work, but, with the input of website visitors, a continual work in progress (Diamond 2006). Bev's comment highlights her concern not only for the product of research and scholarly efforts, but also for attending to the intricacies of the process that unfold along the way. Similar to a song website, a web Festschrift of the twenty-first century might be envisioned with interactive potential that allows for responses, an opportunity for dialogue, and, unlike a bound Festschrift, room for inclusivity and openness to diverse voices continually adding to the festivity. Ultimately, this model runs the pleasurable risk of expanding from Festschrift to Fest-sprachen/Festsingen/Festspielen, all appropriate possibilities given our guest of honour.

During our exchanges, many questions also sprang about community and identity, about power and privilege, about access and responsibility, and these questions overlapped and ran parallel to the conversations and discussions happening online. We found ourselves attuned to the process of turning space into place as much as we were about the discussions of individual topics. The process of understanding what constitutes place and how identity, community, and power are intertwined flowed through our communications—through roadblocks and bursts of online activity. While we did not anticipate all of the breakdowns in communication and the challenges we encountered, in the end, they provided us with valuable pedagogical moments to reflect upon the discussions and reconsider our methodology. As Bev noted herself, in this nexus lies hidden riches: "[t]he best theory emerges in the dissonance between what we think we think and what we find ourselves encountering" (Diamond 1998, 14). In retrospect, it seems only fitting that in the process of honouring Bev, we would have another opportunity to use her insights to examine the juncture/disjunc-ture between theory and practice.

Four discussions appear on the webpage at http://www.press.wlu.ca/press/Catalog/elliott.shtml, following from the groups that formed online: music and identity, music and gender, First Nations music, and fieldwork. In addition to the aforementioned desire for accessibility and expansion, the web Festschrift is an appropriate format for this writing for two rea-sons: the length of the contributions varied considerably, and contributors engaged in widely varying writing styles, from more formal analyses to informal musings, all of which are fitting tributes to Bev, and can find their own unique place in an online format. We invite you to join in on our conversations by writing in on the main blog page.

Our attempt to craft this work in Bev's honour by exploring an elec-tronic medium through which to engage a diversity of voices as a way to work with/in/through the intensities of relationships in the intellectual community surrounding Bev is part and parcel of her influence on us as growing scholars and teachers. She instilled in us the desire to push back at conceptual boundaries both theoretically and practically; she taught us to seek out and envisage ways to see obstacles as productive events in and of themselves. In the online texts, you will read and hear evidence of life-long lessons and practices in the contributions of our colleagues and friends. The gentle energy she brought to many discussions over the years still circulates around her students today, and this is why we will continue to engage one another intellectually with respect, enthusiasm, and commitment for many years to come.

Figure 14.2 Bev's doodles, collected by Maureen Houston and Janice Esther Tulk and artistically arranged by Kelly Best. Maureen is the office administrator of MMaP, Janice is a former student, and Kelly a current student of Bev at Memorial University

Note

1   Elizabeth Church, "Turning the ivory tower into an open book," *The Globe and Mail,*
    21 July 2007, F6.

References

Amit, Vered, and Nigel Rapport. 2002. *The trouble with community: Anthropo-
    logical reflections on movement, identity, and collectivity.* London: Pluto Press.
Diamond, Beverley. 2006. "Reconnecting: University Archives and the Commu-
    nities of Newfoundland." Conference presentation, Canadian Society for Tra-
    ditional Music. Carleton University, Ottawa.
————, with John Shepherd. 1998. "Colloquy/Débat: Theory and Fieldwork."
    Canadian University Music Review 19, no. 1: 4–18.
Marshall, John. 2001. "Cyber-Space, or Cyber-Topos: The Creation of Online
    Space." *Social Analysis* 45: 81–101.
Nancy, Jean-Luc. 1991. *The inoperative community.* Trans. Peter Connor. Min-
    neapolis: University of Minnesota Press.
Stephen, Timothy, and Teresa M. Harrison. 1994. "Conserve: Moving the Com-
    munication Discourse Online." *Journal of the American Society for Informa-
    tion Science* 45, no. 10: 765–70.
Walker, Jill. 2006. "Blogging from Inside the Ivory Tower." In *Uses of blogs,* edited
    by Axel Bruns and Joanne Jacobs, 127–38. New York: Peter Lang.

Appendix
Beverley Diamond—Publications and Lectures

Prior to 1988, Bev's publications use the name Beverley Cavanagh; from 1988 to 1990 some use Beverley Diamond Cavanagh; after 1990 they appear under Beverley Diamond.

Publications

Books and Edited Volumes

1982 *Music of the Netsilik Eskimo: A study of stability and change*, 2 vols., with vinyl recording. Mercury Series, Canadian Ethnology Service Paper 82. Ottawa: National Museums of Canada. Published version of the author's 1979 Ph.D. thesis from the University of Toronto.

1986–89 *Canadian university music review/Revue de musique des universités canadiennes*. English language editor, vols. 7–9.

1987 *Canadian music in the 1930s and 1940s: Proceedings of a conference held at Queen's University, Kingston, Ontario, November 1986*. CanMus Handbooks 2. Kingston: Queen's University Music Department/Toronto: Institute for Canadian Music. Editor.

1994 *Canadian music: Issues of hegemony and identity*. Toronto: Canadian Scholars' Press. Co-edited with Robert Witmer.

1994 *Visions of sound: Musical instruments of First Nations communities in Northeastern America*. Chicago Studies in Ethnomusicology. Waterloo: Wilfrid Laurier University and Chicago: University of Chicago. Co-authored with M. Sam Cronk and Franziska von Rosen.

1994 *Canadian perspectives in ethnomusicology: Canadian University Music Review* 19, no. 2. Co-edited with Robert Witmer.

2000 *Music and gender*. Foreward by Ellen Koskoff. Urbana: University of Illinois. Co-edited with Pirkko Moisala.

2007 *Newfoundland and Labrador Studies*, music issue, 22, no. 1. Co-edited with Glenn Colton and James Hiller.

2008 *Native American music in eastern North America: Experiencing music, expressing culture*. Global Music Series, general eds. Bonnie C. Wade and Patricia Shehan Campbell. New York: Oxford University Press.

2008 *Post-colonial differences: The study of popular music in Canada and Australia*. Newcastle upon Tyne: Cambridge Scholars Publishing. Co-edited with Denis Crowdy and Daniel Downes.

Articles and Chapters in Books

1972   "Annotated Bibliography: Eskimo Music." *Ethnomusicology* 16, no. 3: 479–87.

1973   "Imagery and Structure in Eskimo Song Texts." *Canadian Folk Music Journal* 1: 3–15.

1976   "Some Throat Games of Netsilik Eskimo Women." *Canadian Folk Music Journal* 4: 43–47.

1977   "The Legato Principle in Netsilik Eskimo Music." *Studies in Music from the University of Western Ontario* 2: 15–21.

1981   "In Memoriam: Mieczyslaw Kolinski (1901–1981)." *Ethnomusicology* 25, no. 2: 285–86.

1985   "Les mythes et la musique Naskapis." *Recherches amérindiennes au Québec* 15, no. 4: 5–18. Translated by Robert Larocque and Nicole Beaudry.

1987   "Celebration: Native Events in Eastern Canada." In *Folklife annual*, 70–85. Washington, DC: American Folklife Centre/Library of Congress. Co-authored with M. Sam Cronk and Franziska von Rosen.

1987   "The Performance of Hymns in Eastern Woodlands Indian Communities." *Sing out the glad news*, edited by John Beckwith, 45–56. CanMus Documents 1. Toronto: Institute for Canadian Music.

1987   "Problems in Investigating the History of an Oral Tradition: Reconciling Different Types of Data about Inuit Drum Dance Traditions." *Anuario Musical* 42: 29–52. Edited by Alan Jabbour and James Hardin.

1988   "The Transmission of Algonkian Indian Hymns: Between Orality and Literacy." In *Musical Canada: Words and music honouring Helmut Kallmann*, edited by John Beckwith and Frederick Hall, 3–28. Toronto: University of Toronto Press.

1988   "Vivre ses traditions: fêtes intertribales chez les Amérindiens de l'est du Canada." *Recherches amérindiennes au Québec* 18, no. 4: 5–21. Co-authored with M. Sam Cronk and Franziska von Rosen; translated by Jacqueline Roy and Nicole Beaudry.

1989   "Music and Gender in the Sub-Arctic Algonkian Area." In *Women in North American Indian music: Six essays*, edited by Richard Keeling, 55–66. SEM Special Series no. 6. Bloomington: Society for Ethnomusicology.

1990   "'Not Knowing' and the Study of Native Music Cultures: Introductory Comments"; et al. "Round table discussion: Ethnomusicology in the Canadian university." In *Ethnomusicology in Canada*, edited by Robert Witmer, 57–61 and 349–63. CanMus Documents 5. Toronto: Institute for Canadian Music.

1991   "Canadian Music Studies in University Curricula." *Newsletter of the Association for Canadian Studies* 12, no. 3: 16–18.

1992   "Christian Hymns in Eastern Woodlands Communities: Performance Contexts." *Musical repercussions of 1492: Encounters in text and performance*, edited by Carol E. Robertson, 381–94. Washington: Smithsonian Institution.

1993 "Lessons Learned, Questions Raised: Writing a History of Ethnomusicology in Canada (II)." *Canadian Folk Music Journal* 21: 49–54.

1994 "Introduction: Issues of Hegemony and Identity in Canadian Music" and "Narratives in Canadian Music History." In *Canadian music: Issues of identity and hegemony,* edited by Beverley Diamond and Robert Witmer, 1–21 and 139–71. Toronto: Canadian Scholars' Press.

1995 "Narratives in Canadian Music History." In *Taking a stand: Essays in honour of John Beckwith,* edited by Timothy J. McGee, 273–305. Toronto: University of Toronto Press. [Reprint of the above article.]

1998 "Colloquy: Theory and Fieldwork." *Canadian University Music Review* 19, no. 1: 4–18. Co-authored with John Shepherd.

1998 "When Spirits Sing and Singers Have a Voice." In *Sharing the voices: The phenomenon of singing,* edited by Brian Roberts, 75–88. St. John's: Memorial University.

1999 "Introduction: Canadian Perspectives in Ethnomusicology." *Canadian University Music Review* 19, no. 2: 1–4. Co-authored with Robert Witmer; the two also co-edited this issue of the journal.

1999 "Theory from Practice: First Nations Popular Music in Canada." *Repercussions* 7–8: 397–431.

2000 "Music and Gender: Negotiating Shifting Worlds," co-authored with Pirkko Moisala, and "The Interpretation of Gender Issues in Musical Life Stories of Prince Edward Islanders." In *Music and gender,* edited by Pirkko Moisala and B. Diamond, 1–19 and 99–139. Urbana: University of Illinois Press.

2001 "Re-placing Performance: A Case Study of the Yukon Music Scene in the Canadian North." *Journal of Intercultural Studies* 22, no. 2: 211–24.

2001 "What's the Difference? Reflections on Discourses of Morality, Modernism, and Mosaics in the Study of Music in Canada." *Canadian University Music Review* 21 no. 1: 54–75.

2002 "Native American Contemporary Music: The Women." *World of Music* 44, no. 1: 11–39. Winner of the Society for Ethnomusicology Jaap Kunst Prize.

2003 "In Memoriam: Lise Waxer (1965–2002)." *Canadian Folk Music Bulletin* 37, no. 1: 14.

2005 "Media as Social Action: Native American Musicians in the Recording Studio." *Wired for sound: Engineering and technology in sonic cultures,* edited by Paul Greene and Thomas Porcello, 118–37. Hanover: Wesleyan University Press and the University Press of New England. Winner of the Wachsman Prize for the best book in organology, awarded by the Society for Ethnomusicology for 2005.

2005 "The Soundtracks of Indigenous Film." In *From bean blossom to bannerman, odyssey of a folklorist: A festschrift for Neil V. Rosenberg,* edited by Diane Tye, Martin Lovelace, and Peter Narváez, 125–54. St. John's: Folklore and Language Publications, Memorial University of Newfoundland.

2006 "Canadian Reflections on Palindromes, Inversions, and Other Challenges to Ethnomusicology's Coherence." *Ethnomusicology* 50, no. 2: 324–36.

2006 "There's No Going back." Special issue on *The Future of Music Study in Canada*, edited by Wayne Bowman, *Ecclectica* (an occasional online journal), http://www.ecclectica.ca/issues/2006/2/diamond.ecc.asp.

2007 "'Allowing the Listener to Fly as They Want to': Sámi Perspectives on Indigenous CD Production in Northern Europe." *Worlds of Music* 49, no. 1: 23–49.

2007 "Local Logics and the Gendering of Music Technology: A Newfoundland Case Study." *Intersections: Canadian Journal of Music* 26, no. 2: 49–68.

2007 "Music of Modern Indigeneity: From Identity to Alliance Studies." The John Blacking Distinguished Lecture for 2006. *Journal of the European Seminar for Ethnomusicology*, www.marta-dahlig.com/esem/pdf/ml/JBML 2006-Diamond.pdf.

2007 "Reconnecting: University Archives and the Communities of Newfoundland," and "Whither CSTM? How We Can Look to the Past to Find a Good Path for the Future." *Folk music, traditional music, ethnomusicology: Canadian perspectives, past and present*, edited by Anna Hoefnagels and Gordon E. Smith, 3–12 and 231–36. Newcastle upon Tyne: Cambridge Scholars Publishing.

2007 "Santu's Song Revisited." *Newfoundland and Labrador Studies* 22, no. 1: 229–59.

2008 "Deadly or Not: Indigenous Music Awards in Canada and Australia." *Postcolonial distances: The study of popular music in Canada and Australia*, edited by B. Diamond, D. Crowdy, and D. Downes, 175–90. Newcastle upon Tyne: Cambridge Scholars Publishing.

Dictionary and Encyclopedia Articles

1981 "Binnington, Doreen," "Ethnomusicology," "Inuit," "Kolinski, Mieczslaw," "Witmer, Robert." In *Encyclopedia of music in Canada*, edited by Helmut Kallmann, Gilles Potvin, and Kenneth Winters. Toronto: University of Toronto Press.

1984 "Kalukhaq," "Kelutviaq," "Kilaut," "Shishikwun," "Tautirut," "Teueikan" (articles on Inuit and Algonqkian sound-producing instruments). In *The new Grove dictionary of musical instruments*, edited by Stanley Sadie. London: Macmillan.

1986 "Inuit [Eskimo]." In *The new Grove dictionary of American music*, edited by H. Wiley Hitchcock and Stanley Sadie. London: Macmillan.

1992 "Innu Nikamu," "Kolinski, Mieczyslaw," "Witmer, Robert," "Ethnomusicology," co-authored with James Robbins, and "Native North Americans in Canada," co-authored with seven others. In *Encyclopedia of music in Canada*, 2nd ed., edited by Helmut Kallmann et al. Toronto: University of Toronto Press.

2000 "Susan McClary." In *Encyclopedia of feminist theory*, edited by Lorraine Code. London: Routledge.

2001 "Musical Identity, Diversity, and Interaction in Canada" (1056–65); "Overview: Musical Culture in Canada" (1066–1100); "Canadian Musical Heritage Society" (1108–9); "Acadian Music" (1235–57); "Northern Canada" (1274–78); "Snapshot: Popular Music in Northern Canada" (1279–81); "Snapshot: Musical Interaction on the Canadian Prairies" (1249–51). In *The United States and Canada*, edited by Ellen Koskoff. *Garland encyclopedia of world music*, vol. 3. New York/London: Garland.

2001 "Ethnomusicology." In *Canadian encyclopedia*, edited by James Marsh. Toronto: McClelland and Stewart, http://www.thecanadianencyclopedia .com/index.cfm?PgNm=TCE&Params-A1ARTA0009597.

2005 "First Nations and Métis," "Inuit," "Yukon, Northwest Territories, Nunavut, and Nunavik." *Encyclopedia of popular music of the world*, edited by John Shepherd et al. London: Routledge.

Reviews

1977 Bradley, Ian. *A selected bibliography of musical Canadiana*, rev. ed. Victoria: University of Victoria, 1976; Bradley, Ian, and Patricia Bradley. *A Bibliography of Canadian Native Arts*. Agincourt: GLC, 1977. *Canadian Music Educators Journal* 19, no. 1: 60–2.

1981 "*Inuit Games and Songs/Chants et jeux des Inuit*. Unesco Collection, Musical Sources. Phillips 6586 036. LP recording. *Ethnomusicology* 25, no. 2: 349–52.

1982 Lewis, Larry C., ed. *Union list of music periodicals in Canadian Libraries*, 2nd ed. Ottawa: Canadian Assn of Music Libraries, 1981; Toomey, Kathleen M., and Stephen C. Willis, eds. *Musicians in Canada: A bio-bibliographical finding list*, 2nd ed. Ottawa: Canadian Association of Music Libraries, 1981. *Canadian University Music Review* 2: 231–33.

1983 "Ethnomusicology of Canada's Native Peoples." Review of three books: Canadian Ethnology Service Papers 79, 83, 86 by Maija Lutz, Anton F. Kolstee, and Robert Witmer. *Canadian Ethnic Studies* 15, no. 2: 139–45.

1983 Krummel, D.W., et al., comp. *Resources of American music history: A directory of source materials from colonial times to World War II*. Urbana: University of Illinois, 1981. *Ethnomusicology* 27, no. 1: 126–27.

1983 Lutz, Maija M. *Musical traditions of the Labrador Coast Inuit*. Ottawa: National Museums of Canada, 1982. *Ethnomusicology* 27, no. 3: 540–42.

1983 Pelinski, Ramón Adolfo. *La musique des Inuit du Caribou: cinq perspectives méthodologiques*. Montreal: Presses de l'Université de Montréal, 1981. *Canadian Folklore* 3, no. 2: 167–70.

1985 Beland, Madeleine. *Chansons de voyageurs, coureurs de bois et forestiers*. Quebec: Presses de l'Université Laval, 1982. *University of Toronto Quarterly* 54, no. 4: 515–17.

1985 Cosbey, Robert C. *All in together girls: Skipping songs from Regina, Saskatchewan*. Regina: University of Regina, 1980. *Ethnomusicology* 29, no. 1: 114–16.

1985 Falck, Robert, and Timothy Rice, eds. *Cross-cultural perspectives on music: Essays in memory of Mieczyslaw Kolinski from his students, colleagues, and friends*. Toronto: University of Toronto, 1982. *University of Toronto Quarterly* 54, no. 4: 517–19.

1985 Gibbons, Roy W. *The CCFCS collection of musical instruments: Volume one, Aerophones*. Ottawa: National Museums of Canada, 1982. *Canadian Ethnic Studies* 16, no. 3: 169–70.

1985 "North America: Indian and Inuit Music." Review of entries in the *New Grove dictionary of music and musicians*. *Ethnomusicology* 29, no. 2: 337–42.

1986 Russel, Kelly, producer; text/photos by Kenneth Peacock and Edith Fowke. *Songs of the Newfoundland Outports*. Pigeon Inlet Productions PIP 7319, 1984. LP recording. *Yearbook for Traditional Music* 18: 192–93.

1987 "Audio Report: The Canadian Broadcasting Corporation and Native Music Records." Review of LP recordings. *Yearbook for Traditional Music* 19: 161–65.

1990 McIntosh, Dale. *The history of music in British Columbia, 1850–1950*. Victoria: Sono Nis, 1989. *BC Studies* 86: 90–92.

1991 Nettl, Bruno. *Blackfoot musical thought: Comparative perspectives*. Kent: Kent State University, 1989. *Canadian Folklore* 13, no. 1: 97–102.

1991 Asch, Michael. *Kinship and the drum dance in a Northern Dene community*. Edmonton: Boreal Institute for Northern Studies, 1988; Cronk, M. Sam, comp. *Sound of the drum*. Brantford: Woodland Cultural Centre, 1990; Deiter McArthur, Patricia, comp. *Dances of the northern plains*. Saskatoon: Saskatchewan Indian Cultural Centre, 1987; Ridington, Robin. *Trail to heaven: Knowledge and narrative in a northern Native community*. Vancouver: Douglas and McIntyre, 1988; and *Little bit know something: Stories in a language of anthropology*. Vancouver: Douglas and McIntyre, 1990. *Canadian University Music Review* 11, no. 2: 158–62.

1992 Herndon, Marcia, and Susanne Ziegler, eds. *Music, gender, and culture*. Wilhelmshaven: Florian Noetzel Verlag, 1990. *Canadian University Music Review* 12, no. 1: 146–49.

1993 Lefebvre, Marie-Thérèse. *La création musicale des femmes au Québec*. Montreal: Éditions du remue-ménage, 1991. *Journal of Musicological Research* 13, no. 1–2: 113–15.

1992 Kartomi, Margaret J. *On concepts and classifications of musical instruments*. Chicago and London: University of Chicago, 1990. *Asian Music* 24, no. 1: 141–45.

1995 "Discussing Border Crossings: A Conversational Review of *Border Crossings: Future Directions in Music Studies.*" *Review of Popular Music* (IASPM-Canada) 22: 20–23. Co-authored with Val Morrison.

1995 Kallmann, Helmut et al., eds. *Encyclopedia of music in Canada*, 2nd ed. Toronto: University of Toronto, 1992. *Canadian Historical Review* 76, no. 1: 115–20.

1996 Keil, Charles, and Steven Feld. *Music grooves.* Chicago: University of Chicago, 1994. *Canadian Folklore* 18, no. 1: 124–31.

1996 Nattiez, Jean-Jacques, prod., and Artur Simon, ed. *[Chants des] Inuit Iglulik (Canada).* Museum Collection Berlin, CD 19 [CD recording]. *Ethnomusicology* 40, no. 2: 358–61.

1996 Schabas, Ezra. *Sir Ernest MacMillan: The importance of being Canadian.* Toronto: University of Toronto, 1994. *Canadian Historical Review* 77, no. 4: 625–28.

1997 Heth, Charotte, ed. *Native American dance: Ceremonies and social traditions.* Washington: National Museum of the American Indian, Smithsonian Institution/Starwood, 1992. *Ethnomusicology* 41, no. 1: 116–21.

1998 Enrico, John, and Wendy Boss Stuart. *Northern Haida songs: Studies in the anthropology of North American Indians.* Lincoln/London: University of Nebraska, 1996. *Canadian University Music Review* 18, no. 2: 111–14.

1998 Sugarman, Jane C. *Engendering song: Singing and subjectivity at Prespa Albanian weddings.* Chicago Studies in Ethnomusicology. Chicago: University of Chicago, 1997. *Women and Music* 2: 158–60..

1999 Greenhill, Pauline, and Diane Tye, eds. *Undisciplined women: Tradition and culture in Canada.* Montreal/Kingston: McGill-Queen's University Press, 1997. *Canadian Folk Music Journal* 27: 44–47.

2001 "Musically Imagined Communities": Review of Georgina Born and David Hesmondhalgh, eds. *Western music and its others: Difference, representation, and appropriation in music.* Berkeley: University of California, 2000. *Topia* 6: 105–9.

2002 Elliott, Robin, and Gordon E. Smith, eds. *Istvan Anhalt: Pathways and memory.* Montreal/Kingston: McGill-Queen's University Press, 2001. *Canadian Association of Music Libraries, Archives, and Documentation Centres Review* 30, no. 1: 29–33.

2003 Barkin, Elaine, and Lydia Hamessley, eds. *Audible traces: Gender, identity, and music.* Zurich: Carciofoli Verlagshaus, 1999; Magrini, Tullia, ed. *Music and gender: Perspectives from the Mediterranean.* Chicago: University of Chicago, 2003. *Canadian University Music Review* 24, no. 1: 118–25.

2003 "Heartbeat 2: More Voices of First Nations Women." CD recording. *Ethnomusicology* 47, no. 3: 414–17.

2003 Lehtola, Veli-Pekka. *The Sámi people: Traditions in transition.* Trans. Linna Weber Muller-Wille. Inari: Kustannus-Puntsi, 2002. *Ethnologies* 25, no. 2: 242–46.

2003 Muller, Carol Ann. *Rituals of fertility and the sacrifice of desire: Nazarite women's performance in South Africa.* Chicago: University of Chicago, 1999. *World of Music* 45, no. 1: 159–61.

2004 Koskoff, Ellen. *Music in Lubavitcher life.* Urbana: University of Illinois, 2001. *Women and Music* 8: 92–94.

2007 "Landscape and Diversity in Canada's Music Culture": Review of Elaine Keillor. *Music in Canada.* Montreal/Kingston: McGill-Queen's University Press, 2006. *Topia* 18: 152–57.

2007 Review Essay: Pisani, Michael. *Imagining Native America in music.* New Haven: Yale University, 2005; Ellis, Clyde, et al., eds. *Powwow.* Lincoln: University of Nebraska, 2005; Samuels, David. *Putting a song on top of it: Expression and identity on the San Carlos Apache reservation.* Tucson: University of Arizona, 2004; Wright-McLeod, Brian. *The encyclopedia of Native music: More than a century of recordings from wax cylinder to the Internet.* Tucson: University of Arizona, 2005. *Ethnomusicology* 51, no. 3: 507–16.

Other Publications

2005 *It's time for another one: Songs from the south coast of Newfoundland.* CD and 40-page booklet. Author of booklet and co-producer of CD with Jesse Fudge. MMaP Archive Recordings no. 1. B. Diamond, series producer. St. John's: Memorial University.

2006 *Folklore of Newfoundland and Labrador: A sampler of songs, stories, and tunes.* CD and 50-page booklet. Peter Narváez, producer. B. Diamond, transcriptions and miscellaneous. MMaP Archive Recordings no. 2. B. Diamond, series producer. St. John's: Memorial University.

2007 *Saturday nite jamboree.* CD and booklet. Neil Rosenberg, producer. MMaP Archive Series no. 3. B. Diamond, series producer. St. John's: Memorial University.

2007 *MacEdward Leach and the songs of Atlantic Canada.* Website produced by graduate students in Folklore under the supervision of B. Diamond. 2004. Expanded site with 300 songs added, relaunched January 2007, http://www.mun.ca/folklore/leach/.

2008 *Bellows and bows: Traditional instrumental music in Canada.* Sherry Johnson, volume producer. MMaP Archive Series no, 4. B. Diamond, series producer. St. John's: Memorial University.

2008 *We'ltaq (it sounds good): Historic recordings of Mi'kmaqi.* Janice Esther Tulk, volume producer. MMaP Archive Series no. 5. B. Diamond, series producer. St. John's: Memorial University.

As Subject of Articles

1980 "Beverley Cavanagh Returns to Faculty of Music." *University of Toronto Faculty of Music News* 17: 14.

1981 Pincoe, Ruth. "Cavanagh, Beverley." In *Encyclopedia of music in Canada,* edited by Helmut Kallmann et al., 165a–b.

1988 "New Faculty Appointments." *Musicology and Ethnomusicology at York* 4: 8.

1992 "Diamond Cavanagh, Beverley." *Encyclopedia of music in Canada,* 2nd ed., edited by Helmut Kallmann et al., 364a–b.

2001 Wood, Eric. "Beverley Diamond Reflects on Her Time at York." *Musicology and Ethnomusicology at York* 17: 1.

2003 "Canada Research Chair in Ethnomusicology at Memorial University of Newfoundland." *Canadian Folk Music Bulletin* 37, no. 1: 13.

2003 "Research Centre for the Study of Music, Media, and Place." *Institute for Canadian Music Newsletter* 1, no. 3: 1.

2003 Carroll, Patrick. "A Song in Her Heart: An Interview with Dr. Beverley Diamond." *Transmission: Culture and Tradition's Newsletter* 5, no. 2: 7–9, http://www.ucs.mun.ca/~culture/trans5–2.pdf.

Lectures

Distinguished/Keynote Lectures

1997 "When spirits sing and singers have a voice," Sharing the Voices: The Phenomenon of Singing International Symposium, organized by Memorial University of Newfoundland in conjunction with Cabot 500 celebrations, St. John's.

2000 "Communities, scenes, and individuals," Community Music Commission of the International Council for Music Education, Toronto.

2002 "Indigenous music in an interconnected world," Second Annual Wanda and Bruno Nettl Distinguished Lecture in Ethnomusicology, University of Illinois, Urbana-Champaign.

2004 "Contemporary indigenous music and the uses of media," Canadian University Music Society Annual Conference, Lethbridge.

2006 "Music of modern indigeneity: From identity to alliance studies," John Blacking Distinguished Lecture. European Seminar for Ethnomusicology, Jokmokk, Sweden.

2007 "Out of place: Ethnomusicology and feminist musicology," Feminist Theory and Music 9, Montreal.

2007 "An ethnography of copyright: A Native American case study," Philips Barry Distinguished Lecture, American Folklore Society, Quebec City.

2008 "Feminism and indigenous studies," MacKay Lecture, Dalhousie University, Halifax.

2008 "Native American music cultures of the Northeast: Issues of access and ownership," Symposium on Native American Music Cultures, Syracuse University, Syracuse.

Invited Lectures and Presentations

1975 "Stability and change in Inuit song," International Congress of Americanists, Mexico City.

1978 "Sounds, songs, and something for ... : Music in the world of the central Canadian Inuit," Music Department, Carleton University, Ottawa.

1987 "Music of the Inuit," Agnes Etherington Art Centre, Kingston.

1987 "The performance of hymns in eastern Woodlands Indian communities," Sing out the Glad News, a conference organized by the Institute for Canadian Music; also presented at the Musical Repercussions of 1492 symposium, Smithsonian Institution, Washington, DC.

1990 "Changing issues in the study of Christian hymns in First Nations communities," Sound of the Drum conference, Woodlands Cultural Centre, Brantford.

1990 "Feminist aesthetics and Canadian women's music," International Conference on Feminist Aesthetics, sponsored by the Goethe Institute, Toronto.

1990 "Musical instruments, sound, and metaphor in Native American communities," World Music Series, Eastman School of Music, Rochester.

1990 "Reflections on teaching North American music history: A Canadian perspective," Sonneck Society, Toronto.

1991 "The locus of meaning: Toward an interpretation of sound-producing instruments in Native communities of the Northeastern Woodlands," Brown University Graduate Colloquium, Providence.

1992 "Recent developments in Canadian music research in western Canada," University of Vienna, Vienna, and the University of Graz, Graz.

1992 "Feminisms and ethno/musicologies in the 1990s," University of Ottawa, Ottawa.

1992 "Feminisms and musics in the 1990s," University of Windsor, Windsor.

1992 "Music and celebrations in First Nations communities," Toronto Symphony Women's Committee Lecture Series, Toronto.

1994 "Visions of sound," International Association of Music Librarians, Ottawa; also on the occasion of the twentieth anniversary of Wilfrid Laurier University, Waterloo.

1995 "Border crossings and alternative metaphors," Border Crossings: The Future of Music Study, University of Ottawa, Ottawa.

1996 "Canadian music: Mapping musical life histories," "Doing field research in Canada: Too big, too cold?" "Feminist musicology?" "Music and identity in a postmodern world: Three Canadian comparisons," "Northern powow," and "Visions of sound: New approaches to studies in organology," University of Alberta, Edmonton.

1996 "The interpretation of gender issues in musical life stories," Musicology Department, University of Turku, Turku, Finland.

1996 "Myths of history," University of Alberta, Edmonton; also given at the Musicology Department, University of Turku, Turku, Finland.

1996 Respondent for panel on Music, Culture, and Citizenship, papers by Martin Allor and Line Grenier, International Association for the Study of Popular Music—Canada, Montreal.

1996 "Strategies for confronting patriarchy in the music school," Music, Gender, and Pedagogics, University of Goteborg, Gothenburg, Sweden.

1997 "Myths of history," Brock University, St. Catharines, and York University, Toronto.

1998 Respondent for a panel on Identity and Pedagogy, Sonneck Society, Kansas City.

1999 "Edges of authenticity: Musical negotiations of cultural diversity in the Canadian North," Harvard University, Cambridge.

1999 "Memory and desire: Reading the musical life stories of Canadian musicians," Graduate Colloquium, University of Western Ontario, London.

1999 "Reading for gender and race in a Yukon recording studio," Graduate Colloquium in Music, University of Toronto, Toronto.

1999 "Re/placing events: Toward a new model for studying musical performance," Graduate Colloquium in Music, McMaster University, Hamilton.

1999 "When spirits sings and singers have a voice," University of Texas, Austin.

2000 "New pathways in music research," Conference on New Directions in Music Research, Åbo Akaemi, Turku, Finland.

2000 "Reading for gender and race in a Yukon recording studio," University of Virginia, Charlottesville.

2000 "Reinventing the 'mainstream': Native American women recording artists," Department of Women's Studies, Åbo Akademi, Turku, Finland.

2001 "Communities, scenes, and individuals," Simon Fraser University, Burnaby.

2002 "Gender issues in the recording studio," Carleton University, Ottawa.

2003 "Indigenous music," respondent for panel at the Canadian University Music Society, Halifax.

2001 "Indigenous music cultures in an interconnected world," Memorial University, St. John's.

2003 Panelist on Cultural Studies and the Fine Arts in Canada, Canadian Association of Cultural Studies, Halifax.

2004 "First Nations recording artists and the uses of media," On Our Own Ground: Mapping Indigeneity within the Academy conference, Harvard University, Cambridge.

2004 "On record: Indigenous voice, audio recording, and identity," the Vice-President's Canada Research Chair Lecture Series, Memorial University, St. John's.

2005 "Reflections on the history of ethnomusicology," plenary paper for the fiftieth anniversary conference of the Society for Ethnomusicology, Atlanta.

2005 "Toronto's many voices: Reflecting on centres and margins," Voicing Toronto: The City and the Arts, University of Toronto, Toronto.

2006 "Contemporary indigenous music: Negotiating identity," Mount Alison University, Sackville, and University of Regina, Regina.

2006 "Emerging identities: Native American music in eastern Canada," International Council for Traditional Music Colloquium Emerging Identities: Trans-Atlantic Perspectives, Wesleyan University, Middletown.

2006 "Emerging identities in Native American communities in Atlantic Canada: Teaching challenges when the textbooks and oral history don't agree," Symposium on Applied Ethnomusicology, Ljubljana, Slovenia.

2006 "The MMaP Research Centre," conference on Intangible Cultural Heritage, St. John's.

2006 "Music cultures of First Nations in Atlantic Canada: Some issues of representation," Mount Alison University Canadian Music Lecture Series, Sackville; also presented at the University of Regina, Regina.

2006 "Music of modern indigeneity: From identity to alliance studies," New York University, New York; also in 2008 for the UCLA Ethnomusicology Program and Mellon Fellows Program, Los Angeles.

2006 Respondent for Gender and Sexuality panel, Society for Ethnomusicology, Honolulu.

2006 "Whither CSTM?: Five things we might learn from the past in order to find a good path to the future," Canadian Society for Traditional Music, fiftieth anniversary meeting, Ottawa.

2007 "An ethnography of copyright," International Council for Traditional Music, Vienna, and in a colloquium series at the University of California, Berkeley.

Conference Presentations (incomplete list before 1985)

1978 "Problems in investigating the history of an oral tradition: Reconciling different types of data about Inuit drum dance traditions," International Council for Traditional Music Colloquium, Wiepersdorf, East Germany.

1980 "The current state of research on the Inuit drum dance," Society for Ethnomusicology, Bloomington.

1980 "Naskapi myth performance," International Council for Traditional Music, Seoul, Korea.

1986 "Gender and music in the Sub-Arctic Algonquian area," Society for Ethnomusicology, Ann Arbor; also in 1988 for the York University Graduate Colloquium in Music, Toronto.

1988 "Inter-tribal celebrations in Native communities in eastern Canada," York University Graduate Colloquium in Anthropology, Toronto.

1988 "Women in the field," Niagara Chapter of the Society for Ethnomusicology, Geneseo.

1989   "Narratives in Canadian music history," Canadian University Music Society, Laval University, Quebec City.

1989   "Re-cycling methodologies?: Complementary perspectives on Eastern Woodlands disc rattles as cultural symbols," Society for Ethnomusicology, Boston; also for the York University Graduate Colloquium in Music, Toronto.

1990   "First Nations research and accountability," co-organizer and presenter in a panel for the Canadian Society for Musical Traditions, Calgary.

1991   "Legitimation and contemporary musics," York University Graduate Colloquium, as part of a panel with Alan Lessem and James Tenney, Toronto.

1991   "Towards a framework for interpreting gender and music," Canadian University Music Society, Queen's University, Kingston.

1992   "Lessons learned, questions raised: Writing a history of ethnomusicology in Canada," co-presenter with James Robbins, Canadian Society for Musical Traditions, Montreal.

1992   "'Turtle Island' and the musical knowledge of place," Canadian University Music Society, University of Prince Edward Island, Charlottetown.

1992   "Why are we here?" Festival of Composers: World Music, Queen's University, Kingston.

1994   "Myths of history," Society for Ethnomusicology, Milwaukee.

1994   "Persistent colonialism," Canadian University Music Society, Calgary.

1995   "Contemporary Aboriginal musics in Canada: Framing the mediations of identity," International Council for Traditional Music, Canberra, Australia.

1997   "The authority of disciplines," panel member for a round table as part of Music Studies and Cultural Difference, a conference organized by the Open University, London.

1997   "Music in the reconstruction of identities in two national contexts," with co-presenter, Pirkko Moisala, International Council for Traditional Music, Nitra, Slovakia.

1997   "Troubling agendas: Musical diversity and claims of nationhood in Finland and Canada," colloquium with co-presenter Pirkko Moisala for the York University Graduate Colloquium in Music, Toronto.

1998   "http://www.SEMethics.com/net/edu/gov/org/huh?: Ethical issues in Internet technologies," panel organizer and chair, Society for Ethnomusicology, Bloomington.

1998   "Music/gender/nation," Music and Nationalism conference, Royal Irish Academy of Music, Dublin, Ireland.

1999   "'Pathways' as a perspective on multiculturalism," International Council for Traditional Music, Visby, Sweden.

1999   "Reading for gender in a Yukon recording studio," Feminist Music Theory 5, London, UK.

1999   "Re/placing events," Society for Ethnomusicology, Austin.

2000   "First Nations, Inuit, and Métis women singers in the recording studio," Society for Ethnomusicology at Toronto 2000: Musical Intersections; also presented at the Aboriginal Music Festival symposium, Toronto.

2000   "Playing Pamela and Fleurette in an all-male youth opera production,"
       Music and Gender study group of the International Council for Traditional
       Music, Toronto.

2001   "Native Americans in the recording studio: Partners in knowledge?" Amer-
       ican Folklore Society, Anchorage.

2001   "Producing 'indigenous sound': Native Americans and Sámi in the record-
       ing studio," International Council for Traditional Music, Rio de Janeiro.

2003   "Reading for gender and race in a Yukon recording studio," Festival 500:
       Phenomenon of Singing Symposium, St. John's.

2003   "Studio experiences of Native American and Sámi women," Canadian Com-
       munications Association, Halifax.

2003   "Indigenous alliances and the invention of a transnational popular music:
       The Riddu Riddu festival," International Association for the Study of Pop-
       ular Music, Montreal.

2004   "Soundtracks of indigenous film," International Council for Traditional
       Music, Quanzho, China; also for the Folklore Studies Association of Canada,
       Winnipeg.

2004   "The Newfoundland recording industry: The last 25 years," International
       Association for the Study of Popular Music—Canada, Ottawa.

2005   "Deadly or not: Indigenous music awards in Canada and Australia," "Post-
       colonial distances: The study of popular music in Canada and Australia,"
       Memorial University, St. John's.

2005   "Remixing tradition," Society for Ethnomusicology, Tucson; also for the New
       Found Music Festival, St. John's; and in a revised form for the Folklore
       Studies Association of Canada, Université Sainte Anne, Pointe-de-l'Église.

2005   "Rethinking Internet publication: An Atlantic Canadian case study," Inter-
       national Council for Traditional Music, Sheffield, UK.

2005   "Santu's song," Aboriginal Oral Traditions conference, St. Mary's Univer-
       sity, Halifax.

2006   "Reconnecting: University archives and the communities of Newfoundland
       and Labrador," Canadian Society for Traditional Music, Ottawa.

2008   "Indigenous music and dance as cultural property: Finding a good path,"
       Colloquium on Indigenous Music and Dance as Cultural Property: Global
       Perspectives, Toronto.

2008   "'Allowing the listener to fly as they want to': Sámi perspectives on CD
       production in northern Europe." Folklore Studies Association of Canada;
       recorded for TV broadcast for Podium TV, Sydney.

2008   "More dangerous liaisons? Indigenous music and classical art forms," for
       the panel Contemporary Sámi Music: New Audiences, New Issues, B. Dia-
       mond, panel organizer, Society for Ethnomusicology, Middletown.

2008   "Indigenous-centred pedagogies: Teaching from a 'local' perspective," Cana-
       dian Society for Traditional Music, Halifax.

Contributors

John Beckwith, composer, writer, and professor emeritus, Faculty of Music, University of Toronto, was one of Beverley Diamond's teachers at the University of Toronto. His *Arctic Dances* for oboe and piano (1984) are based on her transcriptions of Inuit dance-songs. Recent works include *A New Pibroch* for Highland pipes, strings, and percussion (2003); *Fractions* for microtonal piano and string quartet (2006); and *Beckett Songs* for baritone and guitar (2008). A CD of selected vocal works, *Avowals*, appeared in 2007 from Centrediscs. Beckwith is the author of *Music Papers: Articles and Talks by a Canadian Composer, 1961–1994* (1997), and *In Search of Alberto Guerrero* (2006). Talks given at a symposium in Toronto in 2007 marking his eightieth birthday appear in the *ICM Newsletter* 5, no. 3 (September 2007).

Rob Bowman has been writing professionally about rhythm and blues, rock, country, jazz, and gospel for over a quarter century. Nominated for five Grammy Awards, in 1996 Bowman won the Grammy in the "Best Album Notes" category for a 47,000-word monograph he penned to accompany a 10-CD box set that he also co-produced, *The Complete Stax/Volt Soul Singles Volume 3: 1972–1975* (Fantasy Records). He is also the author of *Soulsville U.S.A.: The Story of Stax Records* (Schirmer Books), winner of the 1998 ASCAP-Deems Taylor and ARSC Awards for Excellence in Music Research. On top of his popular press and liner note work, Bowman played a seminal role in the founding and creation of the Stax Museum of American Soul Music (opened in Memphis in 2003), wrote the four-part television documentary series *The Industry*, and has helped pioneer the study and teaching of popular music in the world of academia. He is a tenured professor at York University in Toronto, and regularly lectures on popular music around the world.

Virginia Caputo received her Ph.D. from the Department of Social Anthropology at York University in 1996, holding a SSHRCC doctoral fellowship. She is associate professor and director of the Pauline Jewett Institute of

Women's and Gender Studies at Carleton University where she has taught since 1997. An ethnomusicologist and social anthropologist, Virginia's research lies at the intersection of feminism, anthropology, and child/girlhood research. Her work addresses theoretical and methodological approaches to research with children with a specific interest in children as social actors. Her research has included work on children's experiences in schools, gender issues in music, children's oral traditions, young women and technology, and third wave feminism.

Beverley Diamond, FRSC, is Canada Research Chair in Traditional Music and Ethnomusicology at Memorial University of Newfoundland. *Music traditions, cultures, and contexts* is a tribute to her outstanding scholarly contributions, which are discussed, along with her life and various aspects of her career, in Chapter 1 of this book.

Robin Elliott studied Canadian music with Beverley Diamond as an undergraduate student at Queen's University. He is professor of musicology in the Faculty of Music, University of Toronto, where he holds the Jean A. Chalmers Chair in Canadian music, is the director of the Institute for Canadian Music, and is associate dean, undergraduate education. He has co-edited *Istvan Anhalt: Pathways and memory* (2001), *Music and literature in German romanticism* (2004), and *Centre and periphery, roots and exile: Interpreting the music of Istvan Anhalt and György Kurtág* (forthcoming from Wilfrid Laurier University Press). He is a senior fellow at Massey College.

Charlotte J. Frisbie is professor emerita of anthropology at Southern Illinois University, Edwardsville (SIUE). A former president of the Society for Ethnomusicology and co-founder, in 1982, of the Navajo Studies Conference, Inc., she continues both anthropological and ethnomusicological research. At present, her Navajo work focuses on ethnohistory, historic preservation and restoration, traditional foods and their preparation, traditional indigenous knowledge, repatriation and other responses to NAGPRA, and autobiographies. Other continuing interests include indigenous peoples of North America, gender studies, ritual drama, language and culture, Native American hymnody, action anthropology, collaborative/reciprocal ethnography, history of SEM and its early women, and the history of the Quercus Grove southern Illinois farming community where she and her family live. A music major in college years ago, Charlotte also maintains a lively interest in church music and performs it as a bell-ringer and an organist.

Jocelyne Guilbault is professor of ethnomusicology in the Music Department of the University of California, Berkeley. Since 1980, she has done extensive fieldwork in the French Creole- and English-speaking islands of the Caribbean on both traditional and popular music. She has published articles on ethnographic writings, aesthetics, the cultural politics of Western Indian music industries, and world music. She is the author of *Zouk: World music in the West Indies* (1993) and the co-editor of *Border crossings: New direction in music studies* (1999–2000). Her recent book, *Governing sound: The cultural politics of Trinidad's Carnival musics* (2007), explores the ways the calypso music scene became audibly entangled with projects of governing, audience demands, and market incentives.

Ellen Koskoff is professor of ethnomusicology at the University of Rochester's Eastman School of Music and director of the Eastman School's ethnomusicology programs as well as its Balinese gamelan angklung. She has published widely on Jewish music and on gender and music, and is the editor of *Women and Music in Cross-Cultural Perspective* (1987) and the author of *Music in Lubavitcher Life* (2000), which won the 2002 ASCAP Deems-Taylor award. Koskoff is a contributor to the *New Grove Dictionary of Music and Musicians* and is the general editor of the *Garland Encyclopedia of World Music*, vol. 3, "The United States and Canada." She is also the general editor of the University of Rochester Press's Eastman/Rochester Studies in Ethnomusicology Series and a former president of the Society for Ethnomusicology.

Pirkko Moisala is the professor of ethnomusicology at Helsinki University. Currently she is the president of Finland's Society for Ethnomusicology. From 1993 to 2000 she was the co-chair of the Music and Gender Study Group of the International Council for Traditional Music. Her research embraces the cultural study of all kinds of music, with particular specializations in Nepal and Finland. She co-edited *Music and gender* (2000) with Beverley Diamond, and is the author of *Cultural cognition in music: Continuity and change in the Gurung music of Nepal* (1991), the co-author of *Gender and qualitative methods* (2003), and the author of *Kaija Saariaho* (2009).

Bruno Nettl was born in Prague, received his Ph.D. at Indiana University, and spent most of his career teaching at the University of Illinois, where he is now professor emeritus of music and anthropology. His main research interests are ethnomusicological theory and method, music of Native American cultures, and music of the Middle East, especially Iran. He has been concerned in recent years with the study of improvisatory musics, and with the intellectual history of ethnomusicology. Among his books, the most recent are *The study of ethnomusicology* (1983), which, after over twenty years, appeared in a revised edition in 2005; and *Encounters in ethnomusicology* (2002), a professional memoir. He has served as president of the Society for Ethnomusicology and in 2002 completed a second term as editor of its journal, *Ethnomusicology*.

Kip Pegley is an associate professor in the School of Music at Queen's University, Kingston, Ontario, with cross-appointments to the Department of Film and Media, and the Department of Women's Studies. Her recent book, *Coming to you wherever you are: MuchMusic, MTV, and youth identities*, was published with Wesleyan University Press in 2008. She is currently co-editing (with Susan Fast, McMaster University) a volume of essays entitled *Music, violence and geopolitics*, which explores the role of music in geopolitical conflicts from the twentieth and twenty-first centuries, including wars, revolutions, protests, genocides, and the post-9/11 "war on terror."

Regula Burckhardt Qureshi, FRSC, is professor of music and director of the Folkways Alive Project, as well as founder and director of the Canadian Centre for Ethnomusicology at the University of Alberta. She has a special interest in ethnography, documentation, and collaborative research as well as music-making. Her publications focus on music as a social, cultural, and spiritual practice. A cellist and sarangi player, her numerous publications include *Sufi music in India and Pakistan: Sound, context, and meaning in Qawwali* (1986); *Music and Marx: Ideas, practice, politics* (2002); and *Master musicians of India: Hindustani musicians speak* (2007); she also co-edited *Muslim society in North America* (1983) and *Muslim families in North America* (1991).

Neil V. Rosenberg is professor emeritus at Memorial University in St. John's, Newfoundland, where he taught in the Department of Folklore from 1968 to 2004. A fellow of the American Folklore Society and recipient of the Folklore Studies Association of Canada's Marius Barbeau Award for lifetime achievement, he has published extensively on Canadian and American folk music topics. His books include *Bluegrass: A history* (2005) and *Transforming tradition: Folk music revivals examined* (1993). He has been playing the banjo since 1959.

Kay Kaufman Shelemay, the G. Gordon Watts professor of music and professor of African and African American Studies at Harvard University, has carried out fieldwork in Africa (Ethiopia and Ghana), the Middle East (Israel), and the United States. A former president of the Society for Ethnomusicology and a member of the Board of the American Folklife Center at the Library of Congress, Shelemay's most recent books include the textbook *Soundscapes: Exploring music in a changing world* (2nd ed., 2006), and *Pain and its transformations: The interface of biology and culture* (2007), co-edited with Sarah Coakley. Shelemay has held fellowships from the National Endowment for the Humanities, the Guggenheim Foundation, and the American Council for Learned Societies, and was named the chair for Modern Culture at the John W. Kluge Center of the Library of Congress. Her current research focuses on Ethiopian music and musicians new to North America.

Gordon E. Smith is professor of ethnomusicology at Queen's University, Kingston, Ontario. Formerly director of the School of Music, he is currently associate dean in the Faculty of Arts and Science. He is co-editor of *Istvan Anhalt: Pathways and memory* (2000), *Folk music, traditional music, ethnomusicology: Canadian perspectives, past and present* (2007), and *Marius Barbeau: Modelling twentieth-century culture* (2008). He is editor of *MUSICultures* (formerly *The Canadian Journal for Traditional Music/La Revue de musique folklorique canadienne*), and his current research also includes fieldwork in the Mi'kmaw community of Eskasoni, Cape Breton Island, Nova Scotia.

Index

Note: Page numbers in italics refer to illustrations and music illustrations.